ACTIVITY ANALYSIS
AND GENERAL EQUILIBRIUM MODELLING

CONTRIBUTIONS
TO
ECONOMIC ANALYSIS

125

1931 N·H 1981
P C

NORTH-HOLLAND PUBLISHING COMPANY
AMSTERDAM · NEW YORK · OXFORD

ACTIVITY ANALYSIS AND GENERAL EQUILIBRIUM MODELLING

VICTOR A. GINSBURGH and JEAN L. WAELBROECK
University of Brussels

NORTH-HOLLAND PUBLISHING COMPANY
AMSTERDAM · NEW YORK · OXFORD

ISBN 0 444 86011 8

Publishers:

NORTH-HOLLAND PUBLISHING COMPANY
AMSTERDAM · NEW YORK · OXFORD

Sole distributors for the U.S.A and Canada:

ELSEVIER NORTH-HOLLAND INC.
52 VANDERBILT AVENUE
NEW YORK, N.Y. 10017

PRINTED IN THE NETHERLANDS

Introduction to the series

This series consists of a number of hitherto unpublished studies, which are introduced by the editors in the belief that they represent fresh contributions to economic science.

The term "economic analysis" as used in the title of the series has been adopted because it covers both the activities of the theoretical economist and the research worker.

Although the analytical methods used by the various contributors are not the same, they are nevertheless conditioned by the common origin of their studies, namely theoretical problems encountered in practical research. Since for this reason, business cycle research and national accounting, research work on behalf of economic policy, and problems of planning are the main sources of the subjects dealt with, they necessarily determine the manner of approach adopted by the authors. Their methods tend to be "practical" in the sense of not being too far remote from application to actual economic conditions. In addition they are quantitative rather than qualitative.

It is the hope of the editors that the publication of these studies will help to stimulate the exchange of scientific information and to reinforce international cooperation in the field of economics.

The Editors

To Lara and Nathanael
Alles! Alles! Lieb und Leid!
Und Welt und Traum! (G. Mahler)

V. G.

A Isabelle, aux cinq qui sont sept et seront...

L'homme est ainsi fait, quand un
sujet s'enflamme...
Quatre Mathusalem bout à bout
ne pourraient
Mettre fin à ce qu'un seul désire
(La Fontaine)

J. W.

Contents

III. A GENERAL EQUILIBRIUM MODEL OF WORLD TRADE

Introduction

This book sums up the results of research on modelling general equilibrium using Koopmans' activity analysis concepts. The *activity analysis general equilibrium* (AGE) approach can be used to represent any general equilibrium, with the sole qualification that the preferences of agents have to be concave rather than quasiconcave.

Two avenues had been followed to model the behavior of market economies. Johansen, and others after him, have built neoclassical models in which the preferences of consumers and the production possibilities are represented by utility and production functions specific enough to generate demand and supply functions defined by closed form expressions. Excess demand can then be expressed as an explicit function of prices and the model's solution is a price vector ensuring zero excess demand for all goods.

Several years before Johansen, Manne and others had proposed the use of activity analysis to model markets: the behavior of agents is represented by mathematical programs in which utility or profits are maximized subject to inequality constraints representing production possibilities. This approach is inherently more complex than Johansen's, since the maximization problems of agents have to be solved numerically for each set of prices instead of being solved analytically once and for all when the model is specified. The representation is however more general, since closed form demand and supply functions exist only for a narrow class of utility and production functions. It also has the unique advantage of being able to use engineering data describing technologies and the characteristics of available resources or factors of production.

Both the contributions of Johansen and Manne suffered from a common shortcoming: the models built along these lines usually represented an aggregate consumer–producer (a country) trading with one other agent (the rest of the world) whose prices or net trades were fixed. Therefore, no income effects on demand could be generated by the model. Income effects however do appear in *true* general equilibrium systems, once there are at least two agents. The first Johansen and Manne-type models did not take these into account. The Manne approach had even more defects;

indeed, almost all applications had used linear programming, with objective functions much too simple to represent the preferences of consumers, and had also made free use of miscellaneous *ad hoc* constraints with no rigorous theoretical meaning.

It is only recently that Adelman and Robinson (1978) have extended the Johansen approach. They built a computable general equilibrium (CGE) model of the Korean economy which analyzes market interactions between several groups of consumers (and producers) and takes into account the income effects.

We, on the other hand, have tried to overcome the problems posed in the activity analysis approach, and this book presents a fully worked out methodology, free from the above mentioned criticisms, which we apply to a general equilibrium model of world trade.

Our goal of presenting a complete picture of the methodological bases of AGE models has resulted in a rather long and complex book. One reason for this is that this field is a new one. Equally important is the fact that general equilibrium modelling is a subtle and complex discipline. Both of us have experience in building and solving the widely used Keynesian macro models; one of us has used the CGE as well as the AGE approaches to modelling of general equilibrium. We have derived from that experience a strong conviction that general equilibrium modelling requires far more care and rigour than the building of a Keynesian model. General equilibrium involves a pervasive interdependence which has no parallel in Keynesian models. Equilibrium theory also imposes strong constraints on the results obtained, especially for welfare changes, and it is striking to see how easily they can be disrupted by even minor errors in specifying or coding the model. Keynesian models are much more robust because the underlying theory does not imply very precise properties; because they are less complex it is easier to detect errors which distort their results. The complexity of general equilibrium models, however, poses challenging and interesting intellectual problems. It was only gradually that we discovered the correct rules of the game; hopefully what we have found and set out in this book will help on their way others who wish to apply activity analysis to country or to world problems.

Some remarks may be useful on the relative merits of the CGE and AGE approaches. As we stated at the outset, activity analysis is more general; it is however also more expensive from the computational viewpoint. It is however possible to use both methods simultaneously. The specification of GEM illustrates that components based on linear programming may be combined with components involving CGE supply and demand functions. This suggests that general equilibrium models should be of a mixed type where activity analysis is used only to describe the parts of the system on which technological data is available. Other parts would involve smooth and cheaply solved demand and supply functions.

We conclude with some remarks on the need for a model-building technique capable of analyzing in a unified framework both technological and other data. If there is a vision which has motivated our research, it is the one eloquently expressed in Koopmans' presidential address to the ninety-first meeting of the American Economic Association. Koopmans emphasized the need for a framework capable of analyzing the economy-wide implications of technological problems. "With increasing frequency", he stressed, "natural and social scientists are indeed finding themselves thrown together in the study of new problems that are of great practical importance for society, and essentially interdisciplinary in character. Prominent among these are problems of environmental policy, such as the protection of air and water quality. Another class of problems concerns a desirable long-range mix of technologies of energy supply, conversion, and use. These two classes of problems overlap, for instance, with respect to the disposal of nuclear wastes, heat rejection to the environment, and—in the case of fossil fuels—the as yet poorly understood global and regional effects of sustained large releases of carbon dioxide into the atmosphere."

And indeed there has sprung into being a host of models designed to analyze problems of this type, namely those which study energy in an economy-wide context, marrying a representation of technology with equations describing consumer demand. The specification of these models has so far not been based on a rigorous theoretical framework; we feel that this is wrong, and that it would be desirable to make explicit use of the analytical tools provided by general equilibrium theory.

Koopmans pleaded for an interdisciplinary collaboration, able to marry the economist's understanding of the overall functioning of the economy with the engineer's grasp of what is technologically feasible. Johansen or CGE-type models cannot provide a basis for such collaboration because the engineer does not recognize in their production function his vision of a productive system. Hopefully, the approach outlined in the book will contribute to providing such an intellectual framework.

The book is divided into three parts. In the first part we develop ways of describing the behavior of economic agents (consumers and producers), using linear programming. In Chapter 1 we deal with general equilibrium concepts which are translated into the linear framework in Chapter 2. We show that linearity is by no means restrictive, but makes it possible to use efficient computer codes which are currently available. Chapters 3 and 4, more specifically, deal with two important issues encountered in linear (planning) macroeconomic models: (a) inelasticity of foreign demand and the correct representation of the balance of payments (budget) constraint, and (b) saving behavior and the static representation of dynamic behavior. As will be seen, although every agent's allocation problem is linear, the search for a general equilibrium solution is highly nonlinear and cannot be solved neither by linear nor nonlinear programming.

Part II is devoted to general equilibrium solution algorithms. Chapter 5 discusses the various computational strategies which determine the dimension of the space in which the search for equilibrium values is conducted. We discuss in depth two main avenues for solving general equilibrium models: the so-called fixed-point algorithms introduced by Scarf in 1967 and the older Jacobi and tâtonnement methods. If the first are guaranteed to converge, they have a severe drawback as far as efficiency is concerned; the others have no general convergence property but experience so far shows that they converge in surprisingly short computing times. Chapters 6 and 7 are concerned with these two approaches. We show why fixed-point algorithms are slow in converging and how tâtonnement theory suggests efficient ways of carrying out the computation of equilibria. Chapter 8 finally describes four tâtonnement processes, based on different ways of setting up a competitive equilibrium model; the interesting point is that these four processes appear to have different local (and hence certainly global) convergence properties.

Part III finally exploits the ideas put forward in Parts I and II and implements and tests them on a reasonably sized international equilibrium model. This experimental model is however large enough to give rise to the practical problems encountered in building realistic models. Chapter 9 introduces the basic features of the model in terms of linear activity analysis, while the Appendices describe it in more detail and show how a complete set of national accounts can be derived from the equilibrium solution. Chapter 10 reviews the various sources of data and economic theory available to quantify the model. Chapter 11 discusses our and others' computational experience in solving equilibrium models. Finally, in Chapter 12 we present the results of a series of runs aimed at evaluating the effects of various trade liberalization policies.

Acknowledgments

The research with which this book is concerned started during 1972 as part of a broad program on multilevel planning, initiated by the World Bank.[1] The original goal of our work was to evolve ways of representing the world economy by a system of linked linear programming models. The initial research was financed by the World Bank. At no time has the project been a large modelling exercise, but it would not have been possible to keep it alive had we not obtained support from several other sources. The Fonds de la Recherche Fondamental Collective was the most important of those.

Between 1972 and 1979 our ideas, and consequently the model, have undergone a dramatic number of changes, provoking equally dramatic discussions between the authors. We are therefore grateful to a number of institutions where each of us could, alone, sharpen his wit in a stimulating environment, think up new angles of approach, and find time to write draft after draft of the various chapters: Victor Ginsburgh at the Cowles Foundation, Yale University from January 1975 to January 1976, thanks to a generous grant from the Ford Foundation, and at the University of Virginia, Charlottesville, from January to May 1979; and Jean Waelbroeck at the University of British Columbia, Vancouver, from January to June 1974; at the World Bank, from September 1974 to September 1976; and at the International Institute for Applied Systems Analysis (IIASA), Laxenburg, in December 1977 and January 1978, where the "first final draft" was completed. Part of this draft was subsequently lost on a train between Brussels and Paris while one of the authors was correcting the other's corrections.

On occasions when we were simultaneously in Belgium, we bumped into each other in the lounge of the Center for Operations Research and Econometrics, University of Louvain, the scientific environment of which helped us to overcome many doubts and uncertainties. In Brussels, colleagues at the Center for Econometrics and Mathematical Economics

[1]Adelman and Robinson's (1978) work on the CGE approach as well as Goreux and Manne's (1973) and Goreux' (1977) work on multilevel planning started or were on their way at that time. Taylor's (1976) well-known critique of linear programming planning models was also part of that program.

provided useful comments on drafts and, what was even more valuable, sustained pressure to complete the book in finite time. So did our wives.

This book would not have been written without the constant encouragement of Bela Balassa. A summer course by Herb Scarf in 1967, and the intellectual excitement provided by his book and by Koopmans' Activity Analysis of Production and Allocation did a great deal to inspire our research goals. The list of colleagues and friends who influenced our work is too long to be reported in full. Especially in the early years, Jacques Drèze and Erwin Diewert guided our steps to what emerged as a general equilibrium model, while Herb Scarf focused our attention on the desirability of carefully describing the behavior of agents, and restrained us from using his algorithms on our large model.

John Whalley was kind enough to fully read the one but last draft, and gave us several pages of deep comments; Lance Taylor, whose writings were a source of inspiration of Chapters 3 and 4, will hopefully find something of a 1975 version he commented upon. Laurence Wolsey carefully reviewed the mathematics of Chapter 6 and corrected several errors, while Mike Todd and an anonymous referee pointed out some others in a paper which grew into Chapter 8.

Alex Meeraus helped us to uncover the many mysteries of CDC's user manual to Apex, the linear programming software used to solve the model, while Marc Osterrieth's sharp wit and penetrating comments kept us awake during the long dreamless nights at the UNA computing center in McLean, Virginia. We also thank Simon Erlich, who ran some of the final computations at the University of Brussels, when a last minute discovery of a coding error made it necessary to rerun half the solutions of GEM.

Several chapters were taught in graduate courses at the Universities of Brussels, Virginia, and Louvain; students often made unexpected remarks which turned out to be crucial for the clarification of concepts. Michel Allé, Serge Boute, and Marc Osterrieth read chapters of the book and made many valuable comments.

We are grateful to be able to use in chapters 6 and 8 material which was originally published in the *Cahiers de l'ISMEA* and in *The International Economic Review*.

Michelle Papp typed the first final draft with amazing speed and efficiency during Jean Waelbroeck's two month visit to IIASA, while Christiane Fastenaekens devoted her painstaking accuracy to the last two versions, and her good nature to a denumerably large number of corrections and revisions. It took her some time to recover.

PART I

BASIC CONCEPTS

Introduction to Part I

The first four chapters of this book discuss the relation between programming models of national economies and general equilibrium theory. Chapter 1 reviews the basic concepts of general equilibrium theory and states the corresponding results for international trade theory. This provides an opportunity to state for later reference the basic expressions and theoretical concepts which will be used in the volume. Chapter 2 relates these concepts to simple linear programming models of national economies. It shows that linear (and even nonlinear) programming cannot be used to represent general equilibrium of economies with more than one consumer. Chapters 3 and 4 show that the ideas developed point to significant improvements of the specification of linear programming planning models.

CHAPTER 1

The general equilibrium framework

1.1. The concept of a general competitive equilibrium

We will be assuming that there is a finite number r of *commodities* differentiated by time and place, as well as by type. A ton of wheat today in New York is not a ton of wheat available in New York six months from now, or in Rotterdam today. The assumption that the number of commodities is finite, implies that time and space are discretized into a possibly large but finite number of periods and places. Finiteness of the number of time periods in turn implies that the future is cut off at some finite horizon.

Consumers are the only owners and final users of commodities. Each consumer i $(i=1,2,\ldots,m)$ owns an *initial endowment* of commodities, represented by the r-vector ω_i. His consumption bundle or *consumption* is represented by the r-vector x_i.

The set of consumptions which enable consumer i to survive is his *consumption set* X_i. In this book we will assume that consumption sets correspond to the closed non-negative orthant. This simplifies the analysis, and does not affect the results if ability to survive is not an issue considered in the model.

Producer j $(j=1,2,\ldots,n)$ executes production programs represented by the *production* y_j. y_j is an r-vector, the positive components of which are outputs and the negative components, inputs. This production must be feasible, that is to say it must be an element of the *production set* Y_j.

To characterize a competitive market economy, we require two additional concepts:

(1) *prices*, represented by a non-negative r-vector, p, and

(2) coefficients $\theta_{ij} \geqslant 0$ $(i=1,2,\ldots,m;\ j=1,2,\ldots,n,\ \Sigma_i\theta_{ij}=1)$ defining the share of the profits of producer j attributed to consumer i.

Consumer i finally has preferences which can be represented by a *utility function* $U_i(x_i)$. This function has the property that

(a) if i prefers x_i^1 to x_i^2, $U_i(x_i^1) > U_i(x_i^2)$, and

(b) if i is indifferent between consumptions x_i^1 and x_i^2, $U_i(x_i^1) = U_i(x_i^2)$.

In a competitive market economy, producers and consumers are assumed to take prices $\tilde{p}$ as given. The action of each agent can be described as follows.

(1) Consumer i chooses his consumption x_i to maximize his utility subject to his *budget constraint*:

$$\tilde{x}_i \text{ maximizes } U_i(x_i)$$

$$\text{s.t. } \tilde{p}\cdot(x_i-\omega_i)-\sum_j \theta_{ij}\tilde{p}\cdot\tilde{y}_j \leqslant 0,$$

$$x_i \in X_i.$$

(2) Producer j chooses his production $\tilde{y}_j$ to maximize profits:

$$y_j \text{ maximizes } \tilde{p}\cdot y_j$$

$$\text{s.t. } y_j \in Y_j.$$

These consumptions $\tilde{x}_i$ and productions $\tilde{y}_j$ (which are not necessarily unique) will be referred to as the *allocation supported by the prices* $\tilde{p}$.

The *excess demand* on the market is defined by

$$\sum_i \tilde{x}_i - \sum_j \tilde{y}_j - \sum_i \omega_i,$$

where $\tilde{x}_i$ and $\tilde{y}_j$ is an allocation supported by the prices $\tilde{p}$.

An equilibrium will then be defined as a price vector $\bar{p}$, consumptions $\bar{x}_i$, and productions $\bar{y}_j$ supported by $\bar{p}$, such that excess demand be nonpositive and that commodities in excess supply have zero price:

$$\sum_i \bar{x}_i - \sum_j \bar{y}_j - \sum_i \omega_i \leqslant 0,$$

$$\bar{p}\cdot\Big(\sum_i \bar{x}_i - \sum_j \bar{y}_j - \sum_i \omega_i\Big)=0.$$

For the sake of later reference, it is useful to summarize these concepts as follows.

Let x_i and ω_i be r-vectors of consumption and initial endowments held by consumer i ($i=1,2,\ldots,m$) and let y_j be an r-vector of production by producer j ($j=1,2,\ldots,n$). Let X_i denote the consumption set of i, and Y_j the production set of j. Assume that the preferences of consumer i can be represented by a utility function $U_i(x_i)$. Finally, let the r-vector p represent prices and θ_{ij} be the proportion of profit of firm j distributed to consumer i ($\theta_{ij} \geqslant 0$, $\Sigma_i \theta_{ij} = 1$).

Then we define:

Definition 1.1.1. Competitive equilibrium. The allocation $\bar{x}_i$ ($i = 1,2,\ldots,m$), $\bar{y}_j$ ($j=1,2,\ldots,n$) supported by the prices $\bar{p}$, is a *competitive equilibrium* if the following conditions hold.

(a) Equality of demand and supply for nonfree goods:

$$\sum_i \bar{x}_i - \sum_j \bar{y}_j - \sum_i \omega_i \leqslant 0; \qquad \bar{p} \cdot \left(\sum_i \bar{x}_i - \sum_j \bar{y}_j - \sum_i \omega_i \right) = 0.$$

(b) Utility maximization by consumers: $\bar{x}_i$ maximizes $U_i(x_i)$ s.t. $\bar{p} \cdot x_i \leqslant \bar{p} \cdot \omega_i + \Sigma_j \theta_{ij} \bar{p} \cdot \bar{y}_j$, and $x_i \in X_i$, for $i=1,2,\ldots,m$.

(c) Profit maximization by firms: $\bar{y}_j$ maximizes $\bar{p} \cdot y_j$ s.t. $y_j \in Y_j$, for $j=1,2,\ldots,n$.

1.2. Equilibrium and optimum: Fundamental theorems

1.2.1. Basic assumptions

We will make the following assumptions, which are standard.[1]

(1) On the production sets Y_j ($j=1,2,\ldots,n$),
   (a) Y_j is closed;
   (b) Y_j is convex;
   (c) $0 \in Y_j$ (possibility of inaction);
   (b) and (c) imply nonincreasing returns to scale;
   (d) $Y_j \cap \Omega = \{0\}$ with Ω the closed non-negative orthant (no free lunch);
   (e) $\Sigma_j Y_j \cap (-\Sigma_j Y_j) = \{0\}$ (irreversibility of production processes);
   (f) if $y_j^1 \in Y_j$ and $y_j^2 \leqslant y_j^1$, then $y_j^2 \in Y_j$ (free disposal).

[1] To simplify this summary overview, we assume these assumptions to hold throughout, even for particular results for which one or the other assumption is not needed.

(2) On the consumption possibility sets X_i $(i=1,2,\ldots,m)$,
   (g) X_i is the closed non-negative orthant Ω;
   (h) for every $x_i^1 \in X_i$ there exists an $x_i^2 \in X_i$ preferred to x_i^1 (nonsatiation);
   (i) there exists an $x_i^0 \in X_i$ such that $x_i^0 < \omega_i$ (initial endowments are positive and consumer i can survive with endowment ω_i).
(3) On the utility function $U_i(x_i)$ $(i=1,2,\ldots,m)$,
   (j) $U_i(x_i)$ is a continuous real valued quasiconcave function.

1.2.2. Fundamental theorems of mathematical economics

A prior logical problem is existence: is the general competitive equilibrium problem guaranteed to have a solution? The answer is given by the following existence theorem:

Theorem 1.2.1. Existence of equilibrium prices. If assumptions (a)–(j) are satisfied then there exist productions $\bar{y}_j$ and consumptions $\bar{x}_i$ supported by a price vector $\bar{p}$ such that conditions (a), (b), and (c) of definition 1.1.1 hold.

One of the oldest ideas in economics, strongly expressed already by Adam Smith in the Wealth of Nations, is that competitive equilibrium is in a certain sense optimal. Let us define:

Definition 1.2.1. Pareto optimum. A *Pareto optimum* for an economy is a set of productions $y_j \in Y_j$ and consumptions $x_i \in X_i$ satisfying the balance constraints

$$\sum_i x_i - \sum_j y_j - \sum_i \omega_i \leqslant 0,$$

such that there are no other allocations y_j^*, x_i^* satisfying the balance constraints with

$$U_i(x_i^*) \geqslant U_i(x_i), \qquad i=1,2,\ldots,m$$

and strict inequality for at least one consumer.

Theorem 1.2.2. Pareto optimality of competitive equilibria. If assumptions (a)–(j) hold, every competitive equilibrium is a Pareto optimum.

Another concept we will use is that of a Negishi welfare optimum. We first define a welfare optimum.

Definition 1.2.2. Welfare optimum. Let $W[U(x)]=W[U_1(x_1),\ldots,U_m(x_m)]$ be a concave increasing function of the $U_i(x_i)$ and consider the mathematical program max $W[U(x)]$ s.t. $\Sigma x_i-\Sigma y_j-\Sigma\omega_i\leqslant 0$, $x_i\in X_i$ $(i=1,\ldots,m)$, $y_j\in Y_j$ $(j=1,\ldots,n)$. An allocation $\tilde{x}_i$, $\tilde{y}_j$ which maximizes the objective function subject to the constraints, is a *welfare optimum*.

Negishi (1960) has considered the important special case where the welfare function is linear in the utilities of agents

$$W[U(x)]=\sum_{i=1}^{m}\alpha_iU_i(x_i)\qquad(\alpha_i>0,\ \Sigma\alpha_i=1),$$

and where assumption (j) is replaced by (j′):

(j′) $U_i(x_i)$ is a continuous real valued concave function.[2]

Definition 1.2.3. Negishi welfare optimum. The allocation resulting from $\max\Sigma_{i=1}^{m}\alpha_iU_i(x_i)$ s.t. $\Sigma x_i-\Sigma y_j-\Sigma\omega_i\leqslant 0$, $x_i\in X_i$ all i, $y_j\in Y_j$ all j will be called a *Negishi welfare optimum*. The α_i will be called *welfare weights*. Negishi proved:

Theorem 1.2.3. Existence of equilibrium welfare weights [Negishi]. There exists at least one set of strictly positive welfare weights $\bar{\alpha}_i$, $\Sigma\bar{\alpha}_i=1$, for which the solution of the Negishi welfare optimum and the dual prices $\bar{p}$ associated with the balance constraints are an equilibrium.

[2]This assumption is stronger than (j) which only required the utility function to be quasiconcave. The consequent loss of generality need not concern us in this book since the sets of linear inequalities which we will use to represent utility functions are able to approximate only concave functions. In any case, as remarked by Diewert (1973, p. 120): "From an empirical point of view, it is impossible to distinguish concave from quasiconcave functions." A function is concave if the set $\{x,U\mid U\leqslant U(x)\}$ is convex. A function is quasiconcave if for any $x^*\in X$, the set $\{x\mid U(x)\geqslant U(x^*)\}$ is convex.

1.2.3. Equilibrium theory and computation

The equivalence between the three problems described in theorems 1.2.1, 1.2.2, and 1.2.3 is potentially useful for computation, since it implies that an equilibrium can be calculated by solving any one of the three problems. Theorem 1.2.1 suggests searching for equilibrium prices, 1.2.2 for a vector of equilibrium utilities, and 1.2.3 for a vector of equilibrium welfare weights.

1.3. Equilibrium in international trade

1.3.1. Definitions

The general equilibrium concept is readily applied to the field of international trade to which much of this book is devoted. In the pure theory of international trade the agents are countries which are both producers and consumers and whose budget constraints are the balances of payments.[3] We make the usual assumption that each consumer owns domestic producers. This implies that an *international competitive equilibrium* is a general competitive equilibrium in which agents are countries. It is customary in international trade theory to distinguish between traded goods, which can be transported, and nontraded goods which cannot. This can be reflected in the general equilibrium framework by assuming that some commodities can be used only by the producer/consumer agent who owns or produces these commodities.

Assuming that it is countries which produce and consume is of course a fiction. Except in centrally planned economies, trade is conducted by individual agents rather than by governments. In the free trade situation, which characterizes international competitive equilibria, it may be acceptable to disregard this dichotomy and reason as though countries behaved like competitive agents. Such a treatment is not appropriate in the presence of barriers to trade.

Indeed, by imposing tariffs or by enforcing other barriers to trade, governments can drive a wedge between world and domestic prices of

[3] The pure trade literature assumes that the preferences of consumers can be represented by a social welfare function having the properties of a utility function. For simplicity of language, we will write as if there were one single consumer. Under suitable aggregation it can be shown that balance of payments equilibrium is necessary and sufficient for him to be on his budget constraint.

traded goods. This leads to considering a *tariff-ridden equilibrium* in which the true worth of imports and exports to the country, equal to world prices, differs from the apparent worth, equal to domestic prices, which guide the decisions of individual agents.

It is convenient at this point to extend the notation used up to now. Let r^1 be the number of traded goods and $r^2 = r - r^1$ the number of nontraded goods.[4]

Let the r-vectors e_i and m_i be the *exports* and *imports* of country i. To be feasible, these must be elements of *export* and *import sets*, E_i and M_i, the first r^1 components of which are non-negative and the r^2 other zero. Partition accordingly into traded and nontraded goods the vectors y_i, x_i, and ω_i.

For the sake of concreteness, it is assumed that tariffs are *ad valorem*.[5] Let tariff rates on exports and imports of country i be defined by r-vectors t_i^{e}, t_i^{m}, with components t_{ik}^{e}, t_{ik}^{m}, $0 \leqslant t_{ik}^{\mathrm{e}}, t_{ik}^{\mathrm{m}} \leqslant 1$ (tariff rates on nontraded goods are of course zero). It will prove convenient to define also the r-vectors $p_i = (\lambda_i p\ p_i^2)$, the first r^1 components of which are international prices of traded goods p multiplied by the exchange rate λ_i, while the r^2 last components are the prices of nontraded goods. Define, finally, the r-vectors p_i^e and p_i^m with components $(1 - t_{ik}^{\mathrm{e}})p_{ik}$ and $(1 + t_{ik}^{\mathrm{m}})p_{ik}$; p_i^{e} and p_i^{m} are respectively prices reduced by the export tariff and increased by the import tariff; p_i^{m} is the price at which imported goods can be supplied to the domestic market i; and p_i^{e} is the price at which foreign countries are willing to import country i's goods. Finally we define *tariff receipts* as $t_i = (p_i^{\mathrm{m}} - p_i)\cdot m_i - (p_i^{\mathrm{e}} - p_i)\cdot e_i$. Then:

Definition 1.3.1. Tariff-ridden equilibrium. The allocation $\bar{y}_i, \bar{x}_i, \bar{e}_i, \bar{m}_i$, $i = 1, 2, \ldots, n$, supported by the non-negative price vectors $\bar{p}_i$, $i = 1, 2, \ldots, n$, is a *tariff-ridden equilibrium* if the following conditions hold (for $i = 1, 2, \ldots, n$).

(a) Equality of exports and imports for traded goods on the international market

$$\sum_i \bar{m}_i - \sum_i \bar{e}_i = 0.$$

(b) Utility maximization by each country: $\bar{x}_i$ maximizes $U_i(x_i)$ subject to the following constraints:

(b1) feasibility: $x_i \in X_i$; $y_i \in Y_i$; $e_i \in E_i$; $m_i \in M_i$;

[4] Production, consumption, and initial endowment in country i of a nontraded commodity of country j are equal to zero.

[5] The formulation is easily modified to take account of specific tariffs, or of price-equalizing tariffs such as those used in the EEC Common Agricultural Policy.

(b2) perceived balance of payments constraint:
$\bar{p}_i^m \cdot m_i - \bar{p}_i^e \cdot e_i \leqslant \bar{t}_i$, where $\bar{p}_i^m$, $\bar{p}_i^e$, and $\bar{t}_i$ are the values of p_i^m, p_i^e, and t_i corresponding to the equilibrium vectors $\bar{p}_i$, $\bar{e}_i$, and $\bar{m}_i$;
(b3) supply–demand equilibrium constraints on national markets:
$\bar{x}_i + \bar{e}_i - \bar{y}_i - \bar{m}_i - \omega_i \leqslant 0$.

As implied by the (b2) constraints, it is assumed that agents in country i regard $\bar{t}_i$, the equilibrium value of tariff receipts, as independent of their individual decisions. This would, for example, be justified if agents were small so that the contribution of each one to tariff receipts was negligible. It is easy to check that the true balance of payments with which the country is faced, $\bar{p}_i \cdot (m_i - e_i) \leqslant 0$, is equivalent to (b2) at equilibrium.

If tariffs are set equal to zero so that free trade is established, we obtain an international competitive equilibrium, defined by

Definition 1.3.2. International competitive equilibrium. The allocation $\bar{y}_i, \bar{x}_i, \bar{e}_i, \bar{m}_i$, $i = 1, 2, \ldots, n$, supported by the non-negative price vectors $\bar{p}_i$, $i = 1, 2, \ldots, n$, is an *international competitive equilibrium* if the following conditions hold (for $i = 1, 2, \ldots, n$).

(a) Equality of exports and imports for traded goods on the international market

$$\sum_i \bar{m}_i - \sum_i \bar{e}_i = 0.$$

(b) Utility maximization by each country: $\bar{x}_i$ maximizes $U_i(x_i)$ subject to the following constraints:
(b1) feasibility: $x_i \in X_i$; $y_i \in Y_i$; $e_i \in E_i$; $m_i \in M_i$;
(b2) balance of payments constraints: $\bar{p}_i \cdot (m_i - e_i) \leqslant 0$;
(b3) supply–demand equilibrium constraints on national markets:
$\bar{x}_i + \bar{e}_i - \bar{y}_i - \bar{m}_i - \omega_i \leqslant 0$.

1.3.2. Individual behavior implied by international equilibria

These definitions of tariff-ridden and international competitive equilibria can be shown to imply that consumers, producers, exporters, and importers are in equilibrium in the different countries. Let λ_i, the "shadow exchange rate", be the dual price associated with the balance of payments constraint, while the r-vectors of "domestic prices" $p_i^* = (p_i^1\ p_i^2)$, are the dual prices associated with the national market balance constraints in the utility maximization problem of each country. Then it can be shown that an international tariff-ridden equilibrium implies familiar relations between different prices:

$$\bar{p}_i^{\mathrm{e}} \leqslant \bar{p}_i^* \leqslant \bar{p}_i^{\mathrm{m}}.$$

Moreover, the productions $\bar{y}_i$ maximize the profits of producers at prices $\bar{p}_i^*$; the exports $\bar{e}_i$ and imports $\bar{m}_i$ maximize the profits $(\bar{p}_i^{\mathrm{e}} - \bar{p}_i^*)\cdot e_i$ and $(\bar{p}_i^* - \bar{p}_i^{\mathrm{m}})\cdot m_i$ of exporters and importers, subject to $e_i \in E_i$ and $m_i \in M_i$; and the consumptions $\bar{x}_i$ maximize the utility of consumers at prices $\bar{p}_i^*$, subject to $\bar{p}_i^* \cdot (x_i - \bar{y}_i - \omega_i) \leqslant \bar{t}_i$ and $x_i \in X_i$:

In the international competitive equilibrium $\bar{p}_i^{\mathrm{e}} = \bar{p}_i^{\mathrm{m}}$, so that $\bar{p}_i^{\mathrm{e}} = \bar{p}_i^* = \bar{p}_i^{\mathrm{m}}$; thus, at equilibrium domestic prices of traded goods are equal to international prices corrected for the exchange rate. $\bar{x}_i$, $\bar{y}_i$, $\bar{e}_i$, and $\bar{m}_i$ are consumptions, productions, exports, and imports supported by the prices p_i^*.

1.3.3. Equilibrium and optimum in international trade

Theorem 1.2.1 can be extended along the lines followed by Shoven (1974):[6]

Theorem 1.3.1. Existence of equilibrium prices. If assumptions (a)–(j) are satisfied, there exist allocations $\bar{y}_i$, $\bar{x}_i$, $\bar{e}_i$, and $\bar{m}_i$, supported by prices $\bar{p}_i$ and exchange rates $\bar{\lambda}_i$, such that definitions 1.3.1 and 1.3.2 hold.

In the sequel we will be concerned with tariff-ridden equilibria only. The concepts for international competitive equilibria can be easily deduced by setting $\bar{p}_i^{\mathrm{e}} = \bar{p}_i^{\mathrm{m}} = \bar{p}_i$.

The following extensions of the ideas developed in theorems 1.2.2 and 1.2.3 have no theoretical meaning but are of computational interest.

[6]For this purpose imports and exports have to be interpreted as the net trades of the countries, rather than as activities undertaken by exporters and importers, as is frequently done in international trade theory.

Definition 1.3.3. Tariff-ridden "Pareto optimum". A tariff-ridden Pareto optimum is a solution of the following mathematical program:

$$\max U_1(x_1)+\sum_{i=1}^{n}\left[(\tilde{p}_i^{\mathrm{e}}-\tilde{p}_i)\cdot e_i+(\tilde{p}_i-\tilde{p}_i^{\mathrm{m}})\cdot m_i\right]$$

$$\text{s.t. } U_i(x_i)\geqslant \tilde{U}_i, \qquad i=2,\ldots,n,$$

$$x_i+e_i-y_i-m_i-\omega_i\leqslant 0, \qquad i=1,2,\ldots,n,$$

$$\sum_i m_i-\sum_i e_i=0,$$

$$x_i\in X_i,\, y_i\in Y_i,\, e_i\in E_i,\, m_i\in M_i, \qquad i=1,2,\ldots,n.$$

The tilde ($\tilde{}$) over variables indicates given values.

Theorem 1.3.2. Pareto optimality of a tariff-ridden equilibrium. If assumptions (a)–(j) hold, every tariff-ridden equilibrium is a tariff-ridden Pareto optimum.

Proof. Check that the solution of the equilibrium solves the tariff-ridden Pareto optimum. Q.E.D.

Definition 1.3.4. Tariff-ridden Negishi optimum. A tariff-ridden Negishi optimum is a solution of the following mathematical program:

$$\max \sum_{i=1}^{n}\left[\tilde{\alpha}_i U_i(x_i)+(\tilde{p}_i^{\mathrm{e}}-\tilde{p}_i)\cdot e_i+(\tilde{p}_i-\tilde{p}_i^{\mathrm{m}})\cdot m_i\right]$$

$$\text{s.t. } x_i+e_i-y_i-m_i-\omega_i\leqslant 0, \qquad i=1,2,\ldots,n,$$

$$\sum_i m_i-\sum_i e_i=0,$$

$$x_i\in X_i,\, y_i\in Y_i,\, e_i\in E_i,\, m_i\in M_i, \qquad i=1,2,\ldots,n.$$

The tilde ($\tilde{}$) over variables indicates given values.

Definition 1.3.5. Equilibrium welfare weights for the tariff-ridden Negishi optimum. A set of welfare weights $\bar{\alpha}_i$ such that the solution of the tariff-ridden Negishi optimum satisfies the budget constraints is a set of equilibrium weights for the problem.

It can be checked that if the problem is solved with equilibrium weights, the primal and dual variables of a tariff-ridden Negishi optimum are a tariff-ridden equilibrium.

1.4. Extensions of the equilibrium approach

Competitive equilibrium theory is based on restrictive assumptions which will not be met in many practical cases. This section sketches a broader definition of the equilibrium concept which encompasses a broad range of possible economic situations.

It is convenient to define a general equilibrium problem in terms of three components.

(1) *Signals* perceived by agents. These are vectors of variables which agents observe; to be *admissible* these signals may be functions of other variables of the system.

(2) *Rules* which define how agents respond to these signals resulting in the setting of *decisions*.

(3) *System constraints*, which must be satisfied, but which are not taken into account by agents in setting their decisions.

An equilibrium can be defined as a set of admissible signals such that agents' decisions satisfy the system constraints.

We now define formally this general concept. Let $\tilde{p}_{xi}$ $(i=1,2,\ldots,m)$ and $\tilde{p}_{yj}$ $(j=1,2,\ldots,n)$ be the price signals perceived by consumer i and producer j, respectively, and let Ξ be the vector $\Xi=(x_1,\ldots,x_m;\ y_1,\ldots,y_n;\ \omega_1,\ldots,\omega_m;\ p_{x1},\ldots,p_{xm};\ p_{y1},\ldots,p_{yn})$. Define the following signalling functions:

(a) income of consumer i: $\tilde{R}_i=R_i(\tilde{\Xi})$;

(b) external effects on the utility function $\tilde{\zeta}_i=\zeta_i(\tilde{\Xi})$ and the consumption set $\tilde{\xi}_i=\xi_i(\tilde{\Xi})$ of consumer i;

(c) external effects on the production set of producer j: $\tilde{\eta}_j=\eta_j(\tilde{\Xi})$;

(d) prices perceived by consumer i: $\tilde{p}_{xi}=p_{xi}(\tilde{\Xi})$; and

(e) prices perceived by producer j: $\tilde{p}_{yj}=p_{yj}(\tilde{\Xi})$.

Definition 1.4.1. General equilibrium. The allocations $\bar{x}_i$ and $\bar{y}_j$ supported by signals $\bar{R}_i=R_i(\bar{\Xi})$, $\bar{\zeta}_i=\zeta_i(\bar{\Xi})$, $\bar{\xi}_i=\xi_i(\bar{\Xi})$, $\bar{\eta}_j=\eta_j(\bar{\Xi})$, $\bar{p}_{xi}=p_{xi}(\bar{\Xi})$, $\bar{p}_{yj}=p_{yj}(\bar{\Xi})$, all i and j, is a general equilibrium if the following conditions hold.

(a) Equality of demand and supply:[7] $\Sigma_i\bar{x}_i-\Sigma_j\bar{y}_j-\Sigma_i\omega_i=0$.

(b) Utility maximization by consumers: $\bar{x}_i$ maximizes $U_i(x_i,\bar{\zeta}_i)$ s.t. $\bar{p}_{xi}\cdot x_i \leqslant \bar{R}_i$ and $x_i\in X_i(\bar{\xi}_i)$, for $i=1,2,\ldots,m$.

(c) Profit maximization by firms: $\bar{y}_j$ maximizes $\bar{p}_{yj}\cdot y_j$ s.t. $y_j\in Y_j(\bar{\eta}_j)$, for $j=1,2,\ldots,n$.

We now describe a number of models which are covered by the general definition 1.4.1, without discussing the assumptions under which solutions exist.

1.4.1. Competitive equilibrium

The competitive equilibrium is clearly a particular case of our definition, in which the only signals are prices, and these are identical for all consumers and producers; there are no external effects on consumption and production sets nor on utility functions. The incomes of consumers are $\tilde{R}_i=\tilde{p}\cdot\omega_i+\Sigma_j\theta_{ij}\tilde{p}\cdot\tilde{y}_j$.

1.4.2. Equilibrium with an indirect tax redistributing government

We describe only the case of *ad valorem* taxes on consumption. More general cases can easily be constructed; note also that the tariff-ridden equilibrium discussed in section 1.3 is covered by this definition.

Let τ_k be the rate of taxation on commodity k. Instead of paying the price p_k for one unit of commodity k, consumer i will pay $p_k(1+\tau_k)$, so that the price signals are now $p_k(1+\tau_k)$ for consumers and p_k for producers. Assume that the tax-collecting agent redistributes the product of taxes to consumers in the form of lump-sum transfers $\tilde{t}_i=t_i(\tilde{\Xi})$ such that

$$\sum_i\sum_k \tilde{p}_k\tau_k x_{ik}=\sum_i \tilde{t}_i.$$

The income of consumer i is therefore $\tilde{R}_i=\tilde{p}\cdot\omega_i+\Sigma_j\theta_{ij}\tilde{p}\cdot\tilde{y}_j+\tilde{t}_i$, and his behavior will be described by $\max U_i(x_i)$ s.t. $\Sigma_k\tilde{p}_k(1+\tau_k)x_{ik}\leqslant\tilde{R}_i$. Producer j's decision is the result of $\max \tilde{p}\cdot y_j$ s.t. $y_j\in Y_j$.

[7] In some cases other system constraints have to be added.

1.4.3. Equilibrium with externalities

We consider only the case of externalities affecting the utility functions of the consumers. Suppose that consumer i's utility depends not only on his consumption but also on the decisions of some or all other consumers. Then let $\tilde{\zeta}_i = \zeta_i(\tilde{x}_1, \ldots, \tilde{x}_{i-1}, \tilde{x}_{i+1}, \ldots, \tilde{x}_m)$ be a signal for consumer i whose behavior is now described by $\max U_i(x_i, \tilde{\zeta}_i)$ s.t. $\tilde{p} \cdot x_i \leqslant \tilde{p} \cdot \omega_i + \Sigma_j \theta_{ij} \tilde{p} \cdot \tilde{y}_j$, $x_i \in X_i$. The producer will behave as in the competitive equilibrium. It is straightforward to write models in which the consumption set of i and/or the production set of j are affected by the model's variables.

1.4.4. Equilibrium with public goods

A public good is a good the output of which can be entirely consumed by every consumer; this is the case, for instance, of a public park, or TV broadcasting. We describe the formulation in which each consumer i decides on the price p_{xi} he pays for the public good and has to buy the entire amount supplied; therefore, for the producer, the unit price is $p_y = \Sigma_i p_{xi}$. Let $x_i^0 = x^0$ be the consumption of the public good, while y^0 is its production. The consumption of i will be the result of $\max U_i(\tilde{x}^0, x_i)$ s.t. $p_{xi} \cdot \tilde{x}^0 + \tilde{p} \cdot x_i \leqslant \tilde{p} \cdot \omega_i + \Sigma_j \theta_{ij} \tilde{p} \cdot \tilde{y}_j$, $x_i \in X_i$; the producer of the public good will react by maximizing $p_y \cdot y^0$ subject to $y^0 \in Y^0$. Other producers will behave in the usual competitive way. There will be a supply–demand equation for the public stating that $x^0 = y^0 + \omega^0$: every consumer can consume the whole production of the good. The signals are prices for private goods, the production of the public good for consumers, and the price $\tilde{p}_y$ for the producer of the public good.

1.4.5. Equilibrium with monopolistic producers

A firm f has a monopoly on the market for good h if it is the only producer of that good. The demand curve $p_h(y_h)$ of that good is independent of the firm's decisions. The firm will choose a production y_h, implying a price $p_h(y_h)$ to maximize

$$p_h y_h + \sum_{k \neq h} \tilde{p}_k y_{fk}, \qquad y_f \in Y_f, \qquad p_h = p_h(y_h).$$

For the monopolist, the signals are the prices, except for good h, and the demand curve of good h.

The two following concepts are defined only for an exchange economy.

1.4.6. Temporary equilibrium

Consider that a consumer i lives two periods, denoted by superscripts 1 and 2. During the first period he will be faced with decisions concerning his first period *and* his second-period consumption (or his first-period saving). Consumer i attaches utilities to both consumption vectors and his decision will result from the following two-period maximization problem: $\max U_i(x_i^1, x_i^2)$ s.t. $\tilde{p}^1 \cdot x_i^1 + m_i = \tilde{p}^1 \cdot \omega_i^1$, $\tilde{p}^2 \cdot x_i^2 \leqslant m_i + \tilde{p}^2 \cdot \omega_i^2$, $x_i^1 \in X_i^1$, $x_i^2 \in X_i^2$. m_i is his saving which can be transferred to the second period; the other variables are as before. In the classical competitive equilibrium, $\tilde{p}^1$ and $\tilde{p}^2$ are known. In the temporary equilibrium approach the true value of p^2 is unknown and it is assumed that each consumer i forms point expectations $\Psi_i(\bar{p}^1)$ about future prices. The first period, or temporary equilibrium, is then defined as the allocation $\bar{x}_i^1$ $(i = 1,2,\ldots, m)$ supported by the price signals $\bar{p}^1$ and $\Psi_i(\bar{p}^1)$ such that:

(a) consumer i maximizes his utility $U_i(x_i^1, x_i^2)$ subject to $\bar{p}^1 \cdot x_i^1 + m_i = \bar{p}^1 \omega_i^1$, $\Psi_i(\bar{p}^1) \cdot x_i^2 \leqslant m_i + \Psi_i(\bar{p}^1) \cdot \omega_i^2$, $x_i^1 \in X_i^1$, $x_i^2 \in X_i^2$, $i = 1,2,\ldots, m$;

(b) the markets for period 1 are in equilibrium: $\Sigma_i \bar{x}_i^1 = \Sigma_i \omega_i^1$.

1.4.7. Fix-price equilibrium

In many situations one can think of prices which do not adjust fast enough to clear markets. We will assume that prices are set at the beginning of a given period and remain fixed during the period.[8] At these prices, consumers decide on their demands and supplies. In general, these trades will not clear the markets and agents will be rationed: they will not be able to sell or to buy what they supply or demand. We will describe briefly the approach due to Drèze (1975). Further details can be found in Grandmont (1977).

We start with the usual competitive model with one more good, indexed by 0, "money". In addition to prices for the $r+1$ goods, consumers perceive quantity constraints on their trades, for all goods but money. The

[8] One can also assume prices to move between upper and lower bounds. This is of course a more general situation studied, for example, by Drèze (1975).

behavior of consumer i is thus described as follows: $\max U_i(x_i)$ s.t. $\tilde{p}\cdot x_i=\tilde{p}\cdot\omega_i$ and $\underset{\sim}{x}_{ik}\leqslant x_{ik}-\omega_{ik}\leqslant \tilde{x}_{ik}$ for $k=1,2,\ldots,r$, where $\underset{\sim}{x}_{ik}\leqslant\tilde{x}_{ik}$ are lower and upper bounds on the net transactions of commodity k, respectively.

A fix-price Drèze equilibrium can be defined as follows. The allocation $\bar{x}_i$ $(i=1,2,\ldots,m)$ supported by the price signals $\bar{p}$ and the perceived constraints signals $\underset{\sim}{x}_{ik}, \tilde{x}_{ik}$, $k=1,2,\ldots,r$, $i=1,2,\ldots,m$, is a Drèze equilibrium if the following conditions hold.

(a) Equality of demand and supply: $\Sigma_i\bar{x}_i-\Sigma_i\omega_i=0$.

(b) Utility maximization by consumers: $\max U_i(x_i)$ s.t. $\bar{p}\cdot x_i\leqslant\bar{p}\cdot\omega_i$ and $\underset{\sim}{x}_{ik}\leqslant x_{ik}-\omega_{ik}\leqslant\tilde{x}_{ik}$, $k=1,2,\ldots,r$.

(c) For any $k=1,2,\ldots,r$, $\bar{x}_{ik}-\omega_{ik}=\tilde{x}_{ik}$ for some i implies $\bar{x}_{hk}-\omega_{hk}>\underset{\sim}{x}_{hk}$ for all $h\neq i$, $\bar{x}_{ik}-\omega_{ik}=\underset{\sim}{x}_{ik}$ for some i implies $\bar{x}_{hk}-\omega_{hk}<\tilde{x}_{hk}$ for all $h\neq i$.

(d) $\underset{\sim}{x}_{ik}\leqslant 0\leqslant\tilde{x}_{ik}$, all i, h.

Conditions (c) mean that for every commodity k, if there is one consumer whose net demand for k is rationed, no consumer is rationed on the supply side; if there is one consumer who cannot sell as much as what he wants, no consumer will be rationed on the demand side. Conditions (d) imply that no consumer can be forced to supply or consume more than he wants.

The upper and lower bounds will usually be obtained through a specific rationing scheme, for instance a uniform rationing scheme in which all consumers will perceive the same constraints $\underset{\sim}{x}_k$, $\tilde{x}_k$, $k=1,2,\ldots,r$.

CHAPTER 2

Linear programming models and general equilibrium theory

Chapter 1 reviewed, under general assumptions, the relation between equilibria and welfare optima. In a sense there is nothing to add to the results, and there is no need to reiterate for linear programming models propositions which have already been derived for the general case. The goal of Chapter 2 is accordingly to show how linear programming can be used to build quantitative models which have a sound theoretical underpinning. As will be seen in Chapter 3, the linear programming framework is a more flexible tool than is often thought, and can be used to represent equilibrium problems of very general structure.

We deal in Chapter 2 with the relation between equilibrium and optimum in the case of (a) a single consumer (country), and (b) several consumers (countries).

2.1. The single consumer case

When there is only one consumer, any Pareto optimum is a Negishi optimum and conversely. We now show that these optima are also equilibria. It is therefore possible to find an equilibrium by solving a mathematical program.

We restrict definitions 1.1.1 (equilibrium) and 1.3.3 (Negishi optimum) to the case of a single consumer as follows:

Definition 2.1.1. One consumer equilibrium. The allocation $\bar{x}, \bar{y}_j$ ($j = 1, 2, \ldots, n$) supported by prices $\bar{p}$ is a competitive equilibrium if the following conditions hold.

(a) Equality of supply and demand for nonfree goods: $\bar{x} - \Sigma_j \bar{y}_j - \omega \leqslant 0$; $\bar{p} \cdot (\bar{x} - \Sigma_j \bar{y}_j - \omega) = 0$.

(b) Utility maximization by the single consumer: $\bar{x}$ maximizes $U(x)$ s.t. $\bar{p}\cdot x \leqslant \bar{p}\cdot\omega + \bar{p}\cdot\Sigma\bar{y}_j$ and $x \in X$.

(c) Profit maximization by firms: $\bar{y}_j$ maximizes $\bar{p}\cdot y_j$ s.t. $y_j \in Y_j$, for $j = 1, 2, \ldots, n$.

Definition 2.1.2. One consumer Negishi optimum. The allocation resulting from $\max U(x)$ s.t. $x - \Sigma_j y_j - \omega \leqslant 0$, $x \in X$, $y_j \in Y_j$, all j, is a Negishi optimum.

We now prove the following theorem:

Theorem 2.1.1. If assumptions (a)–(j′) of sections 1.2.1. and 1.2.2. hold, the solution of the one consumer Negishi optimum is an equilibrium.

Proof. Note first that the assumptions of theorem 1 of the Mathematical Appendix are satisfied.[1] Then, by theorem 1, the Lagrangian

$$L(x, y, p) = U(x) - p\cdot\left(x - \sum_j y_j - \omega\right)$$

has a saddle point $L(\bar{x}, \bar{y}, \bar{p})$ such that

$$L(x, y, \bar{p}) \leqslant L(\bar{x}, \bar{y}, \bar{p}) \leqslant L(\bar{x}, \bar{y}, p)$$

and

$$\bar{x} - \sum_j \bar{y}_j - \omega \leqslant 0, \bar{p}\cdot\left(\bar{x} - \sum_j \bar{y}_j - \omega\right) = 0, \qquad \bar{p} \geqslant 0,$$

which satisfies condition (a) of definition 2.1.1.

This shows also that at the solution point the budget constraint of the consumer is satisfied. If we now show that $U(x) \leqslant U(\bar{x})$, for every $x \in X$, and $\bar{p}\cdot x \leqslant \bar{p}\cdot\omega + \bar{p}\cdot\Sigma\bar{y}_j$, condition (b) will also be satisfied. But this is obvious from the first saddle point inequality which can be written, after setting $y_j = \bar{y}_j$, all j,

$$U(x) - \bar{p}\cdot(x - \Sigma\bar{y}_j - \omega) \leqslant U(\bar{x}),$$

and clearly $U(x) \leqslant U(\bar{x})$ for every $x \in X$, $\bar{p}\cdot x \leqslant \bar{p}\cdot\omega + \bar{p}\cdot\Sigma\bar{y}_j$.

[1] The less obvious is Slater's condition. Since there exists an $x^0 < \omega$ (assumption (i) of section 1.2.), it is clear that there also exists $x^0 < \omega + \Sigma_j y_j^0$ with $y_j^0 \equiv 0$, all j.

Finally, set $x=\bar{x}$ and $y_j=\bar{y}_j$ except for $j=s$ $(s=1,2,\ldots,n)$. Then, from the first saddle point inequality we have for every $y_s \in Y_s$:

$$\bar{p}\cdot y_s \leqslant \bar{p}\cdot \bar{y}_s, \qquad s=1,2,\ldots,n,$$

which proves that condition (c) holds also. Q.E.D.

It is however worthwhile to prove again this result in the language of linear programming, because this will help to gain greater insight into the economic interpretation of the primal and dual solutions of a linear program. Clear understanding of the general equilibrium meaning of optimal primal and dual variables will suggest in Chapters 3 and 4 ways of improving the specification of linear programming planning models of national economies; it will also help to understand the structure of the GEM model constructed in Chapter 9, and show how its results should be analyzed.

When there are several consumers, the analysis in Chapter 1 tells us that a Pareto or Negishi optimum is not necessarily an equilibrium. Reexamining this fact for linear programming optima will provide insight into the structure of possible algorithms for computing equilibria. Four approaches will be sketched: two based on looking for the equilibrium price vector, the others involving a search for a vector of equilibrium utility levels or of equilibrium Negishi welfare weights. We show how to check that such a vector generates an equilibrium solution; how the search for this vector should be conducted is discussed in Part II of the book.

2.1.1. Linear programming representation of producer behavior in a competitive economy

It is well known that linear programming provides an appropriate framework for the study of the interaction between prices, resource availabilities, and choice of technique. Let us recall the argument. We will designate by A the matrices of technical coefficients of processes j, in which $a_{kj}>0$ indicates that process j produces more of good k than it uses, whereas $a_{kj}<0$ indicates that the process has a net input of good k.

Goods may be produced by several production processes and a process may produce several goods.

We will distinguish between goods and factors of production. The factor input coefficients of the existing production processes are represented by a matrix F containing nonpositive elements.

We first illustrate the linear programming representation of a production set by a simple example which provides an opportunity to recall how linear programming relations can be interpreted in terms of the concepts of general equilibrium theory.

Consider an economy in which each of two producers of a good uses one technique, and the techniques use different factors of production. The selling price of the good is set equal to 1 by normalization; each producer considers prices as given.

Assume that the two available techniques are described by the coefficients matrix:

	Producer 1 Technique 1	Producer 2 Technique 2	Price of good or factor
Output of good	1	1	1
Input of first factor	0.5		$\tilde{p}_2$
Input of second factor		0.5	$\tilde{p}_3$

The aggregate production set of the producers is:

$$Y=\left\{y=\begin{bmatrix}y_1\\y_2\\y_3\end{bmatrix}\middle|\, y\leqslant\begin{bmatrix}z_1+z_2\\-0.5z_1\\-0.5z_2\end{bmatrix},\ z_1 \text{ and } z_2\geqslant 0\right\},$$

where z_1 and z_2 are activity levels denoting the extent to which each technique is used.

Neither producer 1 nor producer 2 can be in equilibrium if $\tilde{p}_2$ and $\tilde{p}_3<2$. If, for example, $\tilde{p}_2=1.5$, the profit from operating technique 1 would be $0.25\,z_1$, a function which has no maximum on $z\geqslant 0$. If $\tilde{p}_2=\tilde{p}_3=2$, then any

$$y=\begin{bmatrix}z_1+z_2\\-0.5z_1\\-0.5z_2\end{bmatrix},\ z_1 \text{ and } z_2\geqslant 0$$

maximizes profits. If $\tilde{p}_2>2$, $\tilde{p}_3=2$ then only producer 2 is willing to produce and any

$$y=\begin{bmatrix}z_2\\0\\-0.5z_2\end{bmatrix},\ z_2\geqslant 0$$

maximizes his profits. If $\tilde{p}_2, \tilde{p}_3 > 2$, the profit maximizing allocation is

$$y = \begin{bmatrix} 0 \\ 0 \\ 0 \end{bmatrix}.$$

The supply behavior of the producer can be expressed more compactly as a linear program. Define $Y(1, \tilde{p}_2, \tilde{p}_3)$, the production supported by the prices 1, $\tilde{p}_2$, and $\tilde{p}_3$, as the set of y values which solve the linear program

$$\begin{aligned} &\max y_1 + \tilde{p}_2 y_2 + \tilde{p}_3 y_3 \\ &\text{s.t. } y_1 - z_1 - z_2 \leqslant 0, \\ &\quad y_2 + 0.5 z_1 \leqslant 0, \\ &\quad y_3 + 0.5 z_2 \leqslant 0, \\ &\quad z_1, z_2 \geqslant 0, \end{aligned}$$

for a given $(\tilde{p}_2, \tilde{p}_3)$. If the linear program has infinite solutions, $Y(1, \tilde{p}_2, \tilde{p}_3)$ is undefined.

More generally let $\begin{pmatrix} A \\ F \end{pmatrix}$ be the matrix of input–output coefficients, where A and F correspond to inputs or outputs of goods and production factors, respectively, and the subscripts g and f denote goods and factors, respectively. The productions $Y(\tilde{p})$ supported by the prices $\tilde{p}$ can be represented by the set $Y(\tilde{p}_g, \tilde{p}_f)$ of y which are solutions of

$$\begin{aligned} &\max \tilde{p}_g \cdot y_g + \tilde{p}_f \cdot y_f \\ &\text{s.t. } y_g - Az \leqslant 0 \quad (u_g), \\ &\quad y_f - Fz \leqslant 0 \quad (u_f), \\ &\quad z \geqslant 0. \end{aligned}$$

2.1.2. *Linear programming representation of consumer behavior in a competitive economy*

It is less well known that linear programming can also be used to express the dependence of consumer demand on prices. We consider in this chapter a very simple case in which the utility function of a consumer is strongly separable, so that it can be written as

$$U(x) = \sum_k U_k(x_k),$$

where x_k is the amount of good k used by the consumer. It will be assumed that the marginal utility of each good is positive and decreasing so that

$$\frac{dU_k}{dx_k} > 0; \qquad \frac{d^2U_k}{dx_k^2} < 0.$$

Each component of the utility function

$$U_k(x_k) = \int_0^{x_k} \frac{dU_k}{d\xi_k} d\xi_k$$

can—as in the theory of the Rieman integral—be approximated with arbitrary accuracy by steps, as illustrated in fig. 2.1.

Then—*provided that marginal utility of each good is a positive decreasing function of consumption of the good*—the utility function can be approximated by the linear program

$$U(x) = \max \sum_k \sum_s g_k^s x_k^s$$

$$\text{s.t.} \quad \sum_s x_k^s \leqslant x_k \qquad (p_{gk}), \quad \text{all } k,$$

$$0 \leqslant x_k^s \leqslant \tilde{x}_k^s \qquad (w_k^s), \quad \text{all } s, k,$$

where the x_k^s will henceforth be called *consumption steps variables*; g_k^s is the average value of the marginal utility of good k on the range s.

Examination of the dual of this linear program will yield insight into its solution. The dual constraints and complementary slackness conditions are

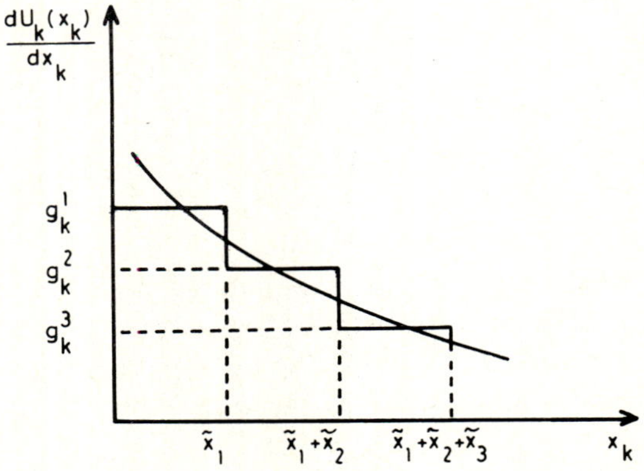

Figure 2.1 Linear approximation of a utility function.

at the optimum,

$$\left.\begin{aligned} &p_{gk}+w_k^s \geqslant g_k^s \\ &x_k^s(p_{gk}+w_k^s-g_k^s)=0 \\ &w_k^s(x_k^s-\tilde{x}_k^s)=0 \end{aligned}\right\}, \quad \text{all } s, k.$$

Let s^* be the last demand step used for product k. Assume that $0<x_k^{s^*}<\tilde{x}_k^{s^*}$, i.e. the step is not fully used. Then $w_k^{s^*}=0$ by complementary slackness, and we see that

$$p_{gk}=g_k^{s^*}=\text{marginal utility of good } k,$$

and

$$w_k^t=g_k^t-p_{gk}=\text{per unit consumer surplus for step } t \leqslant s^*,$$

$$x_k^t w_k^t=\text{total consumer surplus associated with step } t \text{ of the approximated utility function.}$$

Since $x_k^t=0$ for $t>s^*$, no consumer surplus accrues on steps beyond the marginal step s^*.

If $x_k^{s^*}=\tilde{x}_k^{s^*}$ the marginal step is fully used and then marginal utility is not uniquely defined at the point $x_k=\sum_{s=1}^{s^*}x_k^s$. The utility of the *last* unit used is $g_k^{s^*}$, that of the following unit is $g_k^{s^*+1}$, and $g_k^{s^*} \leqslant p_{gk} \leqslant g_k^{s^*+1}$; the other expressions are unchanged.

The dual variables associated with the consumption constraints and consumption upper bounds are therefore interpreted respectively as the marginal utilities of the goods and the consumer surpluses associated with the inframarginal units consumed.

The behavior of the consumer is then to maximize the utility function just defined subject to his budget constraint. The consumer has resources represented by initial holdings of factors of production $\tilde{f}$; he considers prices of goods $\tilde{p}_g$ and factors $\tilde{p}_f$ as given. He therefore choses a consumption x solution of:

$$\begin{aligned} \max &\sum_s \sum_k g_k^s x_k^s \\ \text{s.t.} &\sum_s x_k^s - x_k \leqslant 0, && \text{all } k, \\ & 0 \leqslant x_k^s \leqslant \tilde{x}_k^s, && \text{all } k, s, \\ &\sum_k \tilde{p}_{gk} x_k \leqslant \sum_l \tilde{p}_{fl} \tilde{f}_l. \end{aligned}$$

2.1.3. The competitive equilibrium

A competitive equilibrium of an economy with a single consumer and a set of producers can be calculated by solving the following "full problem" which we write in detached coefficients format as:[2]

Model 2.1

A one-country linear programming model.

	z	$x=y$	x^s		RHS
u_g	$-A$	I		$\leqslant$	0
p_f	$-F$			$\leqslant$	$\tilde{f}$
w^s			I	$\leqslant$	$\tilde{x}^s$
p_g		$-I$	Q	$\leqslant$	0
	$\geqslant$	$\geqslant$	$\geqslant$		$=\min$
Obj.	0	0	g	$=\max$	

where Q is a matrix of 1 and 0 corresponding to the coefficient of the x_k^s in the constraints $\Sigma x_k^s - x_k \leqslant 0$.

Lemma 2.1.1. If $\hat{\zeta}$ and $\hat{v}_1, \hat{v}_2$ is a solution of P_0,

$$\begin{aligned} &\max c\cdot\zeta \\ &\text{s.t. } B_1\zeta \leqslant b_1 \quad (v_1), \\ &\phantom{\text{s.t. }} B_2\zeta \leqslant b_2 \quad (v_2), \\ &\phantom{\text{s.t. }} \zeta \geqslant 0, \end{aligned}$$

[2]We will make extensive use of this convenient representation of linear programs. This detached coefficient table describes a linear program which has as primal

$$\begin{aligned} &\max g\cdot x^s \\ &\text{s.t. } -Az + x \leqslant 0, \\ &\phantom{\text{s.t. }} -Fz \leqslant \tilde{f}, \\ &\phantom{\text{s.t. }} x^s \leqslant \tilde{x}^s, \\ &\phantom{\text{s.t. }} -x + Qx^s \leqslant 0, \end{aligned}$$

and as dual

$$\begin{aligned} &\min \tilde{f}\cdot p_f + \tilde{x}^s\cdot w^s \\ &\text{s.t. } -u_g\cdot A - p_f\cdot F \geqslant 0, \\ &\phantom{\text{s.t. }} u_g - p_g \geqslant 0, \\ &\phantom{\text{s.t. }} w^s + p_g\cdot Q \geqslant g. \end{aligned}$$

The primal and dual non-negativity constraints are assumed to hold unless stated otherwise.

then:

(1) $\zeta=\hat{\zeta}$, $v_3=1$, and $v_2=\hat{v}_2$ is a solution of P_1

$$\begin{aligned}&\max c\cdot\zeta\\ &\text{s.t. } \tilde{v}_1\cdot B_1\zeta\leqslant\tilde{v}_1\cdot b_1 \quad (v_3),\\ &\qquad B_2\zeta\leqslant b_2 \qquad\qquad (v_2),\end{aligned}$$

with $\tilde{v}_1$ given and equal to $\hat{v}_1$ of P_0.

(2) $\zeta=\hat{\zeta}$, $\xi=b_1$, and $v_1=\hat{v}_1$ is a solution of P_2

$$\begin{aligned}&\max c\cdot\zeta-\tilde{v}_2\cdot B_2\zeta-\tilde{v}_1\cdot\xi\\ &\text{s.t. } B_1\zeta-\xi\leqslant 0 \quad (v_1),\\ &\qquad \zeta\geqslant 0,\end{aligned}$$

with $\tilde{v}_1, \tilde{v}_2$ given and equal to $\hat{v}_1$ and $\hat{v}_2$ of P_0.

Proof. Check that these solutions are feasible for both the primal and the dual of P_0, P_1, and P_2. Q.E.D.

Theorem 2.1.2. The solution of model 2.1 is a competitive equilibrium.

Proof. Using lemma 2.1.1 we define

$$B_1=\begin{bmatrix}-A & I & 0\\ -F & 0 & 0\end{bmatrix}; \qquad b_1=\begin{bmatrix}0\\ \tilde{f}\end{bmatrix}; \qquad v_1=\begin{bmatrix}u_g\\ p_f\end{bmatrix},$$

$$B_2=\begin{bmatrix}0 & 0 & I\\ 0 & -I & Q\end{bmatrix}; \qquad b_2=\begin{bmatrix}\tilde{x}^s\\ 0\end{bmatrix}; \qquad v_2=\begin{bmatrix}w^s\\ p_g\end{bmatrix},$$

$$\zeta=\begin{bmatrix}z\\ x\\ x^s\end{bmatrix}; \qquad c=\begin{bmatrix}0\\ 0\\ g\end{bmatrix}.$$

Denote by a circumflex (ˆ) the optimal solution of model 2.1.

Putting model 2.1 in the form of P_1, with $\tilde{u}_g=\hat{u}_g$ and $\tilde{p}_f=\hat{p}_f$ given, we obtain

$$\begin{aligned}&\max g\cdot x^s\\ &\text{s.t. } -\tilde{u}_g\cdot Az+\tilde{u}_g\cdot x-\tilde{p}_f\cdot Fz\leqslant\tilde{p}_f\cdot\tilde{f} \quad (v_3),\\ &\qquad x^s\leqslant\tilde{x}^s \qquad\qquad\qquad\qquad\qquad\qquad (w^s),\\ &\qquad +Qx^s-x\leqslant 0 \qquad\qquad\qquad\qquad\quad (p_g),\end{aligned}$$

the solution of which is, by lemma 2.1.1, $x^s=\hat{x}^s$, $z=\hat{z}$, $x=\hat{x}$, $v_3=1$, $w^s=\hat{w}^s$, and $p_g=\hat{p}_g$. But, by complementary slackness in model 2.1, we know that

$$(\hat{u}_g \cdot A + \hat{p}_f \cdot F)\hat{z} = 0,$$

$$\hat{u}_g \cdot \hat{x} - \hat{p}_g \cdot \hat{x} = 0.$$

Hence, $x^s=\hat{x}^s$, $x=\hat{x}$ is a solution of

$$\begin{aligned} &\max g \cdot x^s \\ &\text{s.t. } \tilde{p}_g \cdot x \leqslant \tilde{p}_f \cdot \tilde{f}, \\ &\qquad x^s \leqslant \tilde{x}^s, \\ &\qquad Qx^s - x \leqslant 0, \end{aligned}$$

which is the utility maximization problem of the consumer and $\hat{x}$ is a consumption supported by the prices $\tilde{p}_g$ and $\tilde{p}_f$.

Putting model 2.1 in the form of P_2 with $\tilde{u}_g=\hat{u}_g$, $\tilde{p}_f=\hat{p}_f$, $\tilde{w}^s=\hat{w}^s$, $\tilde{p}_g=\hat{p}_g$ given, we obtain

$$\begin{aligned} &\max(g-\tilde{w}^s-\tilde{p}_g Q)\cdot x^s + \tilde{p}_g \cdot x - \tilde{u}_g \cdot \xi_1 - \tilde{p}_f \cdot y_f \\ &\text{s.t. } -Az + x - \xi_1 \leqslant 0 \quad (u_g), \\ &\qquad -Fz - y_f \leqslant 0 \qquad (p_f), \end{aligned}$$

the solution of which is, by lemma 2.1.1, $x^s=\hat{x}^s$, $z=\hat{z}$, $x=\hat{x}$, $\xi_1=0$, $y_f=\tilde{f}$, $u_g=\hat{u}_g$, $p_f=\hat{p}_f$. But, by complementary slackness in model 2.1, we know that

$$(g-\hat{w}^s-\hat{p}_g Q)\cdot \hat{x}^s = 0.$$

Hence, $y_g=\hat{x}$ and $y_f=\tilde{f}$ is a solution of

$$\begin{aligned} &\max \tilde{p}_g \cdot y_g - \tilde{p}_f \cdot y_f \\ &\text{s.t. } y_g - Az \leqslant 0, \\ &\qquad -y_f - Fz \leqslant 0, \end{aligned}$$

which is the profit maximization problem of the producer and y_g, y_f is a production supported by the prices $\tilde{p}_g$, $\tilde{p}_f$.

As supply–demand constraints are obviously satisfied by the solution of the model, it follows that the consumptions $\tilde{x}$ and productions $\tilde{y}_g=\tilde{x}$, $\tilde{y}_f=f$ supported by the prices $\tilde{p}_g$, $\tilde{p}_f$ are a competitive equilibrium. Q.E.D.

2.2. Construction of national accounts

We turn now to the construction of national accounts for model 2.1. This will illustrate principles which are applicable to much more general models.

That a balanced set of accounts can be constructed results from the fact that, by complementary slackness,

$$\underset{\text{(income)}}{\bar{p}_f\cdot\tilde{f}} = -\bar{p}_f\cdot F\bar{z} = \underset{\text{(value added)}}{\bar{u}_g\cdot A\bar{z}} = \underset{\text{(expenditure)}}{\bar{u}_g\cdot\bar{x}} .$$

Consumers' surplus is, using the complementary slackness conditions again,

$$\begin{aligned}\bar{w}^s\cdot\tilde{x}^s &= g\cdot\bar{x}^s - \bar{p}_g\cdot Q\bar{x}^s \\ &= g\cdot\bar{x}^s - \bar{p}_g\cdot\bar{x},\end{aligned}$$

i.e. utility minus the value of consumption, as expected.

Finally, we note that if there are no free goods ($\bar{u}_g>0$) so that $-A\bar{z}+\bar{x}=0$, $\tilde{p}\cdot A\bar{z}=\tilde{p}\cdot\bar{x}$ for arbitrary $\tilde{p}$, i.e. national expenditure equals value added even if goods are valued at nonequilibrium prices such as the market prices of an earlier year. This justifies the familiar equality of expenditures and value added at constant prices. However, equality of these aggregates with factor incomes is obviously *not* preserved if prices differ from equilibrium prices as $\bar{p}_f\cdot F\bar{z}\neq\bar{u}_g\cdot A\bar{z}$ usually if prices are arbitrary; whence the well-known remark that it is not, in general, possible to define a constant price income concept which can be fitted into a balanced set of national accounts.

The constant price national income concept is however useful if the prices are those of the equilibrium solution. By the Kuhn–Tucker conditions,

$$\bar{p}_f\cdot F+\bar{u}_g\cdot A=\bar{\theta}\text{ say},\quad \bar{\theta}\leqslant 0,$$

where the components of $\bar{\theta}$ are the unit profits incurred by using the various activities which are zero for activities used at the optimum and nonpositive for others. Also, $\tilde{f}\geqslant -Fz$ for admissible z. Hence, as $\bar{p}_f\geqslant 0$,

$$\bar{p}_f\cdot\tilde{f}\geqslant -\bar{p}_f\cdot Fz\geqslant\bar{u}_g\cdot Az=\bar{u}_g\cdot x,$$

i.e. for any feasible nonequilibrium solution, national income at constant equilibrium prices will tend to exceed constant price value added and expenditure.[3] The excess (if any) will be the sum of two components:

(a) $\bar{p}_f \cdot (\tilde{f} + Fz)$, which is positive if the alternative solution does not use all of the available resources of one or more factors which are not free at equilibrium, and

(b) $-\bar{p}_f \cdot Fz - \bar{u}_g \cdot Az = -\bar{\theta} \cdot z$, which is positive if the alternative solution uses activities which are unprofitable at equilibrium prices.

These two components can be interpreted as indicators of the two sources of waste caused by distorting the equilibrium pattern of production. Their sum provides a convenient measure of the waste caused by tariffs and other types of market distortions.

This waste clearly results from misallocations in the sphere of production. A similar concept can be defined for consumption misallocations. We have to add to the GNP loss measured by $\bar{p}_f \cdot \tilde{f} - \bar{u}_g \cdot x$ the difference between the consumer surpluses in the two solutions. This is $g \cdot x^s - \bar{p}_g \cdot Qx_s \leqslant \bar{w}^s \cdot x^s \leqslant \bar{w}^s \cdot \tilde{x}^s$, where the first term is the consumer surplus of the alternative solution and the last one on the right is the consumer surplus of the competitive equilibrium solution. As for the waste caused by production misallocations, the sign of the inequality is unambiguous.

2.3. Input–output and general equilibrium

It is interesting to use the analysis of section 2.1 to show why the solution of an input–output model is a general equilibrium.

Let a closed system of *input–output quantity equations* be described by

$$(A - I)z + cR = 0,$$

$$l \cdot z = 1,$$

where A is a matrix of input–output coefficients, c $(\Sigma c_i = 1)$ a vector of coefficients reflecting the pattern of spending of consumers, and $l > 0$ a vector of labor coefficients; the labor supply is set equal to 1 by an appropriate choice of units. The variables z are the activity levels of industries and R is the national product.

[3] Note that national income at constant equilibrium prices $\bar{p}_f \cdot \tilde{f}$ is independent of z; any shortfall of GNP as compared to this income is thus a direct measure of the inefficiency of the feasible production program z.

The quantity equations imply that the supply and demand of commodities are in balance; the corresponding *input–output price equations* reflect the equality of selling price and cost of production. These are, if the wage rate is represented by the scalar p_l,

$$p_g \cdot (A-I) + p_l l = 0,$$
$$p_g \cdot c = 1,$$

which implies that for each good j the selling price p_{gj} is equal to the cost of intermediate inputs $\Sigma_i a_{ij} p_{gi}$ plus the labor cost $p_l l_j$. The second equation serves as a normalization rule.

We now show that the input–output quantity and price equations solve an appropriate linear program defined by model 2.2, the solution of which is an equilibrium.

Model 2.2

Linear programming formulation of the closed input–output model.

	z	R		RHS
p_g p_l	$A-I$ l	c 0	$\leq$ $\leq$	0 1
	$\geq$	$\geq$		$=\min$
	0	1	$=\max$	

Theorem 2.3.1. The solution of the closed input–output model is a competitive equilibrium.

Proof. We first show that the solution of the closed input–output model is a solution of model 2.2.

If A is productive, the input–output quantity equations can be shown to have a solution with $\tilde{z} > 0$ and $\tilde{R} > 0$.[4] This is obviously a basic feasible solution of model 2.2; the corresponding value of the primal objective function is $\tilde{R}$.

[4] A is productive if there exists an $x^* \geq 0$ such that $Ax^* < x^*$. For the existence of a positive R, see Gale (1960, pp. 294 *et seq.*). The assumption $c > 0$ can be relaxed to $c \geq 0$, $c \neq 0$ and A indecomposable. See Gale (1960, pp. 294 *et seq.*).

The input–output price equations likewise define a basic feasible solution of the dual of model 2.2, with $\tilde{p}_l>0, \tilde{p}_g>0$; the corresponding value of the dual objective function is $\tilde{p}_l$.

We now show that $\tilde{p}_l=\tilde{R}$, which implies that $(\tilde{z}, \tilde{R}, \tilde{p}_g, \tilde{p}_l)$ is an optimal solution of model 2.2. Premultiplying the quantity equations by $(\tilde{p}_g, \tilde{p}_l)$ shows that

$$\tilde{p}_g\cdot(A-I)\tilde{z}+\tilde{R}\tilde{p}_g\cdot c+\tilde{p}_l l\cdot\tilde{z}=\tilde{p}_l,$$

while postmultiplying the price equations by $(\tilde{z}, \tilde{R})$ shows that

$$\tilde{p}_g\cdot(A-I)\tilde{z}+\tilde{R}\tilde{p}_g\cdot c+\tilde{p}_l l\cdot\tilde{z}=\tilde{R},$$

so that $\tilde{p}_l=\tilde{R}$.

We now prove that the solution of model 2.2 solves the competitive equilibrium problem defined below:

(a) Equality of supply and demand $x-y=\omega$.

(b) Utility maximization of the single consumer: for the consumer we assume that

  (i) his initial endowment is a vector $\omega=\begin{bmatrix}0\\1\end{bmatrix}$, the RHS of the linear program;

  (ii) his consumption set is $X=\Omega$, the closed non-negative orthant; and

  (iii) his utility function is $U=\min_k x_k/c_k$ (its form is illustrated in fig. 2.2).

(c) Profit maximization of firms. Let the production sets of producers be

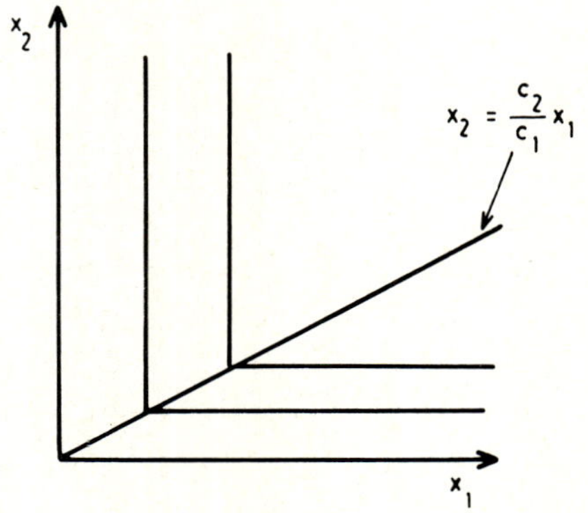

Figure 2.2 Indifference map of the utility function $U=\min\{x_1/c_1, x_2/c_2\}$.

defined by

$$Y_j = \{y_j \mid y_j = a_j z_j,\ z_j \geqslant 0\} \qquad (j=1,2,\ldots,n),$$

where a_j is a vector with components $(-a_{1j}, -a_{2j}, \ldots, 1-a_{jj}, \ldots, -a_{nj}, -l_j)$. Thus the production sets are rays from the origin.

Indeed, the prices $\tilde{p}=(\tilde{p}_g, \tilde{p}_l)$, the productions $\tilde{y}_j = a_j \tilde{z}_j$, and the consumption $\tilde{x}=\tilde{R}c$ satisfy conditions (a), (b), and (c) and are therefore an equilibrium of the economy.

Condition (a) is satisfied because $(\tilde{z}, \tilde{R})$ satisfy the input–output quantity equations.

Condition (b) is satisfied. Indeed, as has been seen, $\tilde{p}_l = \tilde{R}$. But $\tilde{p}_l = \tilde{p}\cdot\omega$, $\tilde{R}=\tilde{p}\cdot\tilde{x}$, so that $\tilde{p}\cdot\tilde{x} = \tilde{p}\cdot\omega$: the consumer is on his budget constraint. It is then trivial to see that $\tilde{x}=c\tilde{R}$ solves the consumer's utility maximization problem which can obviously be written

$$\begin{aligned} &\max\left(\min_k x_k/c_k\right) \\ &\text{s.t.}\quad \tilde{p}\cdot x \leqslant \tilde{p}\cdot\omega, \\ &\qquad\ \ x \geqslant 0. \end{aligned}$$

Condition (c), finally, is also satisfied. The profits of producers are

$$\tilde{p}\cdot y_j = z_j\left(\tilde{p}_{gj} - \Sigma a_{kj}\tilde{p}_{gk} - l_j \tilde{p}_l\right) = 0,$$

as implied by the fact that $(\tilde{p}_g, \tilde{p}_l)$ satisfy the input–output price equations. Profits are zero for all values of z and thus for $z=\tilde{z}$. Hence, $\tilde{y}_j = a_j \tilde{z}_j$ is a production supported by the prices $\tilde{p}$. Q.E.D.

2.4. General equilibrium when there are several consumers

2.4.1. Some simple examples

In models 2.1 and 2.2 it was not necessary to specify explicitly the budget constraint; it was satisfied automatically at the optimum. This is not true when there are several consumers and several goods.

That such constraints are indeed necessary can be illustrated by an almost trivial example. Consider an exchange economy in which there is only one good and no production. There are two consumers with positive initial endowments ω_1, ω_2 of the good, and linear utility functions $U_1(x_1)= g_1x_1$, $U_2(x_2)=g_2x_2$, $g_1, g_2>0$. The optimal allocation of the good between the consumers can be described by

Model 2.3

A two-consumers one-good model.

$$\begin{array}{ll} \max & g_1x_1+g_2x_2 \\ \text{s.t.} & x_1+x_2 \leqslant \omega_1+\omega_2 \quad (p) \\ & x_1 \geqslant 0; \qquad x_2 \geqslant 0 \end{array}$$

If $g_1>g_2$, it is optimal to allocate all of the available quantity of the good to consumer 1: $x_1=\omega_1+\omega_2$. The shadow price of the good will be $p=g_1>0$, and since $\omega_2>0$ we have

$$px_1=p(\omega_1+\omega_2)$$

and the budget constraint of consumer 1 is violated since

$$p(\omega_1+\omega_2)>p\omega_1.$$

If $g_2>g_1$, then consumer 2 will get all the available supply of the good and will spend more than he earns. Only if $g_1=g_2$ will there be an optimal solution which is an equilibrium.[5]

In the example it would be possible to enforce the budget balance of the two consumers by introducing an additional (linear) constraint into the model. This constraint, $x_1=\omega_1$, does imply balance of the (bilinear) budget constraint of consumer 1, $px_1=p\omega_1$; as $x_1+x_2=\omega_1+\omega_2$, we have then $px_2=p\omega_2$ so that consumer 2 is also in balance.

This would lead to solving

$$\begin{aligned} \max\ & g_1x_1+g_2x_2 \\ \text{s.t.}\ & x_1+x_2 \leqslant \omega_1+\omega_2, \\ & x_1=\omega_1, \\ & x_1, x_2 \geqslant 0. \end{aligned}$$

[5]In that case, any $0 \leqslant x_1 \leqslant \omega_1+\omega_2$ is an optimal allocation for consumer 1 so that $x_1=\omega_1$ satisfies his budget balance and is an equilibrium consumption. The corresponding allocation of consumer 2, $x_2=\omega_2$, which satisfies his budget balance, is likewise an equilibrium consumption.

The solution of this program is an equilibrium, with $\bar{x}_1=\omega_1$ and $\bar{x}_2=\omega_2$, $\bar{p}=g_2$, and $\bar{\lambda}=g_1-g_2$.[6]

This solution cannot be adopted if there are two or more goods. Assume that the consumers have utility functions $U_1(x_{11}, x_{12})=g_{11}x_{11}+g_{12}x_{12}$, $U_2(x_{21}, x_{22})=g_{21}x_{21}+g_{22}x_{22}$, where the first subscript refers to the consumer and the second to the good. Assume that $g_{11}, g_{12}, g_{21}, g_{22}>0$ and that the initial resources of the consumers are $(\omega_{11}, \omega_{12})$ and $(\omega_{21}, \omega_{22})$. To find an equilibrium we would have to solve a problem of the form:

Model 2.4

A two-consumers two-goods model.

$$\begin{array}{llllll}
\max & g_{11}x_{11}+g_{12}x_{12}+g_{21}x_{21}+g_{22}x_{22} & & & & \\
\text{s.t.} & x_{11} & + x_{21} & & \leqslant \omega_{11}+\omega_{21} & (p_1) \\
 & x_{12} & & + x_{22} & \leqslant \omega_{12}+\omega_{22} & (p_2) \\
 & p_1x_{11}+p_2x_{12} & & & =p_1\omega_{11}+p_2\omega_{12} & (\lambda) \\
 & x_{11}, x_{12}, x_{21}, x_{22}\geqslant 0 & & & &
\end{array}$$

But this problem is not a linear program: the (λ) constraint is bilinear in the primal and dual variables and cannot be linearized by dividing through by one of the prices. For this reason it is not even a classical nonlinear program.[7] In fact there is no general method for solving such programs.[8]

2.4.2. Approaches to solving general equilibrium problems with several consumers and goods

A first approach to solving model 2.4 would be a trial-and-error procedure alternating between function evaluation and parameter revision phases.

(1) Function evaluation. Replace the budget constraint of model 2.4 by $\tilde{p}_1x_{11}+\tilde{p}_2x_{12}\leqslant\tilde{p}_1\omega_{11}++\tilde{p}_2\omega_{12}$, where $\tilde{p}_1$ and $\tilde{p}_2$ are given. Model 2.4 is now a linear program; solve this and calculate the dual variables of the balance constraints $\hat{p}_1$ and $\hat{p}_2$.

[6] Since at the optimum $x_1+x_2=\omega_1+\omega_2$, $x_1=\omega_1$ implies $x_2=\omega_2$, so that it was not necessary to impose consumer 2's budget constraint.

[7] Note that the dual of a nonlinear program may involve products of dual and primal variables; but the primal problem involves primal variables only.

[8] A very special case is considered by Konno in a recent paper (Konno, 1976); but the algorithm presented is not guaranteed to converge, and is not applicable to general equilibrium problems.

(2) Parameter revision. Check whether $\hat{p}_i = \tilde{p}_i$[9] $(i=1,2)$. If so, the solution of the linear program is an equilibrium. If not, use some rule to generate new $\tilde{p}_1$, $\tilde{p}_2$ and go to the function evaluation phase.

A second way of finding an equilibrium price vector is to drop the balance constraints from model 2.4 and solve a linear program[10] consisting of two entirely separate consumer utility maximization problems, which may be solved independently:

$$\begin{aligned} \max\ & g_{11}x_{11} + g_{12}x_{12} \\ \text{s.t.}\ & \tilde{p}_1 x_{11} + \tilde{p}_2 x_{12} \leqslant \tilde{p}_1 \omega_{11} + \tilde{p}_2 \omega_{12}, \\ & x_{11}, x_{12} \geqslant 0, \end{aligned}$$

and

$$\begin{aligned} \max\ & g_{21}x_{21} + g_{22}x_{22} \\ \text{s.t.}\ & \tilde{p}_1 x_{21} + \tilde{p}_2 x_{22} \leqslant \tilde{p}_1 \omega_{21} + \tilde{p}_2 \omega_{22}, \\ & x_{21}, x_{22} \geqslant 0. \end{aligned}$$

Then, if $\tilde{p}_1$, $\tilde{p}_2$ are equilibrium price vectors, there will be an optimal allocation x_{11}, x_{12}, x_{21}, and x_{22} such that the balance constraints are satisfied.

A computational approach might therefore consist of the following phases.

(1) Function evaluation. Solve the above problems for given $\tilde{p}$. Calculate the optimal excess demands.

(2) Parameter revision. If excess demands are nonpositive, the solution is an equilibrium. If not, select another $\tilde{p}$ using some appropriate rule and go to the function evaluation phase.

A third approach involves solving a Pareto optimum problem of the type

$$\begin{aligned} \max\ & g_{11}x_{11} + g_{12}x_{12} \\ \text{s.t.}\ & g_{21}x_{21} + g_{22}x_{22} \geqslant \tilde{U}_2, \\ & x_{11} + x_{21} \leqslant \omega_{11} + \omega_{21}, \\ & x_{12} + x_{22} \leqslant \omega_{12} + \omega_{22}, \\ & x_{11}, x_{12}, x_{21}, x_{22} \geqslant 0, \end{aligned}$$

[9] We will see that proportionality between the two sets of prices is sufficient for equilibrium.

[10] We have to reintroduce consumer 2's budget constraint which was redundant when the balance constraints were present.

and checking whether the solution satisfies the budget constraint of consumer 1. This suggests yet a third two-stage approach which involves the following phases.

(1) Function evaluation. Solve the above linear program for given $\tilde{U}_2$. Calculate optimal demands and prices.

(2) Parameter revision. If the solution satisfies the budget constraints, it is an equilibrium. If not, use some appropriate rule to generate another $\tilde{U}_2$ and go to the function evaluation.

Negishi's theorem finally suggests a fourth computational approach. Write our model as

$$\begin{aligned}
&\max \tilde{\alpha}_1(g_{11}x_{11}+g_{12}x_{12})+\tilde{\alpha}_2(g_{21}x_{21}+g_{22}x_{22})\\
&\text{s.t. } x_{11}+x_{21}\leqslant \omega_{11}+\omega_{21} \quad (p_1),\\
&\qquad x_{12}+x_{22}\leqslant \omega_{12}+\omega_{22} \quad (p_2),\\
&\qquad x_{11}, x_{12}, x_{21}, x_{22} \geqslant 0.
\end{aligned}$$

If $\tilde{\alpha}_2=0$, the optimal solution would allocate all consumptions to consumer 1, who will have a budget deficit; if $\tilde{\alpha}_1=0$, consumer 1 will have a surplus. We can search for $\tilde{\alpha}_1, \tilde{\alpha}_2$ such that both consumers will be in budget equilibrium. In this case, the two-phase algorithm involves the following.

(1) Function evaluation. Solve the linear programming problem for some given welfare weights $\tilde{\alpha}_1, \tilde{\alpha}_2$.

(2) Parameter revision. If the solution satisfies the budget constraints, it is an equilibrium. If not, use some appropriate rule to generate new $\tilde{\alpha}_i$ and go to the function evaluation phase.

CHAPTER 3

Models of national economies and the two-country model of trade theory

In this chapter it will be argued that the so-called "linear programming planning models" provide an incorrect description of national economies. Except when foreign demand and supply are perfectly elastic, a model should be designed along the lines of the "two-country model" of international trade theory, a general equilibrium system describing relations between the country and an explicitly defined "rest of the world". This scheme can be implemented using linear programs of both the country and the rest of the world.

It is often wrongly thought that linear programming cannot be used to construct nonlinear functions. In a recent paper, Taylor (1976) has shown that models using linear functions do lead to absurd conclusions. These difficulties disappear if the functions have a more realistic structure.

3.1. Linear programming planning models for open economies: The curse of linearity?

Consider the following model, written in detached coefficients format.

Model 3.1

A simple linear programming model of an open national economy without investment.

	z	x	$e-m$		RHS
u_g	$-A$	I	I	$\leqslant$	0
u_f	$-F$			$\leqslant$	$\tilde{f}$
λ			$-\tilde{p}$	$\leqslant$	0
	$\geqslant$	$\geqslant$	$\geqslant$		$=\min$
Obj.	0	g	0	$=\max$	

$\tilde{p}$ is a vector of given world prices and g a vector of marginal utilities of consumption; the remaining notation is the same as that used in section 2.2.

The source of difficulty originates in the theorem of linear programming which states that if a linear program is feasible and bounded, there exists an optimal solution in which the number of nonzero variables, including slacks, does not exceed the number of constraints. Thus, if, as is often the case, there is a single factor of production and r goods, only $r+2$ variables and slacks out of $4r+2$ will normally be positive.

It can be shown that this solution will usually correspond to a situation of extreme specialization in which

(a) a single good is produced;
(b) this good is exported;
(c) all other goods are imported; and
(d) a single good is consumed.

Needless to say such results are hardly realistic, and planning models which generate them would not be likely to gain acceptance. We will see how the builders of such models have tried to adapt the basic format to obtain more reasonable results.

Linear programming theory points the way to a solution. Adding constraints will increase the number of optimal basic variables, and thus prevent extreme specialization of production, consumption, and trade. A sound way of adding constraints is to allow for the existence of additional factors of production. However, as Taylor (1976, p. 66) notes, "inventiveness and data tend to run out when three or four types of labor and shiftable capital have been accounted for". Since adding six or seven positive variables is not enough to eliminate overspecialization in a planning model which may cover 30 goods or more, model-builders have tended to resort to *ad hoc* devices.

These devices are to block off by constraints the solutions they do not like. For this, a complex assortment of bounds is imposed on various production, export, import, and consumption activities, without careful justification. Exports are bounded above to take account of the "limited absorptive capacity of foreign markets"; imports are bounded above in recognition of "the government's import substitution policy"; production is bounded above or below in recognition of "resource constraints which limit expansion" or of "the social costs of rapid reduction of output"; consumption is constrained to fluctuate between upper and lower bounds because "the planners' ability to influence consumption patterns is not unlimited"; and in multiperiod models consumption is forced to increase by a minimum target rate of growth which reflects "the distaste of the population for sudden changes in the standard of living".

The result of all this is, in effect, to define a small cage out of which the optimal solution may not escape. This is good diplomacy, since policy-makers can then please governments by presenting solutions which both look reasonable and are claimed to be optimal. But this is neither good economics, nor is it a responsible way of formulating economic policy.

Planners are also asked to compute shadow prices which can be used for project analysis and other forms of decentralized decision-making. But the arbitrary bounds introduced into optimizing models pick up shadow prices which have no clear meaning and which, since all dual prices are interdependant, distort the dual solution. How, for example, should we interpret, in a decentralized decision-making context, the shadow price of a constraint expressing the "population's preference for a steady increase in the standard of living", or "the inability of planners to distort consumption patterns beyond given limits"?[1]

The problem discussed by Taylor results from:

(a) the linearity of the utility function and the use of constant returns in production; and

(b) the assumption that world prices are given.

The first assumption is relaxed in section 3.2; the second is dealt with in section 3.3.

3.2. Linearization of nonlinear utility and production functions

3.2.1. Utility functions

A few models in the literature have replaced the constant marginal utility formulation by a separable utility function with diminishing marginal utilities.[2] Such functions can be represented easily by linear approximations of the type used in model 2.1 (Chapter 2).

It is important to realize, however, that linear programming is capable of approximating arbitrary concave utility functions to any degree.

[1]If these constraints reflected well-defined policy objectives there might be scope to interpret the shadow prices in terms of second-best analysis. In practice, the constraints usually reflect no more than *ad hoc* fiddling to exclude unreasonable solutions.

[2]This assumption is made implicitly in the CHAC model; see Goreux and Manne (1973). The idea is used explicitly by Goreux (1977) who assumes that the utility function has the direct addilog form.

The representation is based on the fact that if $U(x)$ is a concave function, the set $C=\{x,U \mid U\leqslant U(x)\}$, is a convex set in R^{r+1}, bounded above by the graph of the utility function; $U(x)$ can now be defined by

$$U(x)=\max U$$
$$\text{s.t.}\quad (U,x)\in C,\quad \text{for given } x\in X.$$

As a convex set, C can be approximated in two ways, illustrated in fig. 3.1. In the figure a grid $X=(x_1, x_2, x_3,\ldots)$ is defined to approximate the convex set bounded above by a concave function $f(x)$. The inner approximation is defined by

$$C_1=\{x, f_1(x)| x, f_1(x)\in H_1\},$$

where H_1 is the set defined by

$$f_1(x)\leqslant F\theta,$$

$$x=X\theta,$$

$$\varepsilon\cdot\theta=1,$$

$$\theta\geqslant 0.$$

F is the vector $[f(x_1)f(x_2)\ldots]$ and ε is a vector of ones.

The outer approximation is defined by

$$C_2=\{x, f_2(x)| x, f_2(x)\in H_2\},$$

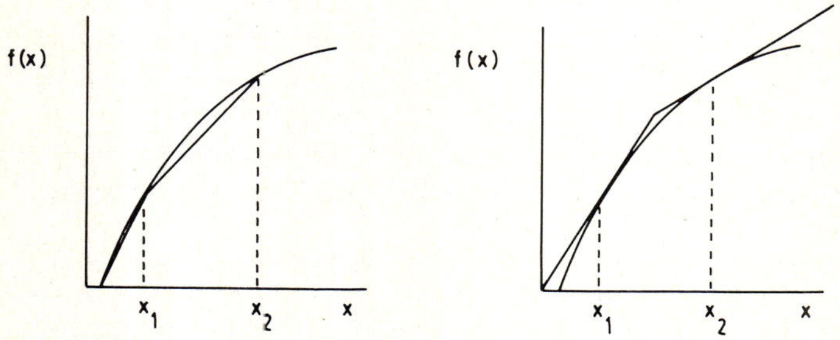

Figure 3.1. Inner and outer approximation of a convex set.

where H_2 is the set defined by

$$\varepsilon f_2(x) \leqslant Gx + \tilde{g}$$

and where G is a vector the components of which are the derivatives $\mathrm{d}f(x)/\mathrm{d}x$ evaluated at $x_1, x_2, \ldots$, and $\tilde{g}$ is a vector the components of which are $f(x_1) - g_1 x_1$, $f(x_2) - g_2 x_2, \ldots$ ($g_i x_i + \tilde{g}_i$ is the first-order Taylor approximation to the function $f(x)$ at the point x_i).

These definitions are readily extended to sets with an arbitrary number of dimensions. X and G will be matrices; the expressions will otherwise not be changed. Also, it is clear that the approximations can be made arbitrarily accurate by suitable refinement of the grid.

In the sequel, we discuss the use in models of the outer approximation only. There are no difficulties in implementing the ideas using the inner approximation.

Using the outer approximation, the utility function $U(x)$ can be approximated by the linear program

$$U(x) = \max U$$
$$\text{s.t.} \quad \varepsilon U - Gx \leqslant \tilde{g}, \quad \text{for given } x \in X$$

which is easy to introduce into a linear programming model of an economy. In detached coefficients format, this would be written:

Model 3.2

Linear programming model of an economy with a general utility function.

	z	x	U		RHS
u_g	$-A$	I		$\leqslant$	0
u_f	$-F$			$\leqslant$	$\tilde{f}$
w		$-G$	ε	$\leqslant$	$\tilde{g}$
	$\geqslant$	$\geqslant$	$\geqslant$		$=\min$
	0	0	1	$=\max$	

The pricing implications of such a representation are straightforward. The primal and dual problems are

$$\begin{aligned} &\max U \\ &\text{s.t.} \quad -Az+x \leqslant 0 \quad (u_g) \\ &\qquad -Fz \leqslant \tilde{f} \quad (u_f), \\ &\qquad -Gx+\varepsilon U \leqslant \tilde{g} \quad (w), \end{aligned}$$

and

$$\begin{aligned} &\min u_f \cdot \tilde{f} + w \cdot \tilde{g} \\ &\text{s.t.} \quad -u_g \cdot A - u_f \cdot F \geqslant 0 \quad (z), \\ &\qquad u_g - w \cdot G \geqslant 0 \quad (x), \\ &\qquad w \cdot \varepsilon \geqslant 1 \quad (U). \end{aligned}$$

Suppose that at the optimum all goods are consumed in positive amounts. Then, from complementary slackness, it follows that $u_g = w \cdot G$ and $w \cdot \varepsilon = 1$. If the optimal x lies in the interior of facet s of the approximated welfare function, only the sth constraint of (w) will hold as an equality and only the sth element of the w-vector will be different from zero, and hence necessarily equal to 1 as can be seen from constraint (U). So, w is the unit vector ε_s.

It is then apparent that, for any x in the interior of some facet s, the primal program is equivalent to

$$\begin{aligned} &\max g^s \cdot x \\ &\text{s.t.} \quad -Az + x \leqslant 0, \\ &\qquad -Fz \leqslant \tilde{f}, \end{aligned}$$

where g^s is the sth row of G. Note that the coefficients g^s of the objective function are obviously approximations of the marginal utilities of the utility function in the region of the consumption set which is defined by facet s.[3] This means that the primal program operates as though switching objective functions when the primal value of x moves between the polyhedral regions over which the welfare function is approximated. This switching ensures that among the alternative objective functions defined by $-Gx+\varepsilon U \leqslant \tilde{g}$ the simplex algorithm automatically selects the function which best describes the welfare function, given the values of x.

[3] The gradient of the hyperplane which approximates the function on this range will correspond to an average value of the total differential of the utility function.

A strongly separable utility function of the type used in Chapter 2

$$U(x) = \sum U_k(x_k)$$

approximated by

$$\max \sum g_k^s x_k^s,$$
$$\text{s.t.} \quad \sum_s x_k^s \leqslant x_k,$$
$$0 \leqslant x_k^s \leqslant \tilde{x}_k^s,$$

has (if there are two goods and two steps for each good) the indifference map shown in fig. 3.2.

In regions A, amounts of goods 1 and 2 with high (low) marginal utility are exchanged for each other. In regions B, high marginal utility amounts of $i=1,2$ are exchanged for low marginal utility amounts of $j=2,1$. In regions C, $x_i^1 + x_i^2$ $(i=1,2)$ has reached its upper limit $\tilde{x}_i^1 + \tilde{x}_i^2$. It is the slack x_i^3 which accounts for the increase of consumption, and as x_i^3 is not in the objective function, the welfare remains unchanged and the indifference curve is parallel to the x_i-axis. In region D, finally, both $x_i^1 + x_i^2$ $(i=1,2)$ have reached their upper limit. All consumption vectors in D are equivalent; they form a thick indifference class.

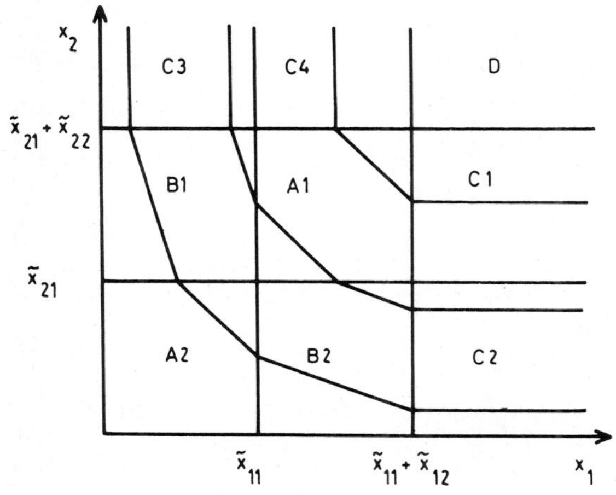

Figure 3.2. Indifference map for a strongly separable utility function.

This approximation of a strongly separable utility function is a special case of the bounding hyperplane representation of welfare functions just defined.[4] The representation used in Chapter 2 is however much simpler.

The ideas just developed can be used to approximate any utility function. The simplest case is that of separable functions, which include the following.

(1) Cobb–Douglas utility functions after transformation to $\log U = \Sigma a_i \log x_i$. More generally, linear expenditure system utility functions of the type $\log U = \Sigma a_i \log(x_i - c_i)$ can be represented for example by shifting the origin of consumption to the vector c.

(2) CES utility functions with an elasticity of substitution exceeding one (so that $-1 \leqslant b < 0$), written as $U = \Sigma d_i x_i^{-b}$.

(3) Direct addilog utility functions, as used by Goreux (1977), of the form $U = \Sigma \alpha_i x_i^{\beta_i}$, where $0 < \beta_i < 1$.

It is possible to approximate in this way utility functions which are not separable. Any strictly concave function can, if it is sufficiently smooth, be approximated locally by a Taylor expansion

$$U \approx U_0 + U'_{x_0}(x - x_0) + \tfrac{1}{2}(x - x_0)' U_{x_0 x_0}(x - x_0),$$

where U_0, the vector U_{x_0}, and the matrix $U_{x_0 x_0}$ are values of the function and of its first two derivatives at a point x_0; $U_{x_0 x_0}$ is negative definite if U is concave and can thus be decomposed as $U_{x_0 x_0} = -C\hat{\Lambda}C'$, where $C' = C^{-1}$ and $\hat{\Lambda}$ is a positive diagonal matrix. But then U can be represented as a

[4] For the case pictured in fig. 3.2 the constraints $-Gx + \varepsilon U \leqslant \tilde{g}$ can be written:

Region of fig. 3.2	x_1	x_2	U		RHS
A1	g_{12}	g_{22}	-1	$\geqslant$	$-(g_{11}-g_{12})\tilde{x}_{11}-(g_{21}-g_{22})\tilde{x}_{21}$
A2	g_{11}	g_{21}	-1	$\geqslant$	0
B1	g_{11}	g_{22}	-1	$\geqslant$	$-(g_{21}-g_{22})\tilde{x}_{21}$
B2	g_{12}	g_{21}	-1	$\geqslant$	$-(g_{11}-g_{12})\tilde{x}_{11}$
C1	0	g_{22}	-1	$\geqslant$	$-[g_{11}\tilde{x}_{11}+g_{12}\tilde{x}_{22}+(g_{21}-g_{22})\tilde{x}_{21}]$
C2	0	g_{21}	-1	$\geqslant$	$-(g_{11}\tilde{x}_{11}+g_{12}\tilde{x}_{12})$
C3	g_{11}	0	-1	$\geqslant$	$-(g_{21}\tilde{x}_{21}+g_{22}\tilde{x}_{22})$
C4	g_{12}	0	-1	$\geqslant$	$-[g_{21}\tilde{x}_{21}+g_{22}\tilde{x}_{22}+(g_{11}-g_{12})\tilde{x}_{11}]$
D	0	0	-1	$\geqslant$	$-(g_{11}\tilde{x}_{11}+g_{12}\tilde{x}_{12}+g_{21}\tilde{x}_{21}+g_{22}\tilde{x}_{22})$

separable function of consumption variables x_* expressed with respect to the base C'; putting $x_* = C'x$ and $x_{*0} = C'x_0$, U can be written

$$U = U_0 + U'_{x_0}C(x_* - x_{*0}) - \tfrac{1}{2}(x_* - x_{*0})'\hat{\Lambda}(x_* - x_{*0})$$

$$= A + Bx_* - \tfrac{1}{2}x'_*\hat{\Lambda}x_*,$$

with

$$A = U_0 - U'_{x_0}Cx_{*0} - \tfrac{1}{2}x'_{*0}\hat{\Lambda}x_{*0},$$

$$B = U'_{x_0}C + x'_{*0}\hat{\Lambda}.$$

3.2.2. Production functions

What has been said of concave utility functions in section 3.2.1 can of course be applied to production functions. In the general case this would lead to describing the profit maximizing problem of the producer as

$$\begin{aligned} &\max\ \tilde{p}_g \cdot y \\ &\text{s.t.}\ \ Hy \leqslant \tilde{h} \quad (u_h), \\ &\qquad y \geqslant 0. \end{aligned}$$

The economic interpretation of this specification is straightforward. The maximand is what is left after subtracting from the value of output the value of all inputs of goods and factors of production: this is the producers' surplus which is to be shared between consumers according to their shares θ_{ij} in the producer's profits. By the duality theorem of linear programming, $\tilde{p}_g \cdot y = \tilde{h} \cdot u_h$, where $\tilde{h} \cdot u_h$ is the rent accruing as a result of decreasing returns to scale.

3.2.3. Final remarks on nonlinear and linearized functions

Overspecialization need not arise in nonlinear programming models; indeed, in a model with diminishing marginal utility of goods it will normally not turn out to be optimal for consumers to spend all their income on a single good. Likewise, if producers are confronted by increasing costs, it will usually not be optimal for them to produce only one good.

For linear programs, Taylor's argument is based on the fact that the number of positive activities does not exceed the number of constraints, and that it is difficult to specify enough constraints. But the use either of step variables or of other approximations of nonlinear functions automatically introduces a large number of additional constraints into the model, freeing the solution from the straitjacket apparently imposed by linear programming theory.

Are linearized programs easier to solve than the nonlinear programs which they approximate? The main advantage of conversion to a linear programming format is to permit the use of existing highly sophisticated softwares. Available solution packages make skilful use of the properties of sparse matrices and provide users with a wide variety of options; nonlinear programming packages are not as highly developed.

It is important to note that linearizing strictly concave nonseparable functions may be costly. A mathematical expression which defines the approximating facets is easily written. But the number of these facets grows exponentially with the number of variables.[5]

3.3. Inelastic foreign demand

The assumption of given world prices implies that the country is confronted with infinitely elastic demand for its exports and supply of its imports. This is not true even if the country is small, except possibly for imports. The inelasticity of foreign demand and supply has a major impact on the structure of foreign trade, limiting, among other things, international specialization.

This is usually reflected by the imposition of arbitrary bounds, a practice which was criticized earlier in the chapter. This section will present a correct solution.

It is usual in international trade theory to represent the behavior of the rest of the world by a trade welfare function. The trade behavior of a country can thus be represented by a "two-country model" in which the second country—the rest of the world—is described by such a function.

Let us briefly recall that such a function relates the welfare of a country to its imports and exports. Let $U_i(x_i)$ be the utility function of country i.

[5]The efficient procedure would then be a cutting plane approach in which facets are generated only as needed. See Wolfe (1963).

The trade welfare function defines the maximum utility the country can reach for given values of exports $\tilde{e}_i \in E_i$, imports $\tilde{m}_i \in M_i$, and initial resources. This is

$$\begin{aligned} &V_i(\tilde{e}_i, \tilde{m}_i) = \max U_i(x_i) \\ &\text{s.t. } x_i - y_i \leqslant \tilde{m}_i - \tilde{e}_i + \omega_i, \\ &y_i \in Y_i,\ x_i \in X_i. \end{aligned}$$

The construction can be illustrated for the familiar case of a two-good economy.[6]

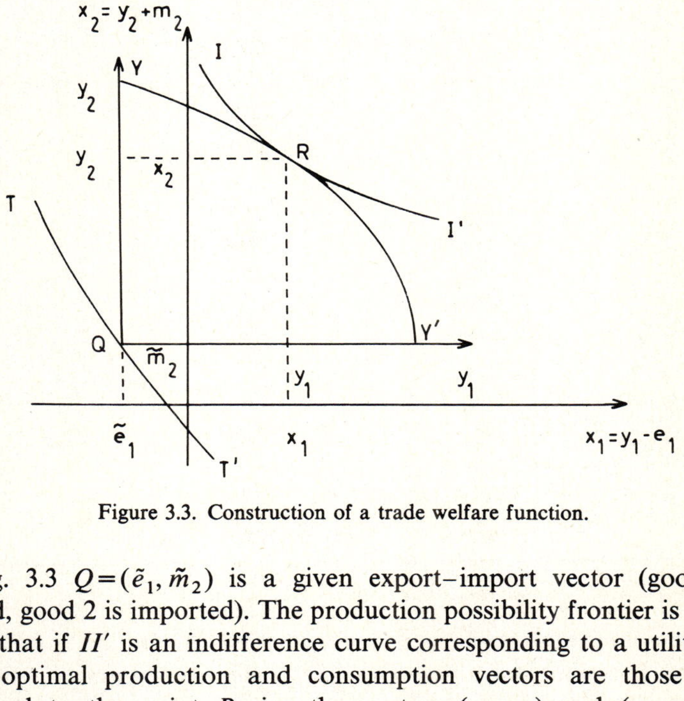

Figure 3.3. Construction of a trade welfare function.

In fig. 3.3 $Q = (\tilde{e}_1, \tilde{m}_2)$ is a given export–import vector (good 1 is exported, good 2 is imported). The production possibility frontier is YY'. It is clear that if II' is an indifference curve corresponding to a utility level $\tilde{U}$, the optimal production and consumption vectors are those which correspond to the point R, i.e. the vectors (y_1, y_2) and (x_1, x_2). So, according to the definition of the trade welfare function given above, $V(\tilde{e}_1, \tilde{m}_2) = U(x_1, x_2) = \tilde{U}$.

The trade indifference curve corresponding to the utility level $\tilde{U}$ can now be generated by sliding the transformation curve YY' along II'. The point Q will trace a curve TT', the locus of the export–import vectors

[6] See, for example, Negishi (1972, p. 32).

which enable the country to reach the utility level $\tilde{U}$. It is clear that this procedure can be used to construct the whole trade indifference map of the country and hence its trade welfare function.

This trade welfare function, which is concave if $U(x)$ is concave and Y_i and X_i convex, can be represented by linear programming, and used to determine exports and imports of the rest of the world. The proper activity analysis model of an open economy facing inelastic foreign demand would then have the form represented by model 3.3 (for the case of a separable welfare function).

Model 3.3

Representation of an open economy facing inelastic demand.

	z	x	x^s	e	m	e^s	m^s		RHS
u_g	$-A$	I		I	$-I$			$\leqslant$	0
u_f	$-F$							$\leqslant$	$\tilde{f}$
p_1		$-I$	Q					$\leqslant$	0
w_1^s			I					$\leqslant$	$\tilde{x}^s$
p_2^e				$-I$		$+Q_e$		$\leqslant$	0
w_{2e}^s						I		$\leqslant$	$\tilde{e}^s$
p_2^m					I		$-Q_m$	$\leqslant$	0
w_{2m}^s							I	$\leqslant$	$\tilde{m}^s$
λ				$-u_g$	u_g			$=$	0
	$\geqslant$	$\geqslant$	$\geqslant$	$\geqslant$	$\geqslant$	$\geqslant$	$\geqslant$		$=\min$
	0	0	g_1^s	0	0	g_{2e}^s	$-g_{2m}^s$	$=\max$	

The model contains a bilinear balance of payments constraint $-u_g \cdot e + u_g \cdot m = 0$. It cannot, therefore, be solved as a pure maximization problem and requires a general equilibrium computational algorithm of the type discussed in Part II of this book. Because there are only two countries, however, the solution is particularly easy to find: low cost tâtonnement processes are guaranteed to converge if there are no more than two countries. This will be discussed in Chapter 7.

It is interesting to relate to the approach just presented, the customary assumption made in planning models, that import and export prices are fixed. The usual representation of such an economy (model 3.4) involves a programming model.

Model 3.4

Programming model of an open economy facing elastic demand.

	z	x	x^s	e	m		RHS
u_g	$-A$	I		I	$-I$	$\leq$	0
u_f	$-F$					$\leq$	$\tilde{f}$
p_1		$-I$	Q			$\leq$	0
w_1^s			I			$\leq$	$\tilde{x}^s$
λ				$-\tilde{p}$	$\tilde{p}$	$=$	0
	$\geq$	$\geq$	$\geq$	$\geq$	$\geq$		$=\min$
	0	0	g_1^s	0	0	$=\max$	

The approach developed in this chapter would require us to represent the situation by a general equilibrium model in which the utility function of the rest of the world is linear. This is done in model 3.5.

Model 3.5

Representation of an open economy facing elastic demand, as a two-country model.

	z	x	x^s	e	m		RHS
u_g	$-A$	I		I	$-I$	$\leq$	0
u_f	$-F$					$\leq$	$\tilde{f}$
p_1		$-I$	Q			$\leq$	0
w_1^s			I			$\leq$	$\tilde{x}^s$
μ				$-u_g$	u_g	$=$	0
	$\geq$	$\geq$	$\geq$	$\geq$	$\geq$		$=\min$
	0	0	g_1^s	$\tilde{p}$	$-\tilde{p}$	$=\max$	

It can easily be checked that, at equilibrium the (e) and (m) dual constraints of model 3.5 imply $(1-\mu)\bar{u}_g=\tilde{p}$, while those of model 3.4 imply $\bar{u}_g=\lambda\tilde{p}$. The optimal solution of model 3.4 satisfies all the primal and dual constraints of model 3.5 if μ is set equal to $(\lambda-1)/\lambda$. Hence, in this special case the programming model 3.4 of an economy does turn out to yield an equilibrium of the two-country model.

CHAPTER 4

Saving and investment in a one-country equilibrium model

In this chapter we discuss several ways of treating saving and investment behavior in a one-country equilibrium model. The difficulties associated with well-known formulations are pointed out and the properties of the formulation used in the GEM model are described.

4.1. Optimal intertemporal investment and saving behavior

The most natural way of describing saving and investment behavior is to assume that they result from an intertemporal decision-making process. Consumers save for the future, producers invest today to obtain returns tomorrow. This idea is readily translated, and since each decision implies and is implied by the next, the result is an infinite horizon intertemporal equilibrium problem. Malinvaud (1953) has shown that, under reasonable assumptions, and if the future is known, there will exist an infinite horizon program with well-defined optimal primal and dual solutions.

We know little about the near future and virtually nothing about the distant future. In practice, it is thus attractive to truncate the future by limiting the model to a finite horizon T. We do this by solving either model 4.1 or 4.2 described below. In model 4.1, the optimal terminal capital stocks $\tilde{K}^T$ are given, while in model 4.2 the prices $\tilde{u}_g^T$ of these terminal stocks are given.[1] Both models 4.1 and 4.2 are set up for $T=2$.

In both models A stands for a matrix of technical coefficients; $-\kappa$ is a matrix of capital output ratios, the components of which are nonpositive; g is a vector of marginal utilities of commodities, and δ is the discount rate. The superscripts i refer to periods $0,1,2$; K^i represents a capital stock vector at the end of period i; $\tilde{u}_g$ is an exogenous capital stock price vector; u_K^i and u_g^i are respectively the dual rental prices of capital goods and the

[1]For the sake of simplicity we assume the $\tilde{K}$ and $\tilde{u}_g$ trajectories to be unique.

Model 4.1

A two-period model when optimal terminal capital stocks $\tilde{K}^2$ are known.

	z^1	x^1	K^1	z^2	x^2		RHS
u_g^1	$-A$	I	I			$\leqslant$	$\tilde{K}^0$
u_K^1	$-\kappa$					$\leqslant$	$\tilde{K}^0$
u_g^2			$-I$	$-A$	I	$\leqslant$	$-\tilde{K}^2$
u_K^2			$-I$	$-\kappa$		$\leqslant$	0
	$\geqslant$	$\geqslant$	$\geqslant$	$\geqslant$	$\geqslant$		$=\min$
		g			$(1+\delta)^{-1}g$	$=\max$	

Model 4.2

A two-period model when optimal terminal capital stock prices $\tilde{u}_g^2$ are known.

	z^1	x^1	K^1	z^2	x^2	K^2		RHS
u_g^1	$-A$	I	I				$\leqslant$	$\tilde{K}^0$
u_K^1	$-\kappa$						$\leqslant$	$\tilde{K}^0$
u_g^2			$-I$	$-A$	I	I	$\leqslant$	0
u_K^2			$-I$	$-\kappa$			$\leqslant$	0
	$\geqslant$	$\geqslant$	$\geqslant$	$\geqslant$	$\geqslant$	$\geqslant$		$=\min$
		g			$(1+\delta)^{-1}g$	$\tilde{u}_g$	$=\max$	

commodity prices in period i; z^i and x^i are respectively vectors of net outputs and consumption at the outset of period i.

Up to T, the solution of the infinite horizon problem is a solution of models 4.1 and 4.2. Reciprocally the solution of 4.1 and the solution of 4.2 leading to capital stocks $\tilde{K}^T$ is obviously consistent with an optimal plan over an infinite horizon. This is simply a consequence of Bellman's optimality principle.

This approach is theoretically unassailable, but is difficult to use in practice. The solution is sensitive to the terminal conditions, although these have to be chosen quite arbitrarily. Setting $\tilde{K}^T$ sharply constrains the optimal path, unless T is quite distant. Small changes of $\tilde{u}_g^T$, on the contrary, often lead to large shifts of the optimal path, and of course we know little about the correct value of $\tilde{u}_g^T$.

The intertemporal allocation of consumption and investment, likewise is sensitive to the social rate of discount. Too low a rate leads to excessive investment, too high a rate to no investment and no growth. But the social rate of discount is a parameter on which we know even less than on terminal conditions.

Finally, it turns out that the pure intertemporal maximization approach of the type described above tends to produce results which imply sharp fluctuations in consumption and saving patterns, thereby contradicting normal behavior.

This has led model-builders to add equations which force the model to reproduce a "normal" behavior. Consumption is forced to grow at least by some minimal rate, some production growth rates are fixed *a priori*, and saving is made a function of income at constant prices instead of being determined by a process of intertemporal optimization. All these *ad hoc* behavioral constraints pick up shadow prices which hardly make sense, and distort the price decentralizing properties one is looking for; the solution of the model cannot be interpreted as an equilibrium. Examples of this are given in section 4.2.

In section 1.4 we considered a number of models in which decision-makers make their plans, taking price *and* other signals as given. These signals are endogenous to the general equilibrium model, but exogenously taken by agents as parameters of their utility or profit maximizing problems; the behavioral or other rules which set the values of these signals are *not* included in the optimization problems faced by agents. In section 4.3 we show how to deal with such rules in the case of saving behavior.

4.2. On the misuse of *ad hoc* behavioral relations

We will illustrate the problem by analyzing two rules of thumb often used to describe terminal investment and saving behavior. The discussion will deal with one-stage planning models derived from intertemporal models by assuming that saving and investment follow a smooth (e.g. linear or exponential) path.

To focus attention on the essential mechanism, we condense the specification of the model studied using the following simplifying device. Start with model 4.3 as it was described in section 2.1.3.

Model 4.3

The full programming model.

	z	x	x^s		RHS
u_g	$-A$	I		$\leq$	0
u_f	$-F$			$\leq$	$\tilde{f}$
p		$-I$	Q	$\leq$	0
w^s			I		$\tilde{x}^s$
	$\geq$	$\geq$	$\geq$		$=\min$
	0	0	g	$=\max$	

It can easily be checked that the optimal solution of model 4.3 will also be an optimal solution of model 4.4 in which $\bar{p}$ is the optimal dual solution of model 4.3.

Model 4.4

The production subproblem of the full programming model.

	z	x		RHS
u_g	$-A$	I	$\leq$	0
u_f	$-F$		$\leq$	$\tilde{f}$
	$\geq$	$\geq$		$=\min$
		$\bar{p}$	$=\max$	

The arguments we want to put forward will therefore not be affected if we work with the representation 4.4. instead of 4.3.

4.2.1. A saving function used in conjunction with a linear path assumption

An approach used by Sandee (1960), for example, is to impose sensible behavior by introducing in the optimization model two behavioral relations: a constant price saving function and capital accumulation equations which reflect the assumption of a linear investment path.[2] These accumulation equations are derived as follows.

To simplify the algebra, we assume that there is a single good and no lag between production and investment.[3] Let I^0 and z^0 represent initial year investment and production, respectively. According to the linear path assumption, investment increases with, say Δ every year, reaching $I^0+T\Delta$ during the terminal year; accumulated investment is then equal to $TI^0+[T(T-1)/2]\Delta$. Since there are no lags and if output in calendar year T is related to investment up to the middle of year T, accumulated investment is $TI^0+(T^2/2)\Delta$. If initial capital were fully employed, it would be equal to $-\kappa z^0$, where $-\kappa$ is a capital–output ratio. Hence terminal capital stock will be equal to

$$-\kappa z^0+TI^0+\frac{T^2}{2}\Delta=\tilde{K}+\frac{T}{2}I^T,$$

where $\tilde{K}=-\kappa z^0+TI^0$ and $I^T=T\Delta$.

We now construct model 4.5 which incorporates Sandee's assumption and uses the simplifying device described in the beginning of this section.

Model 4.5

A one-stage model with terminal investment determined by a linear path assumption.

	z	x	I^T		RHS
u_g	$-A$	I	ε_1	$\leqslant$	0
u_f	$-F$			$\leqslant$	$\tilde{f}$
u_γ		$-\gamma l$	1	$=$	0
r	$-\kappa$		$-T/2$	$\leqslant$	$\tilde{K}$
	$\geqslant$	$\geqslant$	$\geqslant$		$=\min$
		$\bar{p}$		$=\max$	

In model 4.5, $-\kappa$ is a row vector of capital coefficients and ε_1 is the first unit vector (the capital good is the first of the goods listed). T is the length

[2] More complicated procedures have been devised which allow, for example, for exponential paths, see e.g. Manne (1970) and Taylor (1976). Since the particular path assumption is immaterial to the argument, we will use the simple linearity assumption.

[3] The analysis is easily extended to more general cases.

of the planning period, r is the rental price of capital goods, l is a row vector of "ones", and other variables are as before. The r constraint expresses the fact that terminal output is constrained by available initial capacity $\tilde{K}$ and investment.

The saving constraint u_γ asserts that saving is a fraction γ of constant prices consumption $l \cdot x$ (quantity units are assumed to be chosen so that base year prices are equal to unity). Note that this is a behavioral constraint, relating saving to consumption evaluated at the prices of an arbitrary base year, which is hardly consistent with a description of consumer behavior based on utility maximization.

If $I^T > 0$ the I^T dual constraint reads $u_{g1} + u_\gamma = (T/2)r$ imposing that r should be equal to $2/T$ times the sum of the market price of capital goods u_{g1} and the shadow price of the constant price-saving constraint u_γ—hardly a clear concept. For $x > 0$, the x dual constraint shows that $u_g = \bar{p} + \gamma u_\gamma l$; that is to say, market prices of goods u_g are curiously obtained as a weighted average of marginal utilities $\bar{p}$ and base year prices l.

4.2.2. The assumption of given terminal growth rates of production

Another popular formulation is to assume that the growth rates of the capital stocks of different activities in the terminal years are set *a priori* by planners on the basis of their perception of long-term needs. Let $\hat{q}$ be a diagonal matrix of these rates with diagonal elements q_j, and write the planning model as:

Model 4.6

A one-stage model with exogenous terminal growth rates of capital stocks.

	z	x	I^T		RHS
u_g	$-A$	I	ε_1	$\leqslant$	0
u_f	$-F$			$\leqslant$	$\tilde{f}$
r	$-\kappa$		$-T/2$	$\leqslant$	$\tilde{K}$
u_κ	$-\kappa\hat{q}$		-1	$\leqslant$	0
	$\geqslant$	$\geqslant$	$\geqslant$		$=\min$
		$\bar{p}$		$=\max$	

The u_κ constraint defines the terminal growth rates.

The behavioral saving constraint is implicitly taken into account by the choice of terminal growth rates[4] and is therefore absent from the model.

The rental price of the capital good is now $\kappa_j(r+u_\kappa q_j)$; it differs between sectors. This might make sense in an imperfect market, although the particular formula derived does not. Anyway, it makes no sense from a competitive equilibrium point of view. Prices will be distorted as a consequence, leading to inefficiency in the use of resources.

4.2.3. The interest rate calculated using a behavioral formulation of terminal investment and saving behavior is not equal to the marginal productivity of capital

One of the uses of planning models is to derive a measure of the marginal productivity of capital. This is helpful for project analysis. We will show that neither of the approaches described above gives correct results from that point of view.

We have already seen this for model 4.6: different activities pay different prices for a single capital good. This objection can be removed by assuming that all activities grow at the same rate, but this distorts the solution of the primal problem.

According to the first formulation, different industries pay their capital at the same price. But this price is not equal to the marginal product of capital.

This can be seen most clearly by considering a simple form of model 4.4 in which there is a single good produced by a unique activity, used both for consumption and investment; to simplify further, factors other than capital are neglected. Since the goal is to measure the marginal productivity of capital, we want dual prices to represent the derivative of output (instead of consumption only) with respect to the right-hand side of the constraints. To do this we maximize output rather than consumption only.

[4] When terminal growth rates are assumed equal, there is a superficial analogy between this assumption and the relation between growth and interest rates in von Neumann's (1945) model. The analogy has made this formulation of terminal conditions popular, but it is not well founded. The two models are based on different assumptions, in particular the absence of exogenous land and labor constraints in the von Neumann model, and should not be expected to have the same properties.

This simple model is:

Model 4.7

A simple model with linear investment path and saving constraint.

	z	x	I^T		RHS
u_g	-1	1	1	$\leqslant$	0
u_γ		$-\gamma$	1	$=$	0
r	$-\kappa$		$-T/2$	$\leqslant$	$\tilde{K}$
	$\geqslant$	$\geqslant$	$\geqslant$		$=\min$
	0	1	1	$=\max$	

At the optimum all primal and dual constraints will be satisfied as equalities.[5] The marginal productivity of capital is obviously $-1/\kappa$,[6] but the dual price of capital, equal to $-[\kappa(1+T\delta/2\kappa)]^{-1}$ exceeds this ($\delta=\gamma/(1+\gamma)$ is the propensity to consume). This discrepancy arises because the model imputes to capital a productivity which reflects not only what this capital produces, but the productivity of the extra capital generated by the increased saving of consumers. This may be shown by a "reinvestment round" analysis which notes that if the initial capital stock $\tilde{K}$ is increased by one unit, capital, output, and saving will rise as follows:

Round	ΔK	Δz	ΔI
1	1	$-\frac{1}{\kappa}$	$-\frac{\delta}{\kappa}$
2	$-\frac{T\delta}{2\kappa}$	$\frac{T\delta}{2\kappa^2}$	$\frac{T\delta^2}{2\kappa^2}$
3	$\frac{T^2\delta^2}{4\kappa^2}$	$-\frac{T^2\delta^2}{4\kappa^3}$	$-\frac{T^2\delta^3}{4\kappa^3}$
.	.	.	.
.	.	.	.
.	.	.	.
Cumulated impact	$\left(1+\frac{T\delta}{2\kappa}\right)^{-1}$	$-\left(\kappa\left(1+\frac{T\delta}{2\kappa}\right)\right)^{-1}$	$-\delta\left(\kappa\left(1+\frac{T\delta}{2\kappa}\right)\right)^{-1}$

This shows that the dual price of capital is influenced by its productivity, by saver's behavior, and by the horizon T of the plan.

[5] We assume the primal solution set to be bounded.
[6] Remember that, by convention, κ is negative.

In this simple model the distortion is easy to correct.[7] Calculating the proper rate of return is not however straightforward if there are several factors and producing sectors, as the reader can readily verify by investigating an economy with two producing sectors and two factors of production.

4.2.4. *The plan calculated using behavioral relations is not optimal*

Both the formulations discussed in sections 4.2.1 and 4.2.2 generate prices which do not satisfy the classical optimality conditions. Model 4.5 evaluates consumer goods at three sets of prices: l, the base year prices used in defining the saving function; u_g, the producer prices of consumer goods; and $\bar{p}$, their marginal utilities. In model 4.6—except if the terminal rates of growth are the same for all goods—the price of capital differs between producing sectors.

Efficient use of resources implies that goods should be priced uniformly. This leads us to suspect that the "optimal solution" of models 4.5 and 4.6 may not, in fact, imply an efficient use of resources.

We verify this conjecture for model 4.5. To this end, we construct a model which implies the same capital accumulation and investment as 4.4, but does away with the distorting influence of the "behavioral" saving constraint. We then show that the optimal utility level achieved by model 4.4 is at least as large and may be larger than that implied by model 4.5.

We first solve model 4.5 and note the optimal investment $\bar{I}^T$ and capital stock levels $-\kappa\cdot\bar{z}=\bar{K}^T$. We then construct model 4.8.

It is clear, from the way model 4.8 has been constructed, that the optimal solution of 4.5 is feasible for 4.8. Hence the optimum of 4.8 cannot be less than the optimum of 4.5. Examples can be devised showing that the optimum of 4.8 exceeds that of 4.5.[8]

[7] Note that although the rate of return on capital is wrong, the rate of interest r/u_g is equal to $-1/\kappa$ and is therefore correct.

[8] Consider the following example of model 4.5:

$$\begin{array}{lrrrrrl}
 & -z_1 & & +x_1 & & +I^T & \leqslant 0\\
 & 0.1z_1 & -z_2 & & +x_2 & & \leqslant 0\\
 & & & -0.2x_1 & -0.2x_2 & +I^T & =0\\
 & 2z_1 & +4z_2 & & & -4I^T & \leqslant 20.8\\
\max & & & 1.04x_1 & +1.82x_2 & &
\end{array}$$

The optimal solution is $\bar{z}_1=12$; $\bar{z}_2=1.2$; $\bar{x}_1=10$; $\bar{x}_2=0$; $\bar{I}^T=2$. The optimal value of the objective is 10.4. Consider now version 4.8 for this example, where the third constraint is replaced by $I^T=2$ and the fourth by $2z_1+4z_2\leqslant 28.8$. The optimal solution is $\bar{z}_1=2$; $\bar{z}_2=6.2$; $\bar{x}_1=0$; $\bar{x}_2=6$; $\bar{I}^T=2$. The optimal value of the objective is 10.92.

Model 4.8

A one-stage model with exogenous investment and capital stock.

	z	x	I^T		RHS
u_g	$-A$	I	ε_1	$\leqslant$	0
u_f	$-F$			$\leqslant$	$\tilde{f}$
u_γ			1	$=$	$\bar{I}^T$
r	$-\kappa$			$\leqslant$	$\bar{K}^T$
	$\geqslant$	$\geqslant$	$\geqslant$		$=\min$
	0	$\bar{p}$	0	$=\max$	

4.3. Taking account of a behavioral saving function in two-phase solution algorithms

The procedure used to deal with savings in model 4.8 reflects a view of consumer behavior which differs from that of economic theory. Consider the usual theoretical description of saving-consumption decisions of a consumer over a two-period horizon (the indices refer to periods):

$$\begin{aligned} &\max U_1(x_1)+U_2(x_2) \\ &\text{s.t. } p_1\cdot x_1+p_2\cdot x_2=p_1\cdot\omega_1+p_2\cdot\omega_2, \\ &\qquad x_1\in X_1,\ x_2\in X_2. \end{aligned}$$

Saving in the first period is $\sigma_1=p_1\cdot(\omega_1-x_1)$.

In the real world the prices of period 2 are not known to the consumer when he decides on his period 1 consumption: he has to form expectations which will be stochastic functions of past and current observations. Given these expectations, the optimal first-period consumption is the solution of a complex intertemporal stochastic decision problem.

We feel there is good reason to doubt that consumer behavior is correctly portrayed by this analysis. It appears at least as realistic to assume, as is done in GEM, that saving is the result of "satisficing" rather than optimizing decisions: instead of solving an intertemporal stochastic decision problem which he does not perceive clearly, the consumer uses some sensible rule of thumb to decide how much to set aside out of current income in anticipation of the future.

The consumption decision would then be described as a two-stage process in which saving σ_1 is first decided on as some fairly simple function of income and prices; then, in a second stage, the consumer allocates optimally the remainder of his income over the various commodities which he can buy today. He looks for values of σ_1 and x_1, which solve both $\sigma_1=\sigma_1(p_1,\omega_1)$ where $\sigma_1(p_1,\omega_1)$ represents the rule of thumb the consumer uses to set saving, and

$$\begin{aligned}&\max U_1(x_1)\\&\text{s.t. } p_1\cdot(\omega_1-x_1)=\sigma_1,\\&\qquad x_1\in X_1.\end{aligned}$$

The important feature of this approach is that no new constraint is introduced into the one-period optimization decision problem thereby avoiding the distortions which arise otherwise. Instead, a signal σ_1 appears in the budget constraint which prevents the consumer from consuming today all his income.

If for practical reasons one builds a one-stage model similar to model 4.8 to represent growth over several periods, an assumption has to be made on the path of investment. This other "behavioral equation" yields the value of K^T as a function of terminal investment.

This approach is easy to fit into the two-phase solution procedures used in this book. Such a procedure might work as follows.

Initialization: Choose initial values $\bar{I}^T=I^0$ and $\bar{K}^T=K^0$. Set $t=0$.

Iteration t:

Phase 1: *Function evaluation*. Solve model 4.8.

Phase 2: *Parameter revision*. Using the solution obtained in phase 1, compute saving $\sigma_1(p_1,\omega_1)=\sigma_1(u_g,u_\gamma,r,\bar{I}^t,\bar{K}^t)$ and check whether saving equals investment at current prices.

—If so, terminate.

—If not, use some rule to update $\bar{I}^t$ and $\bar{K}^t$.

Set $t=t+1$ and go to the next iteration.

Although this procedure is not guaranteed to converge, it proved very efficient in the practical cases considered in this book.

PART II

THE COMPUTATION OF EQUILIBRIA

Introduction to Part II

The problem of existence, uniqueness, and stability of equilibria has given rise to an abundant literature in mathematical economics. This literature seems to have surrounded the problem of computing equilibria with an aura of wonder which may be excessive. Theoreticians have focused on cleverly designed special cases in which paradoxical results are shown to hold, leading to an impression that actual equilibria have similar counter-intuitive properties. There is no empirical evidence to suggest this, either from the observation of reality, or from the few general equilibrium models which have been built up to now: these do not appear more difficult to solve than, say, macroeconomic dynamic models inspired by Keynesian theory.

This theoretical literature has led to an accurate understanding of important aspects of the computation of equilibria. A Keynesian macro model-builder just "goes and solves his model" without much guidance from theoreticians. The general equilibrium modeller is surrounded by an array of partial results which it seems worthwhile to review.

After a discussion of the structure of the general equilibrium problem and of the available computational strategies (Chapter 5), we discuss the so-called fixed point algorithms introduced by Scarf (1967a), which are associated in the mind of economists with the computation of equilibria (Chapter 6). The discussion covers recent important gains in the understanding of these algorithms, which may point to ways of improving their efficiency. The tâtonnement approach is discussed in Chapter 7. In Chapter 8 we show that tâtonnement based on the four processes described in Chapter 5 are not necessarily simultaneously stable.

The discussion of computational methods in the book may seem unbalanced: it does not review in detail how to apply the range of standard algorithms which economists use to solve systems of equations. These methods are very promising, but they have been well surveyed elsewhere.[1] The attention paid to Scarf-type algorithms as a means to compute equilibria justifies devoting Chapter 6 to these methods. In Chapter 7 we focus on tâtonnement processes, the approach we used to solve GEM.

[1]See Goldfeld and Quandt (1972, ch. 1) for a nontechnical presentation of these procedures and Ortega and Rheinboldt (1970) for an exhaustive presentation.

CHAPTER 5

Structure of the problem and possible computational approaches

5.1. The master program of the general equilibrium problem

We now present more formally and extend the ideas which were briefly outlined in Chapter 2.

5.1.1. The master program of the general equilibrium problem

The concept of the master program of the general equilibrium problem provides a useful way of clarifying the relation between different approaches to the computation of equilibria.

Definition 5.1.1. Master program. The mathematical program $\max \Sigma_i \tilde{\alpha}_i U_i(x_i)$ $(\tilde{\alpha}_i > 0)$ s.t. $\Sigma x_i - \Sigma \omega_i - \Sigma y_j \leqslant 0$, $\tilde{p} \cdot (x_i - \Sigma_j \theta_{ij} y_j - \omega_i) \leqslant 0$, $x_i \in X_i$, $y_j \in Y_j$, for all i and j, will be referred to as the master program of the general equilibrium problem. The vectors $\tilde{\alpha}$ and $\tilde{p}$ will be referred to as the parameters of the master program.

Note that the master program is simply the Negishi welfare optimum, further constrained by the budget constraints $\tilde{p} \cdot (x_i - \Sigma_j \theta_{ij} y_j - \omega_i) \leqslant 0$, all i.

For easy reference, we briefly recall

Definition 1.1.1. Competitive equilibrium. The allocation $\bar{x}_i$ $(i = 1, 2, \ldots, m)$, $\bar{y}_j$ $(j = 1, 2, \ldots, n)$ supported by the prices $\bar{p}$ is a competitive equilibrium if the following conditions hold.

(a) Equality of demand and supply for nonfree goods:

$$\sum_i \bar{x}_i - \sum_j \bar{y}_j - \sum_i \omega_i \leqslant 0; \qquad \bar{p} \cdot \left(\sum_i \bar{x}_i - \sum_j \bar{y}_j - \sum_i \omega_i \right) = 0.$$

(b) Utility maximization by consumers: $\bar{x}_i$ maximizes $U_i(x_i)$ s.t. $\bar{p}\cdot(x_i - \Sigma_j\theta_{ij}\bar{y}_j - \omega_i) \leqslant 0$ and $x_i \in X_i$ for all i.

(c) Profit maximization by firms: $\bar{y}_j$ maximizes $\bar{p}\cdot y_j$ s.t. $y_j \in Y_j$ for all j.

Theorem 5.1.1. Consider the set of solutions $\{\bar{x}_i\}$, $\{\bar{y}_j\}$, $\{\lambda_i^*\}$,[1] u^* of the master program where u^* and λ_i^* are the Lagrange multipliers associated with the constraints $\Sigma_i x_i - \Sigma_j y_j - \Sigma_i\omega_i \leqslant 0$ and $\tilde{p}\cdot(x_i - \Sigma_j\theta_{ij}y_j - \omega_i) \leqslant 0$, respectively. If $u^* = \tilde{p}$, the allocation $\{\bar{x}_i\},\{\bar{y}_j\}$ supported by the prices $\bar{p} = \tilde{p}$ is a competitive equilibrium. (Such a solution will be referred to as an equilibrium solution of the master program.)

Proof. In view of the Kuhn–Tucker–Uzawa theorem (Mathematical Appendix, theorem 1), if $\{\bar{x}_i\},\{\bar{y}_j\}$ is a solution of the master program, there exist $u^* \geqslant 0$, $\lambda_i^* \geqslant 0$, $i = 1,2,\ldots, m$, such that

$$\sum_i \bar{x}_i - \sum_j \bar{y}_j - \sum_i \omega_i \leqslant 0; \qquad u^*\cdot\left[\sum_i \bar{x}_i - \sum_j \bar{y}_j - \sum_i \omega_i\right] = 0, \qquad \text{(d)–(e)}$$

$$\tilde{p}\cdot\left(\bar{x}_i - \sum_j \theta_{ij}\bar{y}_j - \omega_i\right) \leqslant 0; \quad \sum_i \lambda_i^*\tilde{p}\cdot\left(\bar{x}_i - \sum_j \theta_{ij}\bar{y}_j - \omega_i\right) = 0, \qquad \text{(f)–(g)}$$

and such that for $x_i \in X_i$, all i, $y_j \in Y_j$, all j, $u \geqslant 0$, $\lambda_i \geqslant 0$,

$$\sum_i \tilde{\alpha}_i U_i(x_i) + u^*\cdot\left(\sum_i \omega_i + \sum_j y_j - \sum_i x_i\right) + \sum_i \lambda_i^*\tilde{p}\cdot\left(\omega_i + \sum_j \theta_{ij}y_j - x_i\right)$$

$$\leqslant \sum_i \tilde{\alpha}_i U_i(\bar{x}_i) + u^*\cdot\left(\sum_i \omega_i + \sum_j \bar{y}_j - \sum_i \bar{x}_i\right) + \sum_i \lambda_i^*\tilde{p}\cdot\left(\omega_i + \sum_j \theta_{ij}\bar{y}_j - \bar{x}_i\right)$$

$$\leqslant \sum_i \tilde{\alpha}_i U_i(\bar{x}_i) + u\cdot\left(\sum_i \omega_i + \sum_j \bar{y}_j - \sum_i \bar{x}_i\right) + \sum_i \lambda_i\tilde{p}\cdot\left(\omega_i + \sum_j \theta_{ij}\bar{y}_j - \bar{x}_i\right).$$

(h)

Condition (a) of definition 1.1.1 follows immediately from (d)–(e), and $u^* = \tilde{p} = \bar{p}$. From (f) we see that the budget constraints are also satisfied. If

[1] $\{\bar{x}_i\},\{\bar{y}_j\},\{\lambda_i^*\}$ is a shorthand notation for $\bar{x}_i$, $i = 1,2,\ldots, m$; $\bar{y}_j$, $j = 1,2,\ldots, n$; λ_i^*, $i = 1,2,\ldots, m$.

we show that $U_i(x_i) \leqslant U_i(\bar{x}_i)$ for every $x_i \in X_i$ satisfying i's budget constraint, condition (b) of definition 1.1.1 will also be satisfied. If $u^* = \bar{p}$, note first that

$$\bar{p} \cdot \sum_i \left(\omega_i + \sum_j \theta_{ij} \bar{y}_j - \bar{x}_i \right) = u^* \cdot \left(\sum_i \omega_i + \sum_j \bar{y}_j - \sum_i \bar{x}_i \right) = 0.$$

Together with (f) this implies that for every i,

$$\bar{p} \cdot \left(\omega_i + \sum_j \theta_{ij} \bar{y}_j - \bar{x}_i \right) = 0. \tag{i}$$

Now, set $y_j = \bar{y}_j$ for all j, $x_i = \bar{x}_i$ for all i except s, and $u^* = \bar{p}$. The first inequality in (g) then implies, for every $x_s \in X_s$,

$$\tilde{\alpha}_s U_s(x_s) + (1 + \lambda_s^*) \bar{p} \cdot (\bar{x}_s - x_s) \leqslant \tilde{\alpha}_s U_s(x_s). \tag{j}$$

If $x_s \in X_s$ satisfies the budget constraint, using (i) one has $\bar{p} \cdot x_s \leqslant \bar{p} \cdot \bar{x}_s$ so that the second term in the left-hand side of (j) is non-negative and hence, since $\tilde{\alpha}_s > 0$, $U_s(x_s) \leqslant U_s(\bar{x}_s)$.

Finally, set $y_j = \bar{y}_j$ for all j except s, $x_i = \bar{x}_i$ for all i, and $u^* = \bar{p}$. The first inequality in (h) implies for every $y_s \in Y_s$

$$\left(1 + \sum_i \lambda_i^* \theta_{is} \right) \bar{p} \cdot y_s \leqslant \left(1 + \sum_i \lambda_i^* \theta_{is} \right) \bar{p} \cdot \bar{y}_s.$$

Since $(1 + \Sigma_i \lambda_i^* \theta_{is}) > 0$, clearly $\bar{p} \cdot y_s \leqslant \bar{p} \cdot \bar{y}_s$, which proves condition (c) of definition 1.1.1.

Q.E.D.

We must also prove that for any equilibrium there exists a master program which generates this equilibrium. The proof will provide an opportunity to show that the master program and its solution have degrees of freedom which can be exploited in designing a solution procedure. These ideas are expressed in theorem 5.1.2.

Theorem 5.1.2. Let $\{\bar{x}_i\}, \{\bar{y}_j\}$ be an equilibrium allocation supported by the prices $\bar{p}$; let $\bar{\lambda}_i > 0$, $i = 1, 2, \ldots, m$, be the multiplier associated with the budget constraint in consumer i's utility maximization problem, at prices

$\bar{p}$. The master program

$$\begin{aligned}
&\max \sum \tilde{\alpha}_i U_i(x_i), \qquad \tilde{a}_i > 0, \qquad i=1,2,\ldots,m,\\
&\text{s.t.} \ \sum_i x_i \leqslant \sum_j y_j + \sum_i \omega_i,\\
&\quad \tilde{p}\cdot x_i \leqslant \tilde{p}\cdot\omega_i + \sum_j \theta_{ij}\tilde{p}\cdot y_j, \qquad i=1,2,\ldots,m,\\
&\quad x_i \in X_i,\ y_j \in Y_j, \qquad i=1,2,\ldots,m;\ j=1,2,\ldots,n,
\end{aligned}$$

with $\tilde{p}=\bar{p}$, will have the solution $\{\bar{x}_i\}, \{\bar{y}_j\}, u^*, \{\lambda_i^*\}$ such that $u^*=\bar{p}$ and λ_i^* satisfies $(1+\lambda_i^*)=\tilde{\alpha}_i\bar{\lambda}_i$, $i=1,2,\ldots,m$.

Proof. We must show that $\{\bar{x}_i\}$, $\{\bar{y}_j\}$, u^*, and $\{\lambda_i^*\}$ satisfy conditions (d), (e), (f), (g), and (h) of theorem 5.1.1 and that $u^* \geqslant 0$, $\lambda_i^* \geqslant 0$, all i.

Obviously $u^* \geqslant 0$ since $u^*=\bar{p}$; likewise $\lambda_i^* \geqslant 0$, by construction.

Conditions (d), (e), and (f) follow from the definition of an equilibrium allocation; if the consumer is nonsatiated, at equilibrium, $\bar{p}\cdot(\bar{x}_i-\Sigma_j\theta_{ij}\bar{y}_j-\omega_i)=0$, implying condition (g).

The first saddle-point inequality will follow if:

(1) $\tilde{\alpha}_i U_i(x_i)-(u^*+\tilde{p}\lambda_i^*)\cdot x_i \leqslant \tilde{\alpha}_i U_i(\bar{x}_i)-(u^*+\tilde{p}\lambda_i^*)\cdot\bar{x}_i$, for every $x_i\in X_i$, $i=1,2,\ldots,m$;

(2) $(u^*+\tilde{p}\Sigma_i\lambda_i^*\theta_{ij})\cdot y_j \leqslant (u^*+\tilde{p}\Sigma_i\lambda_i^*\theta_{ij})\cdot\bar{y}_j$, for every $y_j\in Y_j$, $j=1,2,\ldots,n$.

Condition (1) can be shown to hold by writing the saddle-point conditions for the utility maximization problem of consumer i ($i=1,2,\ldots,m$) and by using $u^*=\tilde{p}=\bar{p}$ and $(1+\lambda_i^*)=\tilde{\alpha}_i\bar{\lambda}_i$. We also have $(u^*+\tilde{p}\Sigma_i\lambda_i^*\theta_{ij})=(1+\Sigma_i\lambda_i^*\theta_{ij})\bar{p}$, with $(1+\Sigma_i\lambda_i^*\theta_{ij})>0$; condition (2) then follows since $\bar{y}_j$ maximizes $\bar{p}\cdot y_j$ for $y_j\in Y_j$.

The second saddle-point inequality is implied by $u^* \geqslant 0$, $\lambda_i^* \geqslant 0$, and (d), (e), (f), and (g) for every $x_i\in X_i$, $y_j\in Y_j$. Q.E.D.

Remark 1. The equilibrium value of the marginal utility of income of consumer i can easily be deduced from the solution of a master program, using the relation $(1+\lambda_i^*)=\tilde{\alpha}_i\bar{\lambda}_i$.

Remark 2. Theorem 5.1.2 suggests that the master program implies m degrees of freedom: the $\tilde{\alpha}_i$ ($i=1,2,\ldots,m$) can be chosen arbitrarily.

Remark 3. The equilibrium value of the welfare weights can also be deduced from the solution of a master program by setting $\bar{\alpha}_i=(1+\lambda_i^*)^{-1}\tilde{\alpha}_i$. To prove this, note that inserting $\bar{\alpha}_i$ into expression $(1+\lambda_i)=\alpha_i\bar{\lambda}_i$ results in

$\lambda_i = 0$. Hence, for this choice of α_i the budget constraints have zero shadow prices and can be dropped from the master program, yielding the Negishi welfare optimum.

Remark 4. From a computational point of view it is convenient that the mathematical programs considered can be set up in the same basic format. The Negishi welfare optimum can be obtained by introducing slacks into the budget constraints of the master program. These slacks will give the values of the excess budgets corresponding to each choice of α. Likewise, a competitive equilibrium can be obtained from the master program by introducing slacks into its resource balance constraints; these slacks will give the excess demands corresponding to each choice of p.

5.2. The structure of the general equilibrium problem

5.2.1. The system of equilibrium relations

The abstract formulation used in section 5.1 is not suitable for computation. To be able to calculate solutions, we must specify the sets X_i and Y_j by explicit functional (in)equalities.

We have assumed in Chapter 1 that $X_i = \Omega$, $i = 1, \ldots, m$, where Ω is the non-negative orthant. Y_j can be defined by $Y_j = \{y_j \mid f_j(y_j) \leqslant 0\}$.[2] The Lagrangean of the master program can then be written

$$L(\cdot) = \sum_i \tilde{\alpha}_i U_i(x_i) + u \cdot \left(\sum_i \omega_i + \sum_j y_j - \sum_i x_i \right) + \sum_i \lambda_i \tilde{p} \cdot \left(\omega_i + \sum_j \theta_{ij} y_j - x_i \right) + \sum_j \gamma_j f_j(y_j),$$

where u, λ_i $(i = 1, 2, \ldots, m)$, and γ_j $(j = 1, 2, \ldots, n)$ are multipliers. Assuming $U_i(x_i)$, $f_j(y_j)$ to be concave and differentiable functions, the Kuhn–Tucker conditions for an optimum are:

Equality of supply and demand for nonfree goods

$$\sum_i x_i - \sum_j y_j - \sum_i \omega_i \leqslant 0; \qquad u \cdot \left(\sum x_i - \sum y_j - \sum \omega_i \right) = 0; \qquad u \geqslant 0.$$

[2] Y_j can more generally be defined by $Y_j = \{y_j \mid f_j(y_j, z_j) \leqslant 0,\ z_j \in \Omega\}$; the z_j values are internal activity variables set by the producer j; $f_j(\cdot)$ is a vector function.

Utility maximization by consumers $(i=1,2,\ldots,m)$

$$\tilde{\alpha}_i U_{ix} - \lambda_i \tilde{p} - u \leqslant 0; \qquad x_i \cdot (\tilde{\alpha}_i U_{ix} - \lambda_i \tilde{p} - u) = 0; \qquad x_i \geqslant 0,$$

$$\tilde{p} \cdot \left(x_i - \sum_j \theta_{ij} y_j - \omega_i \right) \leqslant 0; \qquad \lambda_i \tilde{p} \cdot \left(x_i - \sum_j \theta_{ij} y_j - \omega_i \right) = 0; \qquad \lambda_i \geqslant 0,$$

where U_{ix} is the vector of partial derivatives of $U_i(x_i)$ with respect to x_i.

Profit maximization by producers $(j=1,2,\ldots,n)$

$$\gamma_j f_{jy} + \sum_i \theta_{ij} \lambda_i \tilde{p} + u = 0,$$

$$f_j(y_j) \leqslant 0; \qquad \gamma_j f_j(y_j) = 0; \qquad \gamma_j \geqslant 0,$$

where f_{jy} is the vector of partial derivatives of $f_j(y_j)$ with respect to y_j.

For an equilibrium solution of the master program, we require (see theorem 5.1.1):

Equality of dual prices of commodities (u) and prices in the budget constraints $(\tilde{p})$:

$$\tilde{p} = u.$$

The master program, together with the conditions $\tilde{p}=u$, will be referred to as the *equilibrium master program*.

These conditions form a highly interdependent nonlinear structure. The inequalities add to the complexity of the problem. It is not surprising that general equilibrium problems have the reputation of being hard to solve.

5.2.2. *Two-phase solution procedures: A reformulation*

The two-phase solution procedures which were briefly introduced in Chapter 2 provide an efficient way of exploiting the structure of the problem. They involve fixing some parameters and truncating the problem by relaxing provisionally a subset of the constraints chosen so that the truncated problem is a concave maximization problem usually not too difficult to solve. If the solution does not satisfy the constraints which were relaxed, the given parameters are modified and the truncated problem is solved again. The procedures described in Chapter 2 may then be formalized as follows.

Procedure (i). Removal of prices distortions

Phase 1: Function evaluation

(a) Define problem (i) as the truncated equilibrium master program in which the constraints $u=\tilde{p}$ are relaxed, and α and p are set at values $\alpha=\tilde{\alpha}>0$, $p=\tilde{p}$.
(b) Solve problem (i) which is simply the master program.
(c) Define the price distortion correspondence D_{i} as

$$D_{\mathrm{i}}(\tilde{\alpha},\tilde{p})=\{u-\tilde{p}\mid u\in H_{\mathrm{i}}\},$$

where H_{i} is the set of solutions of problem (i).

Phase 2: Parameter revision

(a) If $0\in D_{\mathrm{i}}$, stop. If not, use some rule to revise $\tilde{p}$ and return to phase 1.

Procedure (ii). Search for equilibrium prices

Phase 1: Function evaluation

(a) Define problem (ii) as the truncated equilibrium master program in which the balance constraints $\Sigma_i x_i-\Sigma_j y_j-\Sigma_i \omega_i\leqslant 0$ are relaxed, and α and p are set at values $\alpha=\tilde{\alpha}>0$, $p=\tilde{p}$.
(b) Solve problem (ii).
(c) Define the excess demand correspondence D_{ii} as

$$D_{\mathrm{ii}}(\tilde{\alpha},\tilde{p})=\left\{\sum_i x_i-\sum_j y_j-\sum_i \omega_i \mid \{x_i\},\{y_j\}\in H_{\mathrm{ii}}\right\},$$

where H_{ii} is the set of solutions of problem (ii).

Phase 2: Parameter revision

(a) If $0\in D_{\mathrm{ii}}$, stop. If not, use some rule to revise the given $\tilde{p}$ and return to phase 1.

Procedure (iii). Search for equilibrium utilities

Phase 1: Function evaluation

(a) Define problem (iii) as the truncated equilibrium master problem in which the budget constraints are relaxed, and α_1 and $U_i(x_i)$ ($i=2,\ldots,m$), are set at values $\alpha_1=\tilde{\alpha}_1>0$, $U_i(x_i)=\tilde{U}_i$ ($i=2,\ldots,m$).
(b) Solve problem (iii) which is a Pareto optimum problem.
(c) Define the Pareto optimum correspondence as

$$D_{iii}(\tilde{U}_2,\ldots,\tilde{U}_m,\tilde{\alpha}_1)=\left\{\tilde{p}\cdot\left(x_i-\sum_j\theta_{ij}y_j-\omega_i\right)\mid u,\{x_i\},\{y_j\}\in H_{\text{iii}},\tilde{p}=u\right\},$$

where H_{iii} is the set of solutions of problem (iii).

Phase 2: Parameter revision

(a) If $0\in D_{\text{iii}}(\tilde{U}_2,\ldots,\tilde{U}_m,\tilde{\alpha})$, stop. If not, use some rule to revise the given $\tilde{U}_i$ ($i=2,\ldots,m$) and return to phase 1.

Procedure (iv). Search for equilibrium Negishi welfare weights

Phase 1: Function evaluation

(a) Define problem (iv) as the truncated equilibrium master problem in which the budget constraints are relaxed. Set α at values $\alpha=\tilde{\alpha}>0$.
(b) Solve problem (iv) which is a Negishi welfare optimum.
(c) Define the excess budget correspondence as

$$D_{iv}(\tilde{\alpha})=\left\{\tilde{p}\cdot\left(x_i-\sum_j\theta_{ij}y_j-\omega_i\right)\mid u,\{x_i\},\{y_j\}\in H_{\text{iv}},\tilde{p}=u\right\},$$

where H_{iv} is the set of solutions of problem (iv).

Phase 2: Parameter revision

(a) If $0\in D_{\text{iv}}(\tilde{\alpha})$, stop. If not, use some rule to revise the given $\tilde{\alpha}$ and return to phase 1.

5.2.3. *Alternative computational procedures for the function evaluation phase*

Each function evaluation involves solving a concave programming problem. Three approaches may be envisaged.

(1) The most general is to use a standard nonlinear programming algorithm. This approach is always applicable but may prove expensive.

(2) The model-builder may know enough to predict which activities are not used and which goods are in excess supply. These activities and the balance constraints for these goods can be dropped. The problem solved in the function evaluation phase is then a classical concave maximization problem, and its solution is characterized by first-order conditions expressed by equations. Such problems are easy to solve.

(3) In some very special cases the function evaluation can be performed analytically; this is the case with CES or Cobb–Douglas utility and production functions, in the absence of inequality constraints. This phase is then numerically trivial.

5.2.4. *Alternative computational procedures for the parameter revision phase*

The function evaluations therefore pose no novel computational problem. Discussions have thus focused on phase 2 calculations, i.e. the search for equilibrium values of the phase 1 parameters. Most of the literature is devoted to two approaches, the Scarf-type algorithms (Chapter 6) and tâtonnement (Chapter 7). There has also been recent work on designing algorithms which make use of the structure of particular problems. This is briefly reviewed in Chapter 11.

5.2.5. *Extension to more general models*

In this section we discuss very briefly how the two-phase solution procedures can be used to solve the more general models sketched in section 1.4.

Agents perceive signals (prices, transfers, taxes, externalities, and constraints on their trades); they take these signals as given and, individually, set production and consumption on the basis of the specified rules. If decisions satisfy the system constraints, we have a solution.

From a computational point of view, this solution can be sought as follows.

Phase 1: *Function evaluation*. Compute the decision of every agent for given signals. Check whether the system constraints are satisfied.

Phase 2: *Revision of signals*. If the constraints are satisfied, stop. If not, use some rule to choose a new set of admissible signals and go to phase 1.

CHAPTER 6

Scarf-type algorithms for the computation of equilibria

6.1. Introduction

Algorithms of the type devised initially by Scarf, building on an idea of Lemke, are the best known method of computing equilibria. Their outstanding property is guaranteed convergence to a point which can be chosen to be as close as desired to an equilibrium. As a result, these algorithms have proved to be a flexible tool in theoretical work and in solving any system of equations. At their present stage of development they remain many times less efficient than older computational methods. Their convergence property, however, justifies the active research which continues in this field, and it appears worthwhile to carefully survey these methods.

The beautifully clear basic reference remains Scarf's (1973) monograph, although this is by now somewhat out of date.[1] Todd (1976a) has recently published a very complete and thorough review of the state of the art. This does not cover the recent work by Eaves and Scarf (1976), Smale (1976), Garcia and Gould (1976a, 1976b), and Todd (1976c, 1977), who have significantly increased our understanding of the path followed by Scarf-type algorithms and begun to use this understanding to improve their efficiency.

The aim of this chapter is to present the main ideas from the literature in a way which is as nontechnical as possible; we do not hesitate to make simplifying assumptions if this facilitates proofs. The notation and terminology basically corresponds to that of Todd (1976a), and references

[1]A major drawback of Scarf's presentation, at least from the point of view of the reader new to the subject, is that the argument is conducted in terms of primitive sets and not in terms of simplicial subdivisions, a concept which is easier to grasp and is adopted by now by all authors including Scarf. The two concepts are formally equivalent, but it is not always obvious how results expressed in one set of concepts should be translated into the other set. Scarf (1977) has recently completed an up-to-date survey of the approach in terms of simplicial subdivisions.

to technical details are as much as possible to that book. As a result, the notation of this chapter differs somewhat from that used elsewhere in this book.

6.1.1. *Fixed points and the computation of equilibrium*

A fixed point of a function $f: R^n \to R^n$ is a point x such that $x=f(x)$. The concept can be generalized to point to set mappings. Let $P(R^n)$ be the set of all nonempty subsets of R^n; a fixed point of the mapping $F: R^n \to P(R^n)$ is a point x such that $x \in F(x)$.

This concept is of interest because there exist powerful theorems which assert the existence of such points under given assumptions. These theorems can then be used to prove the existence of solutions of particular systems of equations. Trivially, if $x=f(x)$, then x solves $\phi(x)=0$, where $\phi(x)=f(x)-x$. The relevance of the fixed-point concept is usually more indirect, however.

Suppose we want to solve a set of equations $\psi(x)=0$, and suppose we can define a function $f: R^n \to R^n$, $f(x)=g[\psi(x)]$ such that $x=f(x) \leftrightarrows \psi(x)=0$; then the existence of a fixed point $x=f(x)$ is equivalent to the existence of a solution to $\psi(x)=0$. In general equilibrium theory the existence of an equilibrium is converted to a fixed-point problem as follows.[2] An equilibrium is a price vector $\bar{p}(\bar{p}_k \geqslant 0, \Sigma \bar{p}_k = 1)$ and an allocation $\bar{x}_i$ $(i=1,2,\ldots,I)$, $\bar{y}_j$ $(j=1,2,\ldots,J)$ supported by $\bar{p}$, such that

$$\psi(\bar{p}) = \sum_i \omega_i - \sum_i \bar{x}_i + \sum_j \bar{y}_j \geqslant 0.$$

A corresponding fixed point problem is

$$f_k(p) = \frac{p_k + \max[-\psi_k(p),0]}{1+\sum_l \max[-\psi_l(p),0]}, \qquad k=1,2,\ldots,n.$$

It can be shown that a fixed point $\bar{p}$ of this mapping is an equilibrium.

6.1.2. *The two-door principle*

Following Scarf we can illustrate the underlying logic of the algorithms discussed in terms of a house of a rather special type. Let this house have a finite but arbitrary number of rooms, of which some have two doors,

[2] We consider the case in which excess demands are functions and not correspondences.

others one, and the rest none at all. Only one door opens on the outside. It is intuitively clear that a traveller who enters the house and who leaves each room by a different door than that by which he entered it, must eventually reach a room with a single door. Indeed,

(a) he cannot traverse the same room twice; for this to be possible one room should have three doors at least;

(b) he cannot leave the house; this is excluded by (a) and by the fact that the house has only one door opening on the outside; and

(c) since the house has a finite number of rooms, and no room is traversed more than once, the traveller's path must terminate. As this can happen only in a one-door room, it follows that he must reach such a room.

A second immediate conclusion is that there must be an odd number of one-door rooms. One of these is that reached by the traveller. The number of other one-door rooms is even, since because of (a), (b), and (c) above, a path begun in any one of the other one-door rooms must end in an other such room.

How quickly the traveller will reach his goal cannot be predicted in general. If he is lucky, the first room entered may have as its single door that which opens on the outside. It is also conceivable that he will have to visit every room before stopping. All we know is that

(a) he will not traverse any doorless rooms in the house;

(b) he will enter only one of the house's one-door rooms;

(c) he will not traverse the two-door rooms which are on paths connecting pairs of one-door rooms; and

(d) he also will not traverse those two-door rooms which belong to cyclic paths composed of two-door rooms only.

In practice—this is suggested by experience in using Scarf algorithms—the traveller's journey will end after crossing a small fraction of the rooms in the house.

The classical Scarf algorithms involve a search for a solution of a system of equations over a compact set, usually an n-dimensional simplex which has been divided into "rooms" by a simplicial subdivision. All vertices of the subsimplices of the subdivision are given labels according to a rule which reflects the problem tackled. A second rule uses those labels to identify a set of "eligible faces" among the $(n-1)$-dimensional faces of these subsimplices; these eligible faces are the doors through which the algorithm may enter or exit from a subsimplex. The remaining faces are the walls of the rooms. If (a) no subsimplex has more than two eligible faces; (b) there is only one eligible face on the boundary; and (c) the labelling rule ensures that the vertices of the subsimplices which have a single eligible face are close to equilibrium, then an algorithm which moves between subsimplices through their common eligible faces must eventually reach a subsimplex containing a point close to equilibrium.

6.1.3. *The snake in the tunnel*

Borrowing from another area of economics one of its enlightening similes, it is fair to describe the Scarf approach as joining adjacent simplices into a chain the boundary of which forms a polyhedral tunnel. It will be seen that this tunnel contains a snake which, unlike its EEC brother, never touches the walls which imprison him. Using the two-door principle it is possible to construct a tunnel which leads from an appropriate starting subsimplex to one which contains a point close to equilibrium. The "snake" is continuous and linear in each subsimplex traversed; it terminates at the approximate equilibrium point.

6.2. The fixed-point algorithms

6.2.1. *General definitions*

To give these ideas more precise content, we state some basic definitions. Let $v^i = (v_0^i, \ldots, v_n^i)$ denote a point in R^{n+1} and consider the set of points $v^0, \ldots, v^n$. Then

Definition 6.2.1. Simplex and vertex. An n-simplex S^n is the convex hull of the set of points or vertices $v^0, \ldots, v^n$, assumed to be affinely independent:

$$S^n = \left\{ y \,|\, y = \sum_i x_i v^i,\ \sum_i x_i = 1,\ x_i \geqslant 0\ (i = 0, \ldots, n) \right\}.$$

Examples. A 0-simplex is a single point and a 1-simplex consists of two points and the convex hull of these points (a segment); a 2-simplex consists of all the points in a triangle including the vertices and the faces.

In the sequel, we will only be concerned with the so-called *standard simplex* with vertices $v^0 = (1, 0, \ldots, 0)$, $v^1 = (0, 1, \ldots, 0), \ldots,$ $v^n = (0, 0, \ldots, 1)$, so that we have

$$S^n = \left\{ x \mid \sum_i x_i = 1, x_i \geqslant 0 \ (i=0,\ldots,n) \right\}.$$

The term *simplex* will hereafter refer to the standard simplex.

Definition 6.2.2. Face of a simplex. Consider a subset of the vertices $(v^0, v^1, \ldots, v^n)$ of S^n. The convex hull of the subset of these vertices is a *face* of S^n.

Example. The 2-simplex S^2 has three one-dimensional faces (the sides of the triangle), three zero-dimensional faces (its vertices), and one two-dimensional face, the simplex itself.

Definition 6.2.3. Simplicial subdivision and restricted simplicial subdivision. A *simplicial subdivision* (or more briefly, a subdivision), of S^n is a decomposition of S^n into n-subsimplices σ^i such that the following conditions hold:

(a) $\cup \sigma^i = S^n$, or the subsimplices cover the simplex S^n;

(b) for any pair σ^i, σ^j, either $\sigma^i \cap \sigma^j = \varnothing$, or the intersection is an entire face of both simplices. Such a subdivision will be denoted by G.

A *restricted simplicial* subdivision of S^n is a subdivision which contains no vertices on the faces of S^n other than $(v^0, \ldots, v^n)$.

Property 6.2.1. It follows from definition 6.2.3 that any $n-1$ face of an n-subsimplex of the subdivision is either interior to S^n and hence is the face of exactly two subsimplices of the subdivision, or is on the boundary of S^n and hence is the face of exactly one subsimplex.

Definition 6.2.4. Adjacent subsimplices. Two subsimplices of a subdivision G are said to be *adjacent* if they share a common $(n-1)$-dimensional face.

Definition 6.2.5. Simplex chain. A *simplex chain* is a sequence of subsimplices $\sigma^{r_1}, \ldots, \sigma^{r_k} \in G$ such that each subsimplex σ^{r_i}, $i=2, \ldots, k-1$, is adjacent to subsimplices $\sigma^{r_{i-1}}$ and $\sigma^{r_{i+1}}$ and to no others. If, in addition, simplices σ^{r_1} and σ^{r_k} are adjacent, the chain is said to be cyclic; if not, it is acyclic.

Remark. The boundary of the chain forms a tunnel of the type mentioned in section 6.1.2.

As a consequence of property 6.2.1 we state, without proof,

Theorem 6.2.1. Let G be a simplicial subdivision. Let $x^{j_0},\dots,x^{j_n}$ be the vertices of a subsimplex σ^i. If the vector x^{j_0} is removed there is always a unique replacement vector $x^{j_0'}$ such that the convex hull of the vectors $x^{j_1},\dots,x^{j_n},x^{j_0'}$ is a subsimplex of the subdivision which is adjacent to the subsimplex with vertices $x^{j_0},\dots,x^{j_n}$. There is an exception in the case where the face with vertices $x^{j_1},\dots,x^{j_n}$ lies on the boundary of S^n. Then there is no replacement for x^{j_0}.

Definition 6.2.6. Mesh of a simplicial subdivision. The *mesh of a simplicial subdivision* G is equal to $\max_i(\max_{\sigma^i}|x-y|)$ where $|x-y|$ denotes an appropriate norm.

Definition 6.2.7. Carrier of x. Let $x\in S^n$. The subsimplex spanned by the vertices $\{v^i \mid x^i>0\}$ is called the *carrier of* x. It is in fact the face of lowest dimension of S^n containing x.

Example. Consider the simplex in fig. 6.1. The carrier of x is the face spanned by v^0 and v^1. The carrier of y is the simplex.

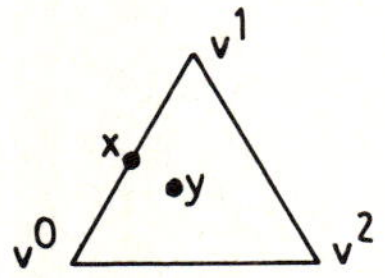

Figure 6.1.

6.2.2. Scalar labelling algorithms

Definition 6.2.8. Scalar labelling rule. A *scalar labelling rule* is a mapping l which assigns to each vertex of a subdivision G of S^n one of the integers $(0,1,\dots,n)$.

Definition 6.2.9. Proper scalar labelling rule. The rule is *proper* if for each vector x, $l(x)=j$ implies that v^j is a vertex of the carrier of x.

This means that the vertices of subsimplices which lie on a face of S^n must be given the label of one of the vertices which span the given face, and that the vertices v^j of S^n must bear the labels $j=0,1,\ldots,n$. Vertices in the interior of S^n may bear any label $0,\ldots,n$.

Examples. S and S' are properly labelled, S'' is not (fig. 6.2).

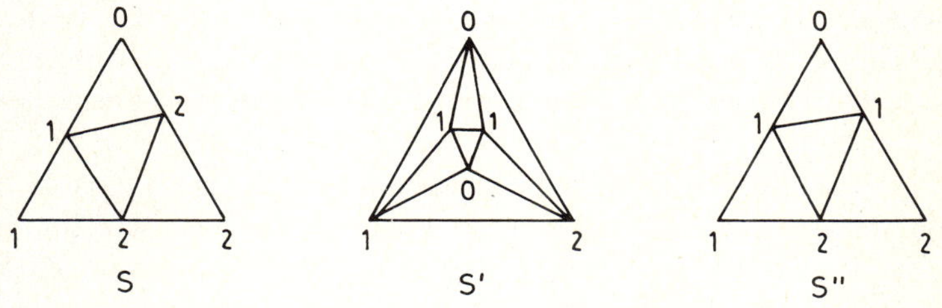

Figure 6.2.

Definition 6.2.10. Complete. A subsimplex is *complete* if its vertices carry all the labels $0,1,\ldots,n$.

Definition 6.2.11. Eligible face. An *eligible face* is an $n-1$ face of a subsimplex of G which is spanned by vertices carrying all the labels $1,\ldots,n$. (Eligible faces are often called *almost complete* faces.)

Remark 1. The argument is symmetric with respect to the choice of labels of eligible faces. These could have been described as faces spanned by vectors carrying all labels $(0,1,\ldots,i-1,i+1,\ldots,n)$ for any given i.

Remark 2. If the subdivision of S^n is restricted, S_0^n—the face carrying labels $1,2,\ldots,n$—is the unique eligible face on the boundary of S^n. If the subdivision is not restricted but its vertices are properly labelled, there may be several eligible faces on the boundary, but they will all lie in S_0^n.

Property 6.2.2. The subsimplices of a subdivision characterized by scalar labels may have 0, 1, or 2 eligible faces. Subsimplices carrying one eligible face are complete; those which have 2 eligible faces have two vertices carrying identical labels.

It is clear that the two-door principle can be used to find a complete subsimplex in a simplex with a restricted subdivision whose vertices are properly labelled. The algorithm will start with the unique subsimplex which has an eligible face on the boundary, move to the unique subsimplex which shares with it an eligible face, forming an acyclic simplex chain as the algorithm moves between adjacent subsimplices through their common eligible faces. The chain will end when it reaches a complete subsimplex. The theorem below describes the procedure in a more formal way.

Theorem 6.2.3. Existence of a complete subsimplex [Scarf]. If there is a unique eligible face on the boundary of S^n, and if the vertices of the subdivision are properly labelled, there exists a complete subsimplex.

Proof. Begin with the unique subsimplex σ^1 which has an eligible face on the boundary, and let x^j be the vertex of this subsimplex which is interior to S^n. If x^j carries the label 0 the theorem is proved. If not, remove the vertex of σ^1 which carries the same label as x^j and replace it by the unique vertex $x^{j'}$, defining σ^2. If $x^{j'}$ carries the label 0, the theorem is proved. If not, remove from σ^2 the vertex which carries the same label as $x^{j'}$ and replace it by a uniquely determined newly introduced vertex. In general, remove at each iteration the vertex which carries the same label as that which has been newly introduced. If this new vertex carries the label 0, end; if not move to the next iteration.

Because no subsimplex has more than two eligible faces, a simplex path initiated on the boundary of S^n cannot cycle (two-door principle). Since the number of subsimplices is finite, the procedure must terminate. It cannot do so by reaching another subsimplex with an eligible face on the boundary, as σ^1 is the only such subsimplex. So termination can only occur upon reaching a subsimplex which has a single eligible face. But such a subsimplex must be complete. Q.E.D.

With subdivisions which are not restricted, it is easy to construct cases in which Scarf's procedure reaches a situation where no replacement of a vertex is possible, so that termination occurs without finding a complete subsimplex. An example of this is given in fig. 6.3. We end up with a subsimplex of which the vertex carrying the label 1 cannot be replaced and the complete subsimplex has not been found.

One way out of the difficulty would be to note that S_0^n is an $n-1$ simplex; Sperner's lemma[3] asserts that if vertices are properly labelled there exists an odd number of complete subsimplices on S_0^n, each of which is an eligible face of the subdivision of S^n. Given proper labelling, there

[3]See, for example, Todd (1976a).

exist no eligible faces on the other faces of S^n. We could thus start with any one of the eligible faces on S_0^n. If the procedure reaches a complete simplex, terminate; if it ends in another eligible face in S_0^n select a third such face and start again. Since the number of eligible faces is odd we must necessarily end up in a complete subsimplex.

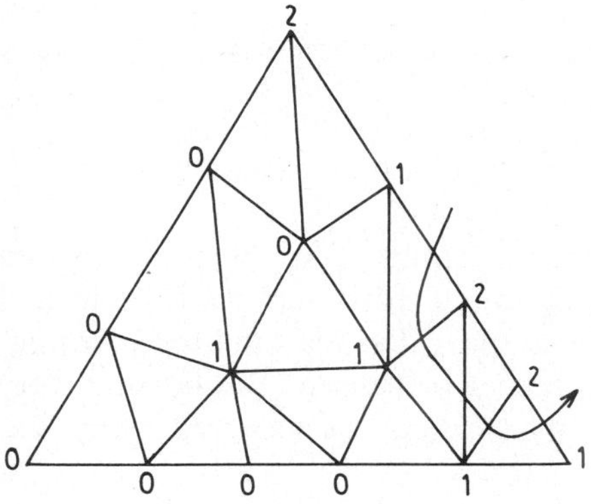

Figure 6.3.

A more convenient way of solving the difficulty is to embed the simplex in a larger simplex, which has a single eligible face on its boundary. Fig. 6.4 illustrates this approach which was first proposed by Kuhn (1968). It is easy to see that if both the original and the enlarged simplices are properly

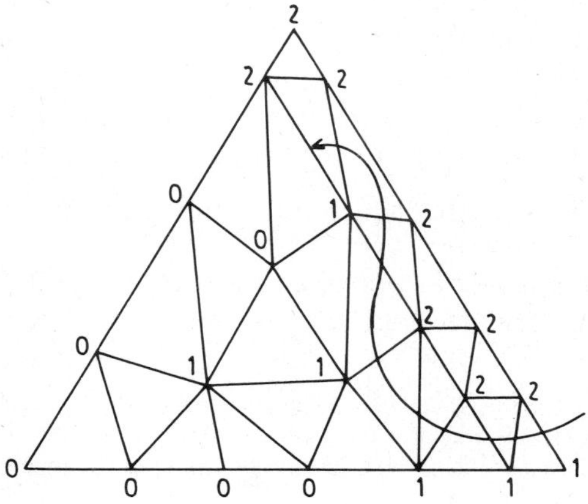

Figure 6.4.

labelled, there exists no complete subsimplex outside of the original simplex and the procedure must terminate within that simplex.

We are now ready to prove

Theorem 6.2.4. [Brouwer]. A continuous mapping $f: S^n \to S^n$ has a fixed point $f(x)=x$.[4]

Proof. Subdivide S^n and label the vertices of the subdivision by the following labelling rule:

$$l(x^j)=i, \quad \text{if } f_i(x^j)-x_i^j \leqslant 0, \qquad x_i^j>0.$$

If several choices are possible, ties must be broken consistently, for example by selecting the smallest index i for which the inequalities are satisfied. It may be checked that the resulting labelling is proper and that such labels can in practice be chosen. Assume that there is a single eligible face on the boundary (this can be achieved using Kuhn's procedure for example).

Theorem 6.2.1 then assures that the algorithm will identify a complete subsimplex. Choosing a sequence of subdivisions whose mesh tends to zero[5] and labelling their vertices according to the rules defined above will generate a sequence of subsimplices which are all complete. Because of the compactness of S^n, a converging subsequence of these vertices can be found which tends to a limit point x. By continuity of f,

$$f_i(x)-x_i \leqslant 0, \quad \text{for all } i.$$

Since

$$\sum_0^n f_i(x)=\sum_0^n x_i=1,$$

necessarily $f_i(x)=x_i$ for all i, which proves the theorem. Q.E.D.

It is of course impossible in practice to construct an "infinite sequence of simplicial subdivisions", to label each of them properly, and to carry out

[4]The conditions of the theorem can be greatly extended (see Todd, 1976a). What we present here is the classical version of the theorem.

[5]Note that this is not possible for restricted subdivisions of the simplex, the mesh of which equals that of the faces of S^n.

the algorithm for each member of the sequence. What is needed is to be assured that carrying out the procedure over a simplicial subdivision with a sufficiently fine mesh will identify a subsimplex the vertices of which are approximate fixed points of the mapping. It is fortunately straightforward to prove, using the continuity of the mapping f and the compactness of S^n, that for each ε there will be a subdivision of mesh δ such that the norm $|f(x^j)-x^j|<\varepsilon$ for all vertices of the complete subsimplex identified. (See Scarf, 1973, p. 52 for details of the argument.) It is *not* true that, if x is a true fixed point of f, the vertices of the simplex identified will lie close to x. This is not important in practice, however, at least for economic applications, since economic mechanisms (and data) are not accurate enough to discriminate sharply between situations of zero excess demand and situations in which excess demands are very small.

6.2.3. *Vector labelling algorithms*

The scalar labelling algorithm described in section 6.2.2 is appropriate only to find the fixed points of point-to-point mappings. Economic theory more generally considers point-to-set mappings. For example, if an isoquant of the production function of a firm is not strictly convex to the origin, the cost minimizing inputs may not be unique, but consist of all the points of a straight-line segment of the isoquant.

Scalar labelling may then break down, as is illustrated in the following example given by Todd (1976a) (fig. 6.5).

Let $F(z)$ be the ellipse containing all points close to x. Then, however fine the grid, it is possible to find a subsimplex containing x with vertices

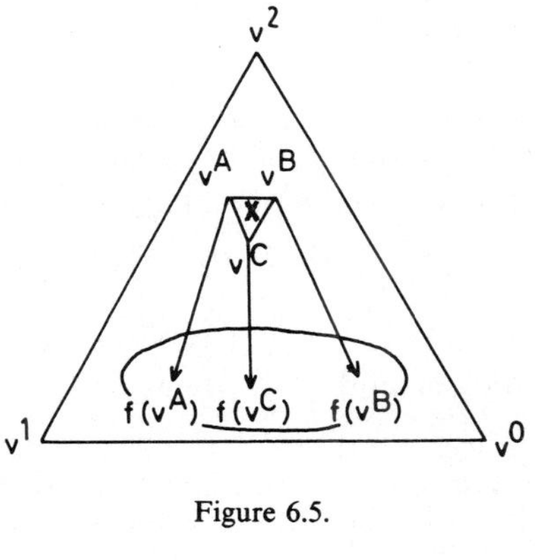

Figure 6.5.

v^A, v^B, and v^C, and points $f(v^A) \in F(v^A)$, $f(v^B) \in F(v^B)$, and $f(v^C) \in F(v^C)$ such that the subsimplex ABC is completely labelled.[6] Yet x is not a fixed point.

This motivates introducing more powerful vector labelling algorithms to find the fixed points of the point-to-set correspondences encountered in economic theory. We shall need the following definitions.

Definition 6.2.12. Vector labels. Let G be a subdivision of S^n with vertices x^j $(j=0,1,\ldots,k)$, and let F be a point-to-set correspondence $F: S^n \to P(\bar{R}^n)$, where $P(\bar{R}^n)$ is the set of all nonempty subsets of $\bar{R}^n$, and $\bar{R}^n$ is the affine subspace of R^{n+1} containing S^n. Let $f(x^j) \in F(x^j)$ and $l(x^j) = f(x^j) - x^j$; we define the *vector label matrix* L associated with the vertices of G as

$$L = \begin{bmatrix} 1 \ldots\ldots 1 \\ l(x^0) \ldots l(x^k) \end{bmatrix}.$$

Note that by construction the components of $l(x^j)$, for all j, add up to 0. The label matrix L_σ of a subsimplex σ with vertices $x^{j_0} \ldots x^{j_n}$ will likewise be defined by

$$L_\sigma = \begin{bmatrix} 1 \ldots\ldots 1 \\ l(x^{j_0}) \ldots l(x^{j_n}) \end{bmatrix}.$$

Definition 6.2.13. Complete subsimplex. A subsimplex σ is said to be *complete* if the system $L_\sigma w = t^0$ has a non-negative solution $w \geqslant 0$; $t^0 = (1,0,\ldots,0)'$ is the first unit vector. It is clear that, given the specification of the label matrix, $\Sigma_0^n w_i = 1$.

Definition 6.2.14. Almost complete subsimplex. A subsimplex σ is said to be *almost complete* if the system $L_\sigma w + c\lambda = t^0$ has a non-negative solution $w \geqslant 0$, $\lambda \geqslant 0$; c is a given vector, the first element of which is 1 and the sum of the remaining elements is 0. Again, this implies that $\Sigma_0^n w_i + \lambda = 1$.

Remark. Definitions 6.2.13 and 6.2.14 imply that a complete subsimplex is always almost complete and that an almost complete subsimplex is

[6] It is readily checked that $v_0^A > f_0(v^A)$, so that vertex A carries the label 1; that $v_0^B < f_0(v^B)$, $v_1^B > f_1(v^B)$ so that vertex B carries the label 2; and that $v_0^C < f_0(v^C)$, $v_1^C < f_1(v^C)$, $v_2^C > f_2(v^C)$ so that vertex C carries the label 3.

complete if $\lambda=0$. Notice also that the solutions of $L_\sigma w+c\lambda=t^0$ are necessarily bounded since $\Sigma w_i+\lambda=1$ and $w_i, \lambda \geqslant 0$.

The system $L_\sigma w+c\lambda=t^0$ has $n+1$ independent equations in $n+2$ variables.[7] We will make the following assumption:

Assumption 6.2.1. Nondegeneracy. Every solution $w \geqslant 0$, $\lambda \geqslant 0$ of this system has at most one component which is zero, all others being strictly positive.[8]

We will now, in the same way as in linear programming, pivot in and out variables w_k and λ. Assume that w_i is pivoted in; because of nondegeneracy and boundedness of the solution set we will find exactly one other variable (w_j or λ) which will go to zero (i.e. which is pivoted out).

Definition 6.2.15. Eligible face. The face of a subsimplex σ opposite vector x^{j_i} is said to be *eligible* if the system $L_\sigma w+c\lambda=t^0$ has a solution with $w_i=0$, $w_k>0$, $k\neq i$ and $\lambda>0$.

Property 6.2.3. Number of eligible faces of a subsimplex. The system $L_\sigma w+\lambda c=t^0$ will always have zero or exactly two solutions. The following possibilities exist indeed:

(a) the system has no non-negative solution; then the subsimplex which it defines has no eligible face ("no door");

(b) the system has two solutions, one in which $\lambda=0$ and the other in which say $w_i=0$; then the subsimplex is complete: it has one eligible face ("one door");

(c) the system has two solutions, one in which $w_i=0$ and the other in which $w_j=0$ $(i\neq j)$. The subsimplex has two eligible faces ("two doors").

This suggests an algorithm to find a complete subsimplex, which has formal properties similar to those of the scalar labelling algorithm. For this, we also need

Assumption 6.2.2. Uniqueness of starting simplex. We assume that there is a unique eligible face on the boundary of S^n.

Remark. This could be assured by specifying an appropriate choice of the vector c, together with a "proper labelling rule" as for the scalar labelling

[7] By construction, the $n+1$ last equations add up to 0.

[8] This assumption can be relaxed, using lexicographic pivoting rules. See, for example, Todd (1976a).

algorithm. Such rules are however difficult to visualize, except for restricted subdivisions, so that assumption 6.2.2 is useful in simplifying the presentation.[9]

We now prove

Theorem 6.2.5. Existence of a complete subsimplex [Scarf]. If assumptions 6.2.1 and 6.2.2 hold, there exists a complete subsimplex.

Proof. Start with the unique subsimplex which has an eligible face on the boundary of S^n. If this subsimplex is complete (i.e. $\lambda=0$), the theorem is proved. If not (i.e. $\lambda>0$), the subsimplex has a second eligible face. Consider the unique subsimplex which shares with the first one this eligible face. If this is complete the procedure ends; if not, identify the subsimplex's other eligible face, and continue.

Each step in the procedure involves pivoting in the vertex which lies opposite an eligible face. If c is pivoted out ($\lambda=0$), then the subsimplex is complete. If another vertex is pivoted out, the face opposite that vertex is eligible.

Because of the boundedness of the solution set it will always be possible to move to an adjacent subsimplex if such a subsimplex exists, except if the subsimplex reached is complete. There could be no adjacent subsimplex if at some point the new eligible face identified by the procedure was on the boundary of the simplex. But this is excluded by assumption 6.2.2. Since the procedure has started in this subsimplex and cannot cycle because of the two-door principle, the new eligible faces identified by the algorithm will all lie in the interior of S^n.

Finally, since the number of subsimplices is finite, the procedure must end in a complete subsimplex. Q.E.D.

Theorem 6.2.5 implies Kakutani's fixed-point theorem. To show this we need a few more definitions.

Definition 6.2.16. Upper hemi-continuous correspondence from $R^{n+1}\to P(R^{n+1})$. The mapping $F: R^{n+1}\to P(R^{n+1})$ is said to be *upper hemi-continuous* if, for every sequence $x^k\to x^*$, $z^k\to z^*$, $z^k\in F(x^k)$, we have $z^*\in F(x^*)$.

[9] A proper labelling rule could be based on corollary 3.2 of Todd (1976a, p. 61) which defines a boundary condition useful for general equilibrium problems.

We do not discuss in detail this well-known concept which is one of the mathematical foundations of general equilibrium theory. We will not work with F as such but with an approximation.

Definition 6.2.17. Piecewise linear approximation of a mapping F. Let $f(x) \in F(x)$, and $x^{j_0} \dots x^{j_n}$ be the vertices of a subsimplex σ^j of G. We approximate linearly the mapping in σ^j by

$$\left.\begin{aligned} f(x) &= \sum_{i=0}^{n} y_i f(x^{j_i}) \\ x &= \sum_{i=0}^{n} y_i x^{j_i} \end{aligned}\right\} \sum y_i = 1, \qquad y_i \geq 0.$$

It is clear that $f(x)$ is a continuous function and we will look for a fixed point of $f(x)$, i.e. an x such that $x = f(x)$. Given the definitions of L_σ and t^0, this means finding $y_i \geq 0$ such that

$$L_\sigma y = t^0.$$

This point x is an approximate fixed point of the mapping F.

To be somewhat more formal, let $P(S^n)$ be the set of nonempty subsets of S^n. We state

Theorem 6.2.6 [Kakutani]. Let $F: S^n \to P(S^n)$ be an upper hemi-continuous convex valued correspondence. Then there exists an x such that $x \in F(x)$.[10]

Proof. We will merely sketch the way in which the theorem can be proved using vector labelling algorithms. Using theorems 6.2.4 and 6.2.5 it is possible to find a complete subsimplex such that $L_\sigma y = t^0, y \geq 0$, which is a fixed point of the piecewise linear approximation of F. Consider a sequence of subdivisions of S^n the mesh of which tends to zero. For each member of the sequence we will find a fixed point. Because of the compactness of the set of possible values of the variables, there must exist a convergent subsequence of these fixed points with limit $[\bar{y}_i, \bar{x}^{j_i}, \bar{f}(x^{j_i})]$. Note that the x^{j_i} tend to a common limit $\bar{x}$, but that under hemi-continuity this may not be true for the $\bar{f}(x^{j_i})$. The limit of the fixed point calculated

[10] The condition of validity of the theorem can be greatly extended. What we present here is the classical version of the theorem.

from the linear approximation to F is then $\Sigma \bar{y}_i \bar{f}(x^{j_i})$. By upper hemi-continuity, $\bar{f}(x^{j_i}) \in F(\bar{x})$; by convexity of $F(\bar{x}), \Sigma \bar{y}_i \bar{f}(x^{j_i}) \in F(\bar{x})$. Hence $\bar{x} \in F(\bar{x})$. Q.E.D.

It is not possible in practice to pass to the limit with finer and finer subdivisions. Because upper hemi-continuity is a capricious property, we cannot be sure that the fixed point $\bar{x}$ obtained in calculations based on a finite grid will make $\bar{x} - f(\bar{x})$ small for $f(\bar{x}) \in F(\bar{x})$. All that can be said is that x is close to some x^* such that $x^* - f(x^*)$ is small.[11]

6.3. Improving the efficiency of the algorithms[12]

The main drawback of Scarf-type procedures is their high cost. A great deal of effort has been devoted to reduce it, and significant progress has been made. However—except for problems with very few variables—these procedures remain much more expensive than other computational approaches.

It is sometimes argued that this weakness is offset by the guaranteed convergence of the procedures. This is not a valid argument for empirical work. No model-builder has unlimited access to computer time. In practical work the best method is one which has the highest probability of convergence in the computer time the user can afford to buy. The convergence proof for Scarf-type algorithms is irrelevant from this point of view because it is based on an exhaustive search argument over the finite but tremendously large number of subsimplices to be examined.

In practice Scarf-type algorithms tend to work better than their convergence proof would lead to hope;[13] but that is an empirical argument which has no more rigorous foundation than the statement that "tâtonnement procedures for computing equilibria work well in practical examples".

It is well known that tâtonnement processes do not converge in general. There are many examples to support this. Todd (1977) has likewise devised an example in which even Scarf-type algorithms keep searching without identifying a fixed point. This example has no economic significance, but there is no guarantee that such a case cannot arise in general equilibrium calculations.

[11] For a more detailed investigation of the accuracy of the approximation, see Scarf (1973).

[12] The survey of recent research orientation does not cover the significant work of Van der Laan and Talman (1979) and Shamir (1979a, 1979b).

[13] The same is true for the simplex algorithm in linear programming.

These remarks show that it is worthwhile to devote time to discussing the computational performance of Scarf-type procedures: why they work in practical problems much better than can be expected, why they are nevertheless so expensive, and how they have and can be made more efficient. We address this in the next sections.

6.3.1. The cost of using the algorithm: Scarf's rule of thumb

It is convenient to organize the discussion of efforts to improve the efficiency of these algorithms around a rough rule of thumb, initially suggested by Scarf as a rough conjecture and strongly confirmed later by the results of numerical experiments. Wolsey (1974) and Todd (1976a) have backed up this conjecture by mathematical arguments under simplifying assumptions about the character of problems studied. The rule of thumb asserts that the number of subsimplices encountered by these procedures will tend to depend on the length of the path μ, the dimension of the problem n, the mesh d of the subdivision, and a unit cost of iteration $(c_1+c_2+c_3)$ which reflects the cost c_1 of identifying the new vertex to be introduced, the cost c_2 of computing its label, and the cost c_3 of identifying the vertex which should be dropped from the subsimplex. The formula is

$$K=\frac{(c_1+c_2+c_3)n^2}{d}\cdot\mu,$$

where K is the average cost of computing fixed points for a path length μ.[14]

The cost c_1 of selecting the new vertex is negligible with the algorithms used today (see section 6.3.2 below). The function evaluation cost, c_2, is highly dependent upon the problem: it is very low in the simple examples considered by Hansen (1968), but amounts to about \$15 for the model presented in this book.[15] The cost, c_3, of pivoting to drop a vertex from the current subsimplex is low with scalar labelling but somewhat higher with vector labelling.

[14]Scarf's version of the rule of thumb does not involve the parameter μ. This is because Scarf was not preoccupied by what might be gained by choosing a starting point close to the suspected equilibrium point: the algorithms he devised had to start on the boundary of the simplex.

[15]See Chapter 11 for more details on the experiments.

6.3.2. Special subdivision of the simplex

We now describe the concept of special subdivisions of the simplex which have reduced to a negligible level the cost c_1 of identifying the next vertex to be considered. The subdivisions in use today partition the unit cube[16] which is replicated to cover R^n. These partitions make it very easy to identify the next vertex to be considered, given the subsimplex last considered and the vertex dropped from it in application of an algorithm. These rules are mechanical and there is no point in describing them in this chapter; a good presentation is given by Todd (1976a) who also surveys the contributions made by individual authors.

6.3.3. Arbitrary starting points and grid refinement

We first describe well-established procedures designed to optimize the grid size and reduce the distance between the starting point and the solution.

In the first generation algorithms the algorithmic path starts on one of the faces of the simplex, which can be selected at will. This provides only weak control over the starting point of the procedure. It is probably a good idea to start on the face which is closest to the suspected location of the equilibrium point, but there is no way of starting as close as would be desirable. The algorithms of Merill (1972), Eaves and Saigal (1972), and Eaves (1971, 1972) have provided a way both to choose freely the starting point and to refine gradually the grid of the simplex on which the search for a fixed point is conducted.[17] In this way it is possible to travel cheaply over most of the path (the d in Scarf's rule is large), switching to a more expensive but more accurate method of search when reaching the neighborhood of the solution.

The basis of these algorithms is really an adaptation of the device proposed by Kuhn to guarantee the existence of a unique starting point (see section 6.2.2. above). Kuhn sandwiched an artificial $n-1$ face *next to* the $n-1$ face of S^n from which the algorithm would otherwise start,

[16]See Todd (1976a, ch. 3).

[17]These algorithms are usually called *homotopy algorithms* because they involve establishing a homotopy between an initial approximation of the function and the function whose fixed point is to be calculated. (If $\Phi_0 : R^n \to R^n$ and $\Phi_1 : R^n \to R^n$ are two mappings, then a homotopy is a continuous mapping $\Psi : R^n \times [0,1] \to R^n$ such that $\Psi(0,x) = \Phi_0(x)$ and $\Psi(1,x) = \Phi_1(x)$ [a simple example which happens to be relevant is $\Psi(t,x) = (1-t)\Phi_0(x) + t\Phi_1(x)$, $0 \leq t \leq 1$].) We do not here pursue this idea which originated in Eaves (1971) and Eaves–Saigal (1972).

extended the subdivision of S^n to that face, and then defined an artificial labelling which guaranteed that the starting point is unique and easy to find. An immediate extension of this idea is Merrill's proposal to add a dimension to S^n so as to be able to sandwich an artificial n simplex *above* S^n. This simplex can be labelled so that the starting point of the procedure is unique and easy to find. Fig. 6.6 illustrates the approaches: Kuhn's sandwich is two-dimensional, Merrill's is three-dimensional.

(a) (b)

Figure 6.6. (a) Kuhn's sandwich for S^2; (b) Merrill's sandwich for S^2.

Merrill's idea can be implemented with both vector and scalar labels; we discuss scalar labels only. Define a simplicial subdivision G of $S^n \times [0,1]$. Label the vertices of $S_0^n = S^n \times \{0\}$ by a scalar labelling rule based on the problem to be solved, and those in $S_1^n = S^n \times \{1\}$ by an artificial rule using only labels $(0,1,\ldots,n)$ and which assures uniqueness of the starting point.

Note that a complete simplex in S_0^n or S_1^n is an eligible face of simplices in $S^n \times [0,1]$. Since no vertex bears a label other than $(0,1,\ldots,n)$, there is no complete simplex in $S^n \times [0,1]$. The procedure can therefore terminate only on the boundary. If S_0^n and S_1^n have been properly labelled, one shows that termination cannot occur elsewhere than on S_0^n or S_1^n. It cannot occur on S_1^n, which carries a unique eligible face from which the procedure was initiated. So it must terminate in an eligible face which is a complete subsimplex of S_0^n. Fig. 6.7 illustrates the procedure for S^1. In the figure the

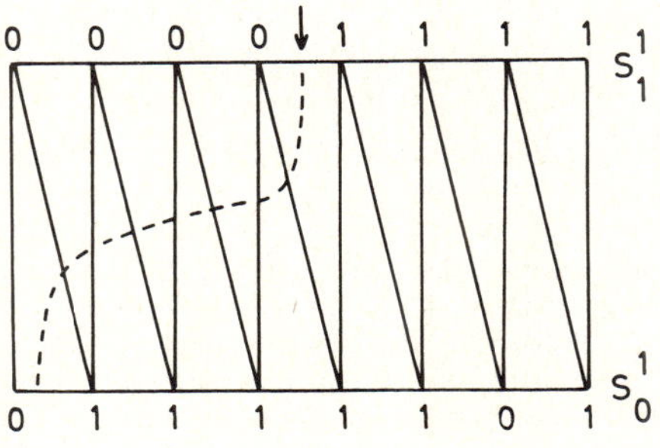

Figure 6.7.

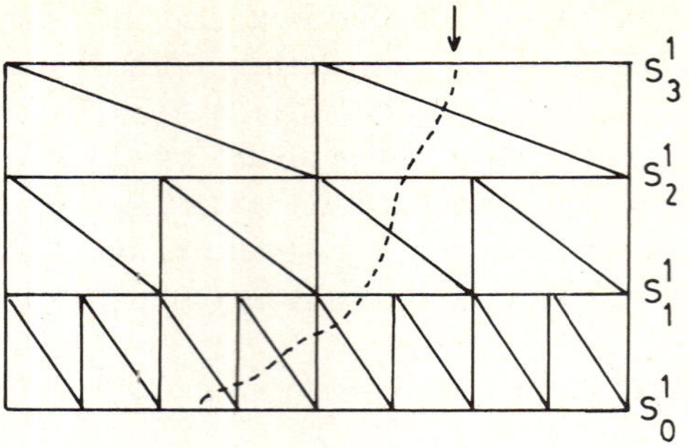

Figure 6.8.

dotted path crosses the successive eligible faces identified by the procedure. It starts from a complete simplex in S_1^1 and ends in a complete simplex in S_0^1.

The approach can obviously be used to control the d parameter by refining in successive steps a fixed point obtained on an initially coarse grid.[18] Fig. 6.8 illustrates the idea, again for S^1. The intersections of the path with the "levels" represented by the simplices S_i^1, $i=0,\ldots,3$, are the approximate fixed points identified at the different stages of the procedure.

In Merrill's algorithm the procedure must be restarted at each "level" reached. This is because the simplicial subdivisions of each layer are not compatible. Eaves proposed to define a single subdivision extending over various levels of grid refinement. Fig. 6.9 illustrates the idea, together with a possible path.

There exist subdivisions other than the one illustrated, but no practical rule is known at present which does better than halving the grid size at successive levels. Note that a grid such as that illustrated can be extended over the half-open set $S^n \times (0,1]$ making possible arbitrarily fine approximations of the fixed point. An interesting feature of the procedure, which distinguishes it from Merrill's, is that it can return to coarse grids if the search on a fine grid fails to locate a fixed point (see the path in fig. 6.9).

[18]The gain from using a coarse grid is somewhat less than is suggested by the rule of thumb, since c_2 generally increases with d. With a fine grid, the last vertex visited is so close to the next one that its label provides an excellent starting point for evaluation of the next label. This offsets to a certain extent the advantage of using a coarse grid, and in practice it is likely that, at least when the functions to be evaluated are not defined by explicit analytic expressions, the cost component $c_2 n^2/d$ decreases less than in inverse proportion to d.

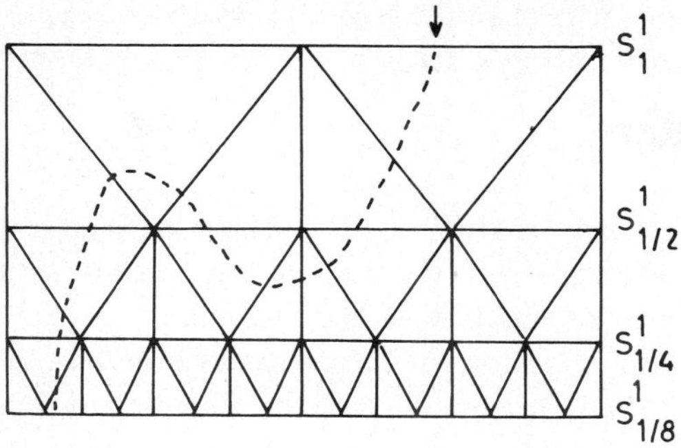

Figure 6.9.

In Merrill's approach the search would continue over the last grid size reached. This might be presumed to increase the efficiency of Eaves' procedures, but this is apparently not confirmed by experience.[19]

6.3.4. The path defined by the algorithm as a generalized Newton path

We must examine whether there are ways of improving the shape of the solution path. There is of course nothing in the logic of the two-door principle which guarantees or even makes probable that a path initiated close to a fixed point will be shorter than a path initiated from further away. It is easy to construct counter-examples to such a conjecture. In practice, however, paths started close to a fixed point do turn out to be short (μ in Scarf's rule of thumb is small). It is worthwhile to understand why this is so, and to see how this understanding points the way to more efficient procedures. The key to this is given in a recent paper by Smale (1976).

Smale has studied the convergence of a "global Newton" differential equation which is closely related to Scarf-type algorithms. We consider functions satisfying

Assumption 6.3.1. C^2 function. $f : M \to R^n$ is a mapping with continuous first and second derivatives. M is an n-dimensional compact set.

[19]See Todd's remark on this point (Todd, 1976a, p. 100).

We look for a zero of f. Using the usual version of Newton's method, this could be done by choosing a sequence of vectors x^i $(i=0,1,\ldots)$ satisfying

$$J(x^{i+1}-x^i)=-f(x^i), \quad x^0 \text{ given},$$

where J is the Jacobian matrix of $f(x)$. There exist many versions of the method, and an extensive literature on the conditions under which $x^i \to \bar{x}$ as $i \to \infty$, where $\bar{x}$ is the solution of the problem.[20]

The basic Newton–Kantorovich theorem asserts that, under appropriate conditions on the function, its derivatives, and its values, it is possible to define a ball around points which are sufficiently close to the solution so that

(a) the solution lies in that ball;

(b) the Newton iterates $(x^0, x^1, \ldots)$ stay within that ball;

(c) they converge to the solution; and

(d) if x^k is close enough to $\bar{x}$, the norm $\| x^k - \bar{x} \|$ decreases at least quadratically at each iteration, by a factor α^{-2k}, where $\alpha < 1$.[21]

This is probably the most powerful result in the literature on numerical methods for solving equations; and this lends great interest to the connection between the Scarf and Newton methods. In particular, it explains why Scarf-type paths tend to be "good paths" instead of wandering at random as is allowed by the logic of the two-door principle.

The discrete increments $x^{i+1}-x^i$ may be replaced by the time derivative $\dot{x}=\mathrm{d}x(t)/\mathrm{d}t$. This leads to a continuous time version of Newton's method which will be designated as the Classical Newton (CN) differential process:

$$J\dot{x}=\frac{\mathrm{d}}{\mathrm{d}t}f[x(t)]=-f[x(t)],$$

initiated at $f[x(t_0)]=f(x^0)=c$.

It is important to note that points on the path of this process satisfy $f[x(t)] \propto c$ or $f[x(t)]=-\lambda(t)c$ and $\mathrm{d}f[x(t)]/\mathrm{d}t=-\dot{\lambda}(t)c$, with $\dot{\lambda}=\mathrm{d}\lambda/\mathrm{d}t$ (λ is a scalar). Also, since $\mathrm{d}f[x(t)]/\mathrm{d}t=-f[x(t)]$, $\dot{\lambda}=-\lambda$. The CN process can therefore be rewritten as

$$\begin{bmatrix} J & 0 \\ 0 & 1 \end{bmatrix}\begin{bmatrix} \dot{x} \\ \dot{\lambda} \end{bmatrix}=\begin{bmatrix} c \\ -1 \end{bmatrix}\lambda,$$

[20] See, for example, Ortega and Rheinboldt (1970).

[21] See Ortega and Rheinboldt (1970, p. 421) for an accurate statement of the theorem.

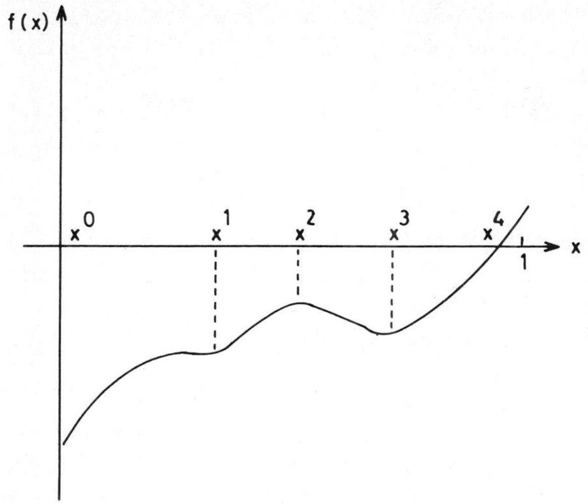

Figure 6.10.

and its path is well defined if J is nonsingular. Then $\lambda \to 0$ exponentially, and so does $f[x(t)] = -\lambda(t)c$.

At singular points, where J does not have full rank, the process is not well defined: the direction of motion of $x(t)$ may be inverted.

This is illustrated in fig. 6.10 for the case $f:[0,1] \to R$. A CN process initiated at $x^0 = 0$ moves successfully beyond the first singularity x^1; but at x^2 the direction of motion switches from $\dot{x} = +\infty$ to $\dot{x} = -\infty$ so that the process stops there.

We now develop a process which does not have these drawbacks.[22] Add to the Newton differential equation a normalization condition, giving the Normalized Newton (NN) process:

$$\begin{bmatrix} J & c \\ \dot{x} & \dot{\lambda} \end{bmatrix} \begin{bmatrix} \dot{x} \\ \dot{\lambda} \end{bmatrix} = \begin{bmatrix} 0 \\ 1 \end{bmatrix}.$$

It is clear that for $\dot{\lambda} > 0$ the normalized process will move along the same

[22]We develop Smale's Global Newton differential equation using elementary mathematics. These are less powerful and elegant than Smale's argument which uses algebraic topology. Hopefully our presentation will be easier to understand for most readers. Our notation differs from his in some respects in order to emphasize the connection with Scarf-type vector labelling algorithms.

path as the Newton differential equation. The speed $\dot{x}\cdot\dot{x}$ of the two processes will however differ: $\dot{x}\cdot\dot{x}\leqslant 1$ for the NN process, whereas $\dot{x}\cdot\dot{x}$ is unbounded for the CN equation.

It is important to note that if any $[\dot{x} \quad \dot{\lambda}]$ satisfies the NN, so does $-[\dot{x} \quad \dot{\lambda}]$: hence the process can move in opposite directions. It is sensible to impose

Consistent orientation rule. Let the direction of the NN process at $t=t_0$ be chosen arbitrarily. Then for $t>t_0$ the direction of motion should be chosen so that the direction vector $[\dot{x} \quad \dot{\lambda}]$ is continuous, i.e. does not suddenly switch sign. In practice the initial choice will be dictated by the problem to be solved.

Remark. This rules out the direction reversal which may characterize the CN process at a point where J is singular. Hence a NN process will cross smoothly such singularities, as is obviously necessary for global convergence.

We will examine paths which satisfy

Assumption 6.3.2. No branch points. The matrix $[J \quad c]$ has full row rank along the path of the NN process.

Remark. The last line of the left-hand side matrix of the (NN) process is orthogonal to the others, so that this matrix has full rank. Assumption 6.3.2 thus implies that the process can move in only one of two alternative directions $[\dot{x} \quad \dot{\lambda}]$ and $-[\dot{x} \quad \dot{\lambda}]$. Hence such paths may consist either of curves, or of closed loops. A path of another type necessarily implies a branch point. It should be remembered that a similar property, resulting from the two-door principle, was a crucial feature of the Scarf algorithm.

Let us examine the behavior of the system at a point $t=\tau$ where J is singular, i.e. at a point where the CN process runs into difficulties. Assumption 6.3.2 implies that if $\det J(\tau)=0$, $\dot{\lambda}(\tau)=0$.

We next examine the sign of $\dot{\lambda}$ in the neighborhood of such a singularity, at points $(\tau+\delta)$, $(\tau-\delta)$, where $J(\tau+\delta)$ and $J(\tau-\delta)$ are nonsingular. Since $\dot{x}(\tau)\cdot\dot{x}(\tau)=1$, at least one component of $\dot{x}(\tau)$, say $\dot{x}_1(\tau)$, is different from zero. By Cramer's rule, we have, solving

$$\begin{bmatrix} J & c \\ \dot{x} & \dot{\lambda} \end{bmatrix}\begin{bmatrix} \dot{x} \\ \dot{\lambda} \end{bmatrix}=\begin{bmatrix} 0 \\ 1 \end{bmatrix}$$

for $\dot{x}_1$:

$$\dot{x}_1 = \frac{\det\begin{bmatrix} 0 & J_{12}\cdots J_{1n} & c_1 \\ \cdots & \cdots & \cdots \\ 0 & J_{n2}\cdots J_{nn} & c_n \\ 1 & \dot{x}_2\cdots\dot{x}_n & \dot{\lambda} \end{bmatrix}}{\det\begin{bmatrix} J & c \\ \dot{x} & \dot{\lambda} \end{bmatrix}} \neq 0,$$

where J_{ij} is the typical element of J.

The determinant in the numerator is bounded away from zero for $t=\tau$. Indeed, if $\dot{x}_1 \neq 0$, the corresponding column J_1 of J is linearly dependent on $J_2 \dots J_n$. But since $[J \quad c]$ has full row rank, $[J_2 \dots J_n \quad c]$ must be nonsingular. Hence, the numerator does not change sign in the interval $[\tau-\delta, \tau+\delta]$.

As $J\dot{x}+c\dot{\lambda}=0$, $\dot{x}\cdot\dot{x}+\dot{\lambda}^2=1$, the determinant in the denominator can be written

$$\det\begin{bmatrix} J & c \\ \dot{x} & \dot{\lambda} \end{bmatrix} = \frac{1}{\dot{\lambda}}\det\begin{bmatrix} J & J\dot{x}+c\dot{\lambda} \\ \dot{x} & \dot{x}\cdot\dot{x}+\dot{\lambda}^2 \end{bmatrix} = \frac{1}{\dot{\lambda}}\det\begin{bmatrix} J & 0 \\ \dot{x} & 1 \end{bmatrix} = \frac{1}{\dot{\lambda}}\det J.$$

But then, since according to the *consistent orientation rule* $\operatorname{sgn}\dot{x}(\tau+\delta) = \operatorname{sgn}\dot{x}(\tau-\delta)$, the sign of $\dot{\lambda}$ must switch if that of $\det J$ changes.

The consistent orientation rule enables the NN process to move smoothly past singularities of J, provided that assumption 6.3.2 holds. In fig. 6.10 above the sign of the direction vector $(\dot{x} \quad \dot{\lambda})$ at t_0 should be chosen so that $\dot{\lambda}(t_0)$ is positive. Then $\dot{\lambda}>0$ in the interval $(0, x^2)$ except at x^1 where $\dot{\lambda}=0$; it is negative in (x^2, x^3), zero at x^2 and x^3, and positive in (x^3, x^4). At x^4, $\dot{x}=\dot{\lambda}=0$ and the process comes to rest at the zero of the function. The NN process has thus converged globally.

The NN process is a special case of Smale's Global Newton (GN) differential equation

$$J\dot{x} = -\dot{\lambda}c,$$

where $\operatorname{sgn}\dot{\lambda}$ is chosen equal to either $\operatorname{sgn}\det J$ or to $-\operatorname{sgn}\det J$; the magnitude of $\dot{\lambda}$ is set in some appropriate way. For this process Smale establishes global convergence subject to a boundary condition:

Assumption 6.3.3. Boundary condition. Let $\operatorname{sgn}\dot{\lambda}$ be chosen equal to $\operatorname{sgn}\det J$ or to $-\operatorname{sgn}\det J$. Then for one of these choices the path $\dot{x} = -\dot{\lambda}J^{-1}c$ must point into M at each $x \in \partial M$.

Remark. This condition forbids paths initiated on the boundary of M to intersect this boundary a second time which is the analogue of a crucial property of simplex chains in Scarf-type algorithms.

Smale then proves

Theorem 6.3.1. If assumptions 6.3.1 and 6.3.3 hold, there is a subset Σ in ∂M such that if $x_0 \in \partial M$, $x_0 \notin \Sigma$, assumption 6.3.2 holds and there exists a unique C^1 solution ϕ: $[t_0, t_1) \to M$ of the GN process starting at $x^0 = \phi(t_0)$ with $\dot{x} \cdot \dot{x} = 1$ and t_1 maximal, $t_1 \leqslant \infty$. This solution converges to a zero of $f(x)$ as $t \to t_1$.

For the proof of this theorem, see Smale (1976).

We can now define

Definition 6.3.1. Continuation curve of the Newton differential equation. The path of Newton's differential equation is called the *continuation curve* of the equation $f(x) = 0$.

The relation to Scarf-type vector labelling algorithms is immediate. Remember the definition of a piecewise linear approximation to $f(x) - x$ as

$$\left.\begin{aligned} l(x) &= \sum_{i=0}^{n} y_i\left[f(x^{j_i}) - x^{j_i}\right] \\ x &= \sum_{i=0}^{n} y_i x^{j_i} \end{aligned}\right\} \sum y_i = 1, \qquad y_i \geqslant 0,$$

where x^{j_i} are the vertices of a subsimplex σ^j and $x \in \sigma^j$. It is easy to see that eligible faces of a subsimplex are those which are intersected by the linear segment defined by

$$l(x) = -\gamma c, \qquad x \in \sigma^j.$$

These linear segments can obviously be joined up to form a piecewise linear path[23] which is the continuation curve of the vector label Scarf algorithm. This is the "snake in the Eaves–Scarf tunnel" referred to in the introduction.

[23] Because each eligible face is intersected at the same point by the linear segments defined in the two adjacent subsimplices.

This is a major finding to which a series of ideas are related.

Charnes, Garcia and Lemke (1977), Garcia (1977), and Garcia and Gould (1976a, 1977) have recently proposed taking the Generalized Newton path really seriously, instead of as a basis for rough guidelines in devising good algorithms. Their procedure involves constructing labelling rules such that a procedure initiated at an arbitrary point x_0 defines a subsimplex chain which contains the continuation curve $\Phi(x) = -\gamma\Phi(x_0)$.[24] Computational experience with this approach is conflicting. The question which comes to mind is that there is no mathematical reason to believe that the Newton path is a good path outside of the "ball of attraction" defined by the Newton–Kantorovich theorem.

Indeed, the main message of this section is perhaps that there is less basic difference between Scarf-type and other computational methods than had been thought until recently. Fixed point algorithms can be made to behave in a way which resembles Newton methods,[25] the gain from using Scarf-type methods being that they cannot cycle and therefore cannot get stuck. The section also points to the possibility of exploiting the "ball of attraction" property of Newton methods: a theme to which we will return (see section 6.3.6).

6.3.5. The number of eligible faces on a solution path: The curse of dimensionality for Scarf-type algorithms

The Achilles' heel of the approach is the term n^2 in Scarf's rule of thumb, compounded by the dependence of c_1, c_2, and c_3 on n, the dimension of the space over which the search for a fixed point is conducted. c_1 (the cost of identifying new vertices) is negligible in practice. c_2 (evaluation of $l(x)$) will tend to increase at least in proportion to n, though this is far from being a general rule.[26] c_3 (the cost of choosing the vector to be dropped) will depend on n for scalar labels and n^2 for vector labels.

[24] The Garcia and Gould papers also show how the path can be generated by scalar rather than by vector labels. Given the way in which the scalar labels are generated it does not seem that this will result in an appreciable cost reduction.

[25] Possibly, labelling rules can be devised to make these algorithms behave like other classical computational methods.

[26] Heuristically, it appears that the cost of evaluating functions on R^n should grow at least linearly with n, except of course if the function depends only on a subset of the coordinates of the space over which it is defined. This is not a general rule of course. The cost of evaluating a quadratic form, for example, depends on n^2; on the other hand, different variants of the model described in this book generate fixed point problems in dimensions which range from 3 to several dozens, with a negligible impact on the cost c_2.

Classical computational methods are far less dependent on n. They involve linear jumps through that space. Each jump is normally more costly if n is large, but the number of jumps required does not depend closely on n.

To understand the origin of the n^2 term, it is necessary to count the number of subsimplices traversed by a continuation curve of given length μ. Equivalently, we can count the number of faces traversed, since the logic of the procedure involves a pivot iteration each time an eligible face is crossed. This is illustrated for the $K1$ simplicial subdivision for $n=2$. We represent a single cube of the subdivision which covers R^2 (fig. 6.11). It is

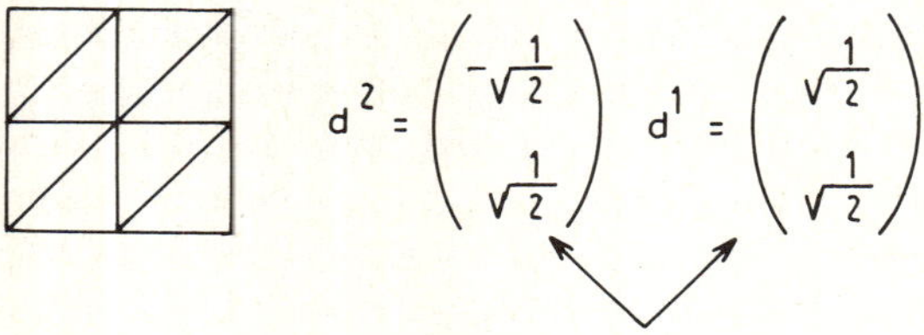

Figure 6.11.

easy to check that the number of faces counted depends on the direction of the search. For instance, a search in the direction d^1 will meet on the average fewer faces than a search in the direction d^2. Let

$$d=\begin{pmatrix} d_1 \\ d_2 \end{pmatrix}$$

be an arbitrary gradient of unit Euclidian length. On average, a sufficiently long linear path of length μ and orientation d will meet $\mu|d_1|$ vertical faces, $\mu|d_2|$ horizontal faces, and $\mu|d_2-d_1|$ oblique faces ($|\cdot|$ is the absolute value).

As shown by Todd (1976b), the formulae generalize for a subdivision of R^n to

(a) $\mu\Sigma_i|d_1|$ intersections of planes parallel to the coordinate planes, and
(b) $\mu\Sigma_{i<j}|d_i-d_j|$ intersections of oblique planes.

By averaging over uniformly distributed directions d, Todd then obtains a formula which implies that (a) the number of intersections of parallel planes is ng_n, and (b) the number of intersections of oblique planes is $n(n-1)g_n/\sqrt{2}$, where g_n is constant. Asymptotically the second term dominates and tends to the n^2 of Scarf's rule of thumb. This dominant n^2 arises for all usual subdivisions.

Simplicial iterations is thus a prohibitively expensive mode of travel over spaces with many dimensions: it is inherently cheaper to travel on a piecewise linear path, as is done by other solution algorithms, than to construct simplex chains. This handicap is not eliminated by the ability of Scarf-type algorithms to refine the grid as the solution is approached, or to start at an arbitrary starting point, since other methods can also use variable step sizes and start from anywhere.

A more radical approach, which Smale intends to implement and which has also been proposed by Kellog, Li and Yorke (1977), is in terms of our simile, "not to mind the tunnel but follow the snake"; i.e. to give up simplicial subdivisions and follow instead the continuation curve obtained by solving the Global Newton differential equation.

In the absence of computational experience it is hard to judge this approach. All that can be said is that the method would be inherently more expensive than classical methods which "jump, look and jump again", because of the need to return to the continuation curve after each jump. As shown by Smale, the Global Newton equation, like Scarf-type algorithms, may have cyclic paths in addition to the acyclic ones which lead to a solution: caution would be needed to avoid switching inadvertently to a cyclic path located close to the one followed by the solution. Finally, it would be desirable to find ways of initiating continuation curves elsewhere than at the boundary of M.

In this connection it is worth mentioning a very interesting paper by Wilson (1978) who has devised a "snake"-type algorithm for general equilibrium problems in which the utility functions and production sets are defined by systems of linear inequalities. His algorithm is simple, but is likely to prove costly to implement for large problems because it implies repeated solution of systems of bilinear equations subject to non-negativity constraints. It is of course possible that shortcuts will be devised to make this approach more practicable; but bilinearity is not easy to eliminate from general equilibrium computations.

The "curse of dimensionality" can of course also be tackled by transforming the fixed-point problem into one which involves a lower number of dimensions. In his book, Scarf noted that if the number of agents is smaller than the number of goods, it might be attractive to define the equilibrium problem in terms of a search for a fixed point over the space of utilities rather than over the space of goods. This approach has since been stressed by Dixon (1975a, 1975b) and is of course emphasized in the present volume.

6.3.6. The fineness of the approximation and the "ball of attraction" property of Newton methods

The ball of attraction property is the outstanding property of Newton methods. The fact that Scarf-type algorithms can be interpreted as Newton methods[27] suggests defining a "subsimplex of attraction" such that a refined grid search initiated in that subsimplex remains inside it, and such that the accuracy of the approximation grows quadratically beyond a certain point. Results of this type have been proved by Saigal (1976) and Saigal and Todd (1976). This implies that high accuracy of the fixed point is not costly beyond a certain point. But given the coarseness of economic data, it is usually not worthwhile to search for highly accurate solutions.

This idea has been exploited by Todd who suggested a mixed procedure in which after an initial simplicial research the algorithm switches to a sequence of quasi-Newton steps carried out using the approximate Jacobian generated by the Scarf algorithm. The procedure is mainly useful for calculating efficiently highly accurate solutions. Very recently Shamir (1979a, 1979b) developed a simplicial subdivision allowing for arbitrary grid refinement which appears to be capable of calculating highly accurate fixed points much more efficiently than pure fixed-point methods. Shamir does not however claim that his method is more efficient than Todd's mixed procedure.

[27] This is at least true for the most widely used variants of the approach.

CHAPTER 7

Tâtonnement and Jacobi procedures for the computation of equilibria: An attempt at rehabilitation

This chapter discusses the convergence properties of Jacobi computational procedures, of which the Gauss–Seidel iterations much used in macroeconomic modelling and the tâtonnement of economic theory are special cases. These procedures are very easy to use since they do not make use of derivatives.

Economic theory has extensively studied the stability of tâtonnement procedures. The disappointing conclusion reached has given rise to a widespread belief that they do not provide a sound approach to the computation of equilibria. We feel that this belief is not entirely justified, because it overlooks essential differences between the economic process which economists wished to represent and the way in which a model-builder solves a model. Indeed,

(a) Computation will be undertaken by an economist who understands the properties of his model and uses, if need be, this understanding to decide how computation should be set up.

(b) This understanding implies at least qualitative knowledge of the structure of the Jacobian of the excess demand functions. This may be based on study of the model and careful examination of the iterations of trial calculation. As will be shown, this knowledge provides useful guidance in designing a Jacobi procedure.

(c) In theoretical work there is little freedom in selecting the form of the adjustment process. It would not make sense to assume that prices drop when excess demand is positive, or that the price of sugar is adjusted in proportion to the excess demand for wheat. There are no such restrictions in computation, and this turns out to be a decisive advantage in difficult cases.

The theoretical literature on the stability of tâtonnement processes, discussed in sections 7.3–7.7, nevertheless yields extremely interesting insights into the problems which may be encountered in solving models.

The most important results are those related to diagonal dominance. It is shown in section 7.8 that, provided that qualitative knowledge of the Jacobian exists, there is no difficulty in solving by Jacobi procedures the classical counter-examples of Scarf (1960) and Gale (see Arrow and Hahn, 1971) on tâtonnement stability.

7.1. Jacobi versus tâtonnement solution processes

The Jacobi approach to computation, or *method of simultaneous displacement*, is probably the simplest way of solving equations. The basic principle can be illustrated by considering the system

$$f(z)=0,$$

where $f: R^{n+1}\to R^{n+1}$ and to solve it by a succession of iterations $\tau=0,1,\ldots,$ in which the x_i^τ are adjusted simultaneously according to values of the components of $f(x^\tau)$. The basic step is to solve for z_i $(i=0,1,\ldots,n)$ simultaneously the equations

$$f_i(z_0^\tau, z_1^\tau,\ldots, z_{i-1}^\tau, z_i, z_{i+1}^\tau,\ldots, z_n^\tau)=0,$$

and to set $z_i^{\tau+1}=z_i$ $(i=0,1,\ldots,n)$.

A variant, the Gauss–Seidel procedure or *method of successive displacement* has proved extremely effective in solving macroeconomic models and has come to be almost universally used for that purpose.[1] The basic step, in this case, is to solve for z_i $(i=0,1,\ldots,n)$ successively the equations

$$f_i(z_0^{\tau+1}, z_1^{\tau+1},\ldots, z_{i-1}^{\tau+1}, z_i, z_{i+1}^\tau,\ldots, z_n^\tau)=0$$

and to set $z_i^{\tau+1}=z_i$ $(i=0,1,\ldots,n)$.

Two important remarks are in order.

(a) The ordering of $f_i(\cdot)$ is in general independent of the ordering of z_i. Define a permutation j_i of $i=0,1,\ldots,n$. Then, the Jacobi iterations can also be defined by

$$f_{j_i}(z_0^\tau,\ldots, z_{i-1}^\tau, z_i, z_{i+1}^\tau,\ldots, z_n^\tau)=0.$$

[1]See Fromm and Klein's (1969) paper which had a great influence in promoting use of the method.

(b) There is in general no need to set $z_i^{\tau+1}=z_i$. It may prove advantageous to set

$$z_i^{\tau+1}=z_i^{\tau}+\Phi_i(z_i-z_i^{\tau}),$$

where $\Phi_i(\cdot)$ is some sign-preserving function.

The method can thus be restated as: solve for z_i ($i=0,1,\ldots,n$) simultaneously the equations

$$f_{j_i}(z_0^{\tau},\ldots,z_{i-1}^{\tau},z_i,z_{i+1}^{\tau},\ldots,z_n^{\tau})=0,$$

and set $z_i^{\tau+1}=z_i^{\tau}+\Phi_i(z_i-z_i^{\tau})$ ($i=0,1,\ldots,n$).

The permutation j_i of $i=0,1,\ldots,n$ and the selection of the $\Phi_i(\cdot)$ does not change the principles of Jacobi's method; it will however affect the convergence properties of the path of the iterations. The method may in fact converge only for appropriate choices of the j_i and the $\Phi_i(\cdot)$ values.

The Jacobi approach is attractive if one can easily solve $f_i(\cdot)$ for z_i. This is so if $f_i(\cdot)=0$ can be written as

$$z_i-g_i(z_0,\ldots,z_{i-1},z_{i+1},\ldots,z_n)=0,$$

where $g_i(\cdot)$ has a simple analytic form. This would lead to the following iterates:

$$z_i=g_i(z_0^{\tau},\ldots,z_{i-1}^{\tau},z_{i+1}^{\tau},\ldots,z_n^{\tau}),$$

$$z_i^{\tau+1}=z_i.$$

If $g_i(\cdot)$ does not have a simple form, one could think of using an alternative, but not completely equivalent version of the method in which z_i is set by:

$$z_i=z_i^{\tau}+\Phi_i[f_i(z_0^{\tau},\ldots,z_{i-1}^{\tau},z_i,z_{i+1}^{\tau},\ldots,z_n^{\tau})],$$

$$z_i^{\tau+1}=z_i,$$

where $\Phi_i(\cdot)$ is a sign-preserving function.[2]

[2] If $f_i(\cdot)=z_i-g_i(\cdot)$ and $\Phi_i=-1$, it is easy to see that this expression reduces to

$$z_i=g_i(z_0^{\tau},\ldots,z_{i-1}^{\tau},z_{i+1}^{\tau},\ldots,z_n^{\tau}),$$

and the two methods are equivalent.

The tâtonnement approach considered in the theoretical literature is the continuous version of these iterates.

The simplicity of the approaches is indeed attractive for computational and theoretical reasons. In solving equations, there is no matrix inversion and no evaluation of derivatives. In theoretical work, tâtonnement has been used to describe how markets adjust, with minimal computation and exchange of information.

Economic tâtonnement resembles Jacobi algorithms, except that the class of processes described is narrower. First, it is not permissible to reverse the signs of a subset of the functions $f_i(\cdot)$ since the $f_i(\cdot)$ values have natural signs.[3] Secondly, the possibility of permuting the indices so that z_i adjusts to $f_{j_i}(z)$ is ruled out since each component z_i can be reasonably assumed to adjust to a unique component $f_i(\cdot)$ of f.[4]

Jacobi iterates can therefore be made to converge for problems where no economic tâtonnement would converge. Examples will be given in section 7.8.

This does not imply that tâtonnement theory is irrelevant for computation. There are only few cases which theory has completely clarified; but the theory sheds a good deal of light on other situations which resemble these cases.

7.2. Calculating the Jacobian of the system

The key to convergence of tâtonnement or Jacobi calculations is the Jacobian of the functions of which a zero is sought. Every model-builder has an idea of this from study of equations or of trial calculations. If need be, it can be calculated. It is standard practice for model-builders to calculate "model multipliers", i.e. the change of the value of the endogenous variables when one exogenous variable is changed. If the equations are excess demand functions, and the "exogenous" variables are prices, the multipliers which correspond to changing one price are a secant approximation of the corresponding column of the Jacobian.[5] Such calculations can easily be made using a slightly modified version of a Jacobi solution package.

[3] For example, in price tâtonnement $f_i(z)$ is excess demand for good i at prices z.

[4] For example, it would be unreasonable to adjust the price of i to excess demand for good $j_i \neq i$.

[5] They are multipliers of the equilibrium model, run as an excess demand system.

We will give examples of how knowledge of the structure of the Jacobian suggests easy ways of solving "hard" problems (section 7.8.). In practice, it will often turn out that evaluation of the Jacobian or of some of its columns reveals that lack of convergence was not due to the intrinsic weaknesses of tâtonnement procedures, but to a coding or specification error: switching to a more powerful but more costly solution algorithm would then hardly have been the correct response to the difficulty.[6]

7.3. General formulation of tâtonnement and Jacobi processes

Consider the system

$$f(z) \leqslant 0,$$

where $f : R^{n+1} \to R^{n+1}$. Define $Z = \{z \mid z \geqslant 0, z \neq 0\}$, and $\mathring{Z} = \{z \mid z > 0\}$. Denote finally by $\bar{Z}$ the solution set $\{\bar{z} \mid \bar{z} \in Z, f(\bar{z}) \leqslant 0\}$.

The assumptions made in section 7.3 will be assumed to hold in all the theorems of this chapter, and will be stated explicitly only when this is useful to understanding of the proof.

Assumption 7.3.1. Well-behaved function. The function $f(z)$ is single valued, continuous, and differentiable on $\mathring{Z}$.

Assumption 7.3.2. Walras' law. The function $f(z)$ is orthogonal to its arguments: $z \cdot f(z) = 0$.

Remark. The property obviously implies

$$\sum_{i=0}^{n} z_i \frac{\partial f_i(z)}{\partial z_j} = -f_j(z), \qquad j = 0, 1, \ldots, n.$$

Assumption 7.3.3. Homogeneity. $f(z)$ is homogeneous of degree zero in z, i.e. $f(\lambda z) = f(z)$, for all $\lambda > 0$.

Remark. The property obviously implies, by Euler's rule, that

$$\sum_{j=0}^{n} z_j \frac{\partial f_i}{\partial z_j} = 0, \qquad i = 0, 1, \ldots, n.$$

[6]Scarf-type and Newton-type algorithms, of course, also generate Jacobians, directly or indirectly; and they generate a whole array of these. Examination of a single Jacobian is however usually sufficient to suggest what is wrong.

Assumption 7.3.4. Interior solution. $\bar{Z} \subset \mathring{Z}$.

Remark. Assumptions 7.3.2 and 7.3.4 together imply that $f(\bar{z})=0$ for all solution vectors $\bar{z} \in \bar{Z}$.

Before stating the next assumption, we must define adjustment rules. Consider attempting to solve $f(z)=0$ by adjusting z to $f(z)$ according to either of the following rules.

Definition 7.3.1. Tâtonnement adjustment rule (rule T). This is defined by the following set of differential equations:

$$\begin{cases} \dot{z}_0 = 0, & \\ \dot{z}_i = 0, & \text{if } f_i(z) < 0 \text{ and } z_i = 0 \ (i = 1, 2, \ldots, n), \\ \dot{z}_i = \kappa_i f_i(z), & \text{otherwise, where } \kappa_i > 0 \ (i = 1, 2, \ldots, n). \end{cases}$$

Economic theory has focused on the properties of rule T, which may be taken as an idealization of market behavior. But in computation, there is no reason to set $\kappa_i > 0$, or to consider as possible one assignment of $\dot{z}_i$ to $f_i(z)$.

Rule T will sove many problems, but there may be occasions when it is useful to resort to the more flexible rule

Definition 7.3.1′. Jacobi adjustment rule (rule J). Let j_i be any permutation of the indices $i = 0, 1, \ldots, n$. A Jacobi adjustment rule is defined by the following set of differential equations:

$$\begin{cases} \dot{z}_0 = 0, & \\ \dot{z}_i = 0, & \text{if } f_{j_i}(z) < 0 \text{ and } z_i = 0 (i = 1, 2, \ldots, n), \\ \dot{z}_i = \kappa_i f_{j_i}(z), & \text{otherwise, where } \kappa_i \neq 0 (i = 1, 2, \ldots, n). \end{cases}$$

We will assume throughout the analysis of stability that

Assumption 7.3.5. Tâtonnement adjustment rule. The z obey the differential equations T.

Remark 1. The rule describes the limiting case of a continuous time adjustment process; in practice z would be adjusted to $f(z)$ by discrete jumps.

Remark 2. The κ_i determine the speeds of adjustment of each of the z_i and are assumed to be constants for the sake of simplicity. We will, on occasion, assume them to be functions $\kappa_i(z)>0$.

Remark 3. The rule defined is the normalized adjustment rule of economic theory, in which one argument of the functions, the "numeraire", is kept constant throughout the process. The choice of numeraire may in some cases determine whether the tâtonnement process satisfies known convergence criteria.

Definition 7.3.2. Well behaved path. Denote by $z[t \mid z(0)]$ the path of rule T corresponding to initial condition $z(0)$. The path is well behaved if

(a) $z[t \mid z(0)]$ is continuous in $z(0)$ and uniquely determined by $z(0)$;
(b) $z[t \mid z(0)]$ is bounded for all t and $z(0) \in \mathring{Z}$; and
(c) $z[t \mid z(0)] \in \mathring{Z}$ for all t and $z(0) \in \mathring{Z}$.

Assumption 7.3.6. Well behaved path. The path $z[t \mid z(0)]$ is well behaved.

Remark 1. Assumptions 7.3.1, 7.3.4, and 7.3.6 can, in many instances, be proved from more basic assumptions about the behavior of agents. We will not discuss how this can be done, but simply accept that the assumptions are satisfied.[7]

Remark 2. Assumptions 7.3.3, 7.3.4, and 7.3.6 imply that any one of the z_i can be selected as numeraire and set equal to 1 for all t.

7.4. Uniqueness and stability: Basic concepts

7.4.1. Global and local uniqueness of solutions

Uniqueness of solutions is an important property from the modelling point of view. One of the main uses of models is comparative statics or comparative dynamics reflecting different values of parameters or exogenous variables. Such an exercise would make no sense if the solution procedure jumped from one equilibrium to another in alternative variants, or in successive years of a dynamic path.

[7] These properties are however important for computation, and the model-builder will have to worry about f being a function and not a correspondence, about boundedness of solution paths, and non-negativity of solutions.

Definition 7.4.1. Global uniqueness. The system $f(z)=0$ has a globally unique solution if the set $\bar{Z}$ contains a unique element $\bar{z}$.

To prove global uniqueness we will need

Definition 7.4.2. Gale property. Let A be a square matrix and T a diagonal matrix of the same order as A, with diagonal elements ± 1. If v is a column vector, A will be said to have the Gale property if for all $T, TATv \geqslant 0$, $v \geqslant 0$ has only the solution $v=0$.

Remark. It can be proved that the Gale property is necessary and sufficient for the matrix A to be Hicksian, i.e. for all principal minors of $-A$ to be positive.

Definition 7.4.3. Jacobian of the system. We will denote by

$$J=\left[\frac{\partial f_i(z)}{\partial z_j}\right]=\left[J_{ij}\right] \qquad (i, j=1,\ldots,n)$$

the matrix of partial derivatives of the last n components $f_1(z),\ldots, f_n(z)$ of $f(z)$ with respect to the last n arguments $z_1,\ldots, z_n$. Occasionally, J will be defined for $i, j=0,1,\ldots, n$.

Assumption 7.4.1. Gale property. The Jacobian J has the Gale property for all $\bar{z}\in\bar{Z}$.

Theorem 7.4.1. If J has the Gale property at all $\bar{z}\in\bar{Z}$, the solution of $f(z)=0$ is globally unique.

Proof. See Arrow–Hahn (1971, pp. 211–215). Q.E.D.

Local uniqueness is a more straightforward concept. We have the theorem

Theorem 7.4.2. If $\| J \| \neq 0$ for $\bar{z}\in\bar{Z}$, there exists a neighborhood of $\bar{z}$ in which $\bar{z}$ is the unique solution.

Proof. Obvious. Q.E.D.

This motivates the assumption

Assumption 7.4.2. Nonsingularity of J at equilibrium. $\| J \| \neq 0$ for all $\bar{z} \in \bar{Z}$.

7.4.2. Global and local stability of adjustment rules and solutions

We need the following definition

Definition 7.4.4. Global stability. If for every $z(0) > 0$, $\lim_{t\to\infty} z[t \mid z(0)] = \bar{z}$, the adjustment rule is globally stable. If $\bar{z}$ is the unique solution, the solution is globally stable.

Definition 7.4.5. Local stability. Let $\bar{z}$ be a solution to the system $f(z) = 0$. If there exists a region θ in which $\bar{z}$ is the unique solution, such that for $z(0) \in \theta$, $\lim_{t\to\infty} z[t \mid z(0)] = \bar{z}$, the solution and the adjustment rule are said to be locally stable.

From these definitions it should be clear that a solution is globally stable only if it is unique. Also, global stability of a solution is a sufficient but not necessary condition for its local stability.

To prove global stability, we will use Lyapunov's theorem which can be stated as follows:

Theorem 7.4.3 [Lyapunov]. Let $V[z(t)]$ be a continuous function which is decreasing on $z[t \mid z(0)]$, for all $z(0) \in Z$, and is constant if and only if $z(t) \in \bar{Z}$. If such a function can be found for an adjustment rule, this rule is globally stable.

Remark. There exists a converse theorem which states that if a differential system is globally stable, then under appropriate assumptions a Lyapunov function exists (see La Salle and Lefschetz, 1961). This is, however, of little practical use since the function may not be easy to find.

Local stability of a differential equation depends on the properties of the linear homogeneous differential equation which approximates its behavior in the neighborhood of a solution. For rule T, this differential equation is

$$\dot{z}_i = \kappa_i \sum_{j=1}^{n} J_{ij}(\bar{z})(z_j - \bar{z}_j), \qquad i = 1, 2, \ldots, n.$$

Let us define

Definition 7.4.6. Stable matrix. A real matrix A is said to be stable if all its latent roots λ_i have negative real parts.

The following theorems are sometimes useful in showing how stable matrices can be characterized in alternative ways.[8]

Theorem 7.4.4 [Routh–Hurwitz]. Let $s_i=(-1)^i$ times the sum of all ith order principal minors of a real $n\times n$ matrix A. A is stable if and only if the following conditions are satisfied:

(1) $s_i>0$ for every $i=1,2,\ldots,n$, and

(2) the following determinantal conditions hold

$$\begin{Vmatrix} s_1 & s_3 \\ 1 & s_2 \end{Vmatrix}>0; \quad \begin{Vmatrix} s_1 & s_3 & s_5 \\ 1 & s_2 & s_4 \\ 0 & s_1 & s_3 \end{Vmatrix}>0\ldots; \quad \begin{Vmatrix} s_1 & s_3 & \cdots & 0 \\ 1 & s_2 & \cdots & 0 \\ \cdots & & & \\ 0 & 0 & \cdots & s_n \end{Vmatrix}>0,$$

where $s_i=0$ for $i>n$.

Theorem 7.4.5 [Lyapunov]. A real $n\times n$ matrix A is stable if and only if there exists a symmetric positive definite matrix B such that $BA+A'B$ is negative definite.

The following well-known theorem holds for a linear equation:

Theorem 7.4.6. Stability of a linear differential equation. The differential equation $\dot{z}=Az$ is stable if and only if A is a stable matrix.

For a nonlinear system, we have

Theorem 7.4.7. Local stability of a nonlinear differential equation. Let $\dot{z}=Az$ be the linear approximation of a nonlinear differential equation in a small neighborhood of the solution. The differential equation is locally stable if A is a stable matrix. The condition is also necessary apart from

[8] See Quirk and Saposnik (1968, pp. 164–166).

borderline cases in which there are latent roots with zero real parts and stability is assured by the second order properties of the system.

Remark. It is well known that, except in particular cases, it is possible to make a stable matrix unstable or vice versa by premultiplying it by a positive diagonal matrix $\hat{\kappa}$. This suggests that an appropriate choice of the κ_i may be an effective way of bringing about convergence of a tâtonnement computational process.[9] This device is in fact much used in solving macroeconomic Keynesian models.

7.5. Global uniqueness and stability basic theorems

In this section we survey the basic theorems on global uniqueness and stability of tâtonnement processes. As will be seen, these involve assumptions which may be difficult to verify for an actual model, except for small ones which make no pretence at realism. Exact verification may not be essential however. It has been our experience that understanding of the principles of tâtonnement theory was quite helpful in suggesting how GEM should be solved, even though precise verification of specific assumptions was not possible. It appears useful, therefore, to stress underlying ideas and intuitions as much as formal proofs of uniqueness and convergence.

The discussion is organized around the four distinct devices used to prove stability. The uniqueness proofs, on the other hand, are usually based on showing that the Gale property holds.

7.5.1. Finding a zero of a continuous function $f: R^1 \to R^1$: The two-variables case

The simplest proof applies to the two-variables case, one of which is the numeraire. The tâtonnement process involves adjusting z_1 to $f_1(z_1)$. It is obvious that if, as in fig. 7.1, points are known such that $z_1^1 < z_1^2$, $f(z_1^1) > 0$, $f(z_1^2) < 0$, the adjustment process $\dot{z}_1 = f(z_1)$ will converge to a solution whether it is initiated at z_1^1 or at z_1^2 (there may, of course, be several solutions between z_1^1 and z_1^2 and the process will find only one of them).

This leads immediately to Assumptions 7.5.1 and 7.5.2.

[9]See Adelman and Robinson (1978) for an example of effective use of this device for a general equilibrium model.

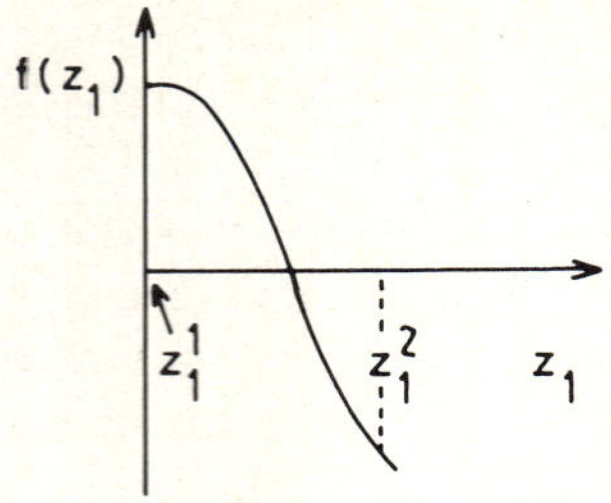

Figure 7.1.

Assumption 7.5.1. Sequence of signs of $f_1(z_1)$. For $z_1^1=0$ and any sufficiently large z_1^2, such that $f(z_1^1)>0$, $f(z_1^2)<0$.

Assumption 7.5.2. Sign of the derivative of $f_1(z_1)$ on the open segment (z_1^1, z_1^2):

$$\frac{\mathrm{d}f_1(z_1)}{\mathrm{d}z_1} \leqslant 0, \quad \text{on } z_1 \in (z_1^1, z_1^2).$$

The following theorem is trivial.

Theorem 7.5.1. Uniqueness and stability when $n=2$. If assumptions 7.5.1 and 7.5.2 hold, there is a unique solution $\bar{z}$ in (z_1^1, z_1^2). If 7.5.1 holds, the tâtonnement process is stable.

When there are more than two variables the problem is more complex. The proofs make use of four Lyapunov functions. These are based either on the Euclidean norm

(a) $\Sigma_l(1/\kappa_l)(z_l-\bar{z}_l)^2$;

(b) $\Sigma_l\kappa_l[f_l(z)-f_l(\bar{z})]^2=\Sigma_l f_l^2(z)$;

or on the maximum norm

(c) $\max_l(z_l-\bar{z}_l)$;

(d) $\max_l(1/\kappa_l)|f_l(z)-f_l(\bar{z})|=\max_l|f_l(z)|$.

These four Lyapunov functions are used to prove stability in the following four cases:

(1) supporting hyperplane: function (a), section 7.5.2;
(2) negative quasidefinite Jacobian: function (b), section 7.5.4;
(3) gross substitutes: function (c), section 7.5.3;
(4) diagonal dominance: function (d), section 7.5.3.

7.5.2. *Moving z toward equilibrium: The supporting hyperplane case*

Assumption 7.5.3. Supporting hyperplane. Let $\bar{z}$ be a solution. If $\bar{z}\cdot f(z)>0$ for all $z\neq\bar{z}$, $f(z)$ has the supporting hyperplane property.

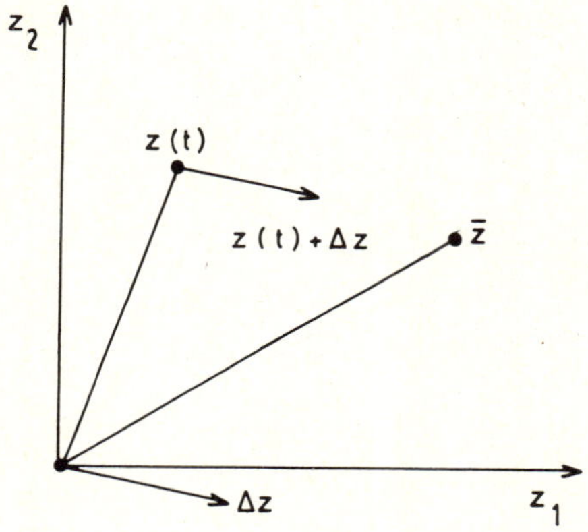

Figure 7.2.

Figure 7.2 is helpful in explaining the underlying idea: $\bar{z}$ is the equilibrium price vector, $z(t)$ is the price vector at time t, and $\Delta z \approx f(z)\Delta t$ indicates the direction of change of prices according to the adjustment process T (it is assumed for the sake of simplicity that the speeds of adjustment κ_i are all equal to unity). Since $\bar{z}\cdot f[z(t)]=\bar{z}\cdot(\Delta z/\Delta t)>0$, Δz and $\bar{z}-z$ define an acute angle.

Then it is easy to check, using $z\cdot f(z)=0$ (Walras's law) that for small Δt

$$\Delta[(z-\bar{z})\cdot(z-\bar{z})]\approx -2\bar{z}\cdot f(z)\Delta t<0.$$

These arguments can be stated more formally as

Theorem 7.5.2. If assumption 7.5.3 holds for $z\in\bar{Z}$, the solution $\bar{z}$ is unique. If it holds for $z\in\mathring{Z}$, the adjustment rule is globally stable.

Proof.

(a) The solution is unique.

Suppose we have two solutions $\bar{z}>0$ and $\tilde{z}>0$ with $\bar{z}\neq\tilde{z}$. Then, $\bar{z}\cdot f(\tilde{z})=0$, contradicting assumption 7.5.3.

(b) The adjustment rule is stable.

Define $V(z)$ by the Euclidian distance between z and the solution $\bar{z}$:

$$V(z)=\tfrac{1}{2}\sum_{l=0}^{n}\frac{1}{\kappa_l}[z_l-\bar{z}_l]^2.$$

Clearly, since z_0 is constant,

$$\dot{V}(z)=\sum_{l=0}^{n}\frac{1}{\kappa_l}\dot{z}_l[z_l-\bar{z}_l]=\sum_{l=1}^{n}\frac{1}{\kappa_l}\dot{z}_l(z_l-\bar{z}_l).$$

Replacing $\dot{z}_l$ with $\kappa_l f_l(z)$ gives

$$\dot{V}(z)=\sum_{l=1}^{n}z_l f_l(z)-\sum_{l=1}^{n}\bar{z}_l f_l(z).$$

Using Walras' law, one has

$$\sum_{l=1}^{n}z_l f_l(z)=-z_0 f_0(z)=-\bar{z}_0 f_0(z).$$

Thus, finally,

$$\dot{V}(z)=-\sum_{l=0}^{n}\bar{z}_l f_l(z),$$

and if $\sum_{l=0}^{n}\bar{z}_l f_l(z)>0$, the distance between z and $\bar{z}$ decreases as long as $z\neq\bar{z}$, and is 0 if and only if $z=\bar{z}$. Q.E.D.

7.5.3. Reduction of $\max_i|f_i(z)|$*: The gross substitutes and diagonal dominance cases*

Again the basic reasoning is easy to grasp. Assume that a matrix A has elements $a_{ij}\geqslant 0$, $\sum_j a_{ij}<1$ for all i. Then it is well known[10] that $\lim_{\tau\to\infty}A^\tau=[0]$; it can likewise be shown that if a_{ij}^τ is a typical element of A^τ, $\max_i|\sum_j a_{ij}^\tau f_j|=\|A^\tau f\|_\infty$ is a decreasing function of τ which tends to zero for $\tau\to\infty$; $\|x\|_\infty$ is the maximum norm of the vector x and f is an arbitrary vector. Non-negativity of a_{ij} can be dispensed with; all that is required then is $\sum_j|a_{ij}|<1$, for all i.

[10]See, for example, Gale (1960).

We have to see how this can be applied to tâtonnement processes.

Definition 7.5.1. Gross substitutes. If $J_{ij}(z)>0$, $i \neq j$, $(i, j=0,1,\ldots,n)$ and $J_{ii}(z)<0$ $(i=0,1,\ldots,n)$ for all $z \in \mathring{Z}$, the functions are said to have the gross substitutes property.

Assumption 7.5.4. Gross substitutes. $f(z)$ has the gross substitutes property.

Remark. The condition can be slightly weakened, at the cost of some extra complication in proving results, to allow for some $J_{ij}(z)=0$, $i \neq j$ (see McKenzie, 1960, p. 48). The resulting gain in generality has no interest for computation, since the margin between the strong and the weak forms of the assumption is not empirically meaningful. We will accordingly discuss only the strong form.

Now consider an adjustment rule which is dependent on z. Let $\kappa(z)$ be equal to z, so that $\dot{z}(t)=\hat{z}(t)f[z(t)]$, where $\hat{z}(t)$ is a diagonal matrix with nonzero components $z_i(t)$. Then if Δt is small

$$
\begin{aligned}
f[z(t+\Delta t)]-f[z(t)] &\approx J[z(t)]\hat{z}(t)\hat{z}(t)^{-1}\dot{z}(t)\Delta t \\
&= J[z(t)]\hat{z}(t)f[z(t)]\,\Delta t,
\end{aligned}
$$

and finally

$$f[z(t+\Delta t)]=\{I+J[z(t)]\hat{z}(t)\Delta t\}f[z(t)].$$

Assumption 7.5.4 implies that if Δt is small $A=\{I+J[z(t)]\hat{z}(t)\Delta t\}$ has non-negative elements; using assumption 7.3.4, and since $J_{i0}(\cdot)z_0>0$ it is easy to check that $\Sigma_j a_{ij}<1$, all i. The matrix A is thus a maximum norm-reducing matrix.

It was pointed out at the beginning of this section that $a_{ij}\geqslant 0$ was not necessary and that $\Sigma_j |a_{ij}|<1$ was enough. The gross substitutes property can therefore be replaced by a weaker property which can be used in two alternative forms.

Definition 7.5.2. Diagonal dominance. If there exist functions $c_j(z)>0$ such that

$$c_i|J_{ii}|>\sum_{j\neq i} c_j|J_{ij}|; \qquad J_{ii}<0, \qquad i=1,2,\ldots,n,$$

the functions $f(z)$ are said to have the diagonal dominance property.

Assumption 7.5.5. Diagonal dominance. $f(z)$ has the diagonal dominance property.

Theorem 7.5.3. If J is diagonal dominant for $\bar{z}\in\bar{Z}$, the solution is unique. If it is diagonal dominant for all $z\in\mathring{Z}$ the tâtonnement process is globally stable.

Proof.[11]

(a) The solution is unique (Arrow and Hahn, 1971).

Let T be a diagonal matrix with diagonal elements ± 1. Suppose there exists some $v \geqslant 0$, $v \neq 0$ and some T such that $TJTv \geqslant 0$. Setting $w_j = v_j/c_j$, we also have $T\tilde{J}Tw \geqslant 0$, where $\tilde{J}_{ij} = c_j J_{ij}$.

Clearly $w_j \geqslant 0$, all j; let $w_k = \max_j w_j$. Then

$$\sum_{j=1}^{n} t_{kk} c_j J_{kj} t_{jj} w_j \geqslant 0.$$

This can also be written as

$$-t_{kk}^2 c_k J_{kk} w_k \leqslant \sum_{j\neq k} t_{kk} c_j J_{kj} t_{jj} w_j \leqslant w_k \sum_{j\neq k} c_j |J_{kj}|,$$

where we have used $w_k = \max_j w_j$ to derive the last inequality.

Since $J_{kk} < 0$, we also have

$$c_k |J_{kk}| \leqslant \sum_{j\neq k} c_j |J_{kj}|$$

contradicting diagonal dominance. Hence, $v=0$ and, appealing to theorem 7.4.1, the solution to the system $f(z)=0$ is unique.

(b) The adjustment rule is globally stable (Arrow, Block and Hurwicz, 1959). Let $V(z) = \max_l (\kappa_l | c_l) | f_l(z)| = (\kappa_L / c_L) | f_L(z)|$. We show that $V(z)$ is always decreasing except for $z = \bar{z}$. Indeed,

$$\dot{V}(z) = \frac{\kappa_L}{c_L} (\text{sign of } f_L) \sum_{j=1}^{n} J_{Lj} \dot{z}_j.$$

[11]The proof of stability is equivalent to showing that $(I + J\hat{c})$ is a norm-reducing matrix in the sense of what preceeds. The $c_j(z)$ are assumed to be constant. Arrow and Hahn (1971) provide a proof for a special $c_j(z)$ function.

In view of the adjustment rule, this is the same as

$$\dot{V}(z)=\frac{\kappa_L}{c_L}(\text{sign of } f_L)\sum_j J_{Lj}\kappa_j f_j(z).$$

At the solution point, $f_j(\bar{z})=0$, all j, and $\dot{V}(z)=0$. Suppose one of the $f_j(z)\neq 0$. Then certainly $|f_L(z)|>0$. Since, by assumption,

$$c_L|J_{LL}|>\sum_{j\neq L} c_j|J_{Lj}|,$$

we must have

$$c_L|J_{LL}||f_L|>\sum_{j\neq L} c_j|J_{Lj}||f_L|,$$

and since

$$\frac{1}{c_L}\kappa_L|f_L|\geqslant\frac{1}{c_j}\kappa_j|f_j|,$$

the inequality can be written

$$c_L|J_{LL}||f_L|>\sum_{j\neq L} c_j|J_{Lj}|\frac{c_L\kappa_j}{\kappa_L c_j}|f_j| = \frac{c_L}{\kappa_L}\sum_{j\neq L}\kappa_j|J_{Lj}||f_j|$$

and

$$\kappa_L|J_{LL}||f_L|>\sum_{j\neq L}\kappa_j|J_{Lj}||f_j|.$$

Since $J_{LL}<0$, the left-hand side of the inequality can be written

$$-\kappa_L(\text{sign of } f_L)J_{LL}f_L$$

and for the right-hand side, we obviously have

$$\sum_{j\neq L}\kappa_j|J_{Lj}||f_j|\geqslant(\text{sign of } f_L)\sum_{j\neq L}\kappa_j J_{Lj}f_j.$$

Collecting the results we get

$$\kappa_L(\text{sign of } f_L)J_{LL}f_L + (\text{sign of } f_L)\sum_{j\neq L}\kappa_j J_{Lj}f_j$$

$$= (\text{sign of } f_L)\sum_j \kappa_j J_{Lj}f_j = \frac{c_L}{\kappa_L}\dot{V}(z) < 0$$

which shows that $\dot{V}(z)$ is decreasing for $z \neq \bar{z}$, and satisfies Lyapunov's theorem. Q.E.D.

7.5.4. *Moving f(z) towards the solution: The negative quasidefinite case*

What condition would assure that the Euclidean distance between $f(z)$ and the origin decreases? The answer is obviously that $f(z)\cdot \mathrm{d}f(z)/\mathrm{d}t = f(z)J\dot{z} = f(z)\cdot Jf(z) < 0$,[12] in other words J should be negative quasidefinite.

This idea is made more precise by the following theorem.

Assumption 7.5.6. Negative quasidefinite Jacobian. J is negative quasidefinite on $z \in \mathring{Z}$.

Theorem 7.5.4. If assumption 7.5.6 holds for $\bar{z} \in \bar{Z}$, the solution $\bar{z}$ is unique. If it holds for all $z \in \mathring{Z}$, the adjustment rule is globally stable.

Proof.

(a) The solution is unique.

Suppose there exists some $v \geqslant 0, v \neq 0$ such that $TJTv \geqslant 0$. But then $[Tv]'J[Tv] \geqslant 0$ contradicting the assumption that J is negative quasidefinite. Hence, theorem 7.4.1 asserts that the solution is unique.

(b) The adjustment rule is globally stable.

Define $V(z)$ by the Euclidian distance between $f(z)$ and the origin:

$$V(z) = \tfrac{1}{2}\sum_{j=1}^{n}\kappa_j f_j^2(z).$$

We show that $V(z)$ is always decreasing, except for $z = \bar{z}$. Indeed,

$$\dot{V}(z) = \sum_j \sum_l \kappa_j f_j(z) J_{jl}\dot{z}.$$

[12] We assume for the sake of simplicity that $\dot{z}_i = f_i(z)$.

Using the adjustment rule, this is also

$$\dot{V}(z)=\sum_j \sum_l \kappa_j f_j(z) J_{jl} \kappa_l f_l(z).$$

Clearly, if the matrix J is negative quasidefinite, $\dot{V}(z)$ is strictly negative and vanishes only at the point $f(\bar{z})=0$. Q.E.D.

7.5.5. The gross substitutes case: Further remarks

The three convergence conditions discussed—supporting hyperplane, diagonal dominance, and negative quasidefinite J—are independent, since one does not imply another. The gross substitutes case is particularly interesting in that it provides a bridge between the three.

Theorem 7.5.5. Homogeneity (assumption 7.3.3) and gross substitutes (assumption 7.5.4) imply diagonal dominance (assumption 7.5.5).

Proof. The proof is immediate, using assumption 7.3.3 in differential form and $J_{i0}>0$ all i. Q.E.D.

A more unexpected result is the following remarkable theorem.

Theorem 7.5.6. Walras' law (assumption 7.3.2) and gross substitutes (assumption 7.5.4) imply the supporting hyperplane property (assumption 7.5.3).

The proof is somewhat long to be given here. It can be found, for example, in Arrow–Hahn (1971, pp. 224–227).

A third result is easily derived. Gross substitutes imply

(a) column diagonal dominance of J close to the solution, by Walras' law in differential form, since for $j=1,2,\ldots,n$:

$$\sum_{i=1}^{n} z_i J_{ij} = -z_0 J_{0j} - f_j(z) \approx -z_0 J_{0j} < 0, \quad \text{in a neighborhood of } \bar{z};$$

(b) row diagonal dominance of J globally, by homogeneity in differential form, since for $i=1,2,\ldots,n$:

$$\sum_{j=1}^{n} z_j J_{ij} = -z_0 J_{i0} < 0.$$

Combining the two results we have $J+J'$ diagonal dominant in a neighborhood of the solution, a result which implies that J is negative quasidefinite in that neighborhood.[13]

This suggests three indirect convergence proofs of stability for the gross substitutes case, appealing to these three properties. The proof based on the properties of $J+J'$ would be local only. In a very ingenious reasoning, McKenzie has, however, exploited the properties of $J+J'$ to derive a global convergence proof. The idea is to note that the column diagonal dominance inequalities are satisfied for the positive components of $f(z)$. Hence, if z and J are partitioned conformably as

$$J=\begin{bmatrix} J^{PP} & J^{PN} \\ J^{NP} & J^{NN} \end{bmatrix}; \qquad z=\begin{bmatrix} z^{P} \\ z^{N} \end{bmatrix},$$

where z^P are the non-negative components of the excess demand vector and z^N the negative components, then J^{PP} is row and column diagonal dominant globally and hence globally negative quasidefinite.

Theorem 7.5.7.[14] If assumptions 7.3.2, 7.3.3, and 7.5.4 hold for $z\in\bar{Z}$, the solution $\bar{z}$ is unique. If these assumptions hold for $z\in\mathring{Z}$, the adjustment rule is globally stable.

Proof.

(a) The solution is unique.

Since gross substitutes imply the supporting hyperplane property, diagonal dominance and negative quasidefiniteness close to the solution, the proof follows from theorems 7.5.2, 7.5.3, or 7.5.4.

(b) The adjustment process is globally stable (McKenzie).

Define $V(z)$ by

$$V(z)=\tfrac{1}{2}\sum_{i\in P}\kappa_i f_i^2(z),$$

where $P=\{i\,|\,f_i(z)\geqslant 0\}$. We show that $V(z)$ is always decreasing except for $z=\bar{z}$. Indeed,

$$\dot{V}(z)=\sum_{i\in P}\sum_{l=0}^{n}\kappa_i f_i(z)J_{il}\dot{z}_l.$$

[13]See, for example, McKenzie (1960, p. 49).

[14]Stability was first proved by Arrow and Hurwicz (1958). The proof given here is due to McKenzie (1960); it applies to the non-normalized process, where the $\dot{z}_i$ adjust to $f_i(z)$ for $i=0,1,\ldots,n$.

Using the adjustment rule, this is also

$$\dot{V}(z)=\sum_{i\in P}\sum_{l=0}^{n}\kappa_i f_i(z)J_{il}\kappa_l f_l(z).$$

Clearly, if $J_{il}>0$ $(i\neq l)$, and since for $i\in P$, $f_i(z)\geqslant 0$ and for $l\notin P$, $f_l(z)<0$, we have

$$\sum_{i\in P}\sum_{l\notin P}\kappa_i f_i(z)J_{il}\kappa_l f_l(z)<0.$$

We must also show that

$$\sum_{i\in P}\sum_{l\in P}\kappa_i f_i(z)J_{il}\kappa_l f_l(z)\leqslant 0.$$

From Walras' law, it follows that

$$\sum_{i=0}^{n} z_i J_{ij}=-f_j(z)$$

and hence, for i, $j\in P$,

$$\sum_{\substack{i\in P\\ i\neq j}} z_i J_{ij}<-z_j J_{jj}$$

or

$$\sum_{\substack{i\in P\\ i\neq j}} z_i|J_{ij}|<z_j|J_{jj}|$$

showing that J^{PP} is dominant diagonal columnwise $(c_i(z)=z_i)$.

From homogeneity it follows that

$$\sum_{\substack{j=0\\ j\neq i}}^{n} z_j J_{ij}=-z_i J_{ii}$$

or

$$\sum_{\substack{j=0\\ j\neq i}}^{n} z_j|J_{ij}|=z_i|J_{ii}|,$$

so that for $i \in P$

$$\sum_{\substack{j \in P \\ j \neq i}} z_j |J_{ij}| < z_i |J_{ii}|.$$

This shows that J^{PP} is dominant diagonal rowwise ($c_j(z) = z_j$).

But then $J^{PP} + J'^{PP}$ is diagonal dominant, so that its roots have negative real parts.[15] Since $J^{PP} + J'^{PP}$ is symmetric, these roots are real. It follows that J^{PP} is negative quasidefinite, so that

$$\sum_{i \in P} \sum_{l \in P} \kappa_i f_i(z) J_{il} \kappa_l f_l(z) < 0$$

unless $f_i(z) = 0$ for all $i \in P$. By assumptions 7.3.2 and 7.3.4, $f_i(z) = 0$ for $i \in P$ implies that $f_i(z) = 0$ for all i. Thus $\dot{V}(z) < 0$ as long as $f_i(z) \neq 0$ for some i, satisfying Lyapunov's theorem and showing that the adjustment rule is globally stable. Q.E.D.

7.5.6. Global stability and speeds of adjustment: Some lessons for computation

Changing speeds of adjustment is one of the standard ways of obtaining convergence of Jacobi computations. It is interesting to examine the global stability proofs for indications on the potential effectiveness of this device.

The proofs are not affected by the choice of a speed of adjustment. Convergence will occur for any adjustment speed vector, although it can probably be accelerated by choosing a vector which generates a fairly direct path to the origin.[16]

It should of course be said that the theorems refer to continuous adjustment processes, whereas computation usually proceeds by discrete jumps. Choosing too large an adjustment speed vector may lead to overshooting equilibrium by the successive iterations; the solution is then, of course, to reduce all adjustment coefficients by the same ratio, bringing the process closer to the continuous type of adjustment envisaged by theory.

Overshooting often produces zigzag paths which are easy to detect from observation of the iterations. In some cases the fact that instability is due

[15] McKenzie (1960, p. 49). Note that J^{PP} and J'^{PP} are dominant diagonal with the same weights z_i.

[16] See the interesting remarks of Adelman and Robinson (1978) which can be interpreted as an application of this idea.

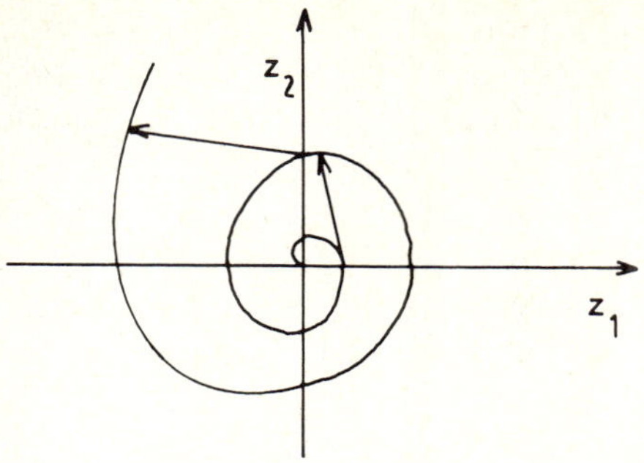

Figure 7.3.

to the adoption of steps which are too large may however be difficult to detect. Fig. 7.3 illustrates the fact that discrete computations may be unstable even when the continuous process is stable: i.e. in badly structured problems calculations will have to proceed by small steps and may prove expensive.

7.6. Local uniqueness and stability

In this section we discuss local uniqueness and stability conditions in terms of their usefulness for the general equilibrium model-builder.

It is usually not possible to check global uniqueness; for a particular solution one can verify whether the Gale property is satisfied; but—at least for a complex model—there is no way of imagining whether the condition is satisfied at other (possibly curious) unknown solutions.

It is, on the other hand, readily possible to verify that the Jacobian is well conditioned in the sense that the condition number $\| A \| \cdot \| A^{-1} \|$ is not much greater than unity (see Ortega and Rheinboldt, 1970, p. 42). If derivatives are continuous and if the determinant $\det J \neq 0$, there will be no other solution in a neighborhood of that identified, and it is unlikely that the solution procedure will jump from one solution to another when solving the model under alternative assumptions. Verification of the property will, of course, in practice be based on the model-builder's understanding of his system and observation of the way in which the solution responds to changes in assumptions.[17]

[17] Ill conditioning of the Jacobian will be revealed by a great sensivity of the solution to small changes in data.

The local stability condition (see definition 7.4.6) which is known is, apart from borderline cases, both necessary and sufficient. For global stability we have only sufficient conditions which are far from necessary: there is a class of cases, which is probably large, for which local stability obtains, but global stability does not. The content of that class is elusive however. No readily interpretable condition is known apparently, which implies that an adjustment process is locally but not globally stable.

7.7. Economic background of the assumptions

7.7.1. Introduction

We survey here results available in the literature.[18] These relate to two interpretations of the adjustment processes discussed: one in which prices adjust to excess demands, the other in which welfare weights are adjusted to consumers' budget surpluses. This involves specializing the $f_i(z)$ as follows.

(I) $f_i(z)=F_i(p)=x_i(p)-y_i(p)-\omega_i$, $i=1,\dots,r$, where $F_i(p)$ represents the excess demand of commodity i at normalized prices $p(p_1=1)$.

(II) $f_i(z)=\alpha_i^{-1}B_i(\alpha)=\alpha_i^{-1}(-p\cdot x_i+\Sigma_{j=1}^n\theta_{ij}p\cdot y_j+p\cdot\omega_i)$, $i=1,2,\dots,m$, where $B_i(\alpha)$ represents the excess budget of consumer i at given positive and normalized welfare weights $\alpha(\alpha_1=1)$.

If $U_i(x_i)$ $(i=1,2,\dots,m)$ is strictly concave and monotonically increasing, and if the production sets Y_j $(j=1,2,\dots,n)$ are strictly convex, closed and bounded from above, these two functions satisfy assumptions 7.3.1 (except differentiability) and 7.3.2 to 7.3.4.

Indeed, for (I)

(a) 7.3.1 holds since for every choice of $p>0$, $F_i(p)$ is unique and depends continuously on p, since $U_i(x)$ is strictly concave and Y_j strictly convex.

(b) 7.3.2 is satisfied by Walras' law, $\Sigma_{l=1}^r p_l F_l(p)=0$.

(c) 7.3.3 is true since every individual demand and supply function is positively homogeneous of degree 0.

(d) 7.3.4 holds if $U_i(x_i)$ is monotonically increasing.

For (II),

(a) 7.3.1 holds; since $U_i(x_i)$ is strictly concave and Y_j strictly convex, the solution of the welfare optimum is unique and continuous in α for every

[18] Some further results are given in Chapter 8.

choice of $\alpha \geqslant 0$; $B_l(\alpha)$ is uniquely defined and depends continuously on α.

(b) 7.3.2 is satisfied since

$$\sum_{l=1}^{m} B_l(\alpha) = -\sum_{l=1}^{r} p_l F_l(p) = 0$$

and the equivalent of Walras' law holds.

(c) 7.3.3 is satisfied since

$$\max \sum_{l=1}^{m} \alpha_l U_l(x_l) \quad \text{and} \quad \max \sum_{l=1}^{m} \lambda \alpha_l U_l(x_l), \qquad \lambda > 0$$

lead to the same (primal) solution of the welfare optimum and dual prices are multiplied by λ so that $B(\alpha) = B(\lambda\alpha)$ obviously.

(d) 7.3.4 is ensured by Negishi's theorem.

The adjustment rules are accordingly adapted as follows:

for (I), $\dot{p}_1 = 0$,
$\dot{p}_i = 0$, if $F_i(p) < 0$ and $p_i = 0$ $(i = 2, 3, \ldots, r)$,
$\dot{p}_i = \kappa_i F_i(p)$, $\kappa_i > 0$, otherwise $(i = 2, 3, \ldots, r)$;

for (II), $\dot{\alpha}_1 = 0$,
$\dot{\alpha}_i = 0$, if $B_i(\alpha) < 0$ and $\alpha_i = 0$ $(i = 2, 3, \ldots, m)$,
$\dot{\alpha}_i = (\kappa_i / \alpha_i) B_i(\alpha)$, $\kappa_i > 0$, otherwise $(i = 2, 3, \ldots, m)$.

Since the assumptions of this chapter are satisfied by both price and welfare weight adjustment, all the theorems presented can be stated for either of the two processes just defined, or for other processes which have the same properties. We will not engage in such an exercise,[19] trusting rather the reader to state for himself the appropriate theorems.

The goal of this section will, instead, be to discuss the economic rationale which may justify the assumptions for the two processes, and the usefulness of these assumptions in suggesting the most effective way of solving models.

7.7.2. The Gale property: Economic interpretation

The Gale property is equivalent to stability in the sense of Hicks. For price equilibrium the property implies that if one price is changed exogenously, any subset of other prices being allowed to adjust while the remaining

[19] How to go about this is illustrated by Dixon's results (Dixon, 1975a, ch. 3), except that Dixon did not specify the welfare weight adjustment process to satisfy the Walras law. Dixon's results were derived independently by Mantel (1971), on whose presentation we rely heavily. Dixon has, however, discussed a "utility adjustment process" not analyzed by Mantel (his process H), which is one of the four processes that we discuss in Chapter 8.

prices are fixed, then demand for the good whose price was increased exogenously will fall. A similar interpretation applies to welfare weights.

7.7.3. The two-goods/two-consumers case

The method of proof is the same in both cases. Arrow and Hurwicz (1958) show that there exists a price of the non-numeraire commodity which is low enough for excess demand for the commodity to be non-negative, and a price high enough for it to be in excess supply. Then, theorem 7.5.1 proves that tâtonnement will converge to equilibrium. Mantel (1971) uses a similar argument for welfare weight tâtonnement.

Mantel's result is probably the more useful of the two, since (see Chapter 3) we have shown that the two-country general equilibrium model of international trade theory should be the basis of models for open economies. The theorem proves that tâtonnement processes will always be capable of solving such models.

7.7.4. Gross substitutes and diagonal dominance

These two assumptions can be treated together since diagonal dominance is a weaker form of the gross substitutes assumption. We will discuss the gross substitutes case mainly, confining ourselves to brief remarks indicating how the diagonal dominance case differs from it.

Both the gross substitutes and the diagonal dominance properties depend on a complex interplay of the preferences and initial holdings of all consumers: they cannot be deduced from the utility and production functions alone.[20] This is because the response of consumer demand to prices depends on the income term of the Slutzky equations, as well as on the supply behavior of producers. Let x_j^h and ω_j^h represent consumption and endowment of good j, consumer h, respectively, and y_j^f production of good j by firm f. Excess demand for good j is

$$f_j(p) = \sum_h x_j^h - \sum_f y_j^f - \sum_h \omega_j^h.$$

It can be shown that the derivative of $f_j(p)$ with respect to the price of

[20] This discussion is close to that of Arrow and Hahn (1971, pp. 225–227 and 296–299).

good i is

$$\frac{\partial f_j(p)}{\partial p_i} = -\sum_h \lambda^h_{ji} + \sum_h \left(x^h_i - \omega^h_i - \sum_f \theta_{hf} y^f_i \right) \phi^h_j - \sum_f \gamma^f_{ji}.$$

In this equation, λ^h_{ji} is the Sutzky substitution term for consumer h, ϕ^h_j his marginal propensity to consume commodity j, and $\gamma^f_{ji} = \partial y^f_j / \partial p_i$.

The sign of the supply response γ^f_{ji} can in principle be inferred from knowledge of the form of the supply functions in the model, although this might not be easy if production sets are described by linear inequalities rather than by explicit functions. The substitution term $\Sigma_h \lambda^h_{ji}$ also depends only on the form of the utility functions from which it can be inferred. So it is the income effect $\Sigma_h (x^h_i - \omega^h_i \Sigma_f \theta_{hf} y^f_i) \phi^h_j$ which causes difficulties since it depends in a complicated way on the interplay of preferences, prices, and initial holdings. It is easy to see that even though $-\Sigma_h \lambda^h_{ji} - \Sigma_f \gamma^f_{ji}$ has the "right" positive sign for $i \neq j$, this may be dominated by a negative income effect so that market demand does not have the gross substitutes property.

At equilibrium prices, $\Sigma_h (\bar{x}^h_i - \omega^h_i - \Sigma_f \theta_{hf} \bar{y}^f_i) = 0$ and the income effect is proportional to the covariance between net trades and propensities to consume. This income effect will be small if net trades are small; if propensities to consume do not differ much; or if net trades and propensities are uncorrelated. There may be good reasons to believe that one of these three conditions holds. The examination of the sign of λ_{ij} and γ_{ij} will make it possible to predict whether a tâtonnement computational process initiated close to equilibrium will then converge.

This is not true at nonequilibrium prices. For then the income effect decomposes into the term discussed above, reflecting the covariance between net trades and propensities to consume, and a term proportional to

$$\sum_h \left(\omega^h_i - x^h_i + \sum_f \theta_{hf} y^f_i \right) \cdot \sum_h \phi^h_j.$$

This can be large far from equilibrium.

What has been said of the possible destabilizing impact of income effects is also true for the budget surplus functions $B_i(\alpha)$ of the welfare weight adjustment process. Mantel (1971, pp. 419–421) has derived an interesting result by showing that if consumers have homothetic utility functions such that excess demand has the gross substitutes property, the $B_i(\alpha)$ functions also have the property. His result is obtained for the pure trade model without production, though it may be possible to generalize it.

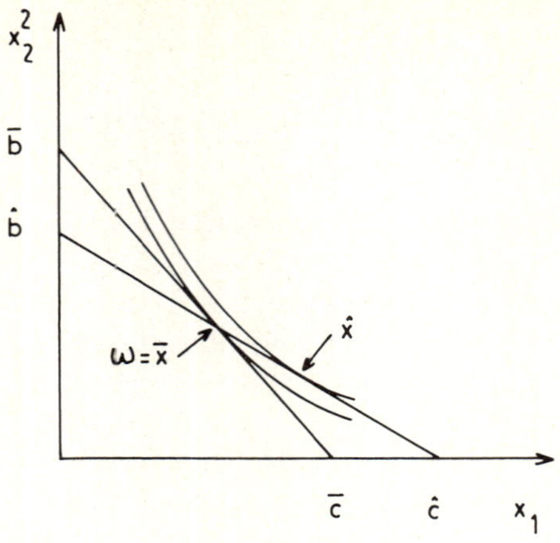

Figure 7.4.

Homothetic utility functions, implying unit income elasticity of demand for all goods, are, of course, not realistic.

7.7.5. *The supporting hyperplane property*

From a theoretical point of view this is the most interesting of the properties because it implies that aggregate demand functions have the same properties as the demand function of a unique consumer. It was pointed out in the last section that total market demand may have properties which differ from those of demand by any of the individuals in the market, because of income effects. Income effects may also jeopardize the hyperplane property. It may be useful to illustrate with diagrams what the property asserts, and how it could be negated by income effects.

It is easy to show that for a one-consumer economy[21] demand functions satisfy the supporting hyperplane assumption. The reasoning is illustrated in fig. 7.4 for the case of two goods, where $\bar{b}\,\bar{c}$ is the budget constraint for the equilibrium price ratio $\bar{p}$, and $\bar{x}=\omega$ (demand equals supply). $\hat{b}\hat{c}$ is the constraint for a nonequilibrium price ratio $\hat{p}$ and $\hat{x}\neq\omega$. $\hat{x}$ is "revealed preferred" to $\bar{x}$, i.e. it is chosen at the disequilibrium price ratio, although $\bar{x}$ does not cost more. The revealed preference principle states that at

[21]We discuss the pure trade case.

equilibrium prices, $\hat{x}$ must have been too expensive to buy: i.e. $\bar{p}\cdot\hat{x}>\bar{p}\cdot\omega=\bar{p}\cdot\bar{x}$. This implies the supporting plane property

$$\bar{p}\cdot(\hat{x}-\omega)>0, \quad \text{since } \bar{p}\cdot(\bar{x}-\omega)=0.$$

An immediate consequence, given theorem 7.5.2, is

Theorem 7.7.1. If there is a single consumer in the economy, the price tâtonnement process is globally stable.

We next illustrate why income effects could negate the property if there are several consumers. Fig. 7.5 describes the behavior of two consumers who have very different marginal propensities to consume two goods; their utility functions imply that there is no substitution effect.

Each consumer owns only one commodity. The first owns two units of the first commodity, the second two units of the second commodity. Their utility functions imply that the prices $\bar{p}=(1,1)$ are equilibrium prices, and that at these prices consumers buy $\bar{x}^1=\bar{x}^2=(1,1)$.

If prices change to a vector $\hat{p}$ where the first good becomes cheaper, the agents demand $\hat{x}^1$ and $\hat{x}^2$. It is easy to check from the figure that $\bar{p}\cdot(\hat{x}^1+\hat{x}^2)<\bar{p}\cdot(\bar{x}^1+\bar{x}^2)$, that is to say the agents spend less out of equilibrium than at equilibrium when their consumption in both situations is valued at equilibrium prices. The supporting hyperplane property does not hold.

The source of the problem is again income effects. Note that the consumer who suffers from the price drop of good 1 happens to have a

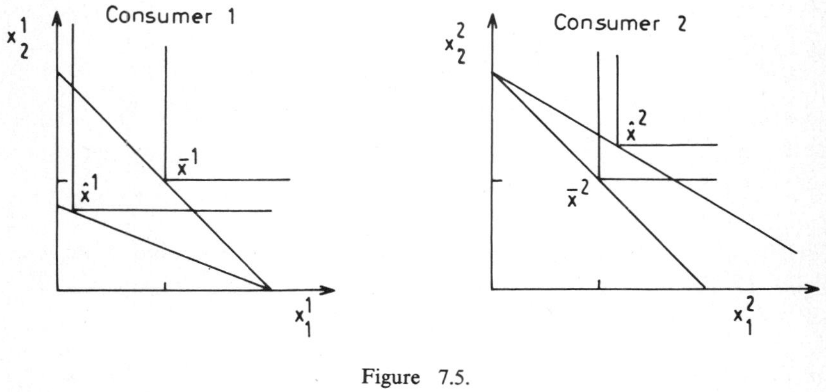

Figure 7.5.

high marginal propensity to consume it. The other consumer could buy more of 1 but has a very low propensity to consume it.

The role of income effects is underlined by the following theorem.

Theorem 7.7.2. If there is no trade at equilibrium, equilibrium is unique and both the price and the welfare tâtonnements are globally stable.

Proof. Strict concavity of the utility functions implies that each consumer satisfies the weak axiom of revealed preference. If in addition there is no trade at equilibrium this axiom is shown to imply the supporting hyperplane property. For detailed proofs, see Arrow–Hurwicz (1958) and Mantel (1971). Q.E.D.

7.7.6. Can the properties of market demand functions be inferred from those of individual demand functions?

The remarks in the last two sections lend great interest to the following question. Is it legitimate to expect that market demand will, *in practice*, have the same properties as demand of individuals?

The theoretical results in this connection are quite disappointing. They show that the market can be expected to behave like an individual only under extremely unlikely assumptions. They also show that the theory of individual consumer behavior imposes very few constraints on the behavior of the market.

Assumption 7.7.1. Identical consumers. All consumers have identical utility functions and initial holdings.

The following theorem is obvious.

Theorem 7.7.3. If assumption 7.7.1 holds, all consumers will behave identically, and market behavior will satisfy all theoretical restrictions satisfied by individual behavior.

Remark. The condition is useful mainly in suggesting a rule for aggregating individuals into groups, each of which is assumed to behave like a single individual.

A more subtle theorem is due to Gorman (1953) and Nataf (1953). We first define

Assumption 7.7.2. Hicksian exchange economy. The economy is said to be Hicksian if all consumers have homothetic utility functions which are identical subject to appropriate monotone transformations.

It can be proved that

Theorem 7.7.4. Behavior of the Hicksian economy. The Hicksian economy behaves as an economy with a single agent.

Theorems 7.7.3 and 7.7.4 together with 7.7.1 imply global stability of the classical adjustment process.

Debreu (1974), Mantel (1974), and Sonnenschein (1973) have proved the other polar result under appropriate technical assumptions:

Theorem 7.7.5. The only restrictions on market demand implied by the theory of individual consumer behavior are Walras' law and positive homogeneity of degree zero of demand with respect to prices.

To top things off, the empirical work of Barten (1969), Jorgenson and Lau (1977), and many others has consistently shown that the theoretical restrictions implied by consumer demand theory are rejected by econometric tests based on aggregate demand data.

Should these results lead to attribute no relevance to the properties of individual demand functions? This is unwarranted. Theory has clarified only two polar cases. It takes extreme assumptions to rule out income effects entirely, whereas if arbitrary income effects are accepted as possible, the Debreu–Mantel–Sonnenschein result holds.

Likewise—if behavior was nonstochastic—Barten and Jorgenson could expect to verify consumer theory from aggregate data for sufficiently large samples only if all agents were identical or had homothetic utility functions which are identical apart from a monotone transformation, and which correspond to the functional form which they tested. To implement their tests they are also forced to make stochastic assumptions which are fairly arbitrary, for the correct way of injecting stochastic elements into consumer demand theory is not evident.

From a practical point of view the useful rule of thumb is probably to look at marginal propensities to consume. If these are not very different across consumers—and econometrics suggests that they do not vary very much[22]—or if they are not related systematically to initial holdings, there is a reason to hope that tâtonnement processes will converge.

[22] See, for example, Houthakker (1957).

7.7.7. Demand function with a negative definite or negative quasidefinite Jacobian

Negative quasidefiniteness of the Jacobian of the demand functions (assumption 7.5.6) can be examined along the same line. This Jacobian can be written as $J=-\Gamma-\Lambda+M$, where Γ is the Jacobian of the supply functions, Λ the Slutzky substitution matrix, and M a matrix with the income effects. The $-\Gamma$ and $-\Lambda$ matrices can be shown to be negative definite, and so is J if the income effects vanish. If income effects are small enough J will still be negative quasidefinite, which is enough to ensure convergence of the adjustment rule.

7.8. Solving "hard problems" with Jacobi processes

7.8.1. Jacobi vs. tâtonnement processes

One of the key ideas of this chapter is that Jacobi processes—of which tâtonnement processes are a subclass and which can be solved as cheaply as the latter—can be relied on to solve equilibrium problems with a high probability of success. Knowledge of the structure of the Jacobian—or the equivalent but vaguer idea of an econometrician's "feel for his model"—will often suggest how a Jacobi solution procedure should be run.

To understand the logic of Jacobi's method, consider solving a system of functions $f_i(z)=0$ $(i=1,\ldots,n)$, each of which depends on a single separate argument.[23] Starting from arbitrary z_i's, Jacobi's method will jump to the solution in a single iteration. It is intuitively clear that Jacobi's method remains very good if the functions have almost this property in the sense that the derivatives $\partial f_i/\partial z_j, j\neq i$, are everywhere small compared to $\partial f_i/\partial z_i$: then Jacobi's method will jump in the first iteration to a point which is close to the solution and converge rapidly. This is obviously the rationale of the dominant diagonal case. In the continuous version of the Jacobi process it is natural to adjust each variable z_i in proportion to the value of one of the functions $f_{j_i}(\cdot)$ so as to reduce, in absolute value, the function most affected by the variable. This leads to

$$\dot{z}_i=\kappa_i\left(-\operatorname{sign}\frac{\partial f_{j_i}}{\partial z_i}\right)f_{j_i}(\cdot),\qquad \kappa_i>0.$$

[23] E.g. $f_1(z_2)=0$, $f_2(z_1)=0$.

The assignment of variable z_i to the function $f_{j_i}(\cdot)$ should, to the extent possible, be such that

$$\left|\frac{\partial f_{j_i}}{\partial z_i}\right| = \max_k \left|\frac{\partial f_{j_i}}{\partial z_k}\right|.$$

(These criteria of course depend on the choice of units.)

7.8.2. Solving Gale's and Scarf's counter-examples

This idea is illustrated by analysis of two well-known counter-examples to the stability of price tâtonnement processes.

The first is due to Gale.[24] Let the utility function of all agents except one be

$$U(x_1, x_2) = 28x_1 + 28x_2 - 2x_1^2 - 3x_1x_2 - 2x_2^2.$$

Each of the agents holds 12 units of the numeraire. In the economy there are stocks of the two goods given by $\omega_1 = 6$, $\omega_2 = 1$. These are held by an agent who is always willing to trade the whole of his stock against numeraire at the going price.

The equilibrium prices are $\bar{p}_1 = 1$, $\bar{p}_2 = 6$. Setting the adjustment speeds equal to 1 gives the Jacobian

$$J(\bar{p}) = \frac{1}{56}\begin{bmatrix} 24 & -60 \\ 10 & -11 \end{bmatrix},$$

both roots of which have positive real parts so that a tâtonnement process is locally unstable.

There would be no difficulty with a Jacobi process; the rule of section 7.8.1 suggests using the market equation for good 1 to explain the second price, and vice versa, and setting κ_1, the adjustment speed for good one, equal to -1, while $\kappa_2 = 1$. This leads to

$$\begin{bmatrix} \dot{p}_1 \\ \dot{p}_2 \end{bmatrix} = \frac{1}{56}\begin{bmatrix} -10 & 11 \\ 24 & -60 \end{bmatrix}\begin{bmatrix} p_1 - \bar{p}_1 \\ p_2 - \bar{p}_2 \end{bmatrix}.$$

[24] As described by Arrow and Hahn (1971, pp. 300–301).

The roots are now both negative and real and the matrix is stable.

Scarf's counter-example[25] is more tricky but is almost as easy to solve provided one knows the general structure of the Jacobian. In the example the utility function is

$$U(x_1, x_2, x_3) = -\left(\frac{\alpha_1^{a+1}}{x_1^a} + \frac{\alpha_2^{a+1}}{x_2^a} + \frac{\alpha_3^{a+1}}{x_3^a}\right)$$

and the initial endowment is $\omega_1, \omega_2, \omega_3$. The equilibrium prices are all equal. The utility function and the initial endowment are permuted cyclically. The situation of the three consumers is given in table 7.1. The excess demand functions are

$$x_1 - \omega_1 = \frac{p_3}{p_1^{\delta}(bp_3^{\gamma} + p_1^{\gamma})} + \frac{bp_1^{\gamma}}{bp_1^{\gamma} + p_2^{\gamma}} - 1,$$

$$x_2 - \omega_2 = \frac{p_1}{p_2^{\delta}(bp_1^{\gamma} + p_2^{\gamma})} + \frac{bp_2^{\gamma}}{bp_2^{\gamma} + p_3^{\gamma}} - 1,$$

$$x_3 - \omega_3 = \frac{p_2}{p_3^{\delta}(bp_2^{\gamma} + p_3^{\gamma})} + \frac{bp_3^{\gamma}}{bp_3^{\gamma} + p_1^{\gamma}} - 1,$$

where $\delta = 1/(1+a)$ and $\gamma = a/(1+a)$. The tâtonnement process is unstable for $b > (a+1):(a-1)$.

Setting $a = 2, b = 5$ the Jacobian at equilibrium is, if p_1 is set equal to unity by normalization,

$$J(\bar{p}) = \frac{1}{(b+1)^2(1+a)}\begin{bmatrix} (ab-a-b-1) & -ab \\ (1+a+b) & (ab-a-b-1) \end{bmatrix}$$

$$= \frac{1}{108}\begin{bmatrix} 2 & -10 \\ 8 & 2 \end{bmatrix},$$

and it is obvious at first glance that it is not dominant diagonal. A tâtonnement computational process will fail to solve it, but a convergent

[25] See Scarf (1960). We discuss only Scarf's general case (see the model on pp. 168–169). But the conclusions are also valid for the simpler model which he presents at the beginning of his paper.

Table 7.1

	α_1	α_2	α_3	ω_1	ω_2	ω_3
Consumer 1	b	1	0	1	0	0
Consumer 2	1	0	b	0	0	1
Consumer 3	0	b	1	0	1	0

Jacobi process is easily defined, which is, in the neighborhood of origin:

$$\begin{bmatrix} \dot{p}_2 \\ \dot{p}_3 \end{bmatrix} = \hat{\kappa}J(p-\bar{p}) = \begin{bmatrix} -1 & 0 \\ 0 & 1 \end{bmatrix} \begin{bmatrix} 8 & 2 \\ 2 & -10 \end{bmatrix} \begin{bmatrix} p_2-\bar{p}_2 \\ p_3-\bar{p}_3 \end{bmatrix}$$

$$= \begin{bmatrix} -8 & -2 \\ 2 & -10 \end{bmatrix} \begin{bmatrix} p_2-\bar{p}_2 \\ p_3-\bar{p}_3 \end{bmatrix}$$

(with $\kappa_1 = -108$, $\kappa_2 = 108$). It can be checked that $\hat{\kappa}J$ is a stable matrix. A more empirical approach to solving the problem has been implemented by Ray Fair who set up the problem for computation in the rough and ready way which is most natural for a macroeconomic model-builder.[26] This also implicitly reverses the assignment of price changes to excess demands, but differs in other respects from the solution given above.

7.8.3. Jacobi processes and the normalization rule used in Gauss–Seidel processes

It is interesting to use the dominant diagonal criterion to analyze a well-known example which is often used to illustrate how the convergence of the Gauss–Seidel computations of a Keynesian macro model may depend on the way in which the equations are formulated. Fig. 7.6 represents the simple Keynesian mutliplier model, where consumption and income (C and Y) are endogenous and investment (I) is exogenous. A Gauss–Seidel process will converge in case 1 and diverge in case 2, as the arrows illustrate.

In the framework of tâtonnement processes, let us write the equations as

$$f_C(Y,C) = aY + b - C = 0,$$
$$f_Y(Y,C) = C + I - Y = 0,$$

[26]See Chapter 11 for additional remarks in Fair's experiment.

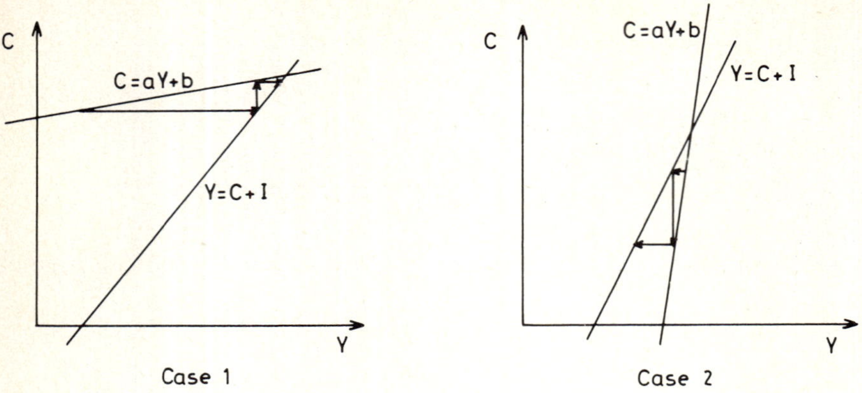

Figure 7.6.

and the process as

$$\begin{bmatrix} \dot{C} \\ \dot{Y} \end{bmatrix} = \begin{bmatrix} \dfrac{\partial f_C}{\partial C} & \dfrac{\partial f_C}{\partial Y} \\ \dfrac{\partial f_Y}{\partial C} & \dfrac{\partial f_Y}{\partial Y} \end{bmatrix} \begin{bmatrix} C-\bar{C} \\ Y-\bar{Y} \end{bmatrix} = \begin{bmatrix} -1 & a \\ 1 & -1 \end{bmatrix} \begin{bmatrix} C-\bar{C} \\ Y-\bar{Y} \end{bmatrix}.$$

It is easy to check that if $|a|<1$, the Jacobian is diagonal dominant; the process will converge (case 1). If $|a|>1$, the Jacobian is not diagonal dominant, and the process will diverge (case 2). But, let us rewrite the equations as

$$f_Y(Y,C) = Y - \frac{C}{a} - \frac{b}{a} = 0,$$

$$f_C(Y,C) = C + I - Y = 0,$$

so that Y is computed from the consumption function and C from the income identity. This simply amounts to changing the assignment of z_i to $f_{j_i}(\cdot)$, in such a way that

$$\left|\frac{\partial f_{j_i}}{\partial z_i}\right| = \max_k \left|\frac{\partial f_{j_i}}{\partial z_k}\right|$$

as suggested above. Now, the tâtonnement process can be rewritten

$$\begin{bmatrix} \dot{C} \\ \dot{Y} \end{bmatrix} = \begin{bmatrix} \dfrac{\partial f_C}{\partial C} & \dfrac{\partial f_C}{\partial Y} \\ \dfrac{\partial f_Y}{\partial C} & \dfrac{\partial f_Y}{\partial Y} \end{bmatrix} \begin{bmatrix} C - \bar{C} \\ Y - \bar{Y} \end{bmatrix} = \begin{bmatrix} 1 & -1 \\ -\dfrac{1}{a} & 1 \end{bmatrix} \begin{bmatrix} C - \bar{C} \\ Y - \bar{Y} \end{bmatrix}$$

with a dominant diagonal and the process will again converge.

CHAPTER 8

Simultaneous stability of four tâtonnement processes

8.1. Introduction

In Chapter 5 we introduced four methods of computing equilibria. These can be formulated as tâtonnement processes, the adjustment being carried out in the parameter revision phase of the algorithms.

Two of these processes—price and welfare tâtonnement—have been discussed fully in Chapter 7. Their properties have been compared in a paper by Mantel (1971). In this chapter we generalize Mantel's paper and a result obtained by Dixon (1975a) in considering two more processes and in giving slightly more general results on simultaneous stability.

To simplify the presentation, the analysis is carried out on the pure trade model, i.e. without production. We have found it useful to restate very briefly some definitions and theorems for this simplified model.

From a practical point of view it is important to note that the four processes are generated from one optimizing model by means of minor changes, so that it is easy to switch to another process when one approach has failed to converge. The model-builder has, so to say, several strings to fit his bow: but is it worthwhile? The answer would be negative if alternative processes were simultaneously stable, so that failure of one implied failure of the others.

It turns out that tâtonnement processes are not simultaneously stable locally, and *a fortiori* globally. It appears worthwhile therefore to make the minor investment in additional programming which permits switching between the four processes instead of being restricted to only one.

8.2. Definition of the tâtonnement processes

Let x_i $(i=1,2,\ldots,m)$ denote the r-dimensional vector of net trades[1] of consumer i and assume his preferences to be represented by the real

[1]In this chapter x refers to net trades and not to consumptions.

valued, monotone and strictly concave twice continuously differentiable utility function $U_i(x_i)$; p is an r-vector of prices. We also assume that the set of net trades which are at least as good as the no-trade position have a lower bound, not attained at the no-trade position. Then, we define a competitive equilibrium as

Definition 8.2.1. A competitive equilibrium (CE) is a bundle of net trades $\bar{x}_1, \bar{x}_2, \ldots, \bar{x}_m$ and a vector of prices $\bar{p}$ such that
(a) $\bar{x}_i$ maximizes $U_i(x_i)$ s.t. $\bar{p}\cdot x_i \leqslant 0$, $x_i \in \mathfrak{R}^r$, $i=1,2,\ldots, m$;
(b) $\Sigma \bar{x}_i \leqslant 0$.

Theorem 8.2.1 [Arrow–Debreu; Negishi]. There exist vectors $\bar{x}_1, \ldots, \bar{x}_m$ and a vector $\bar{p} \geqslant 0$ such that conditions (a) and (b) of the definition are satisfied. There also exist scalars $\bar{\alpha}_1 > 0, \ldots, \bar{\alpha}_m > 0$, such that the vectors $\bar{x}_1, \ldots, \bar{x}_m$ are the solution of the problem $\max \Sigma \bar{\alpha}_i U_i(x_i)$ s.t. $\Sigma x_i \leqslant 0$ and $\bar{p} \geqslant 0$ are the Lagrangian multipliers associated with $\Sigma x_i \leqslant 0$.

Let $G(x) = [U_1(x_1) U_2(x_2) \ldots U_m(x_m)]$ be a vector valued function the elements of which are the utility functions of the m consumers. Consider the following mathematical program:

$$\text{vecmax}\, G(x) \tag{8.1}$$

subject to both or either of the following constraints (8.2)

$$\sum x_i \leqslant 0; \qquad p\cdot x_i \leqslant 0, \quad \text{for } i=1,2,\ldots, m; \tag{8.2}$$

$$x_i \in \mathfrak{R}^r, \qquad \text{for } i=1,2,\ldots, m. \tag{8.3}$$

We show that the four tâtonnement processes, the properties of which will be examined, can formally be derived from the mathematical program (8.1)–(8.3).

Indeed, the classical tâtonnement "search for equilibrium prices" (p-tâtonnement) can be obtained from $\max \Sigma_i U_i(x_i)$ s.t. $p\cdot x_i \leqslant 0$ ($i = 1,2,\ldots, m$). The first-order conditions for a maximum are

$$\frac{\partial U_i(x_i)}{\partial x_i} - \lambda_i p = 0, \qquad i=1,2,\ldots, m, \tag{8.4}$$

$$p\cdot x_i \leqslant 0; \qquad \lambda_i p\cdot x_i = 0; \qquad \lambda_i \geqslant 0, \qquad i=1,2,\ldots, m, \qquad \text{(8.5a)–(8.5c)}$$

where λ_i is a Lagrange multiplier associated to the constraint $p\cdot x_i \leqslant 0$.

Assuming $\lambda_i > 0$ for all i, (8.4) and (8.5a) can be solved, leading to individual excess demand functions $x_i(p)$; aggregation of these functions gives the market excess demand functions $\Sigma_i x_i(p) = f(p)$ and the Walrasian tâtonnement is defined by the system of differential equations $\dot{p} = f(p)$, where $\dot{p} = \mathrm{d}p/\mathrm{d}t$. It is easy to check that a solution $\bar{p}$ of the system of differential equations with $f(\bar{p}) = 0$ satisfies condition (b) of the CE. Condition (a) is satisfied by the individual utility maximization problems.

A second process for "removal of price distortions" (π-tâtonnement) is obtained by consideration of the program $\max \Sigma_i U_i(x_i)$ s.t. $\Sigma x_i \leqslant 0$ *and* $\pi \cdot x_i \leqslant 0$ $(i = 1, 2, \ldots, m)$, where π is a vector of accounting prices used in evaluating the budget constraints.

The first-order conditions for a maximum are

$$\frac{\partial U_i(x_i)}{\partial x_i} - p - \lambda_i \pi = 0, \qquad i = 1, 2, \ldots, m \tag{8.6}$$

$$\sum x_i \leqslant 0; \qquad p \cdot \sum x_i = 0; \qquad p \geqslant 0, \tag{8.7a)–(8.7c}$$

$$\pi \cdot x_i \leqslant 0; \qquad \lambda_i \pi \cdot x_i = 0; \qquad \lambda_i \geqslant 0, \qquad i = 1, 2, \ldots, m. \tag{8.8a)–(8.8c}$$

Assuming $p > 0$, $\lambda_i > 0$ $(i = 1, 2, \ldots, m)$ the system (8.6)–(8.7a)–(8.8a) can be solved for the shadow prices $p(\pi)$ and the π-tâtonnement will be defined by the system of differential equations $\dot{\pi} = p(\pi) - \pi$. To show that for a vector $\bar{\pi}$ such that $p(\bar{\pi}) - \bar{\pi} = 0$ we obtain a CE, we need a version of theorem 5.2.1 specialized to the pure trade case:

Theorem 8.2.2 (Ginsburgh–Waelbroeck). The vectors $\bar{p}$, $\bar{\pi}$, and $\bar{x}_i$ $(i = 1, 2, \ldots, m)$ such that

(i) $\bar{x}_1 \ldots \bar{x}_m$ are a solution of $\max \Sigma_i U_i(x_i)$ s.t. $\Sigma x_i \leqslant 0$ and $\bar{\pi} \cdot x_i \leqslant 0$ $(i = 1, 2, \ldots, m)$;

(ii) $\bar{p} = \bar{\pi}$ ($\bar{p}$ is a vector of multipliers associated to the constraints $\Sigma x_i \leqslant 0$)

are a solution of a CE.

A third "search for equilibrium Negishi welfare weights" (α-tâtonnement) can be obtained by considering Negishi's mathematical program $\max \Sigma \alpha_i U_i(x_i)$ s.t. $\Sigma x_i \leqslant 0$. This problem leads to the following first-order conditions:

$$\alpha_i \frac{\partial U_i(x_i)}{\partial x_i} - p = 0, \qquad i = 1, 2, \ldots, m, \tag{8.9}$$

$$\sum x_i \leqslant 0; \qquad p \cdot \sum x_i = 0; \qquad p \geqslant 0. \tag{8.10a)–(8.10c}$$

If we assume that $\alpha_i > 0$, all i, and $p > 0$, we can solve the system (8.9)–(8.10a), find m net trade vectors $x_i(\alpha)$ $(i=1,2,\ldots,m)$ and a vector $p(\alpha)$, and compute the "savings" of consumer i as $s_i(\alpha) = -p(\alpha)\cdot x_i(\alpha)$; the α-tâtonnement can then very naturally be defined by the differential equations $\dot{\alpha} = s(\alpha)$, where $\dot{\alpha} = \mathrm{d}\alpha/\mathrm{d}t$.

It has been shown by Negishi (1960) that a solution $\bar{\alpha} > 0$, such that $s(\bar{\alpha}) = 0$, satisfies both conditions (a) and (b) of a CE.

The fourth "search for equilibrium utilities" (U-tâtonnement) is obtained from the following mathematical program: $\max U_m(x_m)$ s.t. $U_i(x_i) \geqslant U_i$ $(i=1,2,\ldots,m-1)$ and $\Sigma x_i \leqslant 0$, where U_i are fixed utility levels. Again, the first-order conditions for a maximum are

$$\alpha_i \frac{\partial U_i(x_i)}{\partial x_i} - p = 0, \quad i=1,2,\ldots,m-1, \tag{8.11}$$

$$\frac{\partial U_m(x_m)}{\partial x_m} - p = 0 \tag{8.12}$$

$$-U_i(x_i) + U_i \leqslant 0; \qquad \alpha_i[-U_i(x_i) + U_i] = 0; \qquad \alpha_i \geqslant 0,$$

$$i=1,2,\ldots,m-1, \qquad \text{(8.13a)–(8.13c)}$$

$$\sum x_i \leqslant 0; \qquad p\cdot\sum x_i = 0; \qquad p \geqslant 0. \qquad \text{(8.14a)–(8.14c)}$$

The α_i values $(i=1,2,\ldots,m-1)$ are multipliers associated with the constraints $U_i(x_i) \geqslant U_i$ $(i=1,2,\ldots,m-1)$.

Assuming $p > 0, \alpha_i > 0$ $(i=1,2,\ldots,m-1)$, the system (8.11)–(8.14a) can be solved to give a vector $p(\hat{U})$ and m vectors $x_i(\hat{U})$ $(i=1,2,\ldots,m)$, where $\hat{U}$ is the vector $(U_1, U_2, \ldots, U_{m-1})$; again we can compute the savings of consumer i, $s_i(\hat{U}) = -p(\hat{U})\cdot x_i(\hat{U})$. The U-tâtonnement can now be defined by the system of differential equations $\dot{\hat{U}} = s(\hat{U})$, where $\dot{\hat{U}} = \mathrm{d}\hat{U}/\mathrm{d}t$. Using the same arguments as Negishi (1960), it can be shown that a solution $\bar{\hat{U}}$ such that $s(\bar{\hat{U}}) = 0$ satisfies conditions (a) and (b) of a CE.

We are now faced with four tâtonnement processes:

(1) p-tâtonnement, $\dot{p} = f(p)$;

(2) π-tâtonnement, $\dot{\pi} = p(\pi) - \pi$;

(3) α-tâtonnement, $\dot{\alpha} = s(\alpha)$; and

(4) U-tâtonnement, $\dot{\hat{U}} = s(\hat{U})$.

We show that, locally, they are not necessarily stable or unstable simultaneously.

8.3. Local approximation of the processes

To simplify the analysis we make the following assumptions:

Assumption 8.3.1 (normalization of equilibrium welfare weights). The utility functions are chosen in such a way that, at equilibrium, $\bar{\alpha}_i = 1$ $(i = 1, 2, \ldots, m)$. Since $\bar{\lambda}_i = 1/\bar{\alpha}_i$ at equilibrium, we also have $\bar{\lambda}_i = 1$ $(i = 1, 2, \ldots, m)$.

Assumption 8.3.2 (positiveness of prices at equilibrium). At equilibrium, $\bar{p} > 0$. This will be ensured if the utility functions are strictly monotone.

From these two assumptions it follows that, at equilibrium, $\Sigma \bar{x}_i = 0$, $U_i(\bar{x}_i) = \bar{U}_i$ $(i = 1, 2, \ldots, m-1)$ and $\bar{p} \cdot \bar{x}_i = 0$, all i.

The mathematical derivations which follow are lengthy but not difficult. In each case a local approximation of the tâtonnement process is defined; this approximation is obtained in three steps:

(a) the conditions holding at the optimum of each problem defined in section 8.2 are totally differentiated in the neighborhood of equilibrium;

(b) the resulting linear system is solved for the unknowns;

(c) the tâtonnement is defined in terms of the solution obtained in step (b).

We will need well-known results on the inversion of partitioned negative definite matrices, which we briefly recall in lemmas 8.3.1 and 8.3.2.

Lemma 8.3.1. Let

$$A = \begin{bmatrix} T & R \\ R' & W \end{bmatrix}$$

be a full rank symmetric matrix; if T is a full rank matrix, A^{-1} can be obtained as follows:

$$A^{-1} = \begin{bmatrix} T^{-1} + T^{-1}R(W - R'T^{-1}R)^{-1}R'T^{-1} & -T^{-1}R(W - R'T^{-1}R)^{-1} \\ -(W - R'T^{-1}R)^{-1}R'T^{-1} & (W - R'T^{-1}R)^{-1} \end{bmatrix}. \tag{8.15}$$

If T and W are full rank matrices, then we also have

$$A^{-1}=\begin{bmatrix} (T-RW^{-1}R')^{-1} & -(T-RW^{-1}R')^{-1}RW^{-1} \\ -(W-R'T^{-1}R)^{-1}R'T^{-1} & (W-R'T^{-1}R)^{-1} \end{bmatrix}. \tag{8.16}$$

Lemma 8.3.2. Let A be as in lemma 8.3.1 and negative definite. Then $(W-R'T^{-1}R)^{-1}$ and $(T-RW^{-1}R')^{-1}$ are negative definite.

It will also be useful to define the following matrices:

$V_i=\partial^2U_i(x_i)/\partial x_i^2$ is the $r\times r$ matrix of second derivatives of consumer i's utility function, evaluated at equilibrium;

$$Q=\begin{bmatrix} V_1 & 0 \ldots 0 \\ 0 & V_2 \ldots 0 \\ \ldots & \ldots \\ \ldots & \ldots \\ 0 \ldots 0 & \ldots V_m \end{bmatrix}$$ is a block diagonal $rm\times rm$ matrix;

$J'=[I\ldots I\ldots I]$ is an $r\times rm$ matrix with I the $r\times r$ identity matrix;

$\hat{J}'=$the same matrix as J', with the last row deleted;

$$P=\begin{bmatrix} p\ldots 0\ldots 0 \\ 0\ldots p\ldots 0 \\ \ldots\ldots \\ \ldots\ldots \\ 0\ldots 0\ldots p \end{bmatrix}$$ is an $rm\times m$ matrix; p and 0 are column vectors of r elements; p is the equilibrium price;

$\hat{P}=$the same matrix as P, with the last column deleted.

Note that for the π process we will need a matrix Π, identical to P, but with prices π instead of p. However, since both matrices are evaluated at equilibrium, by theorem 8.2.2, $P\equiv\Pi$. For notational convenience we will express all processes in terms of the P matrix.

$X=[x_1x_2\ldots x_m]$ is an $r\times m$ matrix; x_i is a column vector of r elements (the net trades of consumer i at equilibrium);

$\hat{X}=[x_1 x_2 \ldots x_{m-1}]$;
$\hat{\hat{X}}$ = the same matrix as X, with the last row deleted.

$$F=J'Q^{-1}J=\sum_{i=1}^{m} V_i^{-1}, \tag{8.17}$$

$$\hat{F}=\hat{J}'Q^{-1}\hat{J}, \tag{8.18}$$

$$S=J'Q^{-1}P, \tag{8.19}$$

$$\hat{S}=J'Q^{-1}\hat{P}, \tag{8.20}$$

$$\hat{\hat{S}}=\hat{J}'Q^{-1}P, \tag{8.21}$$

$$D=P'Q^{-1}P, \tag{8.22}$$

$$\hat{D}=\hat{P}'Q^{-1}\hat{P}. \tag{8.23}$$

Two more lemmas will be needed.

Lemma 8.3.3. The matrices $(\hat{F}-\hat{\hat{S}}D^{-1}\hat{\hat{S}}')$ and $(\hat{D}-\hat{S}'F^{-1}\hat{S})$ are negative definite.

Proof. We give the proof for the first matrix. The same type of argument holds through for the second matrix.

(a) We first show that $(\hat{F}-\hat{\hat{S}}D^{-1}\hat{\hat{S}}')$ is negative semidefinite. Using definitions (8.18), (8.21), and (8.22), we have

$$\hat{F}-\hat{\hat{S}}D^{-1}\hat{\hat{S}}'=\hat{J}'\left[Q^{-1}-Q^{-1}P(P'Q^{-1}P)^{-1}P'Q^{-1}\right]\hat{J}=\hat{J}'M\hat{J},$$

with $M=Q^{-1}-Q^{-1}P(P'Q^{-1}P)^{-1}P'Q^{-1}$. It can easily be checked that $M=M'QM$, so that $\hat{J}'M\hat{J}=\hat{J}'M'QM\hat{J}=(M\hat{J})'Q(M\hat{J})$. Q is a block diagonal matrix the blocks of which are negative definite matrices (as matrices of second derivatives of strictly concave utility functions); hence Q is negative definite and $(M\hat{J})'Q(M\hat{J})$ is negative semidefinite. So is $\hat{F}-\hat{\hat{S}}D^{-1}\hat{\hat{S}}'$.

(b) We now show that $\hat{F}-\hat{\hat{S}}D^{-1}\hat{\hat{S}}'$ is nonsingular. Clearly, the matrix $[\hat{J}P]$ has full column rank. Since Q^{-1} is nonsingular, so is

$$\begin{bmatrix} \hat{J}' \\ P' \end{bmatrix} Q^{-1} \begin{bmatrix} \hat{J} & P \end{bmatrix}.$$

But using (8.18), (8.21), and (8.22), we have

$$\begin{bmatrix} \hat{J}' \\ P' \end{bmatrix} Q^{-1} \begin{bmatrix} \hat{J} & P \end{bmatrix} = \begin{bmatrix} \hat{F} & \hat{\hat{S}} \\ \hat{\hat{S}}' & D \end{bmatrix}.$$

Postmultiplying this result by

$$\begin{bmatrix} I \\ -D^{-1} & \hat{\hat{S}}' \end{bmatrix} \text{ gives } \begin{bmatrix} \hat{F}-\hat{\hat{S}}D^{-1}\hat{\hat{S}}' \\ 0 \end{bmatrix}$$

and $\hat{F}-\hat{\hat{S}}D^{-1}\hat{\hat{S}}'$ must be nonsingular.

(c) It is a well-known result that a negative semidefinite matrix is negative definite if it is nonsingular.[2] Hence $\hat{F}-\hat{\hat{S}}D^{-1}\hat{\hat{S}}'$ is negative definite. Q.E.D.

Lemma 8.3.4. Let Q be negative definite and M of full column rank. Then

$$G = \begin{bmatrix} Q & M \\ M' & 0 \end{bmatrix}$$

is nonsingular.

Proof. Consider the system

$$\begin{bmatrix} Q & M \\ M' & 0 \end{bmatrix} \begin{bmatrix} x \\ y \end{bmatrix} = 0.$$

We show that the only solution is

$$\begin{bmatrix} x \\ y \end{bmatrix} = 0.$$

Consider the system $M'x=0$. But $M'x=-M'Q^{-1}My=0$. Since M is of full column rank, $M'Q^{-1}M$ is nonsingular and the only solution is $y=0$. Then, $Qx+My=Qx=0$ has $x=0$ as the only solution. Hence G cannot be singular. Q.E.D.

[2] See, for example, Gantmacher (1960, p. 305).

We are now ready to handle the local approximations.

8.3.1. p-tâtonnement

Total differentiation of (8.4)–(8.5a) with respect to x_i, λ_i, and p gives

$$\left.\begin{aligned} V_i \mathrm{d}x_i - p\,\mathrm{d}\lambda_i - \lambda_i \mathrm{d}p &= 0 \\ x_i' \mathrm{d}p + p' \mathrm{d}x_i &= 0 \end{aligned}\right\} i = 1, 2, \ldots, m.$$

Writing these relations for all consumers, and using assumption 8.3.1 ($\lambda_i = 1$), we have

$$\begin{bmatrix} Q & P \\ P' & 0 \end{bmatrix} \begin{bmatrix} \mathrm{d}x \\ -\mathrm{d}\lambda \end{bmatrix} = \begin{bmatrix} J \\ -X' \end{bmatrix} \mathrm{d}p,$$

where $\mathrm{d}x' = (\mathrm{d}x_1 \ldots \mathrm{d}x_m)$, $\mathrm{d}\lambda' = (\mathrm{d}\lambda_1 \ldots \mathrm{d}\lambda_m)$ and $\mathrm{d}p' = (\mathrm{d}p_1 \ldots \mathrm{d}p_r)$. As is well known, this system defines demand as a zero homogeneous function of prices. As a result, the p-tâtonnement defined in this way converges possibly to a price ray and not to a unique price vector. Usually the difficulty is solved by normalizing the prices. Setting $p_r = 1, \mathrm{d}p_r = 0$, the equations can be written:

$$\begin{bmatrix} Q & P \\ P' & 0 \end{bmatrix} \begin{bmatrix} \mathrm{d}x \\ -\mathrm{d}\lambda \end{bmatrix} = \begin{bmatrix} \hat{J} \\ -X' \end{bmatrix} \mathrm{d}\hat{p},$$

where $\mathrm{d}\hat{p} = (\mathrm{d}p_1 \ldots \mathrm{d}p_{r-1})$.

The matrix on the left-hand side of this last expression has full rank, by lemma 8.3.4. Using (8.15) to invert this matrix, we end up with

$$\mathrm{d}x = \left[Q^{-1}\hat{J} - Q^{-1}P(P'Q^{-1}P)^{-1}P'Q^{-1}\hat{J} - Q^{-1}P(P'Q^{-1}P)^{-1}\hat{X}' \right] \mathrm{d}\hat{p}.$$

Total excess demand $f(p)$ is equal to $J'x$ so that $\dot{p} = \mathrm{d}f = J'\mathrm{d}x$; but we need only $\hat{\dot{p}} = \hat{J}'\mathrm{d}x$. Hence, using (8.18), (8.21), and (8.22), we find

$$\hat{\dot{p}} = \hat{J}'\mathrm{d}x = \left[\hat{F} - \hat{S}D^{-1}(\hat{S}' + \hat{X}') \right] (\hat{p} - \hat{\bar{p}}), \tag{8.24}$$

where $\mathrm{d}\hat{p} = \hat{p} - \hat{\bar{p}}$ is the deviation from the equilibrium value $\hat{\bar{p}}$.

8.3.2. π-tâtonnement

From theorem 8.2.2 it is clear that, at the solution point for which $p=\pi$, one of the constraints $\pi\cdot x_i=0$ or one of the r balances $\Sigma x_i=0$ will be redundant, and can be omitted. If the rth of these balances is omitted, we have as first-order conditions for a maximum

$$\frac{\partial U_i}{\partial x_i}-p-\lambda_i\pi=0, \qquad i=1,2,\ldots,m,$$

$$\sum \hat{\hat{x}}_i=0,$$

$$\pi\cdot x_i=0, \qquad i=1,2,\ldots,m,$$

where $\hat{\hat{x}}_i$ is the vector of net trades of the $r-1$ first commodities for trader i.

Totally differentiating these expressions with respect to x_i, λ_i, and p gives

$$V_i\mathrm{d}x_i-\mathrm{d}p-\lambda_i\mathrm{d}\pi-\pi\mathrm{d}\lambda_i=0, \qquad i=1,2,\ldots,m,$$

$$\sum \mathrm{d}\hat{\hat{x}}_i=0,$$

$$x_i'\mathrm{d}\pi+\pi'\mathrm{d}x_i=0, \qquad i=1,2,\ldots,m.$$

Taking into account that the rth element of both vectors $\mathrm{d}p$ and $\mathrm{d}\pi$ is identically zero (the normalization implies p_r and π_r constant), we can write these equations under matrix form as:

$$\begin{bmatrix} Q & \hat{J} & \Pi \\ \hat{J}' & 0 & 0 \\ \Pi' & 0 & 0 \end{bmatrix}\begin{bmatrix} \mathrm{d}x \\ -\mathrm{d}\hat{p} \\ -\mathrm{d}\lambda \end{bmatrix}=\begin{bmatrix} \hat{J} \\ 0 \\ -\hat{\hat{X}}' \end{bmatrix}\mathrm{d}\hat{\pi}, \tag{8.25}$$

with $\mathrm{d}\hat{p}'=(\mathrm{d}p_1\ldots\mathrm{d}p_{r-1})$ and $\mathrm{d}\hat{\pi}'=(\mathrm{d}\pi_1\ldots\mathrm{d}\pi_{r-1})$. The matrix on the left-hand side of (8.25) is nonsingular (lemma 8.3.4).

Let $N=[\hat{J} \quad \Pi]$ and invert first the matrix $\begin{bmatrix} Q & N \\ N' & 0 \end{bmatrix}$ using (8.15):

$$\begin{bmatrix} Q & N \\ N' & 0 \end{bmatrix}^{-1}=\begin{bmatrix} Q^{-1}-Q^{-1}N(N'Q^{-1}N)^{-1}N'Q^{-1} & Q^{-1}N(N'Q^{-1}N)^{-1} \\ (N'Q^{-1}N)^{-1}N'Q^{-1} & -(N'Q^{-1}N)^{-1} \end{bmatrix}. \tag{8.26}$$

Note that

$$(N'Q^{-1}N)=\begin{bmatrix}\hat{J}'\\ \Pi'\end{bmatrix}Q^{-1}[\hat{J}\quad \Pi]=\begin{bmatrix}\hat{F} & \hat{\hat{S}}\\ \hat{\hat{S}}' & D\end{bmatrix}.$$

We now use (8.16) to invert $(N'Q^{-1}N)$. This gives

$$(N'Q^{-1}N)^{-1}=\begin{bmatrix}(\hat{F}-\hat{\hat{S}}D^{-1}\hat{\hat{S}}')^{-1} & -(\hat{F}-\hat{\hat{S}}D^{-1}\hat{\hat{S}}')^{-1}\hat{\hat{S}}D^{-1}\\ -(D-\hat{\hat{S}}'\hat{F}^{-1}\hat{\hat{S}})^{-1}\hat{\hat{S}}'\hat{F}^{-1} & (D-\hat{\hat{S}}'\hat{F}^{-1}\hat{\hat{S}})^{-1}\end{bmatrix}.$$

Inserting back this result into (8.26), we derive, from (8.25) the following expression for $\mathrm{d}p$:

$$\mathrm{d}\hat{p}=-(\hat{F}-\hat{\hat{S}}D^{-1}\hat{\hat{S}}')^{-1}\left[\hat{F}-\hat{\hat{S}}D^{-1}(\hat{\hat{S}}'+\hat{\hat{X}}')\right]\mathrm{d}\hat{\pi}. \tag{8.27}$$

Since we defined the π-tâtonnement by $\dot{\pi}=p(\pi)-\pi$, locally we have

$$\mathrm{d}p-\mathrm{d}\pi=(p-\bar{p})-(\pi-\bar{\pi})=p-\pi=\dot{\pi}.$$

Hence, we have, after subtracting $\mathrm{d}\hat{\pi}$ from both sides of (8.27),

$$\hat{\dot{\pi}}=-(\hat{F}-\hat{\hat{S}}D^{-1}\hat{\hat{S}}')^{-1}\left[2(\hat{F}-\hat{\hat{S}}D^{-1}\hat{\hat{S}}')-\hat{\hat{S}}D^{-1}\hat{\hat{X}}'\right](\hat{\pi}-\hat{\bar{\pi}}). \tag{8.28}$$

8.3.3. α-tâtonnement

Total differentiation of (8.9)–(8.10a) with respect to x_i, α_i, and p gives

$$\frac{\partial U_i(x_i)}{\partial x_i}\mathrm{d}\alpha_i+\alpha_i V_i\,\mathrm{d}x_i-\mathrm{d}p=0,\qquad i=1,2,\ldots,m,$$

$$\sum_i \mathrm{d}x_i=0.$$

Replacing $\partial U_i(x_i)/\partial x_i$ by p/α_i and taking into account assumption 8.3.1 ($\alpha_i=1$) these equations can also be written for all i as:

$$\begin{bmatrix}Q & J\\ J' & 0\end{bmatrix}\begin{bmatrix}\mathrm{d}x\\ -\mathrm{d}p\end{bmatrix}=-\begin{bmatrix}P\\ 0\end{bmatrix}\mathrm{d}\alpha,$$

where $\mathrm{d}x$ and $\mathrm{d}p$ have already been defined, $\mathrm{d}\alpha' = (\mathrm{d}\alpha_1 \ldots \mathrm{d}\alpha_m)$. The same problem of normalization arises as with the p-tâtonnement.

Setting $\alpha_m = 1$ reduces the system to

$$\begin{bmatrix} Q & J \\ J' & 0 \end{bmatrix} \begin{bmatrix} \mathrm{d}x \\ -\mathrm{d}p \end{bmatrix} = -\begin{bmatrix} \hat{P} \\ 0 \end{bmatrix} \mathrm{d}\hat{\alpha},$$

with $\hat{\alpha}' = (\alpha_1 \ldots \alpha_{m-1})$.

By lemma 8.3.4, $\begin{bmatrix} Q & J \\ J' & 0 \end{bmatrix}$ is nonsingular. Using (8.15), the solution of the system can be written

$$\mathrm{d}x = \left[-Q^{-1} - Q^{-1}J(J'Q^{-1}J)^{-1}J'Q^{-1} \right] \hat{P}\,\mathrm{d}\hat{\alpha}, \tag{8.29}$$

$$\mathrm{d}p = (J'Q^{-1}J)^{-1}J'Q^{-1}\hat{P}\,\mathrm{d}\hat{\alpha}. \tag{8.30}$$

Savings of consumer i are equal to $-p \cdot x_i$. Differentiating this result leads to $\mathrm{d}s_i = -x_i'\mathrm{d}p - p'\mathrm{d}x_i$ or, in matrix notation, for all consumers except consumer m:

$$\mathrm{d}\hat{s} = -\hat{X}'\mathrm{d}p - \hat{P}'\mathrm{d}x.$$

Then, using (8.17), (8.20), (8.23), (8.29), and (8.30), we have

$$\mathrm{d}\hat{s} = \left[\hat{D} - (\hat{S}' + \hat{X}')F^{-1}\hat{S} \right] \mathrm{d}\hat{\alpha}$$

or, since $\dot{\hat{\alpha}} = \mathrm{d}\hat{s}$,

$$\dot{\hat{\alpha}} = \left[\hat{D} - (\hat{S}' + \hat{X}')F^{-1}\hat{S} \right] (\hat{\alpha} - \bar{\hat{\alpha}}), \tag{8.31}$$

where $\hat{\alpha} - \bar{\hat{\alpha}}$ is the deviation from the equilibrium value $\bar{\hat{\alpha}}$.

8.3.4. U-tâtonnement

Total differentiation of (8.11), (8.12), (8.13a), and (8.14a) with respect to x_i, α_i, p, and U_i gives

$$V_m \mathrm{d}x_m - \mathrm{d}p = 0,$$

$$\frac{\partial U_i(x_i)}{\partial x_i}\mathrm{d}\alpha_i + \alpha_i V_i \mathrm{d}x_i - \mathrm{d}p = 0, \qquad i = 1,2,\ldots,m-1,$$

$$\frac{\partial U_i(x_i)}{\partial x_i}\mathrm{d}x_i - \mathrm{d}U_i = 0, \qquad i = 1,2,\ldots,m-1,$$

$$\sum_i \mathrm{d}x_i = 0.$$

Since $\partial U_i(x_i)/\partial x_i = p/\alpha_i$ and $\alpha_i = 1$ at equilibrium, we can write these relations in matrix form as:

$$\begin{bmatrix} Q & J & \hat{P} \\ J' & 0 & 0 \\ \hat{P}' & 0 & 0 \end{bmatrix}\begin{bmatrix} \mathrm{d}x \\ -\mathrm{d}p \\ \mathrm{d}\hat{\alpha} \end{bmatrix} = \begin{bmatrix} 0 \\ 0 \\ \mathrm{d}\hat{U} \end{bmatrix},$$

with $\mathrm{d}\hat{\alpha} = [\mathrm{d}\alpha_1 \ldots \mathrm{d}\alpha_{m-1}]$ and $\mathrm{d}\hat{U} = [\mathrm{d}U_1 \ldots \mathrm{d}U_{m-1}]$. By lemma 8.3.4 the matrix on the left is nonsingular.

Defining $M = [J \quad \hat{P}]$, we first invert the partitioned matrix $\begin{bmatrix} Q & M \\ M' & 0 \end{bmatrix}$ using (8.15). The result is:

$$\begin{bmatrix} Q & M \\ M' & 0 \end{bmatrix}^{-1} = \begin{bmatrix} Q^{-1} - Q^{-1}M(M'Q^{-1}M)^{-1}M'Q^{-1} & Q^{-1}M(M'Q^{-1}M)^{-1} \\ (M'Q^{-1}M)^{-1}M'Q^{-1} & -(M'Q^{-1}M)^{-1} \end{bmatrix}.$$

We now have to invert $(M'Q^{-1}M)$. But

$$M'Q^{-1}M=\begin{bmatrix} J' \\ \hat{P}' \end{bmatrix} Q^{-1}\begin{bmatrix} J & \hat{P} \end{bmatrix}=\begin{bmatrix} F & \hat{S} \\ \hat{S}' & \hat{D} \end{bmatrix}.$$

Using (8.15) we obtain

$$(M'Q^{-1}M)^{-1}$$

$$=\begin{bmatrix} F^{-1}+F^{-1}\hat{S}(\hat{D}-\hat{S}'F^{-1}\hat{S})^{-1}\hat{S}'F^{-1} & -F^{-1}\hat{S}(\hat{D}-\hat{S}'F^{-1}\hat{S})^{-1} \\ -(\hat{D}-\hat{S}'F^{-1}\hat{S})^{-1}\hat{S}F^{-1} & (\hat{D}-\hat{S}'F^{-1}\hat{S})^{-1} \end{bmatrix}.$$

After some further matrix algebra, we end up with

$$\mathrm{d}x=-Q^{-1}(JF^{-1}\hat{S}-\hat{P})(\hat{D}-\hat{S}'F^{-1}\hat{S})^{-1}\mathrm{d}\hat{U},$$

$$\mathrm{d}p=-F^{-1}\hat{S}(\hat{D}-\hat{S}'F^{-1}\hat{S})^{-1}\mathrm{d}\hat{U}.$$

Finally, noting that, as in the α-tâtonnement, $\hat{s}=-\hat{X}'p$ and $\mathrm{d}\hat{s}=-\hat{X}'\mathrm{d}p-\hat{P}'\mathrm{d}x$, we find

$$\mathrm{d}\hat{s}=\left[\hat{X}'F^{-1}\hat{S}+\hat{P}'Q^{-1}(JF^{-1}\hat{S}-\hat{P})\right](\hat{D}-\hat{S}'F^{-1}\hat{S})^{-1}\mathrm{d}\hat{U}$$

$$=-\left[\hat{D}-(\hat{S}'+\hat{X}')F^{-1}\hat{S}\right](\hat{D}-\hat{S}'F^{-1}\hat{S})^{-1}\mathrm{d}\hat{U}$$

and

$$\dot{\hat{U}}=-\left[\hat{D}-(\hat{S}'+\hat{X}')F^{-1}\hat{S}\right](\hat{D}-\hat{S}'F^{-1}\hat{S})^{-1}(\hat{U}-\hat{\bar{U}}), \tag{8.32}$$

where $\hat{U}-\hat{\bar{U}}$ is the deviation from the equilibrium value $\hat{\bar{U}}$.

8.4. Local stability properties

For easy reference, we group the four approximations so far obtained:

$$\dot{\hat{p}}=\left[\hat{F}-\hat{\hat{S}}D^{-1}\left(\hat{\hat{S}}'+\hat{\hat{X}}'\right)\right]\left(\hat{p}-\hat{\bar{p}}\right), \tag{8.33}$$

$$\dot{\hat{\pi}}=-\left(\hat{F}-\hat{\hat{S}}D^{-1}\hat{\hat{S}}'\right)^{-1}\left[2\left(\hat{F}-\hat{\hat{S}}D^{-1}\hat{\hat{S}}'\right)-\hat{\hat{S}}D^{-1}\hat{\hat{X}}'\right]\left(\hat{\pi}-\hat{\bar{\pi}}\right), \tag{8.34}$$

$$\dot{\hat{\alpha}}=\left[\hat{D}-(\hat{X}'+\hat{S}')F^{-1}\hat{S}\right]\left(\hat{\alpha}-\hat{\bar{\alpha}}\right), \tag{8.35}$$

$$\dot{\hat{U}}=-\left[\hat{D}-(\hat{X}'+\hat{S}')F^{-1}\hat{S}\right]\left(\hat{D}-\hat{S}'F^{-1}\hat{S}\right)^{-1}\left(\hat{U}-\hat{\bar{U}}\right). \tag{8.36}$$

We now turn to the question of local stability. We shall see that, in general, the four processes are not necessarily simultaneously stable. To study the question we first recall a few results on the stability of systems of linear differential equations. These results were discussed in Chapter 7.

Lemma 8.4.1.: The system of differential equations $\dot{x}=Ax$ is stable
(a) if all the characteristic roots of A have negative real parts;
(b) (negative definiteness) if A is (quasi) negative definite;
(c) (diagonal dominance) if $a_{ii}<0$, all i, and there exist numbers $c_i>0$ such that $c_i|a_{ii}|>\Sigma_{j\neq i}c_j|a_{ij}|$, all i.

Lemma 8.4.2.[3] Let G be a quasinegative definite matrix and H be a positive definite symmetric matrix. Then the roots of HG (and GH) have negative real parts.

8.4.1. Simultaneously stable systems

There are two general cases in which the four systems can be shown to be stable at the same time. These cases are discussed in the theorems and corollaries which follow.

Theorem 8.4.1. If the income effects vanish, i.e. if $\hat{\hat{S}}D^{-1}\hat{\hat{X}}'=0$ and $\hat{X}'F^{-1}\hat{S}=0$, the processes are simultaneously locally stable.

[3]For a proof, see Karlin (1959, p. 332).

Proof. If $\hat{\hat{S}}D^{-1}\hat{\hat{X}}'$ and $\hat{X}'F^{-1}\hat{S}=0$, we have

$$\dot{\hat{p}}=(\hat{F}-\hat{\hat{S}}D^{-1}\hat{\hat{S}}')(\hat{p}-\bar{\hat{p}}),$$

$$\dot{\hat{\pi}}=-2(\hat{\pi}-\bar{\hat{\pi}}),$$

$$\dot{\hat{\alpha}}=(\hat{D}-\hat{S}'F^{-1}\hat{S})(\hat{\alpha}-\bar{\hat{\alpha}}),$$

$$\dot{\hat{U}}=-(\hat{U}-\bar{\hat{U}}).$$

In lemma 8.3.3 we proved that $\hat{F}-\hat{\hat{S}}D^{-1}\hat{\hat{S}}'$ and $\hat{D}-\hat{S}'F^{-1}\hat{S}$ are negative definite. Processes p and α are thus stable. It is obvious that the π and U processes are stable since $-I$ is negative definite. Q.E.D.

Corollary 8.4.1. If there is no trade at equilibrium, the processes are simultaneously locally stable.

Proof. The no trade at equilibrium situation implies $X=0$, $\hat{X}=0$, and $\hat{\hat{X}}=0$; hence $\hat{\hat{S}}D^{-1}\hat{\hat{X}}'=0$ and $\hat{X}'F^{-1}\hat{S}=0$ and the assumptions of theorem 8.4.1 are satisfied. Q.E.D.

Corollary 8.4.2. If the matrices V_i $(i=1,2,\ldots,m)$ are all identical, the processes are simultaneously locally stable.

Proof. We show that $\hat{\hat{S}}D^{-1}\hat{\hat{X}}'$ and $\hat{X}'F^{-1}\hat{S}$ vanish, as in theorem 8.4.1. Indeed, if all V_i, $V_i=V$ all i, are equal to V, D^{-1} is a diagonal matrix with diagonal terms equal to $(p'V^{-1}p)^{-1}$, a scalar. Hence, $\hat{\hat{S}}D^{-1}\hat{\hat{X}}'=\tilde{D}^{-1}\hat{\hat{S}}\hat{\hat{X}}'=\tilde{D}^{-1}\tilde{J}'Q^{-1}P\hat{X}'=\tilde{D}^{-1}\tilde{I}[V^{-1}p\ldots V^{-1}p]\hat{X}'=\tilde{D}^{-1}\tilde{I}V^{-1}p\Sigma\hat{\hat{x}}_i'=0$ ($\tilde{D}$ is a diagonal $(r-1)$ matrix with diagonal terms equal to $(p'V^{-1}p)^{-1}$; $\tilde{I}$ is the identity matrix with the last row deleted). Likewise, if $V_i=V$, $F=rV^{-1}$ and

$$\hat{X}'F^{-1}\hat{S}=\frac{1}{r}\hat{X}'V[V^{-1}p\ldots V^{-1}p]=\frac{1}{r}\hat{X}'[p\ldots p]=0.$$

The assumptions of theorem 8.4.1 are thus satisfied and the result follows. Q.E.D.

Instability can thus result only from income effects, a well-known conclusion of classical tâtonnement analysis which carries over to the broader range of processes considered here. The "income effects" are, respectively,

$$p \text{ process:} \quad -\hat{\hat{S}}D^{-1}\hat{\hat{X}}',$$

$$\pi \text{ process:} \quad \left[\hat{F}-\hat{\hat{S}}D^{-1}\hat{\hat{S}}'\right]^{-1}\hat{\hat{S}}D^{-1}\hat{\hat{X}}',$$

$$\alpha \text{ process:} \quad -\hat{X}'F^{-1}\hat{S},$$

$$U \text{ process:} \quad \hat{X}'F^{-1}\hat{S}\left[\hat{D}-\hat{S}'F^{-1}\hat{S}\right]^{-1}.$$

It does not seem possible to find general rules about these matrices which would ensure the simultaneous stability of the processes. The only result which can apparently be stated is the weak theorem

Theorem 8.4.2. If the matrix of the p (or α) process is quasinegative definite, then the p and π (or α and U) processes are simultaneously stable.

Proof. The conclusion follows from lemma 8.4.2. Q.E.D.

Corollary 8.4.3. If the matrix $\hat{\hat{S}}D^{-1}\hat{\hat{X}}'$ is quasipositive semidefinite, then the p and the π processes are simultaneously stable. If the matrix $\hat{X}'F^{-1}\hat{S}$ is quasipositive semidefinite, the α and the U processes are simultaneously stable.

Proof. We know that $\hat{F}-\hat{\hat{S}}D^{-1}\hat{\hat{S}}'$ is negative definite. The assumption of the corollary implies that $[\hat{F}-\hat{\hat{S}}D^{-1}(\hat{\hat{X}}+\hat{\hat{S}}')]$ is negative quasidefinite. Using theorem 8.4.2, we see that the p and π processes are stable. A similar reasoning proves the assertion concerning the α and U processes. Q.E.D.

Some other (rather unlikely) cases can be found in which some of the processes would be simultaneously stable. One of them is given in Mantel (1971, p. 429) for the p- and the α-process. Others can be found by imposing severe restrictions on the matrices of the processes which would be meaningless from the economic view point and impossible to check in practice.

8.4.2. Other cases

It is obvious that the conditions stated for simultaneous stability are far from being general. Indeed, it seems, in general, impossible to infer the properties of one procedure from the properties of another. Mantel gives an interesting example of this in showing that if there are two consumers and several goods, the α-tâtonnement will always converge, although the p-tâtonnement is not necessarily convergent.

It seems therefore worthwhile to devise alternative adjustment rules, the properties of which are likely to be different.

PART III

A GENERAL EQUILIBRIUM MODEL OF WORLD TRADE

Introduction to Part III

Part III of the book is concerned with testing the activity analysis specifications and computational approaches developed in Parts I and II, respectively.

The General Equilibrium Model (GEM) of the world economy we have built is large enough to give rise to the kind of problems encountered in manipulating large models. It is however too small to describe adequately the world economy. Indeed, a useful policy model would need to distinguish more regions and probably also more commodities. This would have required a large and absorbing data-gathering effort, and a several fold increase of the model's size. The resulting system would have been a cumbersome tool for the numerous specification and computational experiments required in methodological research like ours.

It seemed important that the model should aim at describing reality. We wanted not only to verify that solutions could be obtained at reasonable costs, but also that these solutions made sense from an economic point of view. For this reason we used as the basis of GEM an experimental linear program of the world economy, the "international model", built for the World Bank and designed to test the feasibility of representing world trade by linear programming. This model was altered in many respects, but its basic structure has remained unchanged.

The "bench testing" function of GEM led us deliberately to distort reality in one important respect. Chapter 7 has shown that it is income effects which may cause tâtonnement computations to diverge. We therefore decided to retain in the model rather low price elasticities of export and import demand in order to test the robustness of the computational procedure. We have, however, also made calculations with coefficients which imply higher elasticities.

Chapters 9 and 10 describe the specification of the model and the data used. Computational and economic results are commented on in Chapters 11 and 12.

CHAPTER 9

The specification of GEM

9.1. GEM: An overview

The model is designed to study the relations between the developing countries of Latin America, Asia, and Africa and the rest of the world, divided into the Middle Eastern oil-producers and developed countries. As the emphasis is on the first three zones, only they are represented by fairly detailed, though still highly aggregated, models. The economy of the oil-producers is represented by a simplified set of equations, since at the time the model was constructed their trade and other relations with developing countries were still relatively small. Finally, to avoid constructing a detailed representation of the economy of developed countries their behavior is described by a trade welfare function.

As explained in Chapter 1, each region acts as an economic agent who, at the same time, produces, consumes, exports, and imports; capital flows net of debt service into Latin America, Asia, and Africa are supposed to be exogenous. In the case of oil-producers, on the other hand, it is assumed that, because of the pull exerted by financial markets in developed countries and their large foreign assets, their surpluses or deficits are covered by building up or drawing down their accumulated financial assets. Only one balance of payments needs to be specified to cover both oil-producers and developed countries. Capital flows are assumed to balance current flows automatically as oil-producers deposit excess balances in developed countries.

Traded goods are aggregated into 13 categories: six primary commodities (noncompeting tropical foods; competing tropical foods; temperate foods; agricultural raw materials; mining and ores; and oil) and seven manufactures (processed foods; textiles; chemicals; nonmetallic products; basic metals; machinery; and other manufactures). However, since commodities produced by different regions are not considered identical, the number of traded goods is close to fifty.[1] In Latin America, Asia, and Africa, nontraded goods (and factors) include construction, services, capital, 13 import substituting commodities, 15 production capacities, 13 export capacities, and rural and urban labor. The reduction of the developed countries model to a trade welfare function means that there are no nontraded goods in that region. Finally, there is only one nontraded good in the Middle East.[2]

The production sets of Latin America, Asia, Africa, and the Middle East are partly linear and partly nonlinear. The latter are approximated by appropriate linear programming objective function terms and constraints, or solved in the revision phase of the algorithm.

The nonlinear utility functions are based on a specification which makes it possible to represent certain nonseparable functions by a small number of variables and constraints. Utility in Latin America, Asia, Africa, and the developed world will be represented in this way, while the function is linear for the Middle East. For Latin America, Asia, and Africa the functions include terms which impute psychological costs to certain types of labor migration.

Our feeling is that it is not appropriate to use general equilibrium models to describe short-run economic behavior which is dominated by expectational phenomena and other types of disequilibria.[3] The ten-year span of GEM is, however, long enough for equilibrium forces to assert themselves. The model describes economic behavior in a one-period framework. This requires that some way is found to cut out a meaningful static equilibrium from the dynamic fabric of possible future developments. How this is done is explained in section 9.2.4.

Given the simplicity of the model, and the defects and lacunae of the data, the emphasis on the general equilibrium underpinning GEM should be taken as a parable rather than as an assertion that world economic equilibrium is truly described. We found the parable useful in that it forced us to adopt theoretically sound formulations. The benefit from the general equilibrium framework is not principally that the results are more accurate than those obtained by less rigorous approaches. There is some gain in accuracy, but of much greater importance is the intellectual discipline which forces the model-builder to avoid using crude heuristics which play

[1] Regions do not necessarily export all goods, so that the number of traded goods is less than $5 \times 13 = 65$.

[2] A full list of commodities produced by each region can be found in Chapter 10.

[3] The temporary equilibrium concept, however, offers a promising approach to the description of this behavior.

such a large role in development planning models. The results then have a clear meaning and provide a sound and rigorous basis for economic analysis.

All econometric models are in any case parables which stress the relevant features of the situation and omit irrelevant ones. Ours emphasizes the substitution mechanisms which determine adjustments in foreign trade and omits details which do not affect them. The aspects of reality stressed are as follows.

(a) *Competition between less developed countries on developed countries' markets* is reflected in the specification of the trade welfare function of developed countries, describing a demand behavior in which overall demand for each commodity is somewhat inelastic, whereas there is strong substitution between different suppliers of each commodity. As transport costs are neglected, the competition between developing areas is not influenced by freight rates.

(b) *Inelasticity of supply of traded commodities in developing countries*. For nonagricultural commodities supply is assumed to be elastic, although, beyond a certain level, increases in exports require additional investment to extend harbor facilities, etc. Constraints on available land recognize the inelasticity of supply of agricultural goods, and also the high cross elasticities of supply which imply that the increase in price of any agricultural good shifts upwards the supply curve of other goods.

(c) *Import substitution*. Latin America, Asia, and Africa are assumed to be capable of replacing imported goods by domestically produced commodities. The cost of this import substituting production increases however quite rapidly as output expands.

(d) *Capital–labor substitution* is described by Cobb–Douglas functions specified for industries producing home goods and import substituting goods.

(e) *Substitution in consumption* is reflected by the utility maximizing behavior of consumers in Latin America, Asia, and Africa (and implicitly by the developed countries' trade welfare function).

(f) *Psychological costs of migration*. It seemed worthwhile to recognize the psychological sacrifices involved in shifting labor between activities. These are thought to be especially significant for movements between primary sectors, which are often geographically far removed from each other; these costs are taken into account by appropriate utility function terms.

The events the model is designed to study are mainly changes in import tariffs by developing and developed countries. The model can also be used to examine the impact of changes in the growth rate of developing and developed countries; in the growth of supply of particular agricultural commodities; and in changes of oil prices (which are exogenous).

9.2. Technical devices used in constructing the equations[4]

9.2.1. Activity analysis representation of production processes

GEM uses four basic specifications of activity analysis to represent production possibilities: (a) constant returns discrete processes; (b) decreasing returns discrete processes; (c) neoclassical processes; and (d) reduced production sets. These will now be described.

(a) *Constant returns discrete processes*. These are the best known and they may be written as

$$y_j \leqslant \begin{bmatrix} A_j \\ F_j \end{bmatrix} z_j,$$

where A_j and F_j are column vectors of constant input–output and factor use coefficients and the activity level z_j is a non-negative scalar variable.

(b) *Decreasing returns discrete processes*. These are processes in which coefficients decrease with the scale of production (as input coefficients are negative, their absolute value increases). They are represented by

$$y_j \leqslant \begin{bmatrix} A_j(z_j) \\ F_j(z_j) \end{bmatrix} z_j,$$

where $A_j(z_j)$ and $F_j(z_j)$ are column vectors of decreasing functions of z_j.

Decreasing returns to a single variable can easily be represented in a linear programming framework by a step approximation of the relation between inputs and outputs and the activity level. Break up the domain of

[4]Notations are defined when used first. A complete list of notations is given in section 9.12, appendix 5. Let us simply state here a few general rules: subscripts i, j, and k will be used respectively for the country, the production process, and the commodity; subscript i will usually be omitted when it is clear we deal with one country; subscript h will be used as a local summation index; superscripts refer to the linear piece of an approximation. Except for technical coefficients (a_{kj}) and labor coefficient (l) we use greek letters for coefficients. Latin letters represent variables; the ($\sim$) indicates right-hand side constants. Functions are usually represented by capital letters.

the activity variable into segments $s=1,2,\dots,S$, and let $\begin{bmatrix} A_j^s \\ F_j^s \end{bmatrix}$ be the average input–output coefficients over segments z_j^s of the domain of z_j. If the activity is characterized by decreasing returns, it can be approximately described over a closed domain by

$$\begin{bmatrix} y_{jg} \\ y_{jf} \end{bmatrix} \leqslant \begin{bmatrix} \sum_s A_j^s z_j^s \\ \sum_s F_j^s z_j^s \end{bmatrix}; \qquad \begin{bmatrix} A_j^s \\ F_j^s \end{bmatrix} \leqslant \begin{bmatrix} A_j^{s+1} \\ F_j^{s+1} \end{bmatrix};$$

$$0 \leqslant z_j^s \leqslant \tilde{z}_j^s; \qquad s=1,\dots,S.$$

(c) *Neoclassical processes*, in which the activity coefficients must belong to a feasible set defined by a given function. I.e.

$$y_j \leqslant \begin{bmatrix} A_j \\ F_j \end{bmatrix} z_j,$$

where A_j and F_j must belong to an isoquant of the production function. Let $\alpha\kappa^a l^{1-a}=1$ be an isoquant of a Cobb–Douglas production function; then $\kappa = \tilde{\kappa} l \exp[(a-1)/a]$ with $\tilde{\kappa}=a\exp(1/\alpha)$ is the capital coefficient while l is the labor coefficient. The representation would then be

$$y \leqslant \begin{bmatrix} 1 \\ -l\tilde{\kappa}\exp\left(\dfrac{a-1}{a}\right) \\ -l \end{bmatrix} z.$$

Such processes can be used to smooth the substitution between labor and capital and avoid the tendency of programming models to emphasize the capital constraint at the expense of the labor constraint or vice versa.

This leads to defining model P:

$$\begin{aligned} \max \quad & c \cdot z \\ \text{s.t.} \quad & Az \leqslant b, \\ & l \cdot z \leqslant \tilde{L}, \\ & \kappa \cdot z \leqslant \tilde{K}, \\ & z \geqslant 0,\ (l, \kappa) \in \Psi, \end{aligned}$$

where z is an n-vector, and Ψ is a set of isoquants $\Psi_1, \ldots, \Psi_n$ of the n constant returns production functions describing how much labor and capital are required to operate each activity at unit level. We now have a model involving nonlinear production functions which can be solved by a combination of a tâtonnement process and the simplex algorithm.

Let w and r denote the "wage rate" and the "price of capital".[5]

Algorithm 9.2.1

Step 1: Function evaluation. For given $\tilde{w}$, $\tilde{r}$, $\tilde{l}_j$, and $\tilde{\kappa}_j$ $(j=1,2,\ldots,n)$ find $\bar{z}$ such that

$$\begin{aligned} &\max c\cdot z,\\ &\quad Az \leqslant b,\\ &\quad (\tilde{w}\tilde{l}+\tilde{r}\tilde{\kappa})\cdot z \leqslant \tilde{w}\tilde{L}+\tilde{r}\tilde{K},\\ &\quad z \geqslant 0.\end{aligned}$$

Step 2: Parameter revision. Compute $\tilde{l}\cdot\bar{z}-\tilde{L}$ and $\tilde{\kappa}\cdot\bar{z}-\tilde{K}$. If these quantities are zero it is obvious that $\bar{z}$ is the optimal solution of problem P, with $l_j=\tilde{l}_j$, $\kappa_j=\tilde{\kappa}_j$ $(j=1,2,\ldots,n)$. The computations are stopped.

Should these quantities be different from zero, use the following tâtonnement process to adjust w and r:

$$\begin{aligned} &\dot{w}=\tilde{l}\cdot\bar{z}-\tilde{L},\\ &\dot{r}=\tilde{\kappa}\cdot\bar{z}-\tilde{K},\end{aligned}$$

yielding new values for the "wage rate" say w, and the "price of capital", say r.

Set $\tilde{r}=r$ and $\tilde{w}=w$ and for given $\tilde{w}$, $\tilde{r}$ find $\bar{l}_j$ and $\bar{\kappa}_j$ values $(j=1,2,\ldots,n)$ such that

$$\begin{aligned} &\min \tilde{w}l_j+\tilde{r}\kappa_j\\ &\quad (l_j,\kappa_j)\in\Psi_j,\end{aligned}$$

for $j=1,2,\ldots,n$.

Set $\tilde{l}_j=\bar{l}_j$ and $\tilde{\kappa}_j=\bar{\kappa}_j$ $(j=1,2,\ldots,n)$ and go to step 1.

[5]Strictly speaking w and r are the wage rate and the price of capital, only if the tâtonnement process described in algorithm 9.2.1 is modified so that the shadow price of the $(\tilde{w}\tilde{l}+\tilde{r}\tilde{\kappa})\cdot z \leqslant \tilde{w}\tilde{L}+\tilde{r}\tilde{K}$ is unity. In practice, only the ratio $\tilde{w}/\tilde{r}$ matters. The algorithm used to solve GEM is designed to find the true wage and interest rates.

(d) *Reduced production sets* which provide an approximate description of production possibilities when there is not enough data to build an accurate description of the production set.

This concept is exemplified by our treatment of agricultural production possibilities.

It is a general observation that some commodities are used by one group of production processes only, and cannot be consumed, exported, or imported. For example, agriculture is the sole user of land; the steel industry is the sole user of blast furnaces. In such cases the production vector y and set Y can be written as:

$$y=y^1+y^2; \qquad y^1 \in Y^1, \qquad y^2 \in Y^2,$$

where the last r^{**} coordinates of $y^1 \in Y^1$ are identically zero. Partitioning y^2 into y^{2*}, y^{2**}, where y^{2**} contains the last r^{**} coordinates of y^2, the national balance constraints imply that any solution of the equilibrium problem must satisfy

$$y=y^1+y^2; \qquad y^1 \in Y^1; \qquad y^2 \in Y^2; \qquad -y^{2**} \leqslant \omega^{**},$$

where ω^{**} contains the r^{**} last coordinates of ω. This leads to defining the reduced production set Y^* composed of $(r-r^{**})$ dimensional vectors as:

$$Y^*(\omega^{**}) = \left\{ y^* \mid y^* = y^{1*} + y^{2*}; \qquad \begin{pmatrix} y^{1*} \\ 0 \end{pmatrix} \in Y^1; \right.$$

$$\left. \begin{pmatrix} y^{2*} \\ y^{2**} \end{pmatrix} \in Y^2; \qquad -y^{2**} \leqslant \omega^{**} \right\}.$$

Replacing Y by Y^* and y by y^* in the definition of a general equilibrium in no way changes the nature of the problem posed,[6] but reduces the number of commodities for which it is necessary to define explicit supply demand constraints.

9.2.2. *Utility functions*

Another extensively used device is a utility function which has a number of useful properties. It involves few parameters and can be approximated by a

[6] The treatment of the energy sector in Goreux and Manne (1973) is an excellent example of this type of production set reduction procedure. The paper does not however give the general formulation of the approach which we provide here.

small number of linear constraints and variables. It is easy to derive parameter values which correspond in a rough way to the results of econometric studies.[7] Since these functions do not seem to have been used by other authors, they will be referred to as "GEM functions".

GEM utility functions have the form

$$U(x)=V\left(\sum_k x_k\right)-\sum_k W_k\left[x_k-\gamma_k-\beta_k\sum_h(x_h-\gamma_h)\right],$$

where V is concave increasing and the W_k are non-negative convex functions which go through the origin. Also, $\Sigma_h\beta_h=1$.

If the W_k are linear, the distinctive property of GEM functions is that all indifference curves can be obtained by sliding a single indifference curve along a ray going through γ. GEM functions are nonseparable, although for W_k linear they can be made weakly separable by a linear transformation. They can accommodate complementarity.

It can be seen that, as the $W_k(\cdot)$ and their derivatives vanish around the origin,

(a) the Engel line corresponding to a situation of equal prices has the equation

$$x_k=\gamma_k+\beta_k\sum_h(x_h-\gamma_h); \tag{9.1}$$

(b) along this line the W_k vanish so that $U(x)=V(\Sigma_h x_h)$;

(c) if $V(\cdot)$ is linear the other Engel lines are parallel to (9.1);

(d) defining V', W_k' as derivatives $\mathrm{d}V/\mathrm{d}(\Sigma x_k)$ and

$$\mathrm{d}W_k/\mathrm{d}\left(x_k-\gamma_k-\beta_k\sum_h(x_h-\gamma_h)\right),$$

the marginal utilities are

$$\frac{\partial U}{\partial x_k}=V'-\left(W_k'-\sum_h\beta_h W_h'\right).^{8} \tag{9.2}$$

Homotheticity might be thought preferable to property (9.2). But since the

[7]The procedure which we have used to quantify these functions is described in Chapter 10.

[8]If V is linear this equation implies parallel Engel curves. See, for example, Blackorby, Boyce and Russel (1978).

function is used to represent preferences in the neighborhood of equilibrium only and not in the large, homotheticity is not an important issue in the present context. The function happens to be computationally convenient because its linearization involves upper bounds which are cheap to handle by linear programming codes.

GEM functions can be approximated by the following linear programming objective function terms and constraints, where subscript k ($k = 1, 2, \ldots, r$) refers to commodity k and superscript s to the sth linear piece:

$$U(\hat{x}) = \max\left[\sum_s \phi^s x^s - \sum_k \sum_s \phi_k^s (x_k^{s+} + x_k^{s-})\right] \tag{9.3}$$

s.t.

$$\sum_s x^s - \sum_k x_k = 0 \qquad (w), \tag{9.4}$$

$$x_k - \beta_k\left(\sum_h x_h - \sum_h \gamma_h\right) - \gamma_k = \sum_s (x_k^{s+} - x_k^{s-}) \qquad (w_k), \tag{9.5}$$

$$x_k^{s+} \leqslant \tilde{x}_k^{s+} \qquad (w_k^{s+}), \tag{9.6}$$

$$x_k^{s-} \leqslant \tilde{x}_k^{s-} \qquad (w_k^{s-}), \tag{9.7}$$

$$x^s \leqslant \tilde{x}^s \qquad (w^s), \tag{9.8}$$

$$x_k = \hat{x}_k \qquad (v_k), \tag{9.9}$$

with $\Sigma_k \beta_k = 1$. We have written, to the right of each constraint, the dual variable associated with the constraint. The first term of the objective function corresponds to the $V(\Sigma x_k)$ of the GEM function: see constraint (9.4). The ϕ^s are approximations of V' over the steps s. Because of the concavity of V, $\phi^{s+1} \leqslant \phi^s$; this ensures that steps enter the solution in the right order.

The second term of the objective function corresponds to

$$\sum_k W_k\left[x_k - \gamma_k - \beta_k \sum_h (x_h - \gamma_h)\right];$$

see (9.5). The ϕ_k^s are approximations of the derivatives W_k'. Once again the convexity of the W_k ensures that $\phi_k^{s+1} \geqslant \phi_k^s$.

The marginal utilities of the goods are obviously equal to the vector v of dual variables associated with constraint (9.9). This leads to studying the dual constraints:

$$w+w^s \geqslant \phi^s \qquad (x^s),$$

$$-w+w_k-\sum_h \beta_h w_h+v_k \geqslant 0 \qquad (x_k),$$

$$w_k^{s+}-w_k \geqslant -\phi_k^s \qquad (x_k^{s+}),$$

$$w_k^{s-}+w_k \geqslant -\phi_k^s \qquad (x_k^{s-}),$$

where the primal variable which corresponds to each constraint is noted in brackets on the right of the constraint.

For the sake of simplicity we will assume that at the optimal point,

$$0<x_k^{s+}<\tilde{x}_k^{s+} \ (\text{or}^9\ 0<x_k^{s-}<\tilde{x}_k^{s-}) \text{ for a step } s^+ \text{ (or } s^-) \text{ and } 0<x^s<\tilde{x}^s$$

for a step s, so that $w^s=w^{s+}$ (or w^{s-})$=0$ by complementary slackness.[10]

Then, the dual variables must obey

$$w=\phi^s, \tag{9.10}$$

$$v_k=w-\left(w_k-\sum_h \beta_h w_h\right), \tag{9.11}$$

$$w_k=\phi_k^s \text{ or } w_k=-\phi_k^s \text{ according to whether } x_k^{s+}>0 \text{ or } x_k^{s-}>0. \tag{9.12}$$

Since ϕ^s and ϕ_k^s are approximations of the derivatives V' and W_k' of the GEM function, it is clear that expression (9.11) is identical to (9.2) which defined marginal utility.

9.2.3. *Behavioral relations*

GEM contains four types of behavioral relations which cannot be accounted for in the function evaluation phase of the solution procedure. They are taken care of in the revision phase along the lines described in Chapters 2–5.

[9] It is easily shown that if $\phi_k^s>0$, $x_k^{s+}\cdot x_k^{s-}=0$.

[10] The reasoning is easily extended if these primal constraints are satisfied as equalities, but the expressions become more complicated.

Import tariffs of the three developing areas are *ad valorem*. These tariffs, which appear in the objective function of the linear program solved in the function evaluation phase are adjusted in the revision phase to make them proportional to the import prices calculated in the most recent function evaluation phase.

Oil export prices are set equal to unity in all solutions so the model involves *fixed price-setting behavior*. This is achieved by introducing in the objective function of the linear program a compensatory levy[11] which is equal to the difference between the cost of production of oil in each zone and its unit world price. The amount of this levy or export tariff is set, in the revision phase, as the difference between the production cost and selling price.

For nonmetallic products and basic metals, cartel behavior is assumed such that the market shares are fixed and export prices are equal to the average of marginal costs of the regions weighted by the export volumes.

Investment is assumed to follow a *linear growth path* in the period covered by the model. The approach was described in section 4.2.1 and leads to an equation of the form $K=\tilde{K}^0+(T/2)x^*$, where $\tilde{K}^0$ is the initial capital endowment, T is the length of the planning period, and x^* is investment.

A *saving investment identity* constrains investment and the terminal capital stock. The saving equation implies that saving is proportional to current price consumption. If x and x^* are the consumption and investment vectors, p the domestic goods price vector, and σ the propensity to consume, the saving investment identity is

$$\sigma p\cdot x=p\cdot x^*.$$

9.3. The submodels for Latin America, Asia, and Africa

9.3.1. Production sets outside agriculture and the oil industry

These sets are represented by activity analysis processes. For each commodity, processes are defined which produce:

(1) a "home good";

(2) for traded goods, a commodity which replaces imports;

[11]Analogous to the compensatory levies used by the Common Market to set domestic agricultural prices independently of world prices.

(3) additional capacities needed for production of the home commodity; and

(4) additional capacities needed for production of the import substituting commodity.

Each of these activities produces one commodity and consumes one or more of the following commodities:

(1) 15 "input–output" goods, referred to hereafter as "home goods";

(2) 13 imported commodities, referred to as "foreign goods";

(3) 15 production capacities for home goods;

(4) 13 production capacities for import substituting commodities;

(5) one urban infrastructure service;

(6) two types of capital goods, machines (good 12) and construction (good 14);

(7) one type of labor; and

(8) 13 export activities for the 13 exported home goods.

The product groups identified in the model are broad aggregates of many different commodities. Of these there will be several for which the country has a competitive advantage; they are the "home goods". Others can find a profitable market only if they benefit from protection or if the domestic exchange rate drops sharply; they are the "import substituting goods".[12]

The parable which we used to represent this situation is that for each type of commodity the "home goods" account for a fixed share of the market. "Foreign goods" account for the rest. They can be imported or produced domestically (import substituting production); the latter however are produced under diminishing returns to capital, and have higher capital requirements at all output levels than the corresponding home goods.

This leads to representing the production sets for home and import substituting goods by linear activity analysis processes using production capacities (the input coefficients corresponding to those capacities are normalized to 1) and other commodity inputs. The activities which "produce" production capacities use capital goods and labor. The output coefficient is unity; the input coefficients are the marginal labor and capital–output ratios. Capacities for production of home and import substituting goods are created by linear and strictly concave processes, respectively.

[12] Ideally import substitution could be represented by a very detailed model based on information on the structure of costs of the goods which can be produced. This data is lacking, and anyway such a detailed treatment of production would have led to a model which could not be built and handled with available means.

Table 9.1.

	Producing activities		Capacity producing activities	
	Home goods	Import subst. goods	Home goods	Import subst. goods
	z_{j_1}	z_{j_2}	i_{j_1}	i_{j_2}
Home goods balance constraints	$\varepsilon_{j_1} - a^{\mathrm{h}}_{j_1}$	$-a^{\mathrm{h}}_{j_2}$		
Foreign goods balance constraints	$-a^{\mathrm{f}}_{j_1}$	$\varepsilon_{j_2} - a^{\mathrm{f}}_{j_2}$		
Production capacity balances, home goods	$-\varepsilon_{j_1}$		ε_{j_1}	
Production capacity balances, import substitution		$-\varepsilon_{j_2}$		ε_{j_2}
Urban infrastructure services balance	$-\nu_{j_1}$	$-\nu_{j_2}$		
Capital balance, machines			$-\kappa_{12,j_1}(l_{j_1})$	$-\phi_{12,j_2}(i_{j_2}) \cdot \kappa_{12,j_2}(l_{j_2})$
Capital balance, construction			$-\kappa_{14,j_1}(l_{j_1})$	$-\phi_{14,j_2}(i_{j_2}) \cdot \kappa_{14,j_2}(l_{j_2})$
Labor balance			$-l_{j_1}$	$-\phi_{l,j_2}(i_{j_2}) \cdot l_{j_2}$

Table 9.2.

	$i_{j_2}^1$	$i_{j_2}^2$	...	$i_{j_2}^S$
Production capacity balances, import substitution	ε_{j_2}	ε_{j_2}	...	ε_{j_2}
Capital balance, machines	$-\rho_{j_2}^1\kappa_{12,j_2}(\cdot)$	$-\rho_{j_2}^2\kappa_{12,j_2}(\cdot)$	...	$-\rho_{j_2}^S\kappa_{12,j_2}(\cdot)$
Capital balance, construction	$-\rho_{j_2}^1\kappa_{14,j_2}(\cdot)$	$-\rho_{j_2}^2\kappa_{14,j_2}(\cdot)$	...	$-\rho_{j_2}^S\kappa_{14,j_2}(\cdot)$
Labor balance	$-\rho_{j_2}^1 l_{j_2}$	$-\rho_{j_2}^2 l_{j_2}$	...	$-\rho_{j_2}^S l_{j_2}$

Let z_{j_1} and z_{j_2} be the processes which produce home goods and import substituting goods and let i_{j_1} and i_{j_2} be the processes which produce the respective capacities. If k is the commodity involved, the production set Y_k can be represented as shown in table 9.1. $a_{j_1}^{\mathrm{h}}(a_{j_1}^{\mathrm{f}})$ and $a_{j_2}^{\mathrm{h}}(a_{j_2}^{\mathrm{f}})$ are column vectors of input coefficients of the different activities numbered j_1 and j_2; ε_{j_1} and ε_{j_2} are the j_1 and j_2 unit column vectors (i.e. vectors with a 1 in position j_1 or j_2 and zeros elsewhere); ν_{j_1} and ν_{j_2} are scalars measuring infrastructure requirements, including schooling and other needs of the labor force. The capital and labor coefficients $\kappa_{k,j_1}(l_{j_1})=l_{j_1}\tilde{\kappa}_{k,j_1}\exp[(a-1)/a]$ ($k=12$ and 14) and l_{j_1} are points on an isoquant of a Cobb–Douglas production function. Finally $\Phi_{12,j_2}(i_{j_2})$, $\Phi_{14,j_2}(i_{j_2})$ and $\Phi_{l,j_2}(i_{j_2})$ are increasing functions of i_{j_2}, reflecting the increasing cost of import substitution.

In practice, $\Phi(i_{j_2})$ is approximated by a piecewise linear function; the i_{j_2} column is thus represented by S columns, as in table 9.2, subject to the linearization constraints $i_{j_2}^s \leqslant \tilde{i}_{j_2}^s$, $s=1,\ldots,S$. Note that as $\Phi(\cdot)$ is a convex function of i_{j_2}, increasing output will tend to be more and more costly in terms of capital and labor inputs. Thus, the ρ^s must be increasing.

9.3.2. Production sets for oil

In each of the three developing zones some countries are capable of producing oil at costs that are comparable to those of the Middle East: Venezuela in Latin America, Malaysia and Indonesia in Asia, and Nigeria, Algeria, and Libya in Africa. The remaining countries which have oil reserves can only exploit them at relatively high costs (e.g. Brazil or Tunisia).

To capture this aspect of reality, it was decided to treat the exported oil of the low cost producers and the import substituting oil of the high cost countries as different products. It is assumed that the low cost oil is demanded only abroad, while the domestic market is supplied either by import substituting oil or by imports. As will be seen later, exported oil is affected by high export tariffs which increase its cost to foreign importers.

These ideas can be expressed by a slight change of the specification presented in the last section. All that is needed is to specify that the z_{j_1} activity for oil produces oil which is exported and not consumed in the home country.

9.3.3. *Production sets for agricultural goods*

The representation of agricultural production sets is far more difficult than for manufacturing and service activities. Agriculture uses a large number of types of land which differ in climate, location, and natural fertility. Most types of land can serve alternative uses, and a principal goal of any model will be to find the optimal allocation of land between different crops.

Mathematical programming offers an excellent framework for analysis of agriculture, as shown by a number of studies.[13] However, successful implementation of this approach requires a large and costly effort even for a single country. Construction of a world agricultural model was not feasible with the means at our disposal.

The representation of agriculture in GEM is the result of a brutal simplification of the complex underlying reality. To understand the equations, we can start from a picture of agricultural production as the sum of productions on numerous types of land, to each of which corresponds a different production function, say

$$f^a(z_j^a, i_j^a, L_j^a) \leqslant \tilde{a}^a, \qquad (9.13)$$

where the subscript j runs over the four agricultural commodities, the superscript a refers to the type of land; $\tilde{a}^a$ is the amount of land of type a which is available; and L stands for labor.

The goal is to describe very crudely by a few constraints the reduced production set obtained by eliminating all the land constraints

[13] See, for example, Duloy and Norton (1973).

(9.13) from the agricultural production set. The linear constraints which are designed to approximate this set reflect the following ideas about its structure.

(a) There are different qualities of land. We distinguish only two: fertile and marginal land.

(b) The more fertile lands will be fully used. As a result, each crop grown on fertile land can be increased only at the expense of other crops. It follows that the production set for that land can next be defined for all agriculture, and not separately for each good as was done for nonagricultural products.

(c) There seems to be a substantial supply of marginal land, even in Asia. There is less likelihood therefore that the expansion of one crop on these lands will limit the possible expansion of other crops.

(d) The yield (and to a certain extent the area) of fertile lands can be increased by investment in irrigation, drainage, and fertilizer production.

(e) Because marginal lands are less fertile, they require higher capital and intermediate goods inputs per unit of production than fertile lands.

These ideas can be represented as follows. Let j_{f} and j_{m} be indices designating the processes which produce an agricultural commodity on fertile and marginal land, respectively, and let j_{p} be the index of the process producing the corresponding import substituting commodity.[14] Let similarly $i_{j_{\mathrm{f}}}$, $i_{j_{\mathrm{m}}}$ and $i^{s}_{j_{\mathrm{p}}}$ $(s=1,\dots,S)$ be production capacities of the processes where, as the notation indicates, capacities for producing import substituting commodities are broken down into steps $s=1,\dots,S$

The production sets for agriculture can be represented by activities which have the same structure as those described in section 9.3.1, supplemented by a number of additional constraints. The $z_{j_{\mathrm{f}}}$, $z_{j_{\mathrm{m}}}$ activities are defined by columns identical to the z_{j_1} column in section 9.3.1; the $i_{j_{\mathrm{f}}}$ and $i_{j_{\mathrm{m}}}$ to the i_{j_1} in section 9.3.1; and the z_{j_p} and $i_{j_{\mathrm{p}}}$ to the z_{j_2} and i_{j_2} in section 9.3.1. The agricultural production set is also subject to linearization constraints which reflect diminishing returns in agriculture. A detailed list of these equations can be found in section 9.8.

9.3.4. Urban infrastructure services

Decreasing returns to urban infrastructure services are represented in table 9.3 where $\Phi_{\mathrm{u}}(i_{\mathrm{u}})$ is an increasing function of i_{u} represented by a piecewise linear approximation, as in the case of i_{j_2} (section 9.3.1).

[14] For the sake of simplicity it is convenient to assume that import substituting goods are produced on one type of land only.

Table 9.3.

	Investment in urban infrastructure i_u
Urban infrastructure services balance	1
Capital balance, machines	$-\phi_{12,u}(i_u)\kappa_{12,u}$
Capital balance, construction	$-\phi_{14,u}(i_u)\kappa_{14,u}$

9.3.5. Export and import sets

In GEM goods imported into a country and goods available on international markets are considered as different commodities; the same holds for exported goods and goods available on these markets. There exist therefore import and export processes which "transport" goods between domestic and international markets.

For each traded good an import process is defined in each developing region which purchases the commodity in fixed proportions on international markets and delivers it to the domestic market as an "imported good". There is therefore no direct price substitution between suppliers of a commodity to developing countries; as will be seen in section 9.5, the same is not true on developed countries' markets. This, we feel, is not a serious weakness of the model, since the share of developed countries on developing countries' markets is so large that substantial shifts in the distribution of these imports are unlikely over the period covered by the model.

The import sets (commodity k and importing country i, the index of which is dropped) is then determined as shown in table 9.4, where i' is the country of origin and $\Sigma_i \mu_{i'k} = 1$.

For exports, likewise, we adopt the convention that there exist export processes which buy each traded good on the domestic market and transform it into an international good. To reflect the infrastructure

Table 9.4

	Import activities m_k
Foreign goods balance	1
World import–export balances	$\mu_{i'k}$

Table 9.5.

	Export activities e_k	Export capacities i_k^e
Home goods balance	1	
Export capacity balance	−1	1
Capital balance, machines		$-\kappa_{12,k}^e$
Capital balance, construction		$-\kappa_{14,k}^e$

bottlenecks which so often hamper the growth of developing countries we assume that these processes require export capacities which can be increased by drawing on the available stock of capital.

The exports sets (commodity k) are defined as shown in table 9.5.

9.3.6. Consumption and migration sets

(a) Sets of feasible consumptions. For traded goods, the consumption processes involve joint inputs of the home-produced and of the corresponding imported goods. For nontraded goods, only the home good is purchased. The consumption sets are thus defined as in table 9.6,[15] where $\lambda_k = 1$ for nontraded goods.

(b) Sets of feasible migration between sectors of the economy. These migrations take place between the four agricultural sectors, nonferrous metals mining, and the rest of the economy. They may take zero, positive, or negative values.

9.3.7. Behavioral relations

As already indicated, a number of behavioral relations are taken care of in the revision phase of the algorithm. These are:

$$\textit{ad valorem}\ \text{import tariffs}\quad \tau_k^{\mathrm{m}} = p_k^{\mathrm{m}} \tau_k^0,$$

[15] The objective function linearization constraints might appear to restrict the consumption set. We feel that this restriction should be disregarded since it depends on the arbitrarily chosen range of the approximation zone. As was pointed out, this zone should be extended wherever the solution is on its boundary.

Table 9.6.

	Consumption activity x_k
Home goods balance	$-(1-\lambda_k)$
Foreign goods balance	$-\lambda_k$

where τ_k^0 is the specific tariff rate;

export tariff on oil $\tau_6^e = 1 - \text{cost}$,

where *cost* = cost of all inputs used (see dual equations);

linear investment path $K_k = \tilde{K}_k^0 + \frac{T}{2} x_k^*$, $k = 12$ and 14;

saving-investment balance $\tilde{A} + \sigma p \cdot x = p \cdot x^*$,

where $\tilde{A}$ is the exogenous amount of aid granted to the country and saving $\sigma p \cdot x$ is proportional to current price consumption $p \cdot x$.

9.3.8. *Summing up the commodity balances*

In the preceding section we defined the elements of the regional domestic supply and demand balances. These balances can be found in section 9.8.

9.3.9. *Utility functions*

The utility functions are linear approximations of

$$U(x, L) = U^*(x) - U^{**}(L)$$

$$= \sum_k x_k - \sum_k W_k\left(x_k - \gamma_k - \beta_k \sum_h (x_h - \gamma_h)\right) - \sum_j V_j^L(L_j),$$

where W_k and V_j^L are convex non-negative functions going through the origin.

The component $U^*(x)$ is a GEM function the first term of which is linear.

The introduction of terms reflecting migration in primary-producing activities is not usual. It accounts for an aspect of economic mechanisms which is very apparent to observers of reality, although it is disregarded in theoretical analysis. Primary-producing activities are usually widely separated geographically so that the labor movements in and out of these areas involve substantial psychological costs which merit recognition as much as the satisfaction associated with the consumption of goods. These costs imply that these activities face upward sloping supply curves for labor. Details can be found in section 9.8.

9.3.10. Import and export tariffs

As explained in Chapter 1, the representation of a tariff-ridden equilibrium requires evaluating the tariff revenue net of subsidies of each country.

Import tariffs τ_k^{m} are taken as *ad valorem* tariffs; the resulting income is therefore $\Sigma_k \tau_k^{\mathrm{m}} m_k$. There are export tariffs only for tropical noncompeting goods, nonferrous metals, and oil (commodities 1, 5, and 6). The first two are thought of as specific. The tariff terms in the objective functions are therefore

$$t^* = \sum_k \tau_k^{\mathrm{m}} m_k + \tau_1^{\mathrm{e}} e_1 + \tau_5^{\mathrm{e}} e_5 + \tau_6^{\mathrm{e}} e_6 .$$

The export tariff on oil accounts for the considerable taxes and royalties which are levied by governments of oil-rich countries. It may also, to a certain extent, reflect the above-average profit margins which oil companies are able to earn as a result of monopolistic collusion.

9.4. The Middle East oil-producers' submodel

GEM was constructed before the oil crisis and at a time when oil-producers were less at the center of attention then today. The Middle Eastern oil-producing countries are accordingly represented by a very simple set of equations since, from the point of view of the world economy, they appeared principally as a reliable source of oil. Their role is much more important and complex today; but the path of their development is still far from clear, and it is not yet easy to see which model would adequately represent their economies.

The economy of this zone is assumed to consist of closely interlinked industries: oil, and industries whose growth depends on the income generated by oil exports. It is thus oil which generates the forward momentum of the whole region.

All goods are aggregated into two commodities: oil and an aggregate good used mainly locally. Oil output is not constrained by initial capacity resources; costs of production are extremely low; and (at least at the time when the model was built) the capital required to produce more crude oil could be easily supplied by the international companies. Unlike other processes in developing countries it was assumed that oil production depended only on demand.

The expansion of the nonoil modern sector depends on the initial productive capacity, increased by the accumulation of capital made possible by oil royalties and by saving in that sector. A small part of the accumulated domestic capital is, however, absorbed by investments in housing and infrastructure which are required for oil production but not financed by the oil companies.

The economy is thus described by the following constraints (the subscripts 6 and 0 refer to oil and other products, respectively).

The oil production balance is

$$-y_6+e_6 \leqslant -\tilde{y}_6,$$

where $\tilde{y}_6$ is exogenous domestic oil consumption.

Capacity in the nonoil sector is given by

$$y_0 \leqslant (\sigma_6-\alpha)y_6+\sigma_0 y_0+\tilde{y}_0.$$

This expression reflects the fact that production is bounded upwards by the initial capacity $\tilde{y}_0$, increased by the capacity which can be created using the savings generated by the oil and nonoil sectors (coefficients σ_6, σ_0), net of the domestic capital used by the oil industry (coefficient α).

Imports are related to activity levels in oil and nonoil production:

$$m_k=\mu_k^6 y_6+\mu_k^0 y_0.$$

The supply–demand balance for the nonoil commodity is

$$x_0=y_0-\sum_{k\neq 6} e_k,$$

and welfare in that region is simply

$$U = x_0.$$

The model finally takes account of export duties on oil:

$$t^* = \tau_6^e e_6$$

$$\tau_6^e = 1 - \text{cost}.$$

9.5. Developed countries' submodel

9.5.1. Import and export sets

Import processes are defined for every commodity originating from every developing region. These activities directly purchase on the international markets. The import set is the non-negative orthant.

Export processes are defined in the same way. They sell directly to international markets. The export set is also the non-negative orthant.

9.5.2. The trade welfare–production function

It had been decided, as explained, to avoid a detailed representation of the economies of developed countries. This is achieved by specifying their trading behavior in terms of the maximization of a trade welfare function. The parable which the formulation expresses may be outlined as follows.

(1) The imports of developed countries are regarded as inputs into a production system which can produce six types of manufactured exports: processed food, textiles, chemicals, basic metals, machinery, and other manufactures; and five primary exports: competing tropical foods, temperate foods, agricultural raw materials, mining and ores and oil; and a single consumption-investment good.[16] At equilibrium, output of that good equals GNP (GNP is equal to national expenditure if the balance of payments is in equilibrium).

(2) Exports of the six manufactured goods to developing countries are a very small fraction of output. It is reasonable to assume that they are produced at constant costs. The trade welfare function is linear in those

[16] There are, of course, other inputs, e.g. the domestic capital stock and labor. They are, however, regarded as exogenous and treated as parameters of the welfare-production function.

goods. The same is true of the single consumption-investment good: output of this good changes too little in alternative solutions to make it necessary to specify a diminishing returns mechanism.

(3) The five primary products are quite homogeneous. Accordingly, net imports are considered to be the arguments of the trade welfare function rather than treating imports and exports as separate arguments.

(4) Imports of primary products are a significant fraction of consumption. Producers of these commodities in developed countries operate in conditions of diminishing returns. It is therefore appropriate to assume diminishing marginal utility of these net imports.

Imports of primary products from different developing regions are highly substitutable. There is less substitutability between imports of manufactures from different regions.

The underlying nonlinear trade welfare function consists of two parts.

(a) A sum of GEM welfare functions for imports of each commodity (except for agricultural products, oil, and mining and ores, for which the arguments of the function are net imports). This sum enters the function with a plus sign.

(b) A sum of exports of manufactured goods of developed countries, with a minus sign.

It appears reasonable to assume that the broad commodity groups considered in the model make separate contributions to the welfare function so that this function may be built up as a sum of components for each group. Each of these is given the form of a GEM function. We first describe the components which correspond to the imports of developed countries. If $m_{0k} = \Sigma_i m_{i0k}$ (i is the country of origin and 0 is the developed zone) each term is written:

$$V_{0k}(m_{0k}, g_0) - \sum_i W_{i0k}(m_{i0k} - \mu_{i0k} m_{0k}).$$

These functions have the following properties:

(a) the functions V_{0k} and W_{i0k} are strictly concave and convex non-negative functions respectively; and

(b) the V_{0k} are increasing functions; the W_{i0k} go through the origin.

The trade welfare components for individual commodities are not separable functions of imports from different regions—separability would indeed violate common sense here. The preferred import baskets, when prices are unity, lie along the ray $m_{i0k} = \mu_{i0k} m_{0k}$ starting at the origin. This ray has the same theoretical significance as the Engel curves of the utility functions described earlier.

The g_0 term reflects the parametric dependence of production in developed countries on their domestic resources, treated as exogenous (see remarks above). The dependence is in principle very complex. In practice all that is possible is to reflect rather crudely the impact of changes of domestic resources on the trade welfare function. The term g_0 is used as a general proxy for the impact of technical progress on production sets and of capital accumulation on initial resources of nontraded goods.

9.5.3. Linearization of the developed countries' submodel

The underlying nonlinear welfare function is therefore (we drop the zone 0 index to lighten notation)

$$U(\cdot) = -\sum_k e_k + \sum_k V_k(m_k, g_0) + \sum_k \sum_i W_{ik}(m_{ik} - \mu_{ik} m_k).$$

This function is represented in the model by a linear approximation the details of which are given in section 9.8.

9.5.4. Tariffs

For the sake of simplicity tariffs are assumed to be specific rather than *ad valorem*. Since these tariffs are not very high, except for temperate foods, it did not seem that the gain in accuracy from specifying *ad valorem* tariffs would have been worthwhile. For temperate foods, an adequate description of the very complex system of import regulations, which protects developed countries' markets, was in any case not possible within the simplistic framework of the model. Tariffs are given by

$$t^* = \sum_k \tau_{0k}^{\mathrm{m}} \sum_s m_k^s.$$

9.6. The international balances

Since commodities of a given type exported by different regions are considered as different commodities, it is necessary to ensure balance between supply and demand of every commodity exported by each country. These balances are simply (i is the exporting country; i' the importing country):

$$e_{ik} \geqslant \sum_{\substack{i'=0 \\ i' \neq i}}^{4} m_{ii'k}.$$

It is useful to recall that the $m_{ii'k}$ have been defined as follows (see sections 9.3.5 and 9.5.3):

$$m_{ii'k} = \mu_{ii'k} m_{i'k}, \qquad i' = 1, \ldots, 4,$$

$$m_{i0k} = \mu_{i0k} \sum_{i'} m_{i'0k} + m_{i0k}^{+} - m_{i0k}^{-}.$$

9.7. The balances of payments

Denote by p_{ik}^{e} the export price of commodity k, country i; then the balance of payments constraint is simply

$$\sum_{k} \left[\sum_{i'} p_{i'k}^{e} m_{i'ik} - p_{ik}^{e} e_{ik} \right] \leqslant \tilde{A}_i \qquad (i = 1, 2 \text{ and } 3),$$

where $\tilde{A}_i$ is the exogenous amount of aid granted to country i.

9.8. Appendix 1: Primal equations[17]

1. Submodels for Latin America, Asia and Africa [18]

(1.1) Supply–demand balances for home goods (except oil)

$$\sum_{j=1}^{4} \left(a_{k,j_t}^{h} z_{j_t} + a_{k,j_m}^{h} z_{j_m} + a_{k,j_p}^{h} z_{j_p} \right) + \sum_{j=5}^{15} \left(a_{k,j_1}^{h} z_{j_1} + a_{k,j_2}^{h} z_{j_2} \right)$$

[demand for good k by producing activities]

$$+ \quad e_k \quad + \quad (1-\lambda_k)x_k \quad + \quad (1-\mu_k)x_k^{*}$$

+ [export of good k] + [consumption of good k] + [investment use of good k]

$$-(\delta_{k,j_t} z_{j_t} + \delta_{k,j_m} z_{j_m} + \delta_{k,j_1} z_{j_1}) \leqslant 0, \qquad k = 1, 2, \ldots, 15, \qquad (p_k)$$

− [production of good k] $\leqslant 0$,

where $x_k^{*} = 0$ except for $k = 12$ (machinery) and $k = 14$ (construction).

[17] Dual variables appear on the right-hand side of each equation.

[18] The region subscript $i = 1, 2, 3$ is dropped to lighten notation.

Supply–demand balance for home oil

$$e_6 \quad - \quad z_{6_1} \quad \leqslant 0, \qquad (p_6)$$

[export – [production ⩽ 0.
of oil] of home oil]

(1.2) Supply–demand balances for foreign goods

$$\sum_{j=1}^{4} \left(a^{\mathrm{f}}_{k,j_{\mathrm{f}}} z_{j_{\mathrm{f}}} + a^{\mathrm{f}}_{k,j_{\mathrm{m}}} z_{j_{\mathrm{m}}} + a^{\mathrm{f}}_{k,j_{\mathrm{p}}} z_{j_{\mathrm{p}}}\right) + \sum_{j=5}^{15} \left(a^{\mathrm{f}}_{k,j_1} z_{j_1} + a^{\mathrm{f}}_{k,j_2} z_{j_2}\right)$$

[demand for "foreign" good k by producing activities]

$$+ \quad \lambda_k x_k \quad + \quad \mu_k x^*_k \quad - \quad m_k$$

+ [demand of "foreign" good k for consumption] + [investment use of "foreign" good k] – [import of good k]

$$- \quad (\delta_{k,j_{\mathrm{p}}} z_{j_{\mathrm{p}}} + \delta_{k,j_2} z_{j_2}) \quad \leqslant 0, \qquad k = 1, 2, \ldots, 13. \qquad (u^{\mathrm{m}}_k)$$

– [domestic production ⩽ 0.
of "foreign" good k]

(1.3) Urban infrastructure services balance and linearization bounds

$$\sum_{j=5}^{15} (v_{j_1} z_{j_1} + v_{j_2} z_{j_2}) \quad - \quad \sum_{s=1}^{S} i^s_u \quad \leqslant 0, \qquad (u_{\mathrm{u}})$$

[consumption of urban infrastructure services] – [capacity infrastructure services] ⩽ 0,

$$i^s_u \leqslant \bar{i}^s_u, \qquad s = 1, 2, \ldots, S. \qquad (v^s_{\mathrm{u}})$$

[linearization bounds]

(1.4) Balances for production capacities of home goods

$$z_{j_{\mathrm{f}}} \quad - \quad i_{j_{\mathrm{f}}} \quad - \quad i^*_{j_{\mathrm{f}}}$$

[activity level] – [additional capacity not requiring land improvement] – [additional capacity requiring land improvement]

$$\leqslant \quad \tilde{i}_{j_f}, \qquad j=1,\ldots,4; \qquad (u_{j_f})$$

$\leqslant$ [initial capacity]

$$z_{j_m} \; - \; i_{j_m} \; \leqslant \; 0 \qquad j=1,\ldots,4; \qquad (u_{j_m})$$

[activity level] − [additional capacity] $\leqslant$ [initial capacity]

$$z_{j_1} \; - \; i_{j_1} \; \leqslant \; \tilde{i}_{j_1} \qquad j=5,\ldots,15. \qquad (u_{j_1})$$

[activity level] − [additional capacity] $\leqslant$ [initial capacity]

(1.5) Balances for production capacities of foreign goods and linearization bounds

$$z_{j_p} \; - \; \sum_{s=1}^{S} i^s_{j_p} \; \leqslant \; 0, \qquad j=1,\ldots,4; \qquad (u_{j_p})$$

[activity level] − [additional capacity] $\leqslant$ [initial capacity]

$$i^s_{j_p} \leqslant \tilde{i}^s_{j_p}, \qquad j=1,\ldots,4; \quad s=1,\ldots,S; \quad (v^s_{j_p})$$

[linearization bounds]

$$z_{j_2} \; - \; \sum_{s=1}^{S} i^s_{j_2} \; \leqslant \; 0, \qquad j=5,\ldots,13; \qquad (u_{j_2})$$

[activity level] − [additional capacity] $\leqslant$ [initial capacity]

$$i^s_{j_2} \leqslant \tilde{i}^s_{j_2}, \qquad j=5,\ldots,13; \quad s=1,\ldots,S. \quad (v^s_{j_2})$$

[linearization bounds]

(1.6) Additional constraints, agriculture

$$i_{j_f} \leqslant \tilde{z}_{j_f}, \qquad j=1,2,\ldots,4; \qquad (v_{j_f})$$

[upperbounds, capacity increase of fertile lands, not requiring land improvement]

$$\sum_{j=1}^{4} i^*_{j_f} \quad \leqslant \quad \sum_{s=1}^{S} i^{*s}_{f}; \qquad (u^*_f)$$

[total demand of land improvement by irrigation] $\leqslant$ [total supply of land improvement by irrigation]

$$i_{\mathrm{f}}^{*s} \leqslant \tilde{i}_{\mathrm{f}}^{*s}, \qquad s=1,\ldots,S; \qquad (v_{\mathrm{f}}^{*s})$$

[linearization bounds, land improvement production function]

$$z_{j_{\mathrm{m}}} \leqslant \tilde{z}_{j_{\mathrm{m}}}, \qquad j=1,\ldots,4. \qquad (v_{j_{\mathrm{m}}})$$

[upper bounds on extension of marginal lands]

Competition for fertile land by agricultural production activities

$$\sum_{j=1}^{2}(z_{j_{\mathrm{f}}}+z_{j_{\mathrm{p}}})-\pi_1\sum_{j=1}^{2}\left(i_{j_{\mathrm{f}}}+i_{j_{\mathrm{f}}}^{*}+\sum_{s=1}^{S}i_{j_{\mathrm{p}}}^{s}\right)\leqslant \pi_1\sum_{j=1}^{2}\tilde{i}_{j_{\mathrm{f}}}; \qquad (u_{1\mathrm{a}})$$

$$\sum_{j=3}^{4}(z_{j_{\mathrm{f}}}+z_{j_{\mathrm{p}}})-\pi_2\sum_{j=3}^{4}\left(i_{j_{\mathrm{f}}}+i_{j_{\mathrm{f}}}^{*}+\sum_{s=1}^{S}i_{j_{\mathrm{p}}}^{s}\right)\leqslant \pi_2\sum_{j=3}^{4}\tilde{i}_{j_{\mathrm{f}}}; \qquad (u_{2\mathrm{a}})$$

$$\sum_{\substack{j=1\\ j\neq 3}}^{4}(z_{j_{\mathrm{f}}}+z_{j_{\mathrm{p}}})-\pi_3\sum_{\substack{j=1\\ j\neq 3}}^{4}\left(i_{j_{\mathrm{f}}}+i_{j_{\mathrm{f}}}^{*}+\sum_{s=1}^{S}i_{j_{\mathrm{p}}}^{s}\right)\leqslant \pi_3\sum_{\substack{j=1\\ j\neq 3}}^{4}\tilde{i}_{j_{\mathrm{f}}}; \qquad (u_{3\mathrm{a}})$$

[production] $-\pi$[additional capacities] $\leqslant \pi$[initial capacities]

π_1, π_2 and $\pi_3 < 1$.

(1.7) Balances for export services

$$e_k - i_k^e \leqslant \tilde{i}_k^e, \qquad k=1,\ldots,13. \qquad (u_k^{\mathrm{e}})$$

[export of good k] − [additional capacity] $\leqslant$ [initial capacity]

(1.8) Cost-minimizing labor and capital coefficients[19]

$$l_{j_{\mathrm{f}}} = \frac{r(1-a_{j_{\mathrm{f}}})}{wa_{j_{\mathrm{f}}}}\cdot\kappa_{j_{\mathrm{f}}}, \qquad \text{(no dual price)}$$

$$\kappa_{j_{\mathrm{f}}} = \frac{rw_0(1-a_{j_{\mathrm{f}}})}{r_0wa_{j_{\mathrm{f}}}}\cdot\tilde{\kappa}_{j_{\mathrm{f}}}, \qquad \text{(no dual price)}$$

$\tilde{\kappa}_{j_{\mathrm{f}}}$ is the capital coefficient when $r_0 = 0.15$ and $w_0 = 1$.

[19]We give the formulae for the $z_{j_{\mathrm{f}}}$ activities. The formulae for the $z_{j_{\mathrm{m}}}$, $z_{j_{\mathrm{p}}}$, z_{j_1}, and z_{j_2} activities are identical except for the indices.

(1.9) Labor balance

$$\sum_{j=1}^{4} (l_{j_f} z_{j_F} + l_{j_m} z_{j_m}) + \sum_{j=5}^{15} l_{j_1} z_{j_1}$$

[labor demand, production of home goods]

$$+ \sum_{j=1}^{4} \sum_{s=1}^{S} \rho^s_{j_p} l_{j_p} i^s_{j_p} + \sum_{j=5}^{15} \rho^s_{j_2} l_{j_2} i^s_{j_2} \leqslant \tilde{L}. \qquad (w)$$

+[labor demand, production of "foreign" goods] ≤ [labor supply]

(1.10) Capital balances

$$\sum_{j=1}^{4} (\kappa_{k,j_f} i_{j_f} + \kappa_{k,j_m} i_{j_m}) + \sum_{j=5}^{15} \kappa_{k,j_1} i_{j_1}$$

[capital goods demand, production of home goods]

$$+ \sum_{j=1}^{4} \sum_{s=1}^{S} \rho^s_{j_p} \kappa_{k,j_p} i^s_{j_p} + \sum_{j=5}^{15} \rho^s_{j_2} \kappa_{k,j_2} i^s_{j_2}$$

+[capital goods demand, production of "foreign" goods]

$$+ \sum_{s=1}^{S} \rho^{*s}_{\mathrm{f}} \kappa^*_{k,\mathrm{f}} i^{*s}_{\mathrm{f}} + \sum_{s=1}^{S} \kappa^s_{k,\mathrm{u}} i^s_{\mathrm{u}}$$

+[capital goods demand, land improvement] +[capital goods demand, urban infrastructure]

$$+ \sum_{j=1}^{13} \kappa^e_{k,j} i^e_j \leqslant K_k, \qquad k = 12, 14. \qquad (rp_k)$$

+[capital goods demand, export services] ≤ [available stock of capital goods]

(1.11) Saving–investment identity

$$p_{12} x^*_{12} + p_{14} x^*_{14} - \sigma \sum_{j=1}^{15} p_j x_j = \tilde{A}. \qquad \text{(no dual price)}$$

[investment] − [saving] = [aid]

(1.12) Linear investment path identity

$$K_k \quad - \quad \frac{T}{2} x_k^* \quad = \quad \tilde{K}_k^0, \qquad k = 12, 14.$$

(no dual price)

$$\begin{bmatrix}\text{terminal}\\ \text{available}\\ \text{stock of}\\ \text{capital}\end{bmatrix} - \begin{bmatrix}\text{accumulated}\\ \text{investment}\end{bmatrix} = \begin{bmatrix}\text{initial}\\ \text{available}\\ \text{stock of}\\ \text{capital}\end{bmatrix}$$

(1.13) Utility function and linearization bounds

Utility function

$$U(\cdot) = \sum_{k=1}^{15} x_k - \sum_{k=1}^{15} \sum_{s=1}^{S} \phi_k^s (x_k^{s+} + x_k^{s-}) - \sum_{j=1}^{6} \sum_{s=1}^{S} \phi_{l,j}^s (L_j^{s+} + L_j^{s-}). \quad (\alpha)$$

[utility] = [utility of commodities consumed] − [disutility of migrations]

Definition of consumption of individual commodities

$$x_k \quad - \gamma_k - \beta_k \sum_{h=1}^{15} (x_h - \gamma_h) - \sum_{s=1}^{S} (x_k^{s+} - x_k^{s-}) = 0, \qquad (u_k^c)$$

$$\begin{bmatrix}\text{consump-}\\ \text{tion}\end{bmatrix} - \begin{bmatrix}\text{consumption on}\\ \text{equal prices}\\ \text{Engel ray}\end{bmatrix} - \begin{bmatrix}\text{deviation}\\ \text{from equal}\\ \text{prices Engel}\\ \text{ray}\end{bmatrix} = 0,$$

$$k = 1, \ldots, 15;$$

$$x_k^{s+} \leqslant \tilde{x}_k^{s+}, \qquad k = 1, \ldots, 15; \qquad s = 1, \ldots, S; \qquad (v_{\phi k}^{s+})$$

$$x_k^{s-} \leqslant \tilde{x}_k^{s-}, \qquad k = 1, \ldots, 15; \qquad s = 1, \ldots, S. \qquad (v_{\phi k}^{s-})$$

[linearization bounds]

Definition of migration flows

$$z_{j_t} + z_{j_m} + z_{j_p} - \varepsilon_j P \qquad - \sum_{s=1}^{S} (L_j^{s+} - L_j^{s-}) \qquad = 0,$$

$$j = 1, \ldots, 4; \qquad (u_j^l)$$

$$z_{j_1}+z_{j_2} \quad -\varepsilon_j P \qquad - \sum_{s=1}^{S} (L_j^{s+} - L_j^{s-}) \quad =0, \qquad j=5; \qquad (u_5^l)$$

$$\sum_{j=6}^{15} (z_{j_1}+z_{j_2}) - \varepsilon_6 P \qquad - \sum_{j=6}^{15} \sum_{s=1}^{S} (L_j^{s+} - L_j^{s-}) \quad =0. \qquad (u_6^l)$$

[divergence between sector growth and overall activity level P] − [indicator of migration flows] = 0.

Definition of the indicator of overall activity level

$$P - \sum_{j=1}^{4} v_{j_f}^{*}(z_{j_f}+z_{j_p}) - \sum_{j=1}^{4} v_{j_m}^{*} z_{j_m} - \sum_{j=5}^{15} v_j^{*}(z_{j_1}+z_{j_2}) = 0; \qquad (u^{*l})$$

[indicator] − [weighted average of activity levels] = 0;

$$L_j^{s+} \leqslant \tilde{L}_j^{s+}, \quad j=1,\ldots,15; \quad s=1,\ldots,S; \qquad (v_{\phi j}^{ls+})$$

$$L_j^{s-} \leqslant \tilde{L}_j^{s-}, \quad j=1,\ldots,15; \quad s=1,\ldots,S. \qquad (v_{\phi j}^{ls-})$$

(1.14) Tariffs

$$-t^{*} \quad + \quad \sum_{k=1}^{13} \tau_k^{\mathrm{m}} m_k \quad + (\tau_1^{\mathrm{e}} e_1 + \tau_5^{\mathrm{e}} e_5 + \tau_6^{\mathrm{e}} e_6) = 0;$$

− [total tariffs] + [*ad valorem* import tariffs] + [specific export tariffs] = 0;

(dual price = 1)

$$\tau_k^{\mathrm{m}} - p_k^{\mathrm{m}} \tau_k^{0} = 0, \quad k=1,\ldots,13; \qquad \text{(no dual price)}$$

[definition of the *ad valorem* tariff rate]

$$\tau_6^{\mathrm{e}} - 1 + \mathrm{cost} = 0. \qquad \text{(no dual price)}$$

[definition of the specific export tariff on oil]

2. Submodel for the Middle East oil-producers[20]

(2.1) Supply–demand balance for oil

$$-y_6 \quad + \quad e_6 \quad \leqslant \quad -\tilde{y}_6. \qquad (p_6)$$

$$-[\text{production}]+[\text{exports}]\leqslant -[\text{domestic use}]$$

(2.2) Supply–demand balance for nonoil commodities

$$-y_0 \quad + \sum_{\substack{k=1\\k\neq 6}}^{13} e_k + \quad x_0 \quad \leqslant 0. \qquad (p_0)$$

$$-[\text{production}]+[\text{exports}]+[\text{domestic use}]\leqslant 0.$$

(2.3) Nonoil production capacity balance

$$y_0 \qquad (\sigma_6-\alpha)y_6-\sigma_0 y_0 \quad \leqslant \quad \tilde{y}_0. \qquad (u_0)$$

$$[\text{production}]-\begin{bmatrix}\text{additional capacity}\\ \text{generated by saving}\end{bmatrix}\leqslant\begin{bmatrix}\text{initial}\\ \text{capacity}\end{bmatrix}$$

(2.4) Imports

$$-m_k \quad + \quad \mu_k^6 y_6+\mu_k^0 y_0 \quad =0, \qquad k=1,\ldots,13. \qquad (u_k^{\mathrm{m}})$$

$$-[\text{imports}]+[\text{domestic requirements}]=0,$$

(2.5) Utility function

$$U(\cdot) \quad = \quad x_0. \qquad (\text{dual price}=1)$$

$$[\text{utility}]=\begin{bmatrix}\text{consumption of the}\\ \text{nonoil commodity}\end{bmatrix}$$

[20]The region subscript $i=4$ is dropped to lighten notation.

(2.6) Tariffs

$$-t^* \quad + \quad \tau_6^e e_6 \quad = 0; \qquad \text{(dual price} = 1)$$

$$-\begin{bmatrix}\text{total}\\ \text{tariffs}\end{bmatrix} + \begin{bmatrix}\text{specific export}\\ \text{tariffs on oil}\end{bmatrix} = 0;$$

$$\tau_6^e - 1 + \text{cost} = 0. \qquad \text{(no dual price)}$$

$$\begin{bmatrix}\text{definition of the specific}\\ \text{export tariff on oil}\end{bmatrix}$$

3. Submodel for the developed countries[21]

(3.1) Trade utility–production function and linearization bounds

Utility function

$$U(\cdot) = \quad x_0.$$

$$[\text{utility}] = \begin{bmatrix}\text{available supply of the}\\ \text{consumption-investment good}\end{bmatrix}$$

Production function

$$x_0 \quad - \sum_{k=1}^{5} \sum_{s=1}^{S} \phi_k^s (m-e)_k^s \quad - \sum_{k=6}^{13} \sum_{s=1}^{S} \phi_k^s m_k^s$$

$$\begin{bmatrix}\text{available supply}\\ \text{of the consumption-}\\ \text{investment good}\end{bmatrix} - \begin{bmatrix}\text{component for net}\\ \text{imports of raw}\\ \text{materials}\end{bmatrix} - \begin{bmatrix}\text{component for imports}\\ \text{of manufactured}\\ \text{commodities}\end{bmatrix}$$

$$+ \sum_{k=6}^{13} \phi_k e_k \quad + \sum_{k=1}^{13} \sum_{i=1}^{4} \phi_{ik} (m_{ik}^+ + m_{ik}^-)$$

$$+ \begin{bmatrix}\text{component for exports}\\ \text{of manufactured}\\ \text{commodities}\end{bmatrix} + \begin{bmatrix}\text{cost of switching}\\ \text{sources of supply}\end{bmatrix}$$

$$-g_0 \quad = \quad 0.$$

$$- \begin{bmatrix}\text{impact of domestic}\\ \text{resources}\end{bmatrix} \quad = \quad 0.$$

(dual price = 1)

[21]The region subscript $i=0$ is dropped to lighten notation.

Net imports of raw materials

$$-(m-e)_k \quad + \quad \sum_{s=1}^{S} (m-e)_k^s + \mu_k g_0 \quad = 0. \qquad (p_k^m)$$

$-$[available net imports] + [demand for net imports] $= 0.$

$k = 1, \ldots, 5.$

Imports of manufactured commodities

$$-m_k \quad + \quad \sum_{s=1}^{S} m_k^s + \mu_k g_0 \quad = 0, \qquad (p_k^m)$$

$-$[available imports] + [demand for imports] $= 0,$

$k = 6, \ldots, 13;$

$(m-e)_k^s \leqslant (m \simeq e)_k^s,$ $\quad k = 1, \ldots, 5; \quad s = 1, \ldots, S; \qquad (v_{\phi k}^s)$

$m_k^s \leqslant \tilde{m}_k^s,$ $\quad k = 6, \ldots, 13; \quad s = 1, \ldots, S. \qquad (v_{\phi k}^s)$

[linearization bounds]

Imports balance for good k from region i

$$-m_{ik} \quad + \quad \mu_{ik} m_k \quad + \quad m_{ik}^+ - m_{ik}^- \quad = 0, \qquad (p_{ik}^e)$$

$-$[imports from region i] + [demand for imports on equal prices Engel ray] + [deviations from equal prices Engel ray] $= 0,$

$i = 1, \ldots, 4; \quad k = 1, \ldots, 13;$

$m_{ik}^+ \leqslant \tilde{m}_{ik}^+,$ $\quad i = 1, \ldots, 4; \quad k = 1, \ldots, 13; \qquad (v_{\phi ik}^+)$

$m_{ik}^- \leqslant \tilde{m}_{ik}^-,$ $\quad i = 1, \ldots, 4; \quad k = 1, \ldots, 13. \qquad (v_{\phi ik}^-)$

[bounds on switching sources of supply]

(3.2) Tariffs

$$-t^* \quad + \quad \sum_{k=1}^{13} \sum_{s=1}^{S} \tau_k^m m_k^s \quad = 0. \qquad \text{(dual price} = 1)$$

$-$[total tariffs] + [specific import tariffs] $= 0.$

4. The international balances[22]

(4.1a) Imports of developing countries and Middle East oil-producers

$$-m_{ii'k} \quad + \quad \mu_{ii'k} m_{i'k} \quad = 0, \qquad (p^e_{ik})$$

$$-\begin{bmatrix}\text{exports from} \\ i \text{ to } i'\end{bmatrix} + \begin{bmatrix}\text{demand by} \\ \text{region } i'\end{bmatrix} = 0,$$

$$i' = 1,\ldots,4; \qquad i = 0,\ldots,4;$$
$$i' \neq i; \qquad k = 1,\ldots,13$$

(4.1b) Imports of developed countries[23]

$$-m_{i0k} \quad + \quad \mu_{i0k} m_{0k} - m^+_{i0k} + m^-_{i0k} \quad = 0, \qquad (p^e_{ik})$$

$$-\begin{bmatrix}\text{exports from} \\ i \text{ to } 0\end{bmatrix} + \begin{bmatrix}\text{demand for imports originating} \\ \text{in region } i\end{bmatrix} = 0,$$

$$i = 1,\ldots,4; \qquad k = 1,\ldots,13.$$

(4.2) International supply–demand balances

$$-e_{ik} \quad + \quad \sum_{\substack{i'=0 \\ i' \neq i}}^{4} m_{ii'k} \quad \leqslant 0, \qquad (p^e_{ik})$$

$$\begin{bmatrix}\text{total export} \\ \text{of region } i\end{bmatrix} + \begin{bmatrix}\text{imports of other} \\ \text{regions from } i\end{bmatrix} \leqslant 0,$$

$$i = 0,\ldots,4; \qquad k = 1,\ldots,13.$$

(4.3) Balances of payments

$$\sum_{k=1}^{13} \sum_{\substack{i'=0 \\ i' \neq i}}^{4} p^e_{i'k} m_{i'ik} - \sum_{k=1}^{13} p^e_{ik} e_{ik} \leqslant \tilde{A}_i, \qquad i = 1,2,3. \qquad \text{(no dual price)}$$

$$\begin{bmatrix}\text{total value} \\ \text{of imports}\end{bmatrix} - \begin{bmatrix}\text{total value} \\ \text{of exports}\end{bmatrix} \leqslant [\text{aid}],$$

[22]We make explicit here the country index i dropped for the regional models. Hence, the variables m_k and e_k and the prices p^e_k are relabelled m_{ik}, e_{ik}, and p^e_{ik}.

[23]We repeat here, for the convenience of the reader, the import balances for developed countries studied in section 3 of this appendix.

9.9. Appendix 2: Solution of the model[24]

Initialization step

Pick initial values for:
- the utility levels of the three developing zones, say $\tilde{U}_i$, $i=1$, 2 and 3;
- the *ad valorem* tariffs on imports τ_{ik}^{m}, $i=1,2,3$; $k=1,\ldots,13$;
- the tariff on oil exports τ_{i6}^{e}, $i=1,\ldots,4$;
- the investment levels $x_{i,12}^*$ and $x_{i,14}^*$, $i=1,2,3$;
- using eqs. (1.12),[25] compute the right-hand sides $K_{12,i}$ and $K_{14,i}$ of the capital balances (1.10), $i=1,2,3$;
- the ratio w_i/r_i, $i=1,2,3$;
- deduce the cost-minimizing labor and capital coefficients l_{ij} and $\kappa_{12,i,j}$ and $\kappa_{14,i,j}$, using eqs. (1.8).
- the prices $p_{12,i}$ and $p_{14,i}$, $i=1,2,3$.

Step 1: Setting up the aggregate capital and labor resources constraint

Define, for $i=1,2,3$ (we drop the index to lighten notation), the aggregate capital and labor resources constraint, obtained by multiplying (1.9) by w_i/r_i, (1.10) by $p_{k,i}$ ($k=12,14$) and adding.

Step 2: Function evaluation

Solve the following optimization program:

$$\max U_0(\cdot)+U_4(\cdot)-\sum_{i=0}^{4} t_i^*$$

subject to the following constraints:

(a) For Latin America, Asia, and Africa ($i=1$, 2 and 3):

$$U_i(\cdot)\geqslant \tilde{U}_i;$$

[24]We only discuss the "search for equilibrium utilities" algorithm.
[25]Equation numbers here refer to section 9.8, appendix 1.

(1.1) and (1.2) with x_k^* given;

(1.3) – (1.4) – (1.5) – (1.6) – (1.7);

the set of constraints appearing in (1.13);
(1.14) with τ_k^{m} and τ_6^{e} given; and
the aggregate capital and labor resources constraint defined in step 1.

(b) For the Middle East ($i=4$):
(2.1) – (2.2) – (2.3) – (2.4);
(2.6) with τ_6^{e} given.

(c) For the developed world ($i=0$):
the set of constraints appearing in (3.1);
(3.2).

(d) For the international constraints:
(4.1) – (4.2).

Step 3: Revision of parameters

Read the relevant results (primal and dual) of the function evaluation (step 2). Then,

(1) compute the balances of payments, and adjust the welfare $\tilde{U}_i$ according to ($i=1,\ldots,3$)

$$\tilde{\tilde{U}}_i = \sum_k \left[p_{ik}^{\mathrm{e}} e_{ik} - \sum_{i' \neq i} p_{i'k}^{\mathrm{e}} m_{i'ik} \right] + \tilde{A}_i;$$

(2) compute the *ad valorem* tariffs and set ($i=1,\ldots,3$)

$$\tau_k^{\mathrm{m}} = p_k^{\mathrm{m}} \tau_k^0;$$

(3) compute the export tariffs on oil and set ($i=1,\ldots,4$)

$$\tau_6^{\mathrm{e}} = 1 - \mathrm{cos}t,$$

where cost is the value of inputs needed to produce one unit of oil;

(4) compute the capital and labor requirements to achieve the activity levels attained in the solution of the last function evaluation; to do this, compute the left-hand sides of eqs. (1.9) and (1.10) for $k=12$ and 14; this will give $\bar{L}$, $\bar{K}_{12}$, and $\bar{K}_{14}$;

(5) use eqs. (1.12) for $k=12,14$ to compute the terminal investment levels $\bar{x}_{12}^*$ and $\bar{x}_{14}^*$;

(6) use the saving investment balance (1.11) to compute

$$\chi=(p_{12}\bar{x}_{12}^* + p_{14}\bar{x}_{14}^*):\left(\sigma\sum_j p_j x_j + \tilde{A}\right)$$

and correct accordingly the terminal investment levels: $x_k^* = \chi \bar{x}_k^*$, $k=12,14$, and compute, using (1.12),

$$K_k = \tilde{K}_k^0 + \frac{T}{2} x_k^*, \qquad k=12,14;$$

(7) use the following tâtonnement process to adjust w/r:

$$\left(\frac{w}{r}\right)_{\text{new}} = \left(\frac{w}{r}\right)_{\text{old}} \cdot \frac{p_{12}K_{12}+p_{14}K_{14}}{p_{12}\bar{K}_{12}+p_{14}\bar{K}_{14}} \cdot \frac{\bar{L}}{L};$$

(8) set $w/r=(w/r)_{\text{new}}$ and find the l_j and κ_j values (all j) which solve (1.8);

(9) compare the values of the parameters which have just been set with the values of the parameters of the preceding revision.

If these values are approximately equal, stop.

If not, go to step 1.

9.10. Appendix 3: Dual equations and price formation in GEM[26]

1. Price formation in Latin America, Asia, and Africa[27]

(1.1) Prices for home goods in agriculture, cost on fertile lands

$$p_j \leqslant \sum_{q=1}^{15} a_{q,j_f}^{\mathrm{h}} p_q + \sum_{q=1}^{15} a_{q,j_f}^{\mathrm{f}} u_q^{\mathrm{m}} + u_{j_f} + \sum_{q=1}^{3} u_{q_a} + l_{j_f} w + u_j^l - v_{j_f}^* u^{*l}, \qquad (z_{j_f})$$

$j=1,\ldots,4.$

[26] Primal variables appear at the right-hand side of each equation.

[27] The region subscript $i=1,2,3$ is dropped to lighten notation.

(1.2) Prices for home goods in agriculture, cost on marginal lands

$$p_j \leqslant \sum_{q=1}^{15} a^{\mathrm{h}}_{q,j_{\mathrm{m}}} p_q + \sum_{q=1}^{15} a^{\mathrm{f}}_{q,j_{\mathrm{m}}} u^{\mathrm{m}}_q + u_{j_{\mathrm{m}}} + v_{j_{\mathrm{m}}} + l_{j_{\mathrm{m}}} w + u^l_j - v^*_{j_{\mathrm{m}}} u^*_l, \qquad (z_{j_{\mathrm{m}}})$$

$$j = 1, \ldots, 4.$$

(1.3) Prices and costs for home goods in industry

$$p_j \leqslant \sum_{q=1}^{15} a^{\mathrm{h}}_{q,j_1} p_q + \sum_{q=1}^{15} a^{\mathrm{f}}_{q,j_1} u^{\mathrm{m}}_q + v_{j_1} u_u + u_{j_1} + l_{j_1} w + u^l_{5,6} - v^*_{j_1} u^*_l, \qquad (z_{j_1})$$

$$j = 5, \ldots, 15.$$

(1.4) Prices and costs for foreign goods in agriculture

$$u^m_j \leqslant \sum_{q=1}^{15} a^{\mathrm{h}}_{q,j_{\mathrm{p}}} p_q + \sum_{q=1}^{15} a^{\mathrm{f}}_{q,j_{\mathrm{p}}} u^{\mathrm{m}}_q + u_{j_{\mathrm{p}}} + \sum_{q=1}^{3} u_{q\mathrm{a}} + u^l_j - v^*_{j_{\mathrm{p}}} u^*_l, \qquad (z_{j_{\mathrm{p}}})$$

$$j = 1, \ldots, 4.$$

(1.5) Prices and costs for foreign goods in industry

$$u^m_j \leqslant \sum_{q=1}^{15} a^{\mathrm{h}}_{q,j_2} p_q + \sum_{q=1}^{15} a^{\mathrm{f}}_{q,j_2} u^{\mathrm{m}}_q + v_{j_2} u_u + u_{j_2} + u^l_{5,6} - v^*_{j_2} u^*_l, \qquad (z_{j_2})$$

$$j = 5, \ldots, 15.$$

(1.6) Prices for home goods production capacities in agriculture, costs on fertile lands

$$u_{j_{\mathrm{f}}} \leqslant v_{j_{\mathrm{f}}} - \sum_{q=1}^{3} \pi_q u_{q\mathrm{a}} + \sum_{q=12,14} \kappa_{q,j_{\mathrm{f}}} r p_q, \qquad j = 1, \ldots, 4. \qquad (i_{j_{\mathrm{f}}})$$

(1.7) Prices for home goods production capacities in agriculture, costs on marginal lands

$$u_{j_{\mathrm{m}}} \leqslant \sum_{q=12,14} \kappa_{q,j_{\mathrm{m}}} r p_q, \qquad j = 1, \ldots, 4. \qquad (i_{j_{\mathrm{m}}})$$

(1.8) Prices and costs for home goods production capacities in industry

$$u_{j_1} \leqslant \sum_{q=12,14} \kappa_{q,j_1} r p_q, \qquad j=5,\dots,15. \qquad (i_{j_1})$$

(1.9) Prices and costs for foreign goods production capacities in agriculture

$$u_{j_p} \leqslant v^s_{j_p} + v_{j_f} - \sum_{q=1}^{3} \pi_q u_{qa} + p^s_{j_p} l_{j_p} w + \sum_{q=12,14} \rho^s_{j_p} \kappa_{q,j_p} r p_q, \qquad (i^s_{j_p})$$
$$s=1,\dots,S; \qquad j=1,\dots,4.$$

(1.10) Prices and costs for foreign goods production capacities in industry

$$u_{j_2} \leqslant v^s_{j_2} + \rho^s_{j_2} l_{j_2} w + \sum_{q=12,14} \rho^s_{j_2} \kappa_{q,j_2} r p_q, \qquad (i^s_{j_2})$$
$$s=1,\dots,S; \qquad j=5,\dots,15.$$

(1.11) Dual price of the overall activity level definition

$$u^*_l \geqslant \sum_{q=1}^{6} \varepsilon_q u^l_q. \qquad (P)$$

Now replace u_{j_f} in (1.1),[28] u_{j_m} in (1.2), u_{j_1} in (1.3), u_{j_p} in (1.4), u_{j_2} in (1.5) by (1.6), (1.7), (1.8), (1.9), and (1.10), respectively; also, in (1.1)–(1.5), replace u^*_l by (1.11). This leads, after some rearrangements, to eqs. (1.12)–(1.16).

(1.12) Prices for home goods in agriculture, cost on fertile lands

$$p_j \leqslant \sum_{q=1}^{15} a^{\mathrm{h}}_{q,j_f} p_q + \sum_{q=1}^{15} a^{\mathrm{f}}_{q,j_f} u^{\mathrm{m}}_q + v_{j_f} + \sum_{q=1}^{3} (1-\pi_q) u_{qa}$$

[price] ≤ [unit cost of inputs of home goods] + [unit cost of inputs of foreign goods] + [price of fertile land used by sector j]

$$+ l_{j_f} w + u^l_j - v^*_{j_f} \sum_{q=1}^{6} \varepsilon_q u^l_q + \sum_{q=12,14} \kappa_{q,j_f} r p_q.$$

+ [labor cost] + [capital cost]

[28] Equation numbers here refer to the present section.

(1.13) Prices for home goods in agriculture, cost on marginal lands

$$p_j \leqslant \sum_{q=1}^{15} a^{\mathrm{h}}_{q,j_{\mathrm{m}}} p_q + \sum_{q=1}^{15} a^{\mathrm{f}}_{q,j_{\mathrm{m}}} u^{\mathrm{m}}_q + v_{j_{\mathrm{m}}}$$

[price] ⩽ [unit cost of inputs of home goods] + [unit cost of inputs of foreign goods] + [price of marginal land]

$$+ l_{j_{\mathrm{m}}} w + u^l_j - v^*_{j_{\mathrm{m}}} \sum_{q=1}^{6} \varepsilon_q u^l_q + \sum_{q=12,14} \kappa_{q,j_{\mathrm{m}}} r p_q .$$

+ [labor cost] + [capital cost]

(1.14) Prices and costs for home goods in industry

$$p_j \leqslant \sum_{q=1}^{15} a^{\mathrm{h}}_{q,j_1} p_q + \sum_{q=1}^{15} a^{\mathrm{f}}_{q,j_1} u^{\mathrm{m}}_q + v_{j_1} u_{\mathrm{u}}$$

[price] ⩽ [unit cost of inputs of home goods] + [unit cost of inputs of foreign goods] + [cost of urban infrastructure]

$$+ l_{j_1} w + u^l_{5,6} - v^*_{j_1} \sum_{q=1}^{6} \varepsilon_q u^l_q + \sum_{q=12,14} \kappa_{q,j_1} r p_q .$$

+ [labor cost] + [capital cost]

(1.15) Prices and costs for foreign goods in agriculture

$$u^m_j \leqslant \sum_{q=1}^{15} a^{\mathrm{h}}_{q,j_{\mathrm{p}}} p_q + \sum_{q=1}^{15} a^{\mathrm{f}}_{q,j_{\mathrm{p}}} u^{\mathrm{m}}_q + v_{j_{\mathrm{f}}} + \sum_{q=1}^{3} (1-\pi_q) u_{qa}$$

[price] ⩽ [unit cost of inputs of home goods] + [unit cost of inputs of foreign goods] + [price of fertile lands used by sector j]

$$+ \rho^s_{j_{\mathrm{p}}} l_{j_{\mathrm{p}}} w + u^l_j - v^*_{j_{\mathrm{p}}} \sum_{q=1}^{6} \varepsilon_q u^l_q + v^s_{j_{\mathrm{p}}}$$

+ [labor cost] + [rent on import substitution]

$$+ \sum_{q=12,14} \rho^s_{j_{\mathrm{p}}} \kappa_{q,j_{\mathrm{p}}} r p_q .$$

+ [capital cost]

(1.16) Prices and costs for foreign goods in industry

$$u_j^{\mathrm{m}} \leqslant \sum_{q=1}^{15} a_{q,j_2}^{h} p_q + \sum_{q=1}^{15} a_{q,j_2}^{\mathrm{f}} u_q^{\mathrm{m}} + \nu_{j_2} u_{\mathrm{u}}$$

[price] ≤ [unit cost of inputs of home goods] + [unit cost of inputs of foreign goods] + [cost of urban infrastructure]

$$+\rho_{j_2}^{s} l_{j_2} w + u_{5,6}^{l} - \nu_{j_2}^{*} \sum_{q=1}^{6} \varepsilon_q u_q^{l} + v_{j_2}^{s}$$

+ [labor cost] + [rent on import substitution]

$$+ \sum_{q=12,14} \rho_{j_2}^{s} \kappa_{q,j_2} r p_q .$$

[capital cost]

(1.17) Prices and costs of urban infrastructure services

$$u_{\mathrm{u}} \leqslant v_{\mathrm{u}}^{s} + \sum_{q=12,14} \kappa_{q\mathrm{u}}^{s} r p_q, \qquad s=1,\dots,S. \qquad (i_{\mathrm{u}}^{s})$$

[price] ≤ [urbanization rent] + [capital cost]

(1.18) Price of additional fertile lands

$$u_{\mathrm{f}}^{*} \leqslant v_{\mathrm{f}}^{*s} + \sum_{q=12,14} \rho_{\mathrm{f}}^{*s} \kappa_{q\mathrm{f}}^{*} r p_q, \qquad (i_{\mathrm{f}}^{*s})$$

[price] ≤ [rent new fertile lands] + [capital cost of fertile land creation]

$s=1,\dots,S;\quad j=1,\dots,4;$

$$u_{j_{\mathrm{f}}} + \sum_{q=1}^{3} \pi_q u_{q\mathrm{a}} \leqslant u_{\mathrm{f}}^{*}, \qquad j=1,\dots,4. \qquad (i_{j_{\mathrm{f}}}^{*})$$

[value to j of additional capacity on fertile lands] + [differential rent] ≤ [price]

(1.19) Prices for consumption goods

The relevant dual equations are

$$(1-\lambda_j)p_j+\lambda_j u_j^{\mathrm{m}}+\alpha-u_j^{\mathrm{c}}-\sum_{q=1}^{15}\beta_q u_q^{\mathrm{c}}\geqslant 0, \qquad k=1,\ldots,15; \qquad (x_k)$$

$$-\alpha\phi_j^{s+}+u_j^{\mathrm{c}}+v_{\phi j}^{s+}\geqslant 0, \qquad s=1,\ldots,S; \qquad k=1,\ldots,15; \qquad (x_k^{s+})$$

$$-\alpha\phi_j^{s-}-u_j^{\mathrm{c}}+v_{\phi j}^{s-}\geqslant 0, \qquad s=1,\ldots,S; \qquad k=1,\ldots,15. \qquad (x_k^{s-})$$

Replacing u_j^{c} from the second or third equation in the first and defining p_j^{c} as the consumption price of good j, gives

$$p_j^{\mathrm{c}} =(1-\lambda_j)p_j+\lambda_j u_j^{\mathrm{m}}\geqslant F[\alpha,\beta_q,\phi_q^{s+},\phi_q^{s-},v_{\phi q}^{s+},v_{\phi q}^{s-}]$$

[price] = [cost of the consumption good] ⩾ [marginal utility]

in $F(\cdot)$, β_q,ϕ_q^{s+}, etc. is a shorthand notation for β_q, $q=1,\ldots,15$; ϕ_q^{s+}, $q=1,\ldots,15$, etc.

We do not give an analysis of the dual equations corresponding to L_j^{s+} and L_j^{s-}. The notation is complicated, but it can be shown that the wage differential between a sector and the average wage in the economy equals the marginal disutility of migration, plus a consumer surplus term reflecting the fact that some workers who are not very averse to migration obtain a surplus when a large labor demand in a sector causes a large differential between its wage and the average wage.

(1.20) Export prices[29]

$$p_{ij}^{\mathrm{e}} \leqslant p_{ij} + u_{ij}^{\mathrm{e}} + \tau_{ij}^{\mathrm{e}}, \qquad (e_{ij})$$

[export price] ⩽ [domestic price of the home good] + [price of a unit of additional capacity of export services] + [specific tariff]

$j=1,\ldots,13;$

$$u_{ij}^{\mathrm{e}} \leqslant \sum_{q=12,14}\kappa_{iqj}^{\mathrm{e}} rp_q, \qquad j=1,\ldots,13. \qquad (i_{ij}^{\mathrm{e}})$$

[price of a unit of additional capacity of export services] ⩽ [capital cost]

[29]We make explicit here the country index i.

(1.21) Import prices

The dual equation can be written

$$-u_{ij}^{\mathrm{m}}+p_{ij}^{\mathrm{m}}\tau_{ij}^{0}+\sum_{\substack{i'=0\\ i'\neq i}}^{4}\mu_{i'ij}p_{i'j}^{\mathrm{e}}\geqslant 0, \qquad j=1,\ldots,13. \qquad (m_{ij})$$

Since

$$p_{ij}^{\mathrm{m}}=\sum_{\substack{i'=0\\ i'\neq i}}^{4}\mu_{i'ij}p_{i'j}^{\mathrm{e}}$$

has been defined as the average international price of commodity j imported by country i, we get

$$u_{ij}^{\mathrm{m}} \leqslant p_{ij}^{\mathrm{m}} + \tau_{ij}^{0}p_{ij}^{\mathrm{m}}.$$

[price of the foreign good] ≤ [international price] + [*ad valorem* tariff]

2. Price formation in the Middle East oil-producing countries

We only deal here with export and import prices. The other prices are easy to derive, and only foreign trade prices are interesting here.[30] The dual prices for the semireduced form equations which describe this zone are not very meaningful.

(2.1) Export prices for oil

$$p_{46}^{\mathrm{e}} \leqslant p_{46} + \tau_{46}^{\mathrm{e}}. \qquad (e_{46})$$

[export price of oil] ≤ [cost of oil] + [compensatory levy]

(2.2) Export prices for other goods

$$p_{4j}^{\mathrm{e}} \leqslant p_{40}, \qquad j=1,\ldots,13 \text{ except } 6. \qquad (e_{4j})$$

[export price] ≤ [cost of the nonoil commodity]

[30] The country index 4 refers to Middle East oil-producers.

(2.3) Import prices

$$u^{\mathrm{m}}_{4j} \leqslant \sum_{i'=0}^{3} \mu_{i'4j} p^{\mathrm{e}}_{i'j}, \qquad j=1,\ldots,13. \qquad (m_{4j})$$

Again, since by definition

$$p^{\mathrm{m}}_{4j} = \sum_{i'=0}^{3} \mu_{i'4j} p^{\mathrm{e}}_{i'j}$$

is the average international price of commodity j imported by oil-producers:

$$\underset{\text{[import price]}}{u^{\mathrm{m}}_{4j}} \leqslant \underset{\text{[international price]}}{p^{\mathrm{m}}_{4j}}.$$

3. Price formation in developed countries

(3.1) Export prices

$$\underset{\text{[price]}}{p^{\mathrm{e}}_{0j}} \leqslant \underset{\text{[marginal cost]}}{\phi^{s}_{0j} - v^{s}_{\phi j}}, \qquad j=1,\ldots,5; \qquad (e^{s}_{0j})$$

$$\underset{\text{[price]}}{p^{\mathrm{e}}_{0j}} \leqslant \underset{\text{[marginal cost]}}{\phi_{0j}}, \qquad j=6,\ldots,13. \qquad (e_{0j})$$

(3.2) Import prices

$$\underset{\text{[international price]}}{p^{\mathrm{m}}_{0j}} + \underset{\text{[specific tariff]}}{\tau^{\mathrm{m}}_{0j}} \geqslant \underset{\text{[marginal product]}}{\phi^{s}_{0j}} - \underset{\text{[producer surplus]}}{v^{s}_{\phi j}}, \qquad j=1,\ldots,13; \qquad (m^{s}_{0j})$$

$$\underset{\text{[international price]}}{p^{\mathrm{m}}_{0j}} \leqslant \underset{\text{[weighted average of other countries' export prices]}}{\sum_{i'=1}^{4} \mu_{i'0j} p^{\mathrm{e}}_{i'j}} \qquad j=1,\ldots,13; \qquad (m_{0j})$$

$$p^{\mathrm{e}}_{ij} \leqslant \phi_{ij} + v^{+}_{\phi ij}; \qquad (m^{+}_{ij})$$

$$p^{\mathrm{e}}_{ij} \geqslant -\phi_{ij} - v^{-}_{\phi ij}. \qquad (m^{-}_{ij})$$

[export price of country i] $\geqslant$ [marginal product of good j exported by i in developed countries]

9.11. Appendix 4: The national accounting system in GEM[31]

In GEM, national accounts can be computed in the three usual ways:

(1) as the sum of expenditure components (consumption + investment + exports − imports);
(2) as the sum of income components (labor and capital income); and
(3) as the sum of values added.

The two first accounts can be derived from the fact that the values of the primal and dual objective functions are equal at the optimum. The third account is obtained from the cost equations and production levels at the optimum.

1. National expenditure and national income

The primal objective function of the tariff-ridden Negishi welfare optimum can be written as follows.[32, 33]

(1.1) Primal objective function

$$\sum_{i=1}^{3} \alpha_i \left[\sum_{j=1}^{15} x_j - \sum_{s=1}^{S} \sum_{j=1}^{15} \phi_j^s (x_j^{s+} + x_j^{s-}) - \sum_{s=1}^{S} \sum_{j=1}^{6} \phi^s l_j (L_j^{s+} + L_j^{s-}) \right]$$

[utility of the three developing zones]

$$- \sum_{i=1}^{3} t_i^* + \alpha_4 x_{04} - t_4^*$$

− [tariffs levied in the three developing zones] + [utility in the M. East] − [tariffs levied in the M. East]

$$+ \alpha_5 x_{00} - t_5^* .$$

+ [utility in the developed world] − [tariffs levied by developed countries]

[31] See also Chapter 2, section 2.2.

[32] The region index i is dropped in the three developing regions' terms to lighten notation (unless necessary).

[33] Since the welfare weights can be normalized and the Middle East oil-producers and developed countries are considered as one single zone, $\alpha_4 = \alpha_5 = 1$.

We add to this function the value of world exports minus world imports at world prices

$$\sum_{i=0}^{4} \sum_{j=1}^{13} p_{ij}^{\mathrm{e}} e_{ij} - \sum_{i=0}^{4} \sum_{j=1}^{13} p_{ij}^{\mathrm{m}} m_{ij},$$

which is zero and does not change the value of the function.

(1.2) Dual objective function

$$\sum_{i=1}^{3} \Bigg[- \sum_{j=12,14} (1-\mu_j) x_j^* p_j - \sum_{j=12,14} \mu_j x_j^* u_j^{\mathrm{m}} + \sum_{s=1}^{S} \tilde{i}_{\mathrm{u}}^{s} v_{\mathrm{u}}^{s}$$

$$+ \sum_{j=1}^{4} \tilde{i}_{j_{\mathrm{f}}} u_{j_{\mathrm{f}}} + \sum_{j=5}^{15} \tilde{i}_{j_1} u_{j_1} + \sum_{s=1}^{S} \sum_{j=1}^{4} \tilde{i}_{j_{\mathrm{p}}}^{s} v_{j_{\mathrm{p}}}^{s} + \sum_{s=1}^{S} \sum_{j=5}^{15} \tilde{i}_{j_2}^{s} v_{j_2}^{s}$$

$$+ \sum_{j=1}^{4} \tilde{z}_{j_{\mathrm{f}}} v_{j_{\mathrm{f}}} + \sum_{s=1}^{S} i_{\mathrm{f}}^{*s} v_{\mathrm{f}}^{*s} + \sum_{j=1}^{4} \tilde{z}_{j_{\mathrm{m}}} v_{j_{\mathrm{m}}} + \sum_{q=1}^{3} \pi_q \sum_{j} \tilde{i}_{j_{\mathrm{f}}} u_{q\mathrm{a}}$$

$$+ \sum_{j=1}^{13} \tilde{i}_j^{\mathrm{e}} u_j^{\mathrm{e}} + w\tilde{L} + \sum_{j=12,14} rK_j p_j + \sum_{j=1}^{15} \left(\gamma_j - \beta_j \sum_{h=1}^{15} \gamma_h \right) u_j^{\mathrm{c}}$$

$$+ \sum_{s=1}^{S} \sum_{j=1}^{15} \left(\tilde{x}_j^{s+} v_j^{s+} + \tilde{x}_j^{s-} v_j^{s-} \right) + \sum_{s=1}^{S} \sum_{j=1}^{15} \left(\tilde{L}_j^{s+} v_{\phi j}^{ls+} + \tilde{L}_j^{s-} v_{\phi j}^{ls-} \right) \Bigg]$$

[components relative to the three developing zones]

$$+ \tilde{y}_0 u_0 - \tilde{y}_6 p_6$$

[components relative to the Middle East]

$$+ g_0 - \sum_{j=1}^{13} \mu_j g_0 p_j^{m} + \sum_{s=1}^{S} \sum_{j=1}^{5} (m \simeq e)_j^s v_{\phi j}^s + \sum_{s=1}^{S} \sum_{j=6}^{15} \tilde{m}_j^s v_{\phi j}^s$$

$$+ \sum_{j=1}^{13} \sum_{i=1}^{4} (\tilde{m}_{ij}^{+} v_{\phi ij}^{+} + \tilde{m}_{ij}^{-} v_{\phi ij}^{-}).$$

[components relative to the developed countries]

We set (1.1) equal to (1.2),[34] and the components in (1.1) and (1.2) relative to a region equal to each other.[35] After rearrangement of some terms, this leads to the following.

(1.3) Expenditure–income equality for regions 1, 2, and 3

$$\alpha\left[\sum_j x_j - \sum_s \sum_j \phi_j^s (x_j^{s+} + x_j^{s-})\right]$$

[utility of consumption]

$$- \sum_j \Big(\gamma_j - \beta_j \sum_h \gamma_h\Big) u_j^c - \sum_s \sum_j (\tilde{x}_j^{s+} v_j^{s+} + \tilde{x}_j^{s-} v_j^{s-})$$

− [consumer surplus components]

$$- \sum_s \tilde{i}_u^s v_u^s \qquad - \sum_s \sum_j (\tilde{L}_j^{s+} v_{\phi j}^{ls+} + \tilde{L}_j^{s-} v_j^{ls-})$$

− [urban surplus accruing to workers] − [consumer surplus components for migrations]

$$+ \sum_{j=12,14} (1-\mu_j) x_j^* p_j + \sum_{j=12,14} \mu_j x_j^* u_j^m - t^*$$

+ [investment at current prices] − [tariffs]

$$+ \sum_s \sum_j \phi_{lj}^s (L_j^{s+} + L_j^{s-}) + \sum_j p_{ij}^e e_{ij} - \sum_j p_{ij}^m m_{ij}$$

+ [migration components of the utility function] + [exports] − [imports]

$$= wL + \sum_{j=12,14} rK_j p_j + \sum_j \tilde{i}_{j_f} u_{j_f} + \sum_j \tilde{i}_{j_1} u_{j_1} + \sum_j \tilde{i}_j^e u_j^e$$

= [labor income] + [capital income] + [quasirents]

$$+ \sum_s \sum_j \tilde{i}_{j_p}^s v_{j_p}^s + \sum_s \sum_j \tilde{i}_{j_2}^s v_{j_2}^s + \sum_s i_f^{*s} v_f^{*s}$$

+ [import substitution rents]

$$+ \sum_j \tilde{z}_{j_f} v_{j_f} + \sum_j \tilde{z}_{j_m} v_{j_m} + \sum_q \pi_q \sum_j \tilde{i}_{j_f} u_{qa}.$$

+ [agricultural rents]

[34] Equation numbers refer to the present section.

[35] This can be justified along the lines of section 2.2 above.

The first two terms on the left-hand side give consumption at current prices; the left-hand side therefore represents national expenditure at current prices (at factor cost). The right-hand side of the equality is national income.

(1.4) "National accounts" for the Middle East

$$\alpha_4 x_0 \quad - \quad t^* \quad + \sum_j p^e_{4j} e_{4j} - \sum_j p^m_{4j} m_{4j} = \tilde{y}_0 p_0 - \tilde{y}_6 p_6 .$$

[domestic expenditure] − [tariffs] + [exports] − [imports] = [value of nonoil domestic resources]

Since $\alpha_4 = 1$, and there is no consumer surplus, utility of consumption is equal to consumption at current prices. The left-hand side is thus national expenditure, at factor cost. Note that in the very simple model used to describe this zone, the utility function does not distinguish between the (immediate) utility of consumption and the (discounted future) utility of investment.

(1.5) "National accounts" for the developed countries

$$\alpha_5 x_0 \quad - \quad t^* \quad + \sum_j p^e_{0j} e_{0j} - \sum_j p^m_{0j} m_{0j}$$

[utility of consumption (or production)] − [tariffs] + [exports] − [imports]

$$- \sum_j \mu_j g_0 p^m_j + \sum_s \sum_j (m \simeq e)^s_j v^s_{\phi j} + \sum_s \sum_j \tilde{m}^s_j v^s_{\phi j}$$

$$+ \sum_{i=1}^{4} \sum_j (\tilde{m}^+_{ij} v^+_{\phi ij} + \tilde{m}^-_{ij} v^-_{\phi ij})$$

+ [consumer (or producer) surplus terms]

$$= \quad g_0 .$$

= [value of domestic resources].

Again the first term on the left-hand side is domestic expenditure. As for the Middle East, the utility function does not distinguish the (immediate) utility derived from consumption and the (future discounted) utility from investment.

2. Gross national product for regions 1, 2, and 3

Gross national product (GNP) at market prices is obtained as the sum of values added at current prices, in the various sectors (i.e. agriculture and industry, both for home and foreign goods and export services).

If p_j is the price of a good j, $\Sigma_i a_{ij} p_i$ the cost of inputs and z_j the activity level, value added in the sector is $VA_j = (p_j - \Sigma_i a_{ij} p_i) z_j$.

Using the dual equations (1.12)–(1.16) for agriculture and industry and the second equation of (1.20) for export services, GNP can be defined as

(2.1) $$\sum_{j=1}^{4} \left[p_j - \sum_{q=1}^{15} a^{\mathrm{h}}_{q,j_{\mathrm{f}}} p_q - \sum_{q=1}^{15} a^{\mathrm{f}}_{q,j_{\mathrm{f}}} u^{\mathrm{m}}_q \right] z_{j_{\mathrm{f}}}$$

[value added in agriculture on fertile lands, home goods]

$$+ \sum_{j=1}^{4} \left[p_j - \sum_{q=1}^{15} a^{h}_{q,j_m} p_q - \sum_{q=1}^{15} a^{f}_{q,j_m} u^{m}_q \right] z_{j_m}$$

+[value added in agriculture on marginal lands, home goods]

$$+ \sum_{j=1}^{4} \left[u^{\mathrm{m}}_j - \sum_{q=1}^{15} a^{\mathrm{h}}_{q,j_{\mathrm{p}}} p_q - \sum_{q=1}^{15} a^{\mathrm{f}}_{q,j_{\mathrm{p}}} u^{\mathrm{m}}_q \right] z_{j_{\mathrm{p}}}$$

+[value added in agriculture, foreign goods]

$$+ \sum_{j=5}^{15} \left[p_j - \sum_{q=1}^{15} a^{\mathrm{h}}_{q,j_1} p_q - \sum_{q=1}^{15} a^{\mathrm{f}}_{q,j_1} u^{\mathrm{m}}_q \right] z_{j_1}$$

+[value added in industry, home goods]

$$+ \sum_{j=5}^{15} \left[u^{\mathrm{m}}_j - \sum_{q=1}^{15} a^{\mathrm{h}}_{q,j_2} p_q - \sum_{q=1}^{15} a^{\mathrm{f}}_{q,j_2} u^{\mathrm{m}}_q \right] z_{j_2}$$

+[value added in industry, foreign goods]

$$+ \sum_{j=1}^{13} u^{\mathrm{e}}_j e_j .$$

+[value added by export services].

9.12. Appendix 5: Notation

1. *Indexes used in the notation*

Subscript i: regions $i=0,\ldots,4$.
0: developed countries,
1: Latin America,
2: Asia,
3: Africa,
4: Middle East oil-producers.
This index is usually dropped when the context makes it clear which region is concerned.

Subscript j (or k): goods, j (or k)$=1,\ldots,15$.
1: Noncompeting tropical foods
2: Competing tropical foods
3: Temperate foodstuffs
4: Agricultural raw materials
5: Mining and ores
6: Oil
7: Processed food
8: Textiles and clothing
9: Chemicals and fertilizers
10: Nonmetallic products
11: Basic metals
12: Machinery
13: Other industrial goods
14: Construction
15: Other services

Subscript $j_{\mathrm{f}}, j_{\mathrm{m}}, j_{\mathrm{p}}, j_1$ and j_2.
j_{f}: agricultural home good j produced on fertile lands, $j=1,\ldots,4$;
j_{m}: agricultural home good j produced on marginal lands, $j=1,\ldots,4$;
j_{p}: agricultural foreign good j, $j=1,\ldots,4$;
j_1: industrial home good j, $j=5,\ldots,15$;
j_2: industrial foreign good j, $j=5,\ldots,15$.

Superscript s: step s of the linear approximation of a nonlinear function, $s=1,\ldots,S$.

Superscript h, f, e, m, *.
h: home goods,
f: foreign goods,
e: exports,
m: imports,
*: various uses.

Other indexes are used, and will be defined when needed.

2. *General notation*

Coefficients are denoted by greek letters, except for input–output coefficients and labor coefficients.

Right-hand side constants and exogenous variables bear a tilde (~).

Variables are denoted by lower case or upper case latin letters. For dual prices, the letters p, u and v are used. $\delta_{k,q}$ is the Kronecker δ with $\delta_{k,q}=1$ if $k=q$ and zero otherwise.

3. *Coefficients*

Goods input coefficients (k, $j=1,\ldots,15$). Regions 1, 2, and 3.

- $a^{\mathrm{h}}_{k,j_{\mathrm{f}}}$, $a^{\mathrm{h}}_{k,j_{\mathrm{m}}}$, $a^{\mathrm{h}}_{k,j_{\mathrm{p}}}$, a^{h}_{k,j_1}, and a^{h}_{k,j_2}: input coefficient of home good k used in producing one unit of agricultural home good j on fertile lands (j_{f}), on marginal lands (j_{m}), of agricultural foreign good j (j_{p}), of industrial home good j (j_1), or of industrial foreign good j (j_2).
- $a^{\mathrm{f}}_{k,j_{\mathrm{f}}}$, $a^{\mathrm{f}}_{k,j_{\mathrm{m}}}$, $a^{\mathrm{f}}_{k,j_{\mathrm{p}}}$, a^{f}_{k,j_1}, and a^{f}_{k,j_2}: input coefficient of foreign good k used by activities j_{f}, j_{m}, j_{p}, j_1, and j_2.

Labor coefficients[36] ($j=1,\ldots,15$). Regions 1, 2 and 3

- $a_{j_{\mathrm{f}}}$, $a_{j_{\mathrm{m}}}$, $a_{j_{\mathrm{p}}}$, a_{j_1}, and a_{j_2}: labor exponent of the Cobb–Douglas production function in various activities.
- $l_{j_{\mathrm{f}}}$, $l_{j_{\mathrm{m}}}$, and l_{j_1}: labor input coefficients for producing home goods.
- $\rho^s_{j_{\mathrm{p}}} l_{j_{\mathrm{p}}}$ and $\rho^s_{j_2} l_{j_2}$: labor input coefficient on step s of the labor demand curve for producing foreign goods.

[36] It should be noted that these parameters are fixed coefficients when solving the linear program, but that they are endogenously determined by eqs. (1.8) in section 9.8, appendix 1.

Capital coefficients[37] ($k=12,14$; $j=1,\ldots,15$). Regions 1, 2, and 3.

- κ_{k,j_t}, κ_{k,j_m}, and κ_{k,j_1}: capital input coefficients for producing home goods.
- $\rho^s_{j_p}\kappa_{k,j_p}$ and $p^s_{j_2}\kappa_{k,j_2}$; capital input coefficients on step s of the capital input demand curve for producing foreign goods.
- $\rho^{*s}_f\kappa^*_{k,f}$: capital input coefficient on step s of the capital demand curve for land improvement.
- $\kappa^s_{k,u}$: capital input coefficient on step s of the capital demand curve for urban infrastructure.
- $\kappa^e_{k,j}$: capital input coefficient for export services expansions.
- $\tilde{\kappa}_{j_t}$, $\tilde{\kappa}_{j_m}$, $\tilde{\kappa}_{j_p}$, $\tilde{\kappa}_{j_1}$, and $\tilde{\kappa}_{j_2}$: capital coefficients for an interest rate of 15 percent and wage-rate of 1.

Coefficients appearing in the utility functions

(a) Regions 1, 2, and 3.

- ϕ^s_k: change in utility when consumption of commodity k deviates from equal prices Engel ray consumption by the amount x^{s+}_k on step s.
- $\phi^s_{l,j}$: disutility of migrations coefficients.
- β_k and γ_k: coefficients defining the equal prices Engel ray.
- ε_j, $\nu^*_{j_t}$, $\nu^*_{j_m}$, and ν^*_j: coefficients defining the distribution of the labor force when wages are equal in different sectors.

(b) Developed countries

- ϕ^s_k: product of one unit of net imports ($k=1,\ldots,5$) or imports ($k=6,\ldots,13$) on step s of the import demand function.
- ϕ_k: cost of one unit of exports ($k=6,\ldots,13$).
- ϕ_{ik}: cost of switching sources of supply ($i=1,\ldots,4$).
- $\mu_k g_0$: import demand when domestic resources are g_0.
- μ_{ik}: share of total imports of good k from region i ($i=1,\ldots,4$) when export prices of regions are equal.

Other coefficients

(a) Regions 1, 2, and 3.

- λ_k and $(1-\lambda_k)$: share of consumption covered by foreign (and home) goods ($k=1,\ldots,15$).
- μ_k and $(1-\mu_k)$: share of investment covered by foreign (and home) goods ($k=12,14$).

[37] It should be noted that these parameters are fixed coefficients when solving the linear program, but that they are endogenously determined by eqs. (1.8) in section 9.8, appendix 1.

- ν_{j_1} and ν_{j_2}: coefficient of urban infrastructure services consumption by industry home (j_1) and foreign (j_2) goods ($j=5,\ldots,15$).
- π_1, π_2, and π_3: coefficients in agricultural constraints.
- σ: marginal saving propensity.
- τ_k^0: specific import tariffs ($k=1,\ldots,13$).
- τ_k^e: export levies ($k=1$, 5, and 6).

(b) Middle East oil-producers
- $\sigma_6-\alpha$, and σ_0: saving coefficients out of oil and nonoil products, respectively.
- μ_k^6 and μ_k^0: import coefficients for oil and nonoil sectors, respectively ($k=1,\ldots,13$).
- τ_6^e: export levy on oil.

(c) Developed countries
- τ_k^m: specific import tariffs ($k=1,\ldots,13$).

4. *Primal variables*

(a) *Activity levels in regions 1, 2, and 3*
- z_{j_f}, z_{j_m}, z_{j_p}, z_{j_1}, and z_{j_2}: activity levels of activities producing agricultural home goods on fertile and marginal lands, activities producing foreign agricultural goods, activities producing industrial home and foreign goods ($j=1,\ldots,15$).
- x_k: consumption level good k ($k=1,\ldots,15$).
- x_k^*: investment level good k ($k=12,14$).
- e_k: export level good k ($k=1,\ldots,13$).
- m_k: import level good k ($k=1,\ldots,13$).
- i_{j_f}, i_{j_m}, and i_{j_1}: additional capacities for home goods (agriculture on fertile and marginal lands and industry).
- $i_{j_p}^s$ and $i_{j_2}^s$: step s of additional capacity for foreign goods (agriculture and industry).
- $i_{j_f}^*$: additional land improvement demand to produce good j.
- i_f^{*s}: step s of the supply curve of land improvement.
- i_u^s: step s of the supply curve of infrastructure services.
- i_k^e: supply of additional capacity in export services.
- K_k: stock of capital ($k=12,14$).
- x_k^{s+}, x_k^{s-}: increase or decrease in consumption of good k when prices are not all equal (away from the equal prices Engel ray).

- L_j^{s+}, L_j^{s-}: increases or decreases in migrations, sector j, step s.
- P: indicator of general activity level.
- t^*: total tariffs levied.

(b) *Activity levels in the Middle East*
- y_0 and y_6: nonoil and oil production.
- e_k: export of good k ($k=1,\ldots,13$).
- m_k: import of good k ($k=1,\ldots,13$).
- x_0: utility level.
- t^*: total tariffs levied.

(c) *Activity levels in developed countries*
- x_0: utility level.
- $(m-e)_k^s$ or m_k^s: net import or import level on step s of the net imports or imports component of the trade production utility function, good k ($s=1,\ldots,S$; $k=1,\ldots,13$).
- $(m-e)_k$ or m_k: net import or import level of good k ($k=1,\ldots,13$).
- e_k: export level of good k ($k=1,\ldots,13$).
- m_{ik}: import of good k from region $i=1,\ldots,4$.
- m_{ik}^+, m_{ik}^-: increase or decrease of import of good k from region i if prices are not equal.
- g_0: level of domestic resources.
- t^*: total tariffs levied.

5. *Dual variables*

We only list the most important prices. For others, the definition can be found by looking at the constraint for which the price is defined.

(a) Regions 1, 2, and 3, domestic prices.
p_j: domestic prices of home goods ($j=1,\ldots,15$).
u_j^{m}: domestic prices of foreign goods ($j=1,\ldots,13$).
w: wage rate.
r: interest rate.

(b) International prices.
p_{ij}^{m}: import prices in region i ($i=0,\ldots,4$) of good j ($j=1,\ldots,13$).
p_{ij}^{e}: export prices of region i ($i=0,\ldots,4$) of good j ($j=1,\ldots,13$).

6. *Exogenous variables and right-hand side constants*

(a) Regions 1, 2, and 3.
- $\tilde{z}_{j_f}$ and $\tilde{z}_{j_m}$: upper bounds of extension fertile and marginal lands ($j=1,\ldots,4$).
- $\tilde{i}_{j_f}$ and $\tilde{i}_{j_1}$: initial capacities of home goods production in agriculture (fertile lands) and industry ($j=1,\ldots,15$).
- $\tilde{i}^e_k$: initial capacities of export services ($k=1,\ldots,13$).
- $\tilde{i}^s_{j_p}, \tilde{i}^s_{j_2}, \tilde{i}^s_u, \tilde{i}^{*s}_f$: bound on step variable s, supply of capacities for foreign goods (agriculture and industry) ($j=1,\ldots,15$), urban infrastructure and land improvement.
- $\tilde{K}^0_k$: initial capital stock ($k=12,14$).
- $\tilde{L}$: labor supply.
- $\tilde{A}$: aid received.
- $\tilde{x}^{s+}_j, \tilde{x}^{s-}_j$: bound on step variable s, substitution in consumption ($j=1,\ldots,15$).
- $\tilde{L}^{s+}_j, \tilde{L}^{s-}_j$: bound on step variable s, migration ($j=1,\ldots,15$).

(b) Middle East oil-producers.
- $\tilde{y}_0$ and $\tilde{y}_6$: initial capacity of nonoil and oil production.

(c) Developed countries.
- $\tilde{m}^+_{ik}, \tilde{m}^-_{ik}$: bounds on import substitution possibilities originating from various regions ($i=1,\ldots,4$; $k=1,\ldots,13$).

CHAPTER 10

Data

This chapter surveys the data available to construct GEM-type models, and describes the choice of coefficients of GEM. For the most part we did not try to estimate these coefficients directly from the basic statistical sources. This would have involved a very large data-gathering effort, whereas we wanted the main thrust of our effort to bear on the improvement of methodology. Refined estimation of coefficients also would really make sense only for a more disaggregated model distinguishing more regions and commodity categories than GEM.

We chose the coefficients of GEM on the basis of an extensive survey of the available quantitative literature on the world economy and in particular on the economy of developing countries. Our computational experience suggests that it is feasible, today, to solve substantially more detailed GEM-type models, opening the way to practical applications of the approach. What is required is a basic improvement of the data base, which was not adequate at the time the model was built. It appears, however, that as a result of work recently accomplished or underway, such a data base is being created gradually.

Sections 10.1 to 10.3 describe respectively the developing countries' model, the oil-producers' model, and the developed countries' model for the low import price elasticities version. In section 10.4 we turn to the coefficients and data which had to be changed to take into account high import price elasticities in developed countries.

10.1. The models for Latin America, Asia, and Africa

10.1.1. National accounts, international trade, and production

Table 10.1 reproduces for the year 1969 aggregate national accounts for the regions considered in the model. These data were obtained by adding individual national accounts published by the United Nations; the result was extrapolated to cover missing countries.

Table 10.1
Aggregate national accounts, 1969 (billions of $).

	Latin America	Asia	Africa	M. East	Developed
Private and collective consumption	102.0	101.0	46.0	14.0	...
Investments	23.0	19.5	6.5	4.5	...
Exports	11.9	9.0	7.5	10.0	36.2
Imports	12.6	15.7	8.2	3.3	34.7
Gross national product	124.3	113.8	51.8	25.2	1600.0

Table 10.2 breaks down consumption and investment by commodities. Since there is little data on the structure of consumption for individual countries within a region or for the region as a whole, the Mexican structure was adopted for Latin America, the Indian for Asia, and a reasonable structure was used for Africa; 40 percent of investment was allocated to machinery and 60 percent to construction.

Table 10.3 breaks down exports and imports by regions and commodities. Calculations are based on United Nations data.

Table 10.4 gives the production structure in developing regions. These data were generated, using input–output tables (to be described in section 10.1.2) and the estimates of final demand, obtained from tables 10.2 and 10.3, by adding consumption, investment and exports, and subtracting imports.

10.1.2. Input–output coefficients

Although there exists by now a very large number of input–output tables, it is very difficult to compare these across countries or over time. Apart from the European Economic Community (EEC) and the Economic Commission for Europe (ECE), international statistical agencies have not made a systematic effort to collect tables and to make these more comparable by establishing standardized accounting rules of the type which exist for national accounts. Such rules exist only for EEC countries. In the ECE, Skolka and Royer have adjusted the tables of a number of countries, mostly developed, to make them more comparable. Large collections of input–output tables exist in the Center for Research for Economic Growth

Table 10.2
Consumption and investment—breakdown by commodities (millions of $).

	Latin America		Asia		Africa	
	Consumption	Investment	Consumption	Investment	Consumption	Investment
1. Tropical noncompeting foodstuffs	1 020	—	1 310	—	1 380	—
2. Tropical competing foodstuffs	1 940	—	2 630	—	2 760	—
3. Temperate foodstuffs	6 430	—	34 850	—	4 600	—
4. Agricultural raw materials	920	—	1 010	—	460	—
5. Ores and nonferrous metals	—	—	100	—	—	—
6. Oil	18 400	—	300	—	920	—
7. Processed food	16 630	—	12 120	—	6 300	—
8. Textiles	6 940	—	6 770	—	5 110	—
9. Chemicals	3 460	—	1 520	—	1 200	—
10. Nonmetallic products	—	—	300	—	140	—
11. Basic metals	—	—	—	—	—	—
12. Machinery	3 770	9 000	2 830	8 000	1 380	2 500
13. Other industry	1 630	—	3 740	—	1 700	—
14. Construction	—	14 000	—	11 500	—	4 000
15. Services	57 420	—	33 520	—	20 050	—
Total	102 000	23 000	101 000	19 500	46 000	6 500

Table 10.3

International trade—breakdown by commodities and regions (millions of $).

	Latin America		Asia		Africa		Middle East		Developed		Total	
	Exports	Imports	Exports	Imports	Exports	Imports	Exports	Imports	Exports	Imports	Exports	Imports
1. Tropical noncompeting foodstuffs	2 130	10	460	10	1 220	—	—	70	—	3 720	3 810	3 810
2. Tropical competing foodstuffs	1 540	820	1 080	1 440	1 170	810	170	120	2 330	3 100	6 290	6 290
3. Temperate foodstuffs	850	280	120	740	110	190	—	110	1 320	1 080	2 400	2 400
4. Agricultural raw materials	1 270	650	1 890	1 140	1 150	440	30	150	1 200	3 160	5 540	5 540
5. Ores and nonferrous metals	2 030	190	720	240	1 700	60	—	30	560	4 490	5 010	5 010
6. Oil	2 680	550	510	740	1 140	70	9 580	660	950	12 840	14 860	14 860
7. Processed food	220	70	150	80	10	70	—	40	270	390	650	650
8. Textiles	100	330	1 590	970	70	690	30	190	1 930	1 540	3 720	3 720
9. Chemicals	220	1 140	70	1 500	70	860	10	270	3 760	360	4 130	4 130
10. Nonmetallic products	—	40	—	30	160	10	—	10	90	160	250	250
11. Basic metals	290	750	160	930	320	500	—	130	2 320	780	3 090	3 090
12. Machinery	120	5 690	420	5 800	20	3 440	20	1 090	16 020	580	16 600	16 600
13. Other industry	430	2 130	1 840	2 130	370	1 030	140	420	5 420	2 490	8 200	8 200
Total	11 880	12 650	9 010	15 750	7 510	8 170	9 980	3 290	36 170	34 690	74 550	74 550

Table 10.4
Production—breakdown by commodities (millions of $).

	Latin America	Asia	Africa
1. Tropical noncompeting foodstuffs	3 900	2 800	4 100
2. Tropical competing foodstuffs	3 700	3 800	3 900
3. Temperate foodstuffs	9 400	46 500	5 300
4. Agricultural raw materials	4 900	6 600	2 800
5. Ores and nonferrous metals	3 100	2 700	1 700
6. Oil	10 100	3 200	3 700
7. Processed food	22 000	13 700	7 700
8. Textiles	9 700	11 500	6 300
9. Chemicals	6 400	2 000	1 800
10. Nonmetallic products	2 200	1 800	1 300
11. Basic metals	3 800	4 900	1 800
12. Machinery	11 900	10 000	4 900
13. Other industry	4 300	7 800	3 400
14. Construction	14 700	12 200	4 400
15. Services	77 500	36 100	27 100

at Brandeis, and in the group directed by Bottomley at the University of Bradford. This group has aggregated 130 tables into 10 sectors. Stern and Lewis (1977) have recently assembled and analyzed a collection of comparable tables. Last, but not least, the gradual implementation of the UN System of National Accounts as the basis of national accounting systems outside of socialist countries should eventually greatly improve the availability of reasonably comparable input–output tables for different countries.

It is in principle possible to make *ad hoc* corrections for at least the most important discrepancies between tables, and this has been done, e.g. by Lamel et al. (1972), in a study which unfortunately encompassed developed countries mainly. Chenery and Watanabe (1958) have studied how input–output patterns change with economic development. The most exhaustive study, is however, Stern's paper quoted above. None of these studies finds systematic changes in technical coefficients between countries, except for agriculture; it is the relative importance of branches which differs in a systematic way as a function of economic development rather than the structure of their inputs. Comparisons over time of course reveal marked changes in input coefficients in response to technical change.

As Balassa (1971), for example, has noted, differences in prices are a hidden but important cause of discrepancies between input–output tables. Differences in price structure between countries are large and converting input–output matrices into a common price base would change some

Table 10.5
Input–output coefficients—Latin America (per thousand).

	Agriculture								Other sectors[c]										
	Fertile lands[a]				Marginal lands[b]														
	1	2	3	4	1	2	3	4	5	6	7	8	9	10	11	12	13	14	15
1. Tropical noncompeting foodstuffs	54	—	—	—	70	—	—	—	—	—	21	—	—	—	—	—	13	—	—
2. Tropical competing foodstuffs	—	54	—	—	—	70	—	—	—	—	31	—	22	—	—	—	13	—	—
3. Temperate foodstuffs	—	—	54	—	—	—	70	—	—	—	82	—	3	—	—	—	13	—	—
4. Agricultural raw materials	—	—	—	54	—	—	—	70	3	—	99	71	28	—	—	2	13	—	—
5. Ores and nonferrous metals	—	—	—	—	—	—	—	—	163	9	1	—	7	30	68	9	1	11	—
6. Oil	20	20	20	20	25	25	25	25	36	309	15	14	15	87	59	17	47	9	12
7. Processed food	53	53	53	53	66	66	66	66	3	1	164	4	15	2	3	3	4	3	2
8. Textiles	18	18	18	18	23	23	23	23	3	2	3	214	12	5	6	8	6	3	2
9. Chemicals	27	27	27	27	33	33	33	33	27	7	5	59	135	22	8	48	20	16	8
10. Nonmetallic products	—	—	—	—	—	—	—	—	3	1	10	1	7	80	15	5	2	115	—
11. Basic metals	2	2	2	2	3	3	3	3	17	3	5	5	8	14	203	130	7	91	3
12. Machinery	10	10	10	10	13	13	13	13	16	7	15	12	15	24	17	120	20	87	11
13. Other industries	7	7	7	7	9	9	9	9	43	8	23	21	40	78	28	26	146	48	14
14. Construction	4	4	4	4	5	5	5	5	6	3	1	3	2	10	5	1	9	4	5
15. Services	42	42	42	42	53	53	53	53	75	44	113	144	140	131	118	85	107	143	121
Total	237	237	237	237	300	300	300	300	395	394	588	548	449	483	530	422	421	530	178

[a] $a_{kj_f} = a_{kj_p}$ coefficients; $j = 1, \ldots, 4$.
[b] a_{kj_m} coefficients; $j = 1, \ldots, 4$.
[c] $a_{kj_1} = a_{kj_2}$ coefficients; $j = 5, \ldots, 15$.

Table 10.6

Input–output coefficients—Asia (per thousand)

	Agriculture								Other sectors[c]										
	Fertile lands[a]				Marginal lands[b]														
	1	2	3	4	1	2	3	4	5	6	7	8	9	10	11	12	13	14	15
1. Tropical noncompeting foodstuffs	128	—	—	—	185	—	—	—	—	—	46	—	—	—	—	—	9	—	—
2. Tropical competing foodstuffs	—	128	—	—	—	185	—	—	—	—	69	—	5	—	—	—	17	—	—
3. Temperate foodstuffs	—	—	128	—	—	—	185	—	—	—	461	—	—	—	—	—	4	—	—
4. Agricultural raw materials	—	—	—	128	—	—	—	185	—	—	69	218	20	3	—	3	33	16	—
5. Ores and nonferrous metals	—	—	—	—	—	—	—	—	47	—	2	5	33	124	42	2	25	—	34
6. Oil	1	1	1	1	1	1	1	1	—	446	1	1	4	14	4	3	4	3	41
7. Processed food	11	11	11	11	13	13	13	13	—	—	45	3	90	—	—	—	1	—	—
8. Textiles	—	—	—	—	—	—	—	—	—	—	6	317	6	48	—	2	39	—	—
9. Chemicals	11	11	11	11	13	13	13	13	—	10	8	21	140	30	9	17	28	11	—
10. Nonmetallic products	—	—	—	—	—	—	—	—	2	—	2	—	21	12	—	2	—	113	—
11. Basic metals	—	—	—	—	—	—	—	—	—	75	9	1	21	5	288	169	3	174	—
12. Machinery	—	—	—	—	—	—	—	—	32	—	—	1	—	—	—	115	—	—	91
13. Other industries	2	2	2	2	2	2	2	2	41	9	12	23	49	46	24	46	125	72	29
14. Construction	4	4	4	4	5	5	5	5	6	3	1	3	2	10	5	1	9	4	5
15. Services	5	5	5	5	6	6	6	6	532	51	8	2	—	93	57	—	13	—	—
Total	162	162	162	162	225	225	225	225	660	594	739	595	391	385	429	360	310	393	200

[a] $a_{kj_f} = a_{kj_p}$ coefficients; $j = 1,\ldots,4$.

[b] a_{kj_m} coefficients; $j = 1,\ldots,4$.

[c] $a_{kj_1} = a_{kj_2}$ coefficients; $j = 5,\ldots,15$.

Table 10.7

Input–output coefficients—Africa (per thousand).

	Agriculture								Other sectors[c]										
	Fertile lands[a]				Marginal lands[b]														
	1	2	3	4	1	2	3	4	5	6	7	8	9	10	11	12	13	14	15
1. Tropical noncompeting foodstuffs	39	—	—	—	60	—	—	—	—	—	154	—	—	—	—	—	43	—	—
2. Tropical competing foodstuffs	—	39	—	—	—	60	—	—	—	—	51	—	53	—	—	—	43	—	—
3. Temperate foodstuffs	—	—	39	—	—	—	60	—	—	—	51	—	—	—	—	—	43	—	—
4. Agricultural raw materials	—	—	—	39	—	—	—	60	—	—	51	104	158	—	—	—	43	—	—
5. Ores and nonferrous metals	—	—	—	—	—	—	—	—	—	—	2	—	11	—	1	—	—	—	—
6. Oil	10	10	10	10	13	13	13	13	91	—	12	3	2	28	1	9	2	32	40
7. Processed food	4	4	4	4	5	5	5	5	—	—	173	1	18	—	—	—	—	—	—
8. Textiles	4	4	4	4	5	5	5	5	—	—	3	243	4	—	—	1	1	—	8
9. Chemicals	20	20	20	20	25	25	25	25	4	4	8	48	238	4	5	15	19	15	1
10. Nonmetallic products	1	1	1	1	1	1	1	1	6	—	1	—	—	380	1	1	3	109	—
11. Basic metals	1	1	1	1	1	1	1	1	10	—	—	2	—	12	487	137	17	71	—
12. Machinery	28	28	28	28	35	35	35	35	96	14	62	19	58	44	13	356	49	66	29
13. Other industries	4	4	4	4	5	5	5	5	13	2	30	19	32	33	10	34	224	72	21
14. Construction	1	1	1	1	1	1	1	1	3	1	2	1	2	1	1	2	2	10	9
15. Services	64	64	64	64	80	80	80	80	126	12	53	58	76	78	66	59	88	87	136
Total	176	176	176	176	231	231	231	231	349	33	653	498	652	380	585	614	577	462	244

[a] $a_{kj_f} = a_{kj_p}$ coefficients; $j = 1, \ldots, 4$.

[b] a_{kj_m} coefficients; $j = 1, \ldots, 4$.

[c] $a_{kj_1} = a_{kj_2}$ coefficients; $j = 5, \ldots, 15$.

Table 10.8
Import coefficients (per thousand).

	I			II			III
	Latin America	Asia	Africa	Latin America	Asia	Africa	Middle East
1. Tropical noncompeting foodstuffs	—	—	—	—	—	—	6
2. Tropical competing foodstuffs	420	550	290	—	—	—	10
3. Temperate foodstuffs	40	20	40	—	—	—	8
4. Agricultural raw materials	—	—	—	130	170	160	12
5. Ores and nonferrous metals	—	—	—	60	90	40	2
6. Oil	—	—	—	60	230	20	13
7. Processed food	4	10	10	—	—	—	2
8. Textiles	50	140	140	—	—	—	14
9. Chemicals	—	—	—	160	730	480	22
10. Nonmetallic products	—	—	—	20	20	—	—
11. Basic metals	—	—	—	200	190	280	10
12. Machinery	—	—	—	480	580	700	86
13. Other industries	—	—	—	500	270	300	34

I: as per thousand of consumption $(1-\lambda_k)$.
II: as per thousand of production (μ_k).
III: as per thousand of GNP $(\mu_k^6 = \mu_k^0)$.

technical coefficients substantially. The necessary price data is almost totally lacking, however, since in most countries statisticians collect only a limited number of prices, and publish even fewer of them. The recent work by Kravis and associates (1975) on international comparisons of purchasing power improves this situation and opens an avenue to building comparable data on intermediate input costs.

An accurate comparison of input–output technologies is therefore very difficult, if not impossible, at present, and in GEM it was felt best to opt for a simple solution. It was decided to select input–output tables for three countries, one in each continent, and to consider these as representative of the interindustry structure for the whole continent. The three tables are a Mexican tableau (Goreux and Manne, 1973) for Latin America, an Indian tableau (Santhanam and Patil, 1972) for Asia, and one for the Ivory Coast (Goreux, 1977) for Africa. The Mexican and Indian tableaux were used without modification, while the third was modified to eliminate distortions resulting from specific features of the Ivory Coast. These tableaux are reproduced in tables 10.5, 10.6 and 10.7.

The input coefficients a^{h}_{ij} and a^{f}_{ij} for home and foreign goods are derived as follows. Let a_{ij} be an input coefficient of good i into activity j in tables 10.5–10.7. Let μ_i be the import coefficient for good i. Then $a^{\mathrm{h}}_{ij}=(1-\mu_i)a_{ij}$ and $a^{\mathrm{f}}_{ij}=\mu_i a_{ij}$. For the μ_i coefficients see table 10.8.

Except for agriculture,[1] intermediate input coefficients are assumed to be fixed. This is an oversimplification, and there is enough evidence to suggest that a broad range of input coefficients are not insensitive to prices. It would ideally be desirable to specify production alternatives to reproduce substitutions between, say, different textile fibers or energy forms. It is doubtful that this is worth doing in a model which is as strongly aggregated as GEM.

10.1.3. Import coefficients

The import coefficients given in table 10.8 were obtained by dividing 1969 imports of different traded goods derived from trade data by the total use (production or consumption) of each of these goods in Latin America, Asia, and Africa.

It is assumed that the imports of a category of goods into each developing region are allocated in fixed proportions between the various exporters

[1]See section 10.1.8.

Table 10.9
Imports—base year shares of regions in total trade.

	Latin America	Asia	Africa	Middle East	Developed
1. Tropical noncompeting foodstuffs	0.56	0.12	0.32	—	—
2. Tropical competing foodstuffs	0.24	0.17	0.19	0.03	0.37
3. Temperate foodstuffs	0.35	0.05	0.05	—	0.55
4. Agricultural raw materials	0.23	0.34	0.21	0.01	0.21
5. Ores and nonferrous metals	0.41	0.14	0.34	—	0.11
6. Oil	0.18	0.03	0.08	0.65	0.06
7. Processed food	0.33	0.22	0.02	—	0.43
8. Textiles	0.02	0.41	0.02	0.01	0.54
9. Chemicals	0.05	0.02	0.02	—	0.91
10. Nonmetallic products	—	—	0.50	—	0.50
11. Basic metals	0.09	0.05	0.11	—	0.75
12. Machinery	0.01	0.02	—	—	0.97
13. Other industries	0.05	0.22	0.05	0.02	0.66

of that good. It would ideally be desirable to calculate these shares from a detailed table of bilateral trade flows between the five regions of GEM. It appeared simpler to use a shortcut and to infer shares of exporters on each trade partner's market from their shares of world exports of each group of products. Specifically we defined $\bar{\varepsilon}_{ij}$ as

$$\bar{\varepsilon}_{ij} = \frac{e_i^0}{\sum\limits_{k \neq j} e_k^0},$$

where e_i^0 is the total export of zone i in some base year 0. The $\bar{\varepsilon}_{ij}$ matrices are easy to construct and will therefore not be reproduced. The data used to build these matrices are reproduced in table 10.9 which shows the shares of each region in world imports by commodity. Table 10.9 is based on table 10.3.

10.1.4. Initial production capacities

The construction of the capacity balances requires data on initial capacities. These are equal to the capacities available in the base year, increased

Table 10.10
Initial production capacities[a] (millions of $).

	Latin America	Asia	Africa
1. Tropical competing foodstuffs	4 500	3 500	4 500
2. Tropical noncompeting foodstuffs	4 500	4 500	4 500
3. Temperate foodstuffs	11 500	56 000	6 000
4. Agricultural raw materials	6 000	8 000	3 000
5. Ores and nonferrous metals	4 000	3 500	2 000
6. Oil	12 000	4 000	4 000
7. Processed food	30 000	19 000	9 000
8. Textiles	13 500	13 500	8 000
9. Chemicals	12 000	3 500	2 000
10. Nonmetallic products	4 000	3 000	2 000
11. Basic metals	6 500	6 500	2 000
12. Machinery	22 000	15 000	5 500
13. Other industries	6 000	12 000	4 000
14. Construction	20 000	18 000	5 500
15. Services	105 000	54 000	34 000

[a] These capacities are the right-hand sides of the supply–demand balance for capacities for home goods ($\tilde{i}_{j_t}$, $j=1,\ldots,4$; $\bar{i}_{j_1}$, $j=5,\ldots,15$). Initial capacities for import substituting goods are zero.

by investments which are decreasing linearly from the base year level to zero in the terminal year.

To simplify the model it was assumed that base year output consisted entirely of home goods: there was no initial production of import substituting goods.[2]

Further details can be found in section 4.2.1. The data used are given in table 10.10.

10.1.5. Export capacities

The infrastructure bottlenecks which hamper the growth of exports are represented by export capacities. These were fixed at twice the export volume in 1969 (table 10.11).

10.1.6. Production functions describing imports of capital and labor for production of home goods

It was necessary to specify production function for the 15 sectors in the

[2] This can be rationalized by assuming that import substituting activities in the initial year mature sufficiently during the model's ten-year planning period to be considered as home goods producers in the horizon year.

Table 10.11
Export capacities[a] (millions of $).

	Latin America	Asia	Africa
1. Tropical noncompeting foodstuffs	4250	920	2450
2. Tropical competing foodstuffs	3050	2150	2350
3. Temperate foodstuffs	1700	250	220
4. Agricultural raw materials	2550	3800	2300
5. Mining	4050	1450	3400
6. Oil	5360	1020	2290
7. Processed food	450	—	20
8. Textiles	200	3200	130
9. Chemicals	450	140	140
10. Nonmetallic products	—	—	320
11. Basic metals	580	330	650
12. Machinery	250	840	40
13. Other industry	850	3680	740

[a]These capacities are the right-hand sides of the balances for export services ($\tilde{i}_k^e$, $k=1,\ldots,13$).

three developing regions. This implied selecting

(a) the form of the function;
(b) the capital and labor intensities in the different sectors; and
(c) the efficiency of each industry in each region.

As to the first point, there is a large literature on production functions in developing countries but this is very scattered and of uneven quality. Only a few of the existing studies have been published in readily available journals and books. Other estimates are given in journals which do not have a broad international circulation, or in Ph.D. theses.

By and large, Gaude's paper confirms that, as has been found for developed countries, estimates of the elasticity of substitution are very sensitive to differences in samples and estimation procedures. The Cobb–Douglas function appears as a sensible compromise, if only because other more refined functions are not demonstrably superior. On grounds of simplicity, we decided to use Cobb–Douglas functions in GEM to account for the contributions of labor and capital to value added.

Given the efficiency parameter α_j, and the capital and labor elasticities a_j and $(1-a_j)$ of the Cobb–Douglas production function of sector j, the cost minimizing capital and labor coefficients are given by the following functions of wages w and interest rate r:

$$\kappa_j = \frac{1}{\alpha_j}\left[\frac{r(1-a_j)}{wa_j}\right]^{a_j-1},$$

$$l_j = \left[\frac{r(1-a_j)}{wa_j}\right]\kappa_j.$$

It can be checked that the equations are consistent with the relation

$$\kappa_j = l_j^{(a_j-1)/a_j}\alpha_j^{-1/a_j}$$

described in Chapter 9.

The a_j coefficients were chosen on the basis of those used by Goreux and Manne (1973). They were used to divide sectors into three classes: labor-intensive, capital-intensive, and other industries, with capital elasticities $a_j = \frac{1}{3}, \frac{5}{6}$, and $\frac{2}{3}$, respectively. The classification, given in table 10.12, is the same for the three developing regions.

Table 10.12
Capital and labor exponents of Cobb–Douglas functions
(home goods and import substituting goods).

	Capital exponent	Labor exponent
1. Tropical noncompeting foodstuffs[a]	1/3	2/3
2. Tropical competing foodstuffs[a]	1/3	2/3
3. Temperate foodstuffs[a]	1/3	2/3
4. Agricultural raw materials[a]	1/3	2/3
5. Ores and nonferrous metals	5/6	1/6
6. Oil	5/6	1/6
7. Processed food	2/3	1/3
8. Textiles	1/3	2/3
9. Chemicals	2/3	1/3
10. Nonmetallic products	1/3	2/3
11. Basic metals	5/6	1/6
12. Machinery	1/3	2/3
13. Other industries	2/3	1/3
14. Construction	1/3	2/3
15. Services[a]	2/3	1/3

[a]For these sectors the capacity existing at the beginning of the period is assumed to embody "traditional" labor-intensive processes. The labor and capital exponents for this initial capacity are assumed to be equal to 5/6 and 1/6, respectively.

The efficiency parameters α_j were not inferred directly. Instead, we selected capital coefficients $\tilde{\kappa}_j$ assumed to correspond to a base year interest rate of 15 percent and wage rate of 1. Since capital coefficients for given factor prices are inversely proportional to α_j, they are obviously valid indicators of efficiency. The reason for this roundabout approach is that there is much more data on capital coefficients than on comparative efficiency of industries.

There exist some primary data on capital–output ratios, but unfortunately these are very weak for developing countries. In principle, it is possible to determine capital stocks by cumulating investment over a sufficiently long period; but only a few developing countries have detailed series of investment at constant prices. In a few cases there exist industrial censuses; but the information they give on capital stocks reflect historical acquisition costs rather than the current value of the equipment. Finally, when preparing projects most planning offices make use of tables giving the estimated cost of different types of factories. These tables are based on data obtained from engineering firms which specialize in building key on door plants, as well as past experience of state enterprises and investment banks. These data are however not public.

The only readily available data on capital coefficients are the estimates embodied in existing linear programming and dynamic input–output models for developing countries.[3] This is secondary data, however: the coefficients are based on detailed analysis of primary data, but include, to a substantial extent, the judgment of their authors. Since such models only exist for a small number of countries and use different industry classification, they are not accurate enough to allow for valid comparisons between countries.

We therefore used this source of information to ascertain only the order of magnitude of capital and labor intensities of production, and not as a basis of information on intercountry differences in the capital coefficients of industries. For Latin America we adopted the capital coefficients used by Goreux and Manne (1973). The choice of capital coefficients for other regions reflected our *a priori* judgment on the comparative efficiency of industries in different regions.

This judgment was based on the export performance of the three regions for different commodities. In a seminal article, McDougall (1951, 1952) showed that performance in foreign trade is a good indicator of comparative advantage. This result, confirmed by later studies, can be used to infer

[3]See, for example, Goreux and Manne (1973), Clark (1970), Weisskopf (1971), and Eckhaus and Parikh (1968).

Table 10.13

Capital coefficients—production of home goods and land improvement enhancing (per thousand).

	Production of home goods[a]		
	Latin America	Asia	Africa
1. Tropical noncompeting foodstuffs			
Machinery	650	800	950
Construction	750	900	1 100
2. Tropical competing foodstuffs			
Machinery	650	800	950
Construction	750	900	1 100
3. Temperate foodstuffs			
Machinery	650	800	950
Construction	750	900	1 100
4. Agricultural raw materials			
Machinery	650	800	950
Construction	750	900	1 100
5. Ores and nonferrous metals			
Machinery	500	625	700
Construction	450	575	650
6. Oil			
Machinery	250	300	400
Construction	200	250	300
7. Processed food			
Machinery	550	550	650
Construction	400	400	500
8. Textiles			
Machinery	750	750	900
Construction	250	250	300
9. Chemicals			
Machinery	850	1 000	1 200
Construction	300	350	450
10. Nonmetallic products			
Machinery	700	950	1 150
Construction	600	700	850
11. Basic metals			
Machinery	950	1 150	1 350
Construction	400	500	600
12. Machinery			
Machinery	800	800	950
Construction	300	350	450
13. Other industries			
Machinery	850	850	1 000
Construction	700	700	850
14. Construction			
Machinery	150	200	200
Construction	50	60	50
15. Services			
Machinery	900	650	800
Construction	1 900	2 000	2 000

[a] $\tilde{\kappa}_{k,j_t} = \tilde{\kappa}_{k,j_m}$, for $j=1,\ldots,4$; $k=12,14$.
$\tilde{\kappa}_{k,j_1}$, for $j=5,\ldots,15$; $k=12,14$.

As production functions for home goods allow substitution between capital and labor, capital coefficients for these industries depend on the rate of interest. The coefficients given are those which minimize costs when the rate of interest is 15 percent.

the comparative advantages enjoyed by different countries by comparing their export performance. We followed this idea to construct the capital (and implicitly the labor) coefficients for Asia and Africa, on the basis of those for Latin America.

The model should also reflect the overall differences in efficiency between the three developing regions. In Asia, the countries of the Indian subcontinent have been characterized by consistently high capital coefficients.[4] In Africa the situation is even less favorable. The lack of technicians and infrastructure handicaps industry, and while in agriculture land is very abundant, it is not of high quality. The fragmentation of the continent into economically small units makes it difficult to exploit economies of scale and to develop rationally the continent's infrastructure.

The assumed capital coefficients are given in table 10.13. Their level reflects the judgments made in the preceding paragraph. In choosing individual coefficients it appeared reasonable to assume that Asia had a comparative advantage for consumer goods. Africa has a handicap for industries which are technically complex and involve economies of scale.

10.1.7. Import substituting activities

The coefficients and upper bounds of import substituting activities are also based on indirect evidence. There are two decisions to be made:

(a) on the scope for import substitution over the ten-year span of the model, i.e. on the maximum possible range of variation of the import share in sales of different products; and

(b) on the discrepancy in efficiency which would correspond to maximum versus zero import substitution, i.e. how high would be the marginal cost of the most expensive import substituting activity, as compared with the cost of producing similar home goods.

In their recent book Chenery and Syrquin (1975) have used time-series/cross-section data to determine the relation between import shares in GNP, income per head, and country size. Their regressions define the import shares which are normal for countries of given size and economic development, while divergences between actual and these normal shares reflect country specific influences, among which trade policies appear to be by far the most important. The Chenery–Syrquin results show that, even after eliminating the influence of size and economic development, the

[4] The opposite has of course been true for East Asian countries; however, their economic weight is small.

Table 10.14

Capital coefficients—foreign goods and export services (per thousand).

	Foreign goods[a]												Export services[b]		
	Latin America				Asia				Africa				Latin America	Asia	Africa
	1	2	3	4	1	2	3	4	1	2	3	4			
1. Tropical noncompeting foodstuffs															
Machines	—	—	—	—	—	—	—	—	—	—	—	—	200	250	300
Construction	—	—	—	—	—	—	—	—	—	—	—	—	250	300	350
2. Tropical competing foodstuffs															
Machines	—	—	—	—	—	—	—	—	—	—	—	—	200	250	300
Construction	—	—	—	—	—	—	—	—	—	—	—	—	250	300	350
3. Temperate foodstuffs															
Machines	800	1 000	1 100	1 300	900	1 100	1 150	1 350	1 050	1 300	1 400	1 650	200	250	300
Construction	900	1 150	1 300	1 550	1 000	1 200	1 300	1 500	1 200	1 500	1 600	1 900	250	300	350
4. Agricultural raw materials															
Machines	—	—	—	—	—	—	—	—	—	—	—	—	200	250	300
Construction	—	—	—	—	—	—	—	—	—	—	—	—	250	300	350
5. Ores and nonferrous metals															
Machines	600	750	850	1 000	675	825	875	1 025	750	950	1 000	1 200	150	200	200
Construction	550	700	750	900	625	775	825	975	700	900	950	1 150	150	150	200
6. Oil															
Machines	1 400	1 700	1 850	2 150	1 550	1 850	1 950	2 250	1 800	2 100	2 250	2 600	300	350	400
Construction	1 150	1 400	1 550	1 800	1 300	1 550	1 650	1 850	1 500	1 800	1 900	2 200	250	300	350

7. Processed food															
Machines	650	850	950	1 150	600	750	800	950	700	900	950	1 150	150	150	200
Construction	500	600	700	800	450	550	600	700	550	700	750	900	100	100	150
8. Textiles															
Machines	900	1 150	1 300	1 550	850	1 000	1 100	1 250	1 000	1 200	1 300	1 500	250	250	250
Construction	300	400	450	550	300	350	400	450	350	400	450	500	100	100	100
9. Chemicals															
Machines	1 000	1 300	1 450	1 750	1 100	1 350	1 450	1 700	1 300	1 600	1 750	2 050	250	300	350
Construction	350	450	500	600	400	450	500	550	500	600	650	750	100	100	150
10. Nonmetallic products															
Machines	850	1 050	1 200	1 400	1 050	1 300	1 400	1 650	—	—	—	—	—	—	350
Construction	700	900	1 000	1 200	750	950	1 000	1 200	—	—	—	—	—	—	250
11. Basic metals															
Machines	1 150	1 450	1 600	1 900	1 250	1 550	1 650	1 950	1 500	1 800	1 950	2 250	200	350	400
Construction	500	600	700	800	550	700	750	900	650	800	900	1 050	100	150	200
12. Machinery															
Machines	950	1 200	1 350	1 600	900	1 100	1 150	1 350	1 050	1 300	1 400	1 650	100	250	300
Construction	350	450	500	600	400	450	500	550	500	600	650	750	100	100	150
13. Other industries															
Machines	1 000	1 300	1 450	1 750	950	1 150	1 250	1 450	1 100	1 350	1 450	1 700	200	250	300
Construction	850	1 050	1 200	1 400	750	950	1 000	1 200	950	1 250	1 250	1 550	200	200	250

[a] $\rho^s_{j_p}\tilde{\kappa}_{k,j_p}$, for $j=1,\ldots,4$; $s=1,\ldots,4$; $k=12,14$.

$\rho^s_{j_1}\tilde{\kappa}_{k,j_1}$, for $j=5,\ldots,15$; $s=1,\ldots,4$; $k=12,14$.

[b] $\kappa^e_{k,j}$, $j=1,\ldots,13$; $k=12,14$.

As production function for import substituting goods allow substitution between capital and labor, capital coefficients for these industries depend on the rate of interest. The coefficients given are those which minimize costs when the rate of interest is 15 percent.

Table 10.15
Linearization bounds—foreign goods[a] (millions of $).

	Latin America	Asia	Africa
1. Tropical noncompeting foodstuffs	—	—	—
2. Tropical competing foodstuffs	—	—	—
3. Temperate foodstuffs	50	140	35
4. Agricultural raw material	—	—	—
5. Ores and nonferrous metals	35	50	10
6. Oil	110	150	15
7. Processed food	10	15	10
8. Textiles	65	200	140
9. Chemicals	230	300	170
10. Nonmetallic products	10	5	—
11. Basic metals	150	190	100
12. Machinery	1 150	1 160	690
13. Other industries	420	420	200

$\tilde{i}^s_{j_P}$, for $j=1,\ldots,4$; $s=1,\ldots,4$.
$\tilde{i}^s_{j_2}$, for $j=5,\ldots,15$; $s=1,\ldots,4$.
The four steps are equal.

trading intensities of countries vary by more than a factor of 1 to 2. The observations for such countries as Brazil, Taiwan, and Korea suggest that these shares respond strongly and quickly to changes in trade policies. On the basis of the results, we have set import substitution bounds so as to allow import shares to fluctuate over a range of 1 to 2.

In GEM, activities producing home goods and import substituting goods have similar intermediate input coefficients; differences in their efficiency are reflected only in their inputs of labor and capital. It is therefore the levels of effective tariffs which should be taken as indicators of the discrepancy in efficiency between import substituting and home producing activities. Unless these are set at unnecessary high levels, they should reflect the cost of producing the most costly of the import substituting goods. Recent studies[5] suggest that effective protection rates in developing countries range in many cases up to around 100 percent; substantially higher rates have been recorded. It was felt reasonable to assume that, at the upper range of import substitution possibilities, the productivity of labor and capital in production of import substituting goods is only half that for home goods.

The coefficients and other data appear in tables 10.12, 10.14, and 10.15.

[5]See, for example, Balassa (1971); Bhagwati and Desai (1970); and Little, Scitovsky and Scott (1970).

10.1.8. Agricultural supply

There are three sources of information on agricultural supply response:

(a) a very large number of econometric studies measuring the response of acreage and crops to market prices;

(b) linear programming and recursive programming models of the agricultural sector from which supply response can be derived; and

(c) agricultural production functions.

Each approach has its specific sources of bias. We briefly describe each of them in turn.

(a) *Econometric studies* relate farmers' response to a nonobservable expected price; this price is deduced by assuming expectations to be determined by a mechanical feedback rule. This is, at best, an imperfect description of human judgment, so that regressions are affected by errors in variables. Econometrics is also a poor way of ascertaining the slow shifts in supply response which reflects the adjustment of capital, fertilizers, and organization to the profitability of crops. It is theoretically possible to sweep up this response into a crop response function with very long lags but, in practice, this is likely to involve asking too much of the data. Both of the imperfections mentioned will lead to underestimating the supply response of outputs.

Econometric studies focus on the partial response of one crop to its price and to that of products which compete closely with it for land. An overwhelming proportion of studies deals with the supply response for a single crop, or pairs of crops such as jute/paddy, sugarcane/paddy, millet/groundnuts, soybeans/corn and similar instances where two commodities compete closely for the same land. There is nothing to guarantee that the behavior implied by these functions is consistent with the overall land, labor, and capital constraints to which agriculture is subject. It is therefore difficult to judge the relevance of such partial studies to a general equilibrium model of agriculture.

Results on econometric estimates of supply response are very scattered. Labys (1975) has provided a convenient list of results. Other surveys are provided by Usda (1978) and Behrman (1968). Recently, Adams and Behrman (1976) have estimated world supply functions for wheat, rice, sugar, cotton, wool, vegetable oils, coffee, cocoa, and tea.

As is to be expected, these and other sources imply widely dispersed elasticity estimates. There is a definite clustering of values over the 0.5–1.0 range which may be taken to be typical for these types of estimates.

(b) *Linear and recursive programs*, on the other hand, tend to overestimate the flexibility of response of agricultural output. With this approach it is possible to account for only some of the reasons why farmers are reluctant to shift the assortment of their crops. Examples of these are rotation rules reflecting the desirability of particular sequences of crops; land suitability constraints excluding, for example, most types of rice from unirrigated land; seasonal factor constraints causing farmers to select a cropping pattern which smoothes out peaks in utilization of land and labor. Some other causes of inflexibility, such as market imperfections or the desire to diversify crops to minimize weather and marketing risks, can be modelled heuristically only by *ad hoc* constraints (see Hazell, 1971). But this approach cannot reflect accurately the enormous diversity in land quality which prevails even over geographically limited areas: it is assumed that crop yields are in fixed ratios for a limited number of types of land, an assumption which practitioners know to be unrealistic.

In linear programming models the supply of capital is usually assumed to be fixed; this technique therefore cannot adequately take into account this important determinant of the supply response. This problem is tackled by the *recursive programming* approach introduced by Day (1963), who solves a dynamic sequence of linear programs: in each of them specific constraints (in particular those involving capital) are shifted in response to the solution of the preceding year's program.

(c) *Production functions* provide a third way of assessing the response of production to changes in demand and supply of factors. A classical study is that by Heady and Dillon (1961).

It is worth noting that these functions, usually estimated from cross-section data, may overestimate the scope for substitution between labor and capital at the economy-wide level. This is because the sample will include farms which specialize in capital- and labor-intensive crops. The data will reveal large difference in factor intensities, reflecting the specialization of individual farms. The assortment of output could not vary as much for the economy as a whole.

The results obtained using the Chac model constructed by Duloy and Norton (1973) may be taken to be typical of what is implicit in detailed economy-wide models of agriculture in developing countries. Its authors have calculated that Chac implies a supply elasticity of 1.4 for field crops; it should be remarked that, since the supply of capital is fixed, the result does not reflect the response to prices of the available supply of capital.

This response is allowed for in the Singh and Ahn (1978) recursive programming model of the wheat/livestock sector in Southern Brazil. This model, validated by simulations over the past, implies very high supply elasticities, i.e. of the order of 10 for a ten-year period. The study, covering a rapidly expanding sector in a country which has large amounts of unused land, cannot be taken to represent the normal response of supply in developing countries; but it does show how important changes in the capital stock may be in enhancing the response of agricultural supply to price changes.

An excellent application of the production function approach is the well-known study by Tweeten and Leroy Quance (1969). This disaggregates US agriculture into animal and crops sectors, and estimates the aggregate supply response of US agriculture using a variety of approaches. The supply elasticity they obtain is close to that which results from Duloy's and Norton's work.

The constraints in our model (tables 10.16 and 10.17) were chosen not on the basis of specific data, but by a trial-and-error procedure meant to ensure that agricultural supply behaves in a way consistent with the results of available more detailed quantitative studies. The extent to which this was achieved may therefore best be judged by computing the elasticities implied by the various general equilibrium solutions. Relevant measures are as follows.

(a) The average elasticity of substitution, i.e. the elasticity of the ratio of agricultural production to constant prices GNP, with respect to the ratio of the price of that value added to the GNP price index. This is calculated by comparing different solutions to the reference variant.

Table 10.16
Right-hand side of agricultural constraints (millions of $).

	Latin America	Asia	Africa
1. Limitation of fertile land ($\tilde{z}_{j_t}$)			
Tropical noncompeting foodstuffs	7 800	5 600	8 200
Tropical competing foodstuffs	7 400	7 600	7 800
Temperate foodstuffs	18 800	93 000	10 600
Agricultural raw materials	9 800	13 200	5 600
2. Limitation of marginal land ($\tilde{z}_{j_m}$)			
Tropical noncompeting foodstuffs	1 000	800	1 000
Tropical competing foodstuffs	1 000	1 000	1 000
Temperate foodstuffs	2 000	10 000	1 000
Agricultural raw materials	1 000	1 500	1 000
3. Competition between crops ($\pi_i \Sigma_j \tilde{z}_{j_t}$)			
$\pi_1 \Sigma \tilde{z}_{j_t}$	12 200	10 500	13 000
$\pi_2 \Sigma \tilde{z}_{j_t}$	20 000	21 000	17 600
$\pi_3 \Sigma \tilde{z}_{j_t}$	23 000	85 000	12 800

Table 10.17

Decreasing returns to land, improvement by irrigation (linearization bounds in millions of $; capital coefficients in per thousand).

Steps	Latin America			Asia			Africa		
	Bounds[a]	Capital coefficients[b]		Bounds[a]	Capital coefficients[b]		Bounds[a]	Capital coefficients[b]	
$s=1$	2500	80	95	2500	100	115	700	120	135
$s=2$	1500	165	190	3800	200	225	1000	240	275
$s=3$	2000	245	280	5200	300	340	1400	355	415
$s=4$	∞	325	375	∞	400	450	∞	475	550

[a] $\tilde{i}_{f}^{*s}$; $s=1,\ldots,4$.
[b] $\kappa_{12,f}^{*s}$ and $\kappa_{14,f}^{*s}$; $s=1,\ldots,4$.

(b) The average elasticity of substitution of individual crops with respect to other crops: the variables studied are proportional changes in gross production and in the ratio of the prices of the four categories of products distinguished in the model.

The values of these elasticities are 0.5 and 5.1, respectively.

10.1.9. Decreasing returns in urban infrastructure

Experience strongly suggests that sharp increases of investments in the industrial sector decrease their productivity. A recent dramatic example is the wastefulness of investment programs initiated by oil-producing countries since the recent increase in oil prices. Planners, who are very much aware of this relation, account for it loosely in terms of the inadequacy of the economy's absorption capacity for investment.

Although the underlying mechanisms which account for this phenomenon have not been researched systematically, their nature is generally understood. Sharp increases in investment cause infrastructure bottlenecks, particularly in the transport sector. There are not enough good investment projects to absorb available funds, and major investments are initiated without adequate preparation. It is necessary to recruit untrained workers who are not very productive.

In GEM the view is taken for simplicity's sake that it is infrastructure which constitutes the critical bottleneck. This reflects the cost of overcoming transport bottlenecks and, to a certain extent, also the social infrastructure costs which results from a very rapid build-up of the labor force.

Because of Latin America's much higher *per capita* income social infrastructure costs are assumed to be higher than for other regions.[6] Coefficients and right-hand sides of the constraints for the three regions are given in tables 10.18 and 10.19.

10.1.10. Saving functions

Work by Kuznets, Chenery and others on the patterns of economic growth indicates that the average rate of saving tends to rise with the rate of

[6] Empirical studies show that demand for public services increases with income as much if not more rapidly than private consumption. See Chenery and Syrquin (1975) or Barten (1970). This relation between public services and income is likely to involve the stock of social capital as well as current government expenditures.

Table 10.18

Decreasing returns in urban infrastructure (linearization bounds in millions of \$; capital coefficients in per thousand).

	Latin America		Asia		Africa	
Steps	Bounds[a]	Capital coefficients[b]	Bounds[a]	Capital coefficients[b]	Bounds[a]	Capital coefficients[b]
$s=1$	60 000	0	40 000	0	24 000	0
$s=2$	3 000	60	2 000	30	950	30
$s=3$	3 000	100	2 000	60	950	60
$s=4$	∞	130	∞	90	∞	90

[a] $\tilde{i}_u^s$; $s=1,\ldots,4$.
[b] $\kappa_{12,u}^s$ and $\kappa_{14,u}^s$; $s=1,\ldots,4$.

Table 10.19
Urban infrastructure—input coefficients[a]

	Latin America	Asia	Africa
5. Ores and nonferrous metals	0.029	0.036	0.041
6. Oil	0.066	0.080	0.090
7. Processed food	0.071	0.071	0.086
8. Textiles	0.300	0.300	0.360
9. Chemicals	0.086	0.101	0.124
10. Nonmetallic products	0.390	0.500	0.600
11. Basic metals	0.040	0.049	0.042
12. Machinery	0.330	0.346	0.420
13. Other industry	0.116	0.116	0.185
14. Construction	0.060	0.078	0.078
15. Services	0.210	0.200	0.210

[a] $\nu_{j_1} = \nu_{j_2}$; $j = 5,\ldots,15$.

development, with the sharpest rise occurring at low-income levels. This leads to saving functions for which the marginal rate of saving exceeds the average rate. Other patterns have been identified which have important implications for development policies but are less well understood. Thus, domestic saving decreases with the size of capital inflows—a reasonable enough behavior given that there is no reason for countries to save resources received from abroad and consume only what they produce themselves.[7] It is not necessary, however, to introduce such a term into the GEM saving function, since the inflows of aid and foreign capital are the same in all model solutions. Maizels (1971) has found that savings depend on the level of exports. This relation probably reflects the high saving propensities in the dynamic export oriented sectors as well as the tendency of countries whose growth is held back by lack of foreign exchange, to consume savings which they are unable to invest productively (see Weisskopf, 1972). Though this relation is fairly strong statistically, we decided to disregard it in GEM.

Saving propensities are 0.22, 0.17, and 0.18, respectively, for Latin America, Asia, and Africa.

[7] As Papanek (1972) has pointed out, it may be difficult to separate cause and effect in studying the relation between saving and aid, since countries which, like Nigeria or Bangladesh in the past, suffer from sudden political difficulties which reduce their ability to generate savings will also tend to receive a good deal of foreign aid. But as the behavior of countries which have suddenly become the recipients of large amounts of aid from Arab oil-producers indicates, there does seem to be a definite tendency for capital imports to spill over into consumption.

10.1.11. Aid and private capital flows

Aid and private capital exports from developed countries were set at 21 billion dollars, or 0.8 percent of 1969 prices GNP of the developed countries. This is less than the long-term goal of 1 percent proposed by the United Nations Assembly (note that the UN target excludes private capital movements). The figure is somewhat higher however than the 0.6 percent share of private and public capital achieved in the late 1960s. The available aid and capital movements are allocated between Latin America, Asia, and Africa in rough proportion to their GNPs in the basic solution of the model. The amounts assumed are 9500 million, 8200 million, and 3300 million, respectively.

10.1.12. Utility functions: Consumption components

The utility functions which generate the patterns of consumer demand in GEM must reflect available data on demand in developing countries. There have been very few comparative studies of this type.[8] One is the paper by Weisskoff (1971) which estimates income and price elasticities of consumer demand on the basis of time-series/cross-section national accounts. More recently Lluch, Powell and Williams (1977) have applied the extended linear expenditure system (ELES) devised by Lluch to a sample which includes eight developing countries.

The Lluch–Powell–Williams approach is most attractive for a model such as GEM, since the estimated demand equations are consistent with separable utility functions equal to a weighted sum of logarithms of consumptions. Since logarithms are concave functions of their arguments these functions are easily represented by step approximations.

The Lluch–Powell–Williams estimates were not available at the time GEM was constructed. Also, they cover only a limited number of small developing countries, so that we did not feel they provided a good basis for inference on preferences in the regions of GEM.

This led to using an approach which is simpler but which lacks a rigorous justification.

(1) *Derivation of GEM-type utility functions*. The procedure used to construct the GEM-type utility functions from estimates of consumer demand equations can be described as follows.

[8] We do not consider here the fundamental papers by Houthakker (1957) and Goldberger and Gamaletsos (1970) who have compared demand patterns for developed countries only.

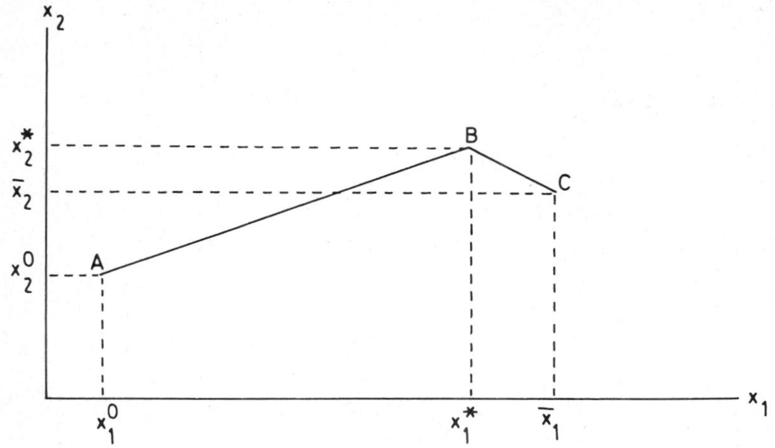

Figure 10.1.

Let the estimated demand curves have the form $x_i = f_i(x, p_i)$, where x_i, x, and p_i are the consumption of good i, total consumption, and the price of good i, respectively. As is very often the case with econometrically estimated demand curves, the consumption of good i depends only on its own price. Assume that, by a suitable normalization of quantities in the base year, all prices are equal to unity. They will remain so along the Engel line, which describes the choices made by consumers when their income increases.

The first step in the procedure is to linearize the curves, obtaining

$$x_i = a_i x - b_i p_i + d_i,$$

where the coefficients are, if need be, adjusted to $\Sigma_i a_i = 1$ and $\Sigma_i(d_i - b_i) = 0$. Since $p_i = 1$ for all i, along the Engel curve this ensures $\Sigma_i x_i = x$.

Let us represent in figs 10.1 and 10.2 the situation for the two-commodity case.

In fig. 10.1 x_1^0 and x_2^0 are the amounts consumed in the initial year, in which, by suitable normalization of quantities, prices are equal to unity. The segment AB is part of the Engel line along which prices remain equal to unity. Point C is a possible consumption basket, and B is the point on the Engel line which satisfies $\bar{x}_1 + \bar{x}_2 = x_1^* + x_2^*$.

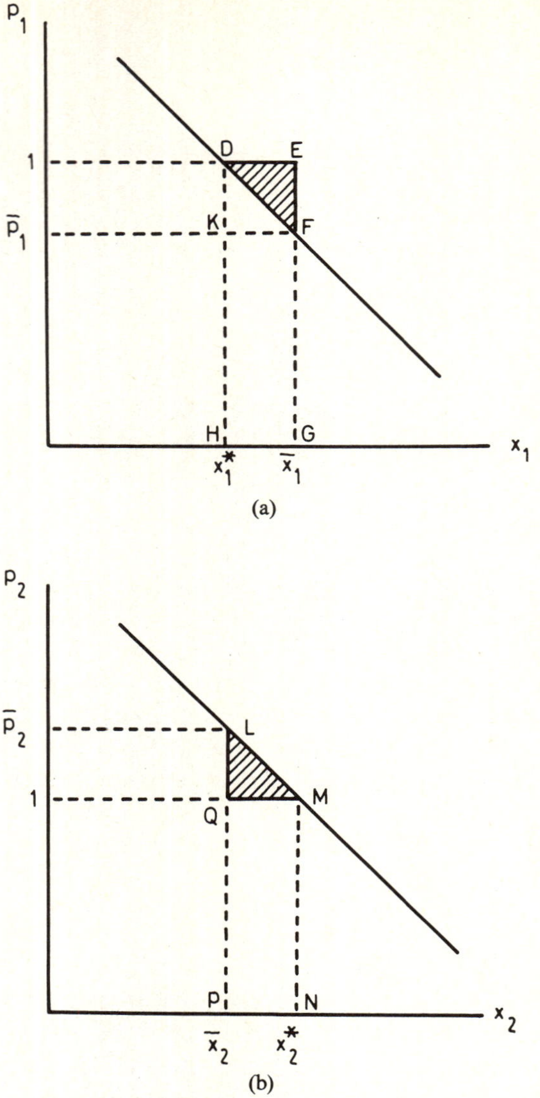

Figure 10.2. (a) Demand curve for good 1; (b) demand curve for good 2.

Table 10.20
Expenditure and price elasticities.

	Latin America		Asia		Africa	
	Expenditure	Price	Expenditure	Price	Expenditure	Price
1. Tropical noncompeting foodstuffs	0.2	0.0	0.8	−0.6	0.8	−0.6
2. Tropical competing foodstuffs	0.6	−0.4	0.8	−0.9	0.8	−0.9
3. Temperate foodstuffs	0.7	−0.4	0.8	−0.9	0.8	−0.9
4. Agricultural raw materials	0.2	−0.4	0.4	−0.9	0.4	−0.9
5. Ores and nonferrous metals	—	—	—	—	—	—
6. Oil	1.0	−0.5	1.0	−1.0	1.0	−1.0
7. Processed food	1.4	−0.6	1.4	−1.2	1.4	−1.2
8. Textiles	1.2	−0.5	1.4	−0.8	1.4	−0.8
9. Chemicals	1.4	−0.2	1.4	−0.5	1.4	−0.5
10. Nonmetallic products	—	—	—	—	—	—
11. Basic metals	—	—	—	—	—	—
12. Machinery	1.7	−1.2	1.4	−1.0	1.4	−1.0
13. Other industry	1.4	−1.2	1.4	−1.0	1.4	−1.0
14. Construction	—	—	—	—	—	—
15. Services	0.9	−0.7	1.1	−0.4	1.1	−0.4

The GEM function is chosen to ensure that, along the Engel curve AB, utility is equal to total consumption.

The calculation of the utility at points such as C, situated elsewhere than on the Engel curve, can be understood starting with fig. 10.2 which describes the demand curves for goods 1 and 2 corresponding to a total consumption $\bar{x}_1+\bar{x}_2=x_1^*+x_2^*$. Notice that $\bar{p}_1<1$ and $\bar{p}_2>1$, as implied by the fact that in fig. 10.1 $\bar{x}_1>x_1^*$ and $\bar{x}_2<x_2^*$.

Using the familiar idea that prices are indicators of utility, so that changes in utility can be approximated by suitable areas below the demand curve,[9] the difference in utility between points B and C is equal to the area of the shaded triangles DEF and LMQ of fig. 10.2a and b. This can be seen as follows. First, since $\bar{x}_1+\bar{x}_2=x_1^*+x_2^*$, $HG=PN$, and the areas $DEGH$ and $QMNP$ are equal. The change in utility in moving from (x_1^*, x_2^*) to $(\bar{x}_1, \bar{x}_2)$ is equal to the area $LMNP$ minus the area $DFGH$. The difference between these areas is DEF plus LMQ.

This reasoning can be extended to more than two goods and makes it possible to construct a utility function from demand curves.

(2) *Choice of coefficients*. The choice of coefficients was mainly based on the paper by Weisskopf (1971). Weisskopf did not try to estimate demand functions consistent with the theory of choice, and his demand curves do not satisfy the constraints implied by theory. Although about two-thirds of Weisskoff's price elasticity coefficients are negative, some of the estimated values seem too high or too low. He has computed separate estimates for a number of groups of countries, but the differences between coefficients for different groups are often hard to explain and generally not significant. We therefore used his results only as a general guideline on the pattern of consumer demand.

The expenditure and price elasticities used in constructing the utility functions appear in table 10.20, while table 10.21 describes the coefficients of the utility functions themselves.

10.1.13. Utility functions: Labor migration components

The utility functions for Latin America, Asia, and Africa also contain terms reflecting the psychological cost of migration between primary producing sectors, and between primary producing sectors and industry. A seminal study in this area is the paper by Harris and Todaro (1970), but it

[9] If separability of the utility function is assumed.

Table 10.21

Description of the utility functions—consumption components (linearization bounds in millions of $).

	Latin America			Asia			Africa		
	β	γ	Bounds[a]	β	γ	Bounds[a]	β	γ	Bounds[a]
1. Tropical noncompeting foodstuffs	0.002	900	—	0.010	300	100	0.021	475	100
2. Tropical competing foodstuffs	0.011	850	50	0.020	650	200	0.042	950	200
3. Temperate foodstuffs	0.043	2200	200	0.262	9400	2800	0.071	1600	400
4. Agricultural raw materials	0.002	800	25	0.004	750	100	0.004	475	50
5. Ores and nonferrous metals	—	—	—	—	—	—	—	—	—
6. Oil	0.018	0	100	0.003	0	25	0.018	0	100
7. Processed food	0.222	−5850	1200	0.160	−3800	1700	0.169	−1050	900
8. Textiles	0.080	−1200	400	0.089	−2100	600	0.137	−850	500
9. Chemicals	0.047	−1250	100	0.020	−450	100	0.032	−200	100
10. Nonmetallic products	—	—	—	—	—	—	—	—	—
11. Basic metals	—	—	—	—	—	—	—	—	—
12. Machinery	0.061	−2300	600	0.037	−900	300	0.037	−250	200
13. Other industry	0.021	−600	200	0.050	−1200	400	0.046	−300	200
14. Construction	—	—	—	—	—	—	—	—	—
15. Services	0.493	6450	3500	0.345	−2650	1400	0.423	−850	800

[a]Value of the first step $\tilde{x}^{1+} = \tilde{x}^{1-}$: the value of the second step is twice the value of the first. The ϕ^1 and ϕ^2 coefficients are equal to 0.025 and 0.125, respectively, for all goods.

Table 10.22
Description of the utility functions—labor migration components.

	Latin America				Asia				Africa			
	ε	Bounds[a]	ϕ_l^1	ϕ_l^2	ε	Bounds[a]	ϕ_l^1	ϕ_l^2	ε	Bounds[a]	ϕ_l^1	ϕ_l^2
1. Tropical noncompeting foodstuffs	0.015	200	0.03	0.07	0.021	250	0.03	0.07	0.064	250	0.03	0.07
2. Tropical competing foodstuffs	0.016	200	0.03	0.07	0.018	350	0.03	0.07	0.052	200	0.03	0.07
3. Temperate foodstuffs	0.015	600	0.03	0.07	0.313	3200	0.03	0.07	0.084	350	0.03	0.07
4. Agricultural raw materials	0.025	300	0.03	0.07	0.043	490	0.03	0.07	0.044	200	0.03	0.07
5. Ores and nonferrous metals	0.012	200	0.03	0.07	0.007	250	0.03	0.07	0.021	150	0.03	0.07
6. Other sectors (6–15)	0.883	10000	0.03	0.07	0.581	5500	0.03	0.07	0.735	2900	0.03	0.07

[a]Value of the first step $\tilde{L}^{1+} = \tilde{L}^{1-}$; the second step is unbounded.

Table 10.23
Migration component of the utility functions—weights of sectors in the activity indicator.[a]

	Latin America		Asia		Africa	
1. Tropical noncompeting foodstuffs	0.76	0.70	0.84	0.77	0.82	0.77
2. Tropical competing foodstuffs	0.76	0.70	0.84	0.77	0.82	0.77
3. Temperate foodstuffs	0.76	0.70	0.84	0.77	0.82	0.77
4. Agricultural raw materials	0.76	0.70	0.84	0.77	0.82	0.77
5. Ores and nonferrous metals	0.61		0.34		0.65	
6. Oil	0.61		0.41		0.97	
7. Processed food	0.41		0.26		0.35	
8. Textiles	0.45		0.41		0.50	
9. Chemicals	0.55		0.61		0.35	
10. Nonmetallic products	0.52		0.62		0.42	
11. Basic metals	0.47		0.57		0.42	
12. Machinery	0.55		0.64		0.39	
13. Other industries	0.58		0.69		0.42	
14. Construction	0.47		0.61		0.54	
15. Services	0.82		0.80		0.76	

[a]For sectors 1–4, the first column shows the ν_{jt}^* coefficients, the second column, the ν_{jm}^* coefficients; for sectors 5–15, these are the ν_j^* coefficients.

does not take account of the utility costs of migration. The coefficients used in GEM were chosen by trial and error on the basis of experiments with the model to produce results which seemed reasonable from an empirical point of view. They are listed in tables 10.22 and 10.23.

10.1.14. Import and export tariffs

Studies of protection in developing countries reveal a broad dispersion of tariff and even more of effective tariff rates between commodities and between countries. Levels of protection tend to be higher in Latin American countries than elsewhere. Equipment goods are usually subject to lower duties than other goods.

Developing countries are substantial net exporters of agricultural commodities. Yet paradoxically many of these grant substantial protection to particular high cost agricultural products. Thus, Turkey protects sugar beet, Brazil biases its domestic price structure in favor of wheat, West African countries protect their rice production, while India has tried to become self-sufficient in jute. This explains why GEM provides for fairly high tariffs for agricultural commodities.[10]

[10]These tariffs affect directly only the prices of "foreign" agricultural goods, which are not demanded in large quantities. They, therefore, have only a small impact on the costs of industries which use agricultural imports. It is possible for the prices of home goods to be quite low even though those of foreign goods, both home produced and imported, are high.

Table 10.24
Tariffs.

	Import tariff rates				Specific export tariff rates			
	Ad Valorem			Specific				
	Latin America	Asia	Africa	Developed	Latin America	Asia	Africa	Middle East
1. Tropical competing foodstuffs	—	—	—	0.16	0.20	0.20	0.20	—
2. Tropical noncompeting foodstuffs	0.60	0.40	0.40	0.28				
3. Temperate foodstuffs	0.60	0.40	0.40	0.30				
4. Agricultural raw materials	0.60	0.40	0.40	0.19				
5. Ores and nonferrous metals	0.60	0.40	0.40	0.03	0.20	0.20	0.20	
6. Oil	0.60	0.40	0.40	—	[a]	[a]	[a]	[a]
7. Processed food	0.60	0.40	0.40	0.12				
8. Textiles	0.60	0.40	0.40	0.18				
9. Chemicals	0.45	0.30	0.40	0.12				
10. Nonmetallic products	0.45	0.40	—	—				
11. Basic metals	0.45	0.30	0.30	—				
12. Machinery	0.45	0.30	0.30	0.06				
13. Other industries	0.45	0.40	0.40	0.12				

[a] The tariff is an export levy equal to the difference between the exogenous unit export price and the cost of production of exported oil.

We finally have to assess the export taxes which are a feature of developing countries' trade policies. These are imposed on goods for which exporters perceive they have some monopoly power, and/or use low cost depletable resources. These tax rates vary sharply, both between countries and over time.

This is reflected in GEM by low specific export tariffs for tropical noncompeting foodstuffs (coffee, cocoa, tea) and nonferrous metals. For petroleum it is assumed that prices are fixed exogenously, independently of costs or of demand. The oil export tariff is therefore specified as a flexible compensatory levy, akin to those used in the EEC's Common Agricultural Policy (CAP). Whereas the EEC levies absorb the difference between fluctuating world prices and the fixed domestic prices of the CAP, the oil export tariff offsets the discrepancy between production costs and the fixed world price chosen by exporters.

Tariffs are given in table 10.24.

10.2. The model for Middle East oil-producers

The implemented version of the model is written in a slightly different way from the logic presented in section 9.4.

Value added[11] by domestic factors of production at 1969 prices plays a central role. A first equation (the "oil production balance") relates value added in the oil sector to oil exports:

$$v_6 = 0.58e_6 + 1100.$$

The constant term in the equation reflects domestic uses of oil, which are treated as exogenous since they are quite small. Only a fraction of the value of oil exports accrues to domestic factors of production; the rest corresponds to the cost of imports needed by the industry and to payments to foreign factors of production.

Production of the oil sector is thus assumed to be determined by demand, and the sector generates more capital than it uses so that, as will be seen later, it is not limited by a financing constraint. At the time the model was constructed this sector was largely in the hands of foreign companies, and its expansion was financed from retained profits or from capital imports.

[11] In effect value added at constant prices is taken to be the measure of activity, rather than production as is more customary. It is clear that in a fixed coefficients model the two formulations are equivalent.

The production of the nonoil sector, on the other hand, is limited by the available amount of domestic capital. The corresponding constraint takes account of the following.

(a) Saving in the terminal year equal to $0.28v_6 + 0.14v_0$: the propensity to save from oil income is twice the propensity to save from other income.

(b) Assuming a linear growth of saving over the ten-year period covered, the increase of the capital stock is five times the (exogenous) initial year saving, plus five times that of the terminal year.

(c) A small fraction of this capital will be used for investments required by the oil industry, such as housing and infrastructure financed from local sources; the main user, however, is the nonoil sector, assumed to have a capital coefficient of 2.5.

This leads to the constraint

$$72.500 - (1.4v_6 + 0.7v_0) \geqslant (0.38v_6 + 2.5v_0).$$

(supply of undifferentiated capital) $\geqslant$ (use of undifferentiated capital)

It will be noticed that the oil sector contributes more capital than it uses ($1.4v_6$ rather than $0.38v_6$): an increase in demand for oil increases rather than reduces the amount of capital which is available for other sectors.

Imports finally are related to total value added (instead of production)

$$m_k = \mu_k(v_6 + v_0).$$

The μ_k coefficients appear in table 10.8.

10.3. The model for developed countries

10.3.1. The trade welfare–production function

The trade welfare function, which describes the relation between the welfare of developed countries and their foreign trade, depends on four components.

(i) Gross domestic product at constant prices—used as a proxy to represent the domestic resources available in developed countries.

(ii) Exports of manufactures.

(iii) Imports of manufactures.

(iv) Exports and imports of primary commodities.

The procedure followed to construct the components of the function is similar in principle to that used to construct the Latin American, Asian, and African utility functions (section 10.1.12). There are, however, differences in details.

(a) The Engel ray which describes purchases of a commodity from different sellers when prices are equal to unity passes through the origin for imports. Its coefficients reflect the base year shares of developing exporters in imports of developed countries.

(b) Along that ray the marginal utility is proportional to the price defined by the import demand curve for that product. It decreases therefore along the Engel ray, instead of being constant as in the developing countries' utility function.

Choice of coefficients of the import demand curves. There are no good estimates of import demand for manufactures covering specifically imports from developing into developed countries. There is however a good deal of evidence that import demand for manufactures is quite elastic with respect to price in the long run. This is illustrated by the well-known articles by McDougall (1951, 1952), Junz and Rhomberg (1965), and the book by Kravis and Lipsey (1971) which use very different approaches and sources of data. The price elasticities which we have used appear in table 10.25. Demand for machinery and for chemicals were assumed to have the highest price elasticity reflecting the very low market shares of developing countries for these goods; the lowest elasticity is assumed for "other

Table 10.25
Import elasticities of developed countries.

	Income elasticity[a]	Price elasticity[b]
1. Tropical noncompeting foodstuffs	0.3	−0.3
2. Tropical competing foodstuffs	0.3	−0.8
3. Temperate foodstuffs	0.7	−1.6
4. Agricultural raw materials	0.3	−1.2
5. Ores and nonferrous metals	1.2	−4.1
6. Oil	1.5	—
7. Processed food	1.5	−2.3
8. Textiles	3.0	−2.4
9. Chemicals	3.0	−3.2
10. Nonmetallic products	3.0	—
11. Basic metals	3.0	—
12. Machinery	3.0	−6.4
13. Other industries	3.0	−1.8

[a] With respect to gross national product.
[b] Mean value over the approximation region of the demand curve.

Table 10.26

Description of the trade welfare function—developed countries.

	μ_k (10^{-6})[a]	$\mu_k g^0$	Utility function coefficients, ϕ_k^s															Bounds[b]	Coeff. ϕ_{ik}	Bounds[c]	Coeff. ϕ_k
1. Noncompeting tropical foodstuffs	522	3 280	—	—	—	1.28	1.15	1.07	1.03	1.0	0.96	0.93	0.85	0.75	0.65	0.55	0.45	100	0.009	10 000	—
2. Competing tropical foodstuffs	337	−1 370	—	—	—	1.28	1.15	1.07	1.03	1.0	0.96	0.93	0.85	0.75	0.65	0.55	0.45	170	0.022	10 000	—
3. Cereals and livestock	274	−1 480	2.20	1.66	1.36	1.20	1.11	1.05	1.02	1.0	0.97	0.9	0.89	0.80	0.72	0.64	0.56	60	0.031	10 000	—
4. Agricultural raw materials	344	320	—	—	—	1.33	1.25	1.195	1.17	1.15	1.12	1.10	1.05	0.97	0.90	0.83	0.76	180	0.047	10 000	—
5. Mining	1 940	−1 780	—	—	—	1.12	1.07	1.03	1.01	1.0	0.98	0.97	0.93	0.88	0.80	0.68	0.56	250–600	0.078	10 000	—
6. Oil	21 278	−22 470	—	—	—	1.00	—	—	—	—	—	—	—	—	—	—	—	∞	—	—	1.00
7. Food	503	−460	—	—	—	1.16	1.09	1.04	1.02	1.0	0.98	0.96	0.91	0.84	0.74	0.64	0.54	115–170	0.125	35	1.00
8. Textiles	4 056	−7 440	—	—	—	1.31	1.24	1.19	1.17	1.15	1.13	1.11	1.06	0.99	0.89	0.79	0.69	465–750	0.125	330	1.15
9. Chemicals	943	−1 730	1.62	1.41	1.29	1.23	1.19	1.17	1.16	1.15	1.14	1.13	1.10	1.07	0.97	0.87	0.77	110–350	0.125	220	1.15
10. Nonmetallic products	657	−1 210	—	—	—	1.00	—	—	—	—	—	—	—	—	—	—	—	∞	—	—	1.15
11. Basic metals	1 185	−2 190	—	—	—	1.00	—	—	—	—	—	—	—	—	—	—	—	∞	—	—	1.15
12. Machinery	425	−780	1.47	1.26	1.14	1.08	1.04	1.02	1.01	1.00	0.99	0.98	0.95	0.92	0.82	0.72	0.62	350–1000	0.250	845	1.15
13. Other industries	6 535	−11 980	2.23	1.67	1.44	1.31	1.24	1.19	1.17	1.15	1.13	1.11	1.06	0.99	0.89	0.79	0.69	750–1100	0.125	820	1.15

[a] The coefficients given are $\mu_k = \Sigma_i \mu_{i0k}$; the corresponding μ_{i0k} coefficients can be deduced from table 10.9 and the formulae of section 10.1.3.

[b] When two bounds are given, the smaller applies to the first steps, the higher one to steps 13, 14 and 15; $\widetilde{(m-e)}_k^s$ for $k=1, \ldots, 5$ and $\tilde{m}_k^s$ for $k=6,\ldots,13$.

[c] $\tilde{m}_i^{s+} = \tilde{m}^{s-}$ for $i=1,\ldots,4$; $\tilde{m}_i^{s+} = \frac{1}{2}\tilde{m}_i^{s-}$ for others.

industries", a category which includes handicrafts and similar products for which demand in developed countries is probably rather inelastic.

The income elasticities used are lower than those implied by past changes in GNP and manufactures imports from developing countries. Elasticities estimated from past data implied 1980 levels of imports which we judged to be unrealistically high.

For raw materials the model does not contain separate export supply and import demand components, but functions relating the marginal utility of net imports to the amount purchased. As for manufactures, these functions are built by assuming that the utility of imports equals the area under the import demand curve.

There has been a great deal of work on estimation of import demand for primary commodities, but much of this is not usable. Since these commodities are quite homogeneous the appropriate way of specifying import demand is as the difference between domestic supply and consumption; it is doubtful that the relation between net imports, income, and price is stable enough to be estimated by econometric methods. Some notable studies which have used the former approach are those of Fisher et al. (1972), Usda (1978), and Adams and Behrman (1976), completed after GEM was built.

For tropical noncompeting foodstuffs (coffee, cocoa, tea, and bananas) the price and income elasticities used reflect econometric estimates available in the early 1970s. These goods are not produced in developed countries, and import demand coincides with consumer demand on which there exist numerous studies.

It is more difficult to estimate the elasticity of import demand of the other categories of goods, which are produced as well as consumed by developed countries. The US, Canada, and Australia are large producers of minerals; the US and Australia are the world's largest producers of cotton and wool, respectively. For cereals, Europe and Japan are net importers, but developed countries have in recent years been net exporters to the developing world. In the "competing tropical products" category, developed countries also are large producers of vegetable oils, sugar, and citrus fruits. This is good reason for choosing substantially higher price elasticities than for the tropical noncompeting group.

The coefficients are described in table 10.26.

10.3.2. *Tariffs*

The tariff rates for imports of manufactures into developing countries have been the subject of numerous studies. Balassa (1971) provides an excellent synthesis of this work. The results which he quotes, modified to take account of tariff reductions adopted since the book was written, served as a basis for our estimates of tariff rates on manufactures and mining imports listed in table 10.24.

It is much more difficult to estimate the rate of protection of agriculture in developed countries. The main goal of protection measures is to stabilize the income of farmers at levels set by political decisions. This is achieved by a complex system of variable import levies and quotas, which tend to change from year to year as world prices of agricultural products fluctuate. As a result, estimates of the rate of protection of agriculture give lower results for years in which agricultural prices are high than for years of low prices. The protection rates also differ between countries of course.

There are not enough estimates of this type to make it possible to calculate rates which represent an average of protection rates for different years. It seemed preferable to resort to a more indirect approach.

In an IBRD working paper, Tims (1975) has estimated the impact of the elimination of developed countries' protection against agricultural imports from the developing world. This calculation describes the quantitative impact of eliminating tariffs, other levies, quotas, and other quantitative restrictions.

We aggregated Tims' figures into the four categories of agricultural products of GEM in order to find out how much larger imports of each category of products into developed countries would be if protection was eliminated. Given our estimates of the price elasticity of import demand for agricultural products it was then possible to assess by how much prices would need to drop to bring about such an increase in imports. This price reduction was taken to be an estimate of the tariff equivalent of the diverse protection measures.

10.4. The "high elasticities" variant of GEM

10.4.1. Recent evidence on the price elasticity of demand for foreign goods

The basic version of GEM which has been described so far in this chapter represents a world in which international trade is not very responsive to prices. This reflected the conclusions drawn from our initial survey of available data. But as time went on we gradually became convinced that the model underestimated strongly the long-term sensitivity of exports and imports to prices. GEM, however, describes market adjustments over a ten-year span, a long enough period to permit producers and consumers to adjust rather fully to price changes, and this should be reflected in its coefficients.

For raw materials import demand by developed countries, the new evidence was largely econometric. A number of remarkable commodity models have been built recently; see especially those by Adams and Behrman (1976), Fisher et al. (1972), and Usda (1978) (see Osterrieth, 1978, for an analysis of that model's implications) which feature substantial import demand elasticities in developed countries. These models do not provide equally convincing results for developing countries' import demand.

Econometric research on import demand for manufactures in developed and developing countries is less advanced, but recent history clearly suggests that the long-term price elasticity of demand must be very high. Indeed, developing countries have been able to expand their shares of manufactured goods markets in developed countries very substantially over the last ten to fifteen years without a marked drop in relative price. This success cannot be accounted for by high income elasticities of demand—this explanation is contradicted by the fact that the share of developing countries in developed countries' imports continued to rise rapidly in the recent recession.

History also suggests that the market shares of individual developing countries may change drastically over the years. The share of East Asian exporters of manufactured goods have, for example, risen dramatically, while those of South Asia fell markedly.

The experience of these East Asian countries, and of South American countries which, like them, switched from an import substituting to an export oriented strategy, also shows that the scope for expanding imports is large. How high protection has been in developing countries was revealed by the work of Balassa (1971) and Little, Scitovsky and Scott (1970). No developing country has reduced protection to the levels prevalent in the developed world, yet these countries which have abandoned policies of extreme protection have experienced a large increase of the imports to GNP ratio.

A major revision of the coefficients of GEM appeared necessary therefore if the model was to produce empirically useful results. It was decided, however, not to scrap the first version which we thought served better the methodological goals of our work. As explained in Chapters 7 and 8, it is income effects which make the computation of equilibria difficult. In fact, if prices were constant,[12] computation of equilibria would be a trivial problem. The "low elasticities" initial version of the model was therefore retained as a tool for bench testing solution procedures.

10.4.2. Differences between coefficients of the "high elasticities" and "low elasticities" version of GEM

The "high elasticities" version of GEM differs from the earlier version in the following ways.

(a) The utility function of developed countries implies higher price elasticities of demand for primary commodities and manufactured goods.

(b) These functions also imply higher elasticities of substitution between suppliers to developed countries.

(c) Imports are much more responsive to protection policies.

(d) In the earlier version the initial stock of capital and labor is locked into the available initial production capacities and cannot be reallocated within or between industries (putty–clay assumption). This is not a realistic assumption in the long term; for example, much of the initial capital would be replaced during the ten-year span covered by GEM, so that it is preferable to assume that the initially available capital and labor may be reallocated freely (putty–putty assumption).

It would have been interesting to dovetail the two versions of GEM so that they were comparable in some well-defined sense. For example, the choice of coefficients could have been carried out so that the two models might generate the same base case. Achieving this is possible, but quite difficult. This exercise would also be somewhat pointless since there is no reason to expect that economies with different coefficients would follow the same path under some set of assumptions about the policies pursued by governments.

Since the two versions of GEM represent different economies, we therefore felt free to juggle a number of coefficients to obtain a well-balanced base case solution. One such change involved an increase in the world price of machines which allowed more flexibility of import substitution in that sector. Because this had a significant impact on the balance of payments of developing countries, it was decided to increase the aid which they receive. Apart from aid, these adjustments were limited to capital

[12] Relative prices could be constant in the neighborhood of equilibrium if utility functions imply linear indifference curves.

Table 10.27

Capital coefficients—production of home goods, high elasticities version (per thousand).

	Production of home goods[a]		
	Latin America	Asia	Africa
1. Tropical noncompeting foodstuffs			
Machinery	650	900	900
Construction	750	900	1100
2. Tropical competing foodstuffs			
Machinery	650	900	900
Construction	750	900	1100
3. Temperate foodstuffs			
Machinery	650	900	900
Construction	950	900	1100
4. Agricultural raw materials			
Machinery	650	900	900
Construction	750	900	1100
5. Ores and nonferrous metals			
Machinery	750	625	1400
Construction	750	575	1300
6. Oil			
Machinery	250	300	400
Construction	200	200	300
7. Processed food			
Machinery	800	550	650
Construction	600	400	500
8. Textiles			
Machinery	750	400	1200
Construction	250	150	400
9. Chemicals			
Machinery	850	1000	1200
Construction	300	350	450
10. Nonmetallic products			
Machinery	700	950	1150
Construction	600	700	850
11. Basic metals			
Machinery	950	1150	1350
Construction	400	500	600
12. Machinery			
Machinery	800	400	950
Construction	300	200	450
13. Other industries			
Machinery	850	850	1000
Construction	700	700	850
14. Construction			
Machinery	150	200	200
Construction	50	60	50
15. Services			
Machinery	900	650	800
Construction	1900	2000	2000

[a] $\tilde{\kappa}_{k,j_t} = \tilde{\kappa}_{k,j_m}$, for $j=1,\ldots,4$; $k=12,14$.
$\tilde{\kappa}_{k,j_1}$, for $j=5,\ldots,15$; $k=12,14$.

As production functions for home goods allow substitution between capital and labor, capital coefficients for these industries depend on the rate of interest. The coefficients $\tilde{\kappa}_{j_t}$, $\tilde{\kappa}_{j_m}$ and $\tilde{\kappa}_{j_1}$ given are those which minimize costs when the rate of interest is 15 percent.

Table 10.28
Capital coefficients—foreign goods and export services, high elasticities version (per thousand).

	Foreign goods[a]												Export services[b]		
	Latin America				Asia				Africa						
	1	2	3	4	1	2	3	4	1	2	3	4	Latin America	Asia	Africa
1. Tropical noncompeting foodstuffs															
Machines	—	—	—	—	—	—	—	—	—	—	—	—	200	250	300
Construction	—	—	—	—	—	—	—	—	—	—	—	—	250	300	350
2. Tropical competing foodstuffs															
Machines	—	—	—	—	—	—	—	—	—	—	—	—	200	250	300
Construction	—	—	—	—	—	—	—	—	—	—	—	—	250	300	350
3. Temperate foodstuffs															
Machines	800	1000	1100	1300	1000	1200	1250	1450	1000	1250	1350	1550	200	250	300
Construction	900	1150	1300	1500	1000	1200	1300	1550	1200	1500	1600	1850	250	300	350
4. Agricultural raw materials															
Machines	—	—	—	—	—	—	—	—	—	—	—	—	200	250	300
Construction	—	—	—	—	—	—	—	—	—	—	—	—	250	300	350
5. Ores and nonferrous metals															
Machines	1150	1750	2250	2750	825	1275	1625	2125	1600	1800	2100	2400	150	200	200
Constructions	1150	1650	2000	2700	775	1325	1575	2075	1500	1700	1900	2100	150	150	200
6. Oil															
Machines	1700	2000	2150	2450	850	1300	1450	1900	3800	4100	4250	4600	300	350	400
Construction	1400	1650	1800	2050	750	1200	1250	1550	3200	3500	3600	3900	250	300	350
7. Processed food															
Machines	900	1100	1200	1350	750	850	900	1250	750	1150	1250	1550	150	150	200
Construction	700	800	900	1000	550	650	700	800	600	900	1000	1200	100	100	150

8. Textiles															
Machines	900	1150	1300	1500	1300	1450	1550	1650	1300	1500	1600	1850	250	250	250
Construction	300	400	450	500	450	500	550	600	450	500	550	600	100	100	100
9. Chemicals															
Machines	1150	1600	2000	2350	1600	2200	2600	3200	1500	2000	2300	2900	250	300	350
Construction	450	550	700	850	600	750	950	1050	600	750	900	1150	100	100	150
10. Nonmetallic products															
Machines	850	1050	1200	1400	1250	1500	1600	1800	—	—	—	—	—	—	350
Construction	700	900	1000	1200	900	1100	1150	1350	—	—	—	—	—	—	250
11. Basic metals															
Machines	1350	1850	2150	2650	1600	2100	2600	3350	1800	2250	2650	3250	300	350	400
Construction	550	700	850	1000	850	1000	1250	1500	750	1000	1200	1400	100	150	200
12. Machinery															
Machines	1000	1200	1400	1700	1250	1550	1800	2050	1150	1350	1550	1850	250	250	300
Construction	400	500	600	700	550	650	750	950	550	650	750	950	100	100	150
13. Other industries															
Machines	1150	1600	1850	2250	1450	2200	2650	3500	1300	1600	1900	2400	250	250	300
Construction	1000	1400	1700	2100	1100	1750	2050	2650	1150	1450	1650	2050	200	200	250

[a] $\rho^s_{j_p}\tilde{\kappa}_{k,j_p}$, for $j=1,\ldots,4$; $s=1,\ldots,4$; $k=12,14$.

$\rho^s_{j_1}\tilde{\kappa}_{k,j_1}$, for $j=5,\ldots,15$; $s=1,\ldots,4$; $k=12,14$.

[b] $\kappa^e_{k,j}$, $j=1,\ldots,13$; $k=12,14$.

As production function for import substituting goods allow substitution between capital and labor, capital coefficients for these industries depend on the rate of interest. The coefficients given are those which minimize costs when the rate of interest is 15 percent.

Table 10.29

Description of the trade welfare function—developed countries, high elasticities version.

	μ_k (10^{-6})[a]	$\mu_k g^0$	Utility function coefficients, ϕ_k^s															Bounds[b]	Coeff. ϕ_{ik}	Bounds[c]	Coeff. ϕ_k
1. Noncompeting tropical foodstuffs	522	3 280	—	—	—	1.447	1.403	1.361	1.320	1.280	1.242	1.204	1.168	1.133	1.099	1.066	1.033	see below	0.009	10 000	—
2. Competing tropical foodstuffs	337	−1 370	—	—	—	1.323	1.288	1.125	1.220	1.188	1.157	1.126	1.097	1.068	1.041	1.014	0.988		0.022	10 000	—
3. Cereals and livestock	210	−1 480	1.32	1.28	1.24	1.20	1.16	1.12	1.08	1.04	1.00	0.96	0.92	0.88	0.84	0.80	0.76		0.031	10 000	—
4. Agricultural raw materials	344	320	—	—	—	1.652	1.606	1.563	1.520	1.473	1.439	1.400	1.362	1.326	1.310	1.256	1.223		0.047	10 000	—
5. Mining	1 940	−1 780	—	—	—	1.081	1.150	1.040	1.020	1.000	0.981	0.963	0.944	0.926	0.909	0.892	0.875		0.078	10 000	—
6. Oil	21 278	−22 470	—	—	—	1.00	—	—	—	—	—	—	—	—	—	—	—		—	—	1.00
7. Food	503	−460	—	—	—	1.337	1.314	1.292	1.270	1.248	1.227	1.206	1.186	1.166	1.147	1.128	1.109		0.125	2 500	1.15
8. Textiles	4 056	−7 440	—	—	—	1.374	1.345	1.317	1.290	1.263	1.237	1.211	1.186	1.161	1.136	1.113	1.089		0.125	3 500	1.15
9. Chemicals	180	−1 730	1.090	1.067	1.045	1.023	1.001	0.980	0.959	0.938	0.918	0.898	0.878	0.858	0.838	0.819	0.800		0.125	3 000	1.15
10. Nonmetallic products	657	−1 210	—	—	—	1.00	—	—	—	—	—	—	—	—	—	—	—		—	—	1.15
11. Basic metals	1 185	−2 190	—	—	—	1.00	—	—	—	—	—	—	—	—	—	—	—		—	—	1.15
12. Machinery	163	−780	1.189	1.166	1.144	1.000	1.100	1.079	1.058	1.037	1.017	0.997	0.977	0.957	0.939	0.920	0.901		0.250	2 000	1.55
13. Other industries	1 690	−11 980	1.020	1.001	0.983	0.965	0.948	0.930	0.913	0.896	0.880	0.864	0.848	0.831	0.814	0.798	0.782		0.250	8 000	1.20

Bounds[b]

1. Noncompeting tropical foodstuffs	—	—	—	56	56	57	58	59	59	60	61	61	62	63	64
2. Competing tropical foodstuffs	—	—	—	182	198	215	233	254	275	300	325	354	385	418	454
3. Cereals and livestock	230	230	230	230	230	230	230	230	230	230	230	230	230	230	230
4. Agricultural raw materials	—	—	—	194	215	239	265	294	326	361	400	445	493	546	606
5. Mining	—	—	—	572	750	983	1 287	1 686	2 209	2 893	3791	4965	6 505	8 522	11 163
6. Oil	—	—	—	—	—	—	—	—	—	—	—	—	—	—	—
7. Food	—	—	—	385	528	724	996	1 364	1 871	2 567	3 522	4 832	6 630	9 096	12 480
8. Textiles	—	—	—	372	452	550	669	815	992	1 206	1 469	1 787	2 175	2 647	3 221
9. Chemicals	195	232	277	331	395	471	562	670	800	955	1 139	1 360	1 624	1 939	2 315
10. Nonmetallic products	—	—	—	—	—	—	—	—	—	—	—	—	—	—	—
11. Basic metals	—	—	—	—	—	—	—	—	—	—	—	—	—	—	—
12. Machinery	87	104	124	148	176	211	251	300	358	427	509	607	725	865	1032
13. Other industries	1831	2184	2606	3110	3710	4428	5283	6304	7522	8975	10709	12776	15242	18168	21674

[a] The coefficients given are $\mu_k = \Sigma_i \mu_{i0k}$; the corresponding μ_{i0k} coefficients can be deduced from table 10.9 and the formulae of section 10.1.3.

[b] $(\widetilde{m-e})_k^s$ for $k=1,\ldots,5$ and $\tilde{m}_k^s$ for $k=6,\ldots,13$.

Table 10.30
Exogenous initial stocks of capital and labor, high elasticities version (in billion $).

	Latin America	Asia	Africa
Machinery	39 800	33 600	14 100
Construction	64 100	54 300	22 900
Labor	53 300	64 300	31 100

coefficients in developing countries and to the utility function of developed countries.

The coefficients of the high elasticities version which differ from those of the earlier version are given in tables 10.27–10.30. Table 10.27, which defines the capital coefficients for home goods, may be compared with table 10.13. The capital coefficients for import substitution of table 10.28 replace those of table 10.14, while the linearized utility function of developed countries given in table 10.29 replaces the one of table 10.26.

In the high elasticities variant, the initial capacities of table 10.10 are set equal to zero. The capital and labor existing in the base year of the model is added to the right-hand side of the capital and labor constraints. In the low elasticities version this right-hand side is K_{12}, K_{14}, and L for the two capital and for the labor balance, where K_{12} and K_{14} are the amounts of capital created during the period covered by the model (an endogenous variable), and L is the additional labor which becomes available during the period. In the high elasticities version it is necessary to add the initial stocks of capital $\tilde{K}_{12}$ and $\tilde{K}_{14}$ and labor $\tilde{L}$, so that the right-hand sides become $K_{12}+\tilde{K}_{12}$, $K_{14}+\tilde{K}_{14}$, and $L+\tilde{L}$. The values of $\tilde{K}_{12}$, $\tilde{K}_{14}$, $\tilde{L}$, and L are given in table 10.30.

The amount of aid was increased, as explained above. In the high elasticities variant, aid received by Latin America is equal to 9500 billions, by Asia to 8200 billions, and by Africa to 3300 billions.

CHAPTER 11

Computational experience in solving general equilibrium models

In this chapter we discuss our experiences and those of others in solving general equilibrium problems. In surveying the results of others we do not pretend to be exhaustive, and discuss only work which we have been able to follow fairly closely and which we think is representative of the type of experience that is to be expected in the field.

It may be useful at the outset to say that we define "a general equilibrium model" more narrowly than is sometimes done, e.g. by McKenzie (1976) in his survey. We exclude models in which there is a single agent, for which the difficulties associated with handling of budget constraints do not arise, and models in which agents do not behave as utility or profit maximizers. An example of the latter is linked Keynesian macroeconomic models like the LINK system (see Ball, 1973, and Waelbroeck, 1976)

11.1. A brief description of the models solved in the experiments

The experiments were carried out using two versions of GEM. Those based on the early version were more systematic. Except when otherwise stated, all comments apply to the early version. Table 11.1 roughly describes the characteristics of the early and final versions of GEM.

11.2. Phase 1 computations: Function evaluations

The choice of computational approach has little impact on the complexity of phase 1 computations. Choosing approaches (i), (ii), (iii), or (iv) of section 5.2 changes only a few constraints of the problem solved.

For reasons which are set out below (section 11.6) approaches (i) and (iii) were the only ones used. We also experimented with a mixture of approaches (i) and (iv).

Table 11.1
Characteristics of the models.

	Early version	Final versions
Constraints[a]	360	360
Variables[a]	880	880
of which bounded variables	400	400
Regions	5	5
Commodities	labor excluded	labor included
Balance of payments constraints[b]	3	3
Ad valorem tariffs	39	39
Oil export tariffs	4	4
Cobb–Douglas production functions	—	45
Current price saving constraints	—	3
International trade elasticities	low	low and high

[a] These are approximate numbers since they depend on the way the model is solved.

[b] There is only one balance of payments for the developed countries and the Middle East; one of the four balances of payments is implied by the others.

In each case we attempt to solve a medium-sized linear programming problem, which is a fairly expensive process.

11.3. Dimensionality of the Phase 2 "parameter revision"

The selection of a computational procedure depends also on the dimensionality of the parameter space on which the search for equilibrium must be conducted.

Approach (i) (removal of price distortions) involves searching for a set of 52 balance of payments prices,[1] equal to the dual prices of the international balance constraints, and four export tariffs, equal to the difference between the exogenous price of oil and its cost of production in different regions. Balance of payments prices are non-negative and oil export tariffs may be positive or negative; hence the search should be conducted over $R^4 \times \Omega^{52}$.

[1] In our model *ad valorem* import tariffs are linear functions of these prices.

Approach (iii) (search for equilibrium utilities) implies a search for 3 non-negative utilities (the utility of the remaining regions is maximized), 39 non-negative *ad valorem* import tariffs, and 4 oil export tariffs. So the search is over $R^4 \times \Omega^{42}$.

In the mixed welfare weight-price adjustment procedure described below, the search is over the 3 non-negative welfare weights, 52 export prices, and 4 oil export tariffs, i.e. over $R^4 \times \Omega^{55}$.

These figures refer to the basic versions of the model; in the "free trade" version, for instance, all nominal import tariffs are set equal to zero. The dimension of the search is drastically reduced to $R^4 \times \Omega^3$ for approach (iii).

11.4. Parameter revision using Scarf-type algorithms

The first solution approach we considered was a Scarf-type procedure. Examination of the problem convinced us this would have been too expensive. Experience with Scarf-type algorithms shows that hundreds—possibly thousands—of function evaluations are needed to solve problems with 10 or 15 dimensions and, as was explained in section 6.2, their number tends to depend on the square of the dimension of the search. Each function evaluation of the GEM model is expensive.

Convergence could be speeded up by starting close to the equilibrium; this is what the algorithms of Merril and Eaves and Saigal do. However, there should be no illusion about this being feasible: both prices and quantities in GEM are quite sensitive to changes in parameters, and only rough guesses can be made at how the equilibrium solution will respond to parameter changes.

Another idea is to start the search right away using a fine grid. Then each function evaluation would only require a few simplex iterations. This argument is mathematically, but not computationally, valid because there are fixed costs associated with starting and stopping the simplex algorithm. In particular, checking that a previous basis is still optimal costs 6 s of CPU time on a CDC 6400 for GEM: this is far from a negligible cost if many function evaluations are needed.

11.5. Newton and other Jacobian-based methods

Newton and other methods based on the gradient of functions have powerful convergence properties in the neighborhood of a solution, although they do not have the global convergence of Scarf-type algorithms. The gradients cannot be calculated analytically for our problem because of inequality constraints; but it would have been readily possible to calculate a secant approximation of the Jacobian, to be used in a gradient-based algorithm.

The number of dimensions for the parameter search is large; for example, in the search for equilibrium utilities the dimension is 46, and it would take 47 function evaluations to calculate a secant approximation of the gradient. However, the problem has major (the 3 utility levels) and minor (the 43 tariffs) parameters. It would thus have been possible to compute an approximate gradient in utility space using four function evaluations; methods for choosing approximate values of the nominal tariffs can be devised.

This approach appeared feasible and would have been tried if tâtonnement had failed.

11.6. Designing a tâtonnement solution procedure

The reasons why a tâtonnement procedure is attractive for our problem are easy to understand in the light of the discussion in Chapter 7. The model studies the trade relations between three developing zones: Latin America, Africa, and Asia, and a Middle East oil–Developed countries zone. The developing regions all tend to export primary products and to import manufactures, so that an increase in the exports of any one zone adversely affects the terms of trade and the balance of payments of the others (*gross substitutes property*). The importance of the Middle East oil–Developed countries zone also dictated the *choice of normalization* in utility tâtonnement:[2] it was that region's utility which was maximized in the search for equilibrium utilities approach.

Since we did not want to make things too easy for the algorithm, we kept the import demand elasticities of Middle East–Developed and developing countries at levels which we were beginning to think were rather low.[3] We thought computation would be too easy if price elasticities were

[2] See the remark on normalization in section 11.7.

[3] The import demand elasticities of Middle East–Developed countries, which are reflected in the trade production function for developed countries, had been chosen following conversations with IBRD staff. That they were too low became gradually apparent on the basis of new econometric studies, the most important of which were those of Adams and Behrman (1976). The import demand elasticities of developing countries depend in a complex way on the assumed import substitution mechanism. Experiments with the model suggested that the way in which this had been specified understated the response of imports to changes in tariffs.

high because income effects would be small; and it was shown in Chapter 7 that it is income effects which may jeopardize the stability of tâtonnement processes.

It was necessary to choose the *adjustment speeds* (the κ_i of rule T in Chapter 7). In the continuous case, stability is independent of adjustment speed in the gross substitutes case. But this does not apply to a discrete tâtonnement involving successive "jumps" in which too high a speed of adjustment may well lead to overshooting of the solution and lack of convergence. Originally we considered four processes:

(i) removal of price distortions;
(ii) search for equilibrium prices;
(iii) search for equilibrium utilities; and
(iv) search for equilibrium Negishi welfare weights.

It appeared difficult to guess the correct adjustment speeds for processes (ii) and (iv). We thought that the efficient frontier and the utility frontier which determine the response of excess budgets to welfare weights were rather flat in the GEM model, so that small price and welfare weight changes would lead to large jumps in the solution.[4]

For process (iii) the choice of adjustment speeds seemed obvious. As $\lambda_i = 1/\alpha_i$ is the marginal utility of money for agent i, a unit change in his income corresponds—if prices are constant—to a change in $1/\alpha_i$ of his utility. It therefore was appropriate to choose a speed of adjustment of $1/\alpha_i = \kappa_i$. (In particular, since the α_i values were not very far from unity, κ_i was set equal to 1.)

For process (i) also it was obviously sensible to set the balance of payments prices at each iteration equal to the international dual prices in the preceding iteration. A more precise rule could have been worked out, but again this did not seem worthwhile.

We also experimented with a mixed rule combining (i) and (iv) for which an obvious choice of adjustment speeds is also possible.

It was finally necessary to select a standardized way of starting the algorithm which did not depend on knowledge of a previous equilibrium point. This starting point, the *near equilibrium program*, was a solution of a master program in which international prices and regional welfare weights were chosen equal to arbitrary but reasonable values. We set international prices in the balance of payments constraints equal to prices in the base year (equal to 1 by an appropriate choice of quantity units). For welfare weights we used the fact that utility functions had been calibrated so that

[4]We now think that this fear was exaggerated since prices are quite sensitive to changes in the model's exogenous variables.

utility levels achieved by consumers when all prices are the same equalled consumption at base year prices. The marginal utility of income should then be close to unity (equal if all prices are the same); the α_i values were therefore set equal to unity.

It is the near equilibrium program which determined the increase in the capital stock compatible with the saving investment identity. This program contained a constant price saving constraint.[5] Its solution gives a capital stock equal to the value of construction and machinery evaluated at the near equilibrium dual prices. In later iterations the model was solved without a saving function but with a capital use constraint.[6]

The near equilibrium program used to initialize the three procedures is as follows.

Program P1: Near equilibrium program. $\max \Sigma \tilde{\alpha}_i U_i(x_i)$ $(\tilde{\alpha}_i > 0)$ s.t. $\Sigma_i x_i - \Sigma_i \omega_i - \Sigma_j y_j \leqslant 0$, $\tilde{p} \cdot (x_i - \Sigma_j \theta_{ij} y_j - \omega_i) \leqslant 0$, $x_i \in X_i$ for every i and $y_j \in Y_j$ for every j.

We now describe the three computational procedures.

Computational procedure I: Removal of price distortions.

- Step 1: Set the values of $\tilde{\alpha}, \tilde{p} > 0$.
- Step 2: Solve the mathematical program P1. Check whether u, the optimal values of the Lagrange multipliers associated with the $\Sigma_i x_i - \Sigma \omega_i - \Sigma_j y_j \leqslant 0$ constraints of P1, are proportional to $\tilde{p}$.
- Step 3: Should this be true, we can consider $\tilde{p} = u$ as a fixed point of the mapping $P : p \to p$. If this is not the case, put $\tilde{p} = u$ and go to step 2.

Computational procedure II: Simultaneous search for equilibrium Negishi welfare weights and removal of price distortions.

- Steps 1, 2: These are the same as in computational procedure I.
- Step 3: If $u \neq \tilde{p}$, set $\tilde{p} = u$ as in procedure I. Also, compute a new value for $\tilde{\alpha}_i$ as suggested by theorem 5.1.2, i.e. choose $\tilde{\alpha}_i = \tilde{\alpha}_i : (1 + \lambda_i)$ where, by convention, the left- and right-hand side $\tilde{\alpha}_i$ are the new and old values of the variable; λ_i is the value of the earlier optimal value of λ_i. Go to step 2.

[5] In the final version this was replaced by a theoretically more satisfactory formulation.

[6] Let $\bar{u}_1$ and $\bar{u}_2$, $\bar{K}_1$ and $\bar{K}_2$ be the near equilibrium dual prices and stocks of construction and machinery. Then the capital use constraint is

$$\sum_j (\bar{u}_1 \kappa_{1j} + \bar{u}_2 \kappa_{2j}) z_j \leqslant \bar{u}_1 \bar{K}_1 + \bar{u}_2 \bar{K}_2,$$

where κ_{1j} and κ_{2j} are the capital coefficients of industry j.

We now come to the third procedure, based on the concept of a Pareto optimum; define Program P2 as follows.

Program P2: Pareto optimum. $\max U_1(x_1)$ s.t. $U_i(x_i) \geqslant \tilde{U}(x_i^0)$ $(i=2,\ldots,m)$, $\Sigma_i x_i - \Sigma_i \omega_i - \Sigma_j y_j \leqslant 0$, $x_i \in X_i$ for every i, $y_j \in Y_j$ for every j; $\tilde{U}_i(x_i^0)$ is the value of consumer's i utility when he consumes a given bundle x_i^0.

Computational procedure III: Search for equilibrium utilities.

- Steps 1, 2: These are the same as in computational procedure I.
- Step 3: Set $\tilde{p}=u$ and compute excess budgets $b_i(\tilde{p})=\tilde{p}\cdot(\omega_i+\Sigma\theta_{ij}y_j-x_i)$ where u, y_j, and x_i are solutions of the previous mathematical program solved. If the excess budgets are negligibly small, go to step 6 (or end). If not, go to
- Step 4: Compute the welfares $U_i=U_i(x_i)$ of the last mathematical program solved, and set $\tilde{U}_i=\tilde{U}_i+b_i(\tilde{p})$, where, by convention, the left- and right-hand side U_i refer to the new and old values of U_i.
- Step 5: Set up a new program P2, solve it, and go to step 3.
- Step 6: (Optional) as a way of refining the approximation, set up a program P1 where the $\tilde{\alpha}$ and $\tilde{p}$ vectors are the dual solutions of the previous step 3 program.

11.7. Computational experience

11.7.1. Description of the computations

The computations were run on CDC 6400 and CDC 6600 computers on which a version of the linear programming code Apex I was available. It is useful, at this stage, to go into some detail concerning the code described at full length in CDC's user manual (1972). This will shed some light on the interpretation of the performance.

Apex I can be used as such by simply submitting to the code any linear program in a suitable form (MPS format) and by specifying how the problem should be solved: direction of optimization, name of the objective function, name of the right-hand side and the bounds vector, and type of desired printed output. A precise description of the files on which the various components of the problem are located—input data, advanced basis, etc.—should, of course, also be supplied to the computer. The optimal solution can then be transferred to a disc which is readable by a user-supplied FORTRAN program (USP). This program can compute whatever is needed, change some of the data of the problem, and submit it to Apex for a new solution. The general scheme is thus a series of as many (Apex→USP→Apex) iterations as needed.[7] Of course, such a procedure requires a fairly large number of files stored on disc to go from one function evaluation to the next; this means also that for each of these evaluations the matrix of the linear program must be reconstructed and the optimal solution, including the optimal basis, has to be stored on an external (not in the central memory) file.

Apex I can also be used as a callable subroutine. This means that the user has his own FORTRAN program and wants to employ special subroutines of the Apex I system, for instance the optimization subroutine. With this option the problem can reside in the central memory between the function evaluations; this simplifies the management of the various files, since they stay in core, and also reduces the computing time. There is neither reconstruction of the constraints matrix nor construction of an output file after each evaluation. Of course, there is no free lunch and this way of using Apex requires much more programming work and skill; in fact, it amounts to updating and recompiling the partly FORTRAN-written Apex I program.

We chose to use the first option; it is clear that if several dozens of runs have to be made, the second option would be preferred. We shall try to give an idea of the possible gains in computing time, using the second option.

The computer programs have been written in such a way that every one of the computational procedures required a maximum of eight to ten major iterations, the first of them being in each case the following P1-type program: $\max \sum_i \tilde{\alpha}_i U_i(x_i)$ s.t. $\sum_i x_i - \sum_j y_j - \sum_i \omega_i \leqslant 0$, $\tilde{p}\cdot(x_i - \sum_j \theta_{ij} y_j - \omega_i \leqslant 0$, $x_i \in X_i$, $y_j \in Y_j$, for every i and j where we chose the initial $\tilde{\alpha}_i$ values and $\tilde{p}$ as explained earlier.[8]

The following seven major iterations for procedures I and II are described in section 11.6 above. For procedure III there are six iterations of a P2-type program; the eighth and final iteration is a P1 program constructed as in Step 6 of the procedure.

11.7.2. Computational experience: The early version

The three procedures discussed in Section 11.6 have been tested on five

[7] This notion of iteration is different from the usual simplex iteration. To avoid confusion we use in the sequel the term "function evaluation" as opposed to "simplex iteration".

[8] The data concerning this first iteration will not be given; they are not very meaningful since the computations start with an advanced basis and not from a completely artificial one.

different variants of the same model.[9] The main results are summarized in table 11.2 which gives, for every variant, a measure of the speed of convergence and the total number of simplex iterations needed. The measure of the speed of convergence is the sum of absolute values of excess budgets (in this case the balances of payments) in millions of U.S. dollars. It may help the reader to evaluate the convergence to know that in variant I the equilibrium value of world imports is 178,100 millions.

In all cases convergence was achieved more or less quickly, except for run 2 with procedure I. On average the procedure in utility space (procedure III) performs best with an average of 130 simplex iterations to reach equilibrium, against 165 for procedure I and 172 for procedure II. The number of simplex iterations to achieve equilibrium is small anyway compared to the number needed to solve the P1-type linear program (between 800 and 1000 simplex iterations to achieve near equilibrium), and is only loosely related to the initial "distance" from equilibrium: compare for instance run A with run K.

From a practical point of view it is important to note that the "near equilibrium" prices and allocations give a good enough picture of the system to make it possible to use only the near equilibrium model in the initial exploration of the system. General equilibrium did, however, diverge from the preliminary near equilibrium solutions, especially for the values of excess budgets. As noted above, obtaining true general equilibrium solutions was a little more costly than remaining satisfied with calculations truncated at the near equilibrium stage.

The results shed light on the idea stressed by Dixon (1975a, 1975b) and Ginsburgh and Waelbroeck (1976a) that if the number of agents is less than the number of goods, indirect computation should be cheaper than direct computation because the fixed-point search is restricted to a smaller dimensional space. Procedure III is indeed cheaper than the others, but the gain is small. Since there seemed to be a gain, and our funds were limited, the other methods were not explored further; we preferred to gain more insight into procedure III.

Twelve variants of the model have been computed, including the five described earlier. The results are reproduced in table 11.3 which, basically,

[9]The variants were chosen for their economic meaning and for their value in testing the robustness of the procedure to sharp changes in starting values. The problems are (ordered from A to M in the tables): reference solution; free trade in Latin America; free trade in Asia; free trade in Africa; free trade in the developing countries; world-wide free trade; free trade in the developed world; free trade in developed and 50 percent tariff cut in developing countries; effects of the oil crisis; effects of the oil crisis I and recession in the developed world; effects of the oil crisis II; recession in the developed world, without oil crisis; and generalized preferences.

Table 11.2

Comparative performance of the procedures (early version).

	A			B			E			F			K		
	I	II	III	I	II	III	I	II	III	I	II	III	I	II	III
Function evaluation															
1	3184	3184	3184	10 367	10 367	10 367	17 900	17 900	17 900	13 771	13 771	13 771	8260	8260	8260
2	3342	3342	1154	2 322	2 322	1 742	3 751	3 751	2 794	4 405	4 405	.3 237	2917	2917	480
3	1680	1811	930	714	539	799	629	414	1 088	210	334	384	919	969	482
4	270	501	584	168	389	152	137	30	180	24	70	49	931	132	134
5	70	214	359	38	294	142	52	3	18	5	5	7	18	40	25
6	18	15	72	185	70	40	4	3	4	2	1	3	5	14	5
7	3	2	26	184	12	5	2	3	2	1	1	2	1	10	1
8	3	1	1	188	2	2	1	3	2	1	1	1	1	2	2
Number of simplex iterations	154	175	113	231	239	160	166	147	153	110	120	121	164	182	94

Each column gives the sum of the absolute values of the excess budgets during the iterative procedure.

Table 11.3
Performance of procedure III (early version).

	A		B		C		D		E		F	
	(1)	(2)	(1)	(2)	(1)	(2)	(1)	(2)	(1)	(2)	(1)	(2)
Function evaluation												
1	3 184		10 367		6 370		5 750		17 900		13 771	
2	1 154	51	1 742	73	2 899	67	1246	50	2 794	101	3 237	94
3	930	33	799	44	959	49	232	18	1 088	37	384	19
4	584	10	152	25	124	7	212	8	180	8	49	0
5	359	10	142	6	54	0	50	3	18	0	7	0
6	72	0	40	0	1	0	25	0	4	0	3	0
7	26	0	5	0	1	0	12	0	2	0	2	0
8	1	9	2	12	1	6	1	7	2	7	1	8
Total simplex iterations		113		160		129		86		153		121
Computing time												
Total	307		332		319		309		327		310	
of which LP	205		230		217		207		225		208	

Table 11.3 (*Continued*)

	G		H		I		J		K		L	
	(1)	(2)	(1)	(2)	(1)	(2)	(1)	(2)	(1)	(2)	(1)	(2)
Function evaluation												
1	4069		6824		34 740		27 202		8260		6414	
2	2071	54	1672	52	35 600	152	33 246	168	480	61	531	56
3	854	28	296	10	9 350	118	5 758	138	482	10	76	1
4	199	6	15	0	1 350	50	1 910	26	134	11	2	0
5	570	9	2	0	758	11	1 008	29	25	1	1	0
6	189	0	1	0	266	1	210	13	5	0	1	0
7	60	0	1	0	90	0	204	3	1	0	1	0
8	2	11	1	10	2	14	315	15	2	11	2	9
Total simplex iterations		108		72		345		392		94		66
Computing Time												
Total	313		265		404		451		312		230	
of which LP	211		163		302		349		210		128	

Column (1) gives the sum of the absolute values of the excess budgets.
Column (2) gives the number of simplex iterations for every function evaluation.

gives the same data as table 11.2: column (1) contains the sum of the absolute values of the excess budgets during the iterative process; column (2) gives the number of LP simplex iterations; for each problem we indicate also the total time taken in central processing seconds (the input–output time is negligible since Apex works in core) and the time taken for solving the various linear programs involved. The difference between the two numbers is due to:[10]

(a) the time taken for the construction of the LP matrices, which amounts to some 63 s per problem; this time could be saved if Apex was used as a subroutine, so that the problem would always remain in the memory;

(b) the time taken to prepare the final complete solution of the linear program: 7 s CP time; and

(c) the time for reading each LP solution, computing the excess budgets, and revising the data of the linear program before computing the next function evaluation: 32 s CP time.

It can be seen that, even when starting very far from equilibrium (cases I and J), convergence is achieved (case J would have needed two or three more evaluations) and that computing time is far from being prohibitive once a solution of the linear program including budget constraints is available. As already stated, this amounts to 1000 simplex iterations for our model; however, when alternative solutions are computed, we can start from a fairly good basis, e.g. the one for the reference solution.

11.7.3. Computational experience: The final version

Only procedure III was used; but the reader should bear in mind that a larger number of parameters are revised and that the model is in fact much more elaborate since it includes production functions and current price-saving constraints.

The impact of these modifications is clear; the average number of simplex iterations in the function evaluation phase increases very sharply:

	Simplex iterations
Early version	150
Final version, low elasticities	600
Final version, high elasticities	950

Computing times also increase, of course, but since computations for the

[10] These numbers are averages: the variance, however, is very small (about 2 or 3 percent).

Table 11.4
Performance of procedure III (final version, low elasticities).

	A		B		E		F		G		H		L		M	
	(1)	(2)	(1)	(2)	(1)	(2)	(1)	(2)	(1)	(2)	(1)	(2)	(1)	(2)	(1)	(2)
Function evaluation																
1	540	28	5 180	127	14 548	208	13 208	222	7316	49	2984	141	4856	44	6870	86
2	3 048	61	6 800	167	5 040	255	9 884	165	7698	59	9956	186	5978	73	2264	58
3	3 210	85	4028	316[a]	7 330	166	4 616	108	2634	134	5278	156	3078	92	3 134	37
4	1 052	98	2624	58	3 298	80	4 824	101	1308	72	3820	112	1480	64	1 168	22
5	1 792	74	1 340	51	2 302	22	804	21	2428	32	3388	103	2118	19	564	15
6	572	73	1046	31	542	58	1 386	26	1138	42	482	71	242	23	350	1
7	410	33	490	11	428	8	1 430	11	1062	28	524	46	588	15	114	5
8	364	44	472	11	710	10	384	9	444	18	998	32	390	19	60	0
9	724	34	1056	5	456	4	614	2	70	11	290	41	432	4	76	0
10	430	13	412	6	354	3	154	8	228	5	538	39	260	2	14	0
Total simplex iterations	543		783		814		673		450		927		355		224	
Computing time																
Total	976		1 189		1 188		1072		885		1284		833		723	
of which LP	908		1 120		1 118		1006		817		1220		772		654	

[a] Cycling.

Table 11.5
Performance of procedure III (final version, high elasticities).

	A		B		E		F		G		H		L		M	
	(1)	(2)	(1)	(2)	(1)	(2)	(1)	(2)	(1)	(2)	(1)	(2)	(1)	(2)	(1)	(2)
Function evaluation																
1	24 888	334	27 380	342	36 134	422	60 260	532	42 602	337	56 772	379	36 902	355	21 918	628
2	984	134	19 090	120	19 858	158	23 794	202	4 800	166	10 946	148	1 472	173	804	139
3	39 242	161	18 822	116	8 536	94	18 906	190	40 342	146	25 572	60	42 742	124	39 462	215
4	8 700	175	6 940	65	9 790	34	14 852	77	6 886	195	7 342	140	4 982	122	7 758	176
5	1 648	28	4 288	88	3 048	82	2 640	49	5 816	42	2 422	87	3 154	47	1 878	48
6	1 570	15	1 932	51	904	25	814	42	892	39	820	46	2 876	36	1 882	60
7	1 750	18	1 376	9	546	16	710	4	1 000	26	464	5	546	1	1 708	14
8	230	16	830	4	728	16	400	9	502	7	610	11	306	8	358	9
9	144	0	1 226	0	498	10	282	1	204	1	32	16	212	3	134	1
Total simplex iterations		881		795		857		1106		959		892		869		1290
Computing time																
Total	1 127		1075		1 163		1 373		1 181		1235		1 179		1514	
of which LP	1 083		1032		1 119		1 329		1 137		1 190		1 136		1470	

early and the final versions were not run on the same computer, the comparison is not very meaningful.

The difference between the low and high elasticities versions should not be taken too seriously either. Indeed, all computations have been initialized with the same starting basis; but, as was explained in Chapter 10, the two versions of the model are not the same. And, as is apparent, the starting basis was better for the low elasticities version than for the other: indeed, for the first function evaluation there is a difference of some 300 simplex iterations between the two versions. If we neglect this "starting effect", the number of simplex iterations is approximatively the same in the two cases. This conclusion does not support the intuitive impression that, since high elasticities induce small income effects, tâtonnement would do better than with low elasticities.

It is worth mentioning finally that in early calculations with the high elasticities version, difficulties were encountered when the solution turned out to be outside of the range over which the model is described by a fairly smooth piecewise linear approximation. When the solution was close to a sharp "corner" of the feasible set it sometimes oscillated without converging. Such a corner can of course be smoothed out without changing the basic shape of the feasible area by using a larger number of approximating hyperplanes intersecting sufficiently close to each other.

11.7.4. Possibly cheaper methods of solution

The master program solved for each function evaluation is highly decomposable. The linking constraints are the world import–export balances. The rest of the model is made of decomposable blocks. It might be worth experimenting with an up-to-date program based on the Dantzig–Wolfe decomposition algorithm (see Dantzig, 1963). Experience shows that this approach is less effective than would be expected given its elegant theoretical basis, but it could lead to cost reductions in a highly structured problem like ours.

A possibly even more attractive solution would be to experiment with a tâtonnement process adjusting prices in response to excess demands. Its advantage is that it is the only one which breaks down the model into fully separate linear programs which can be solved independently of each other. This would bring about a reduction of the cost of each iteration, as the cost of solving a linear program rises faster than the number of its constraints. The difficulty would lie in selecting an adjustment speed of prices to excess demands which does not result in overshooting of the solution and hence in instability. We have not had the opportunity to try this approach.

11.8. Other research experiences: A brief survey

We close this chapter by reporting briefly on other work which we have had the opportunity of following.

Dixon (1975b) has applied the tâtonnement approach to problems presented by Scarf (1973) and by Shoven and Whalley (1974a, b). It turned out that the approach was extremely effective, achieving about 1 percent accuracy in four to five function evaluations. By comparison, Hansen and Scarf needed 468 and 913 iterations for the two problems solved by Dixon. The calculations per evaluation are roughly the same for both methods.

The comparison is unfair for two reasons. Scarf-type methods have become more efficient since Hansen, Scarf, Shoven and Whalley made their calculations—although the improvement has not reduced their cost very sharply. More importantly, the problems solved by Dixon were "easy" and were only meant to illustrate the working of the algorithms rather than their ability to solve intractable problems. It is interesting therefore to report calculations of solving Scarf's (1960) well-known counter-example to tâtonnement stability. Neither price nor welfare weight converges in this case (see Chapter 7). This led Osterrieth to apply a gradient procedure to the problem, which converged in a few iterations (depending on the starting point). Fair solved the same problem very quickly using a Gauss–Seidel algorithm, a variant of the tâtonnement procedure, but with a different normalization than that implied by classical tâtonnement.[11]

It is also useful to report experiments with larger models. Dixon (1975a) reported calculations done in 1973 in which he illustrated his joint maximization approach by solving a model of trade between artificial countries, represented by input–output tables for the US economy for three different years. The procedure he used was "search for equilibrium utilities". The utility function was of the max min x_i/c_i form. The problem is simple but not trivial because prices cannot readily be calculated and because tâtonnement algorithms may diverge when there are three agents (or three goods). An accurate solution was found in three iterations.

[11]See the remarks on Fair's choice of normalization in Chapter 7.

Adelman and Robinson (1978) solved a general equilibrium model of the Korean economy; the problem is dynamic, involving a search for a fixed point for several groups of consumers over a ten-year period. The intertemporal links, however, are not strong. The rate of growth of the capital stock is exogenous; the main problem is thus to allocate investment in each year so that the discounted rates of return are equal. An endogenous growth of the capital stock would have made the problem more difficult.

Their computational procedure is interesting in that it uses both a tâtonnement algorithm and a Jacobian-based procedure (the Powell algorithm). The first is used to balance the supply and demand of goods, the second to balance the supply and demand of factors of production. The authors argue that factor demand is more interdependent than demand for goods,[12] and they justify in this way their choice of algorithms. The computations are done in two nested loops:

(a) an inner loop which matches factor supply and demand in each year; and

(b) an outer loop which matches the supply and demand of commodities in each year.

The function evaluation step in their model is cheap since the excess demand functions are defined analytically. There are, however, 2400 of these nonlinear equations. The number of iterations is of the order of 2000; solutions required an average of 90 s on the IBM 360-91 at Princeton University.

The nondifferentiability of functions is a basic problem in solving equilibrium problems. This can be eliminated by appropriate specification, as in the Adelman-Robinson model; but the difficulty is inherent in many economic problems, such as those involving capacity bottlenecks or import and export quotas. This lends interest to the work of Keyzer, Lemarechal and Mifflin on solving a world agricultural trade model in which countries seek to control food prices within the bounds set by import and export quotas. The algorithm used involves two loops: an inner loop, designed by Keyzer (unpublished), which solves the country models subject to given world prices, and an outer loop which solves the world system, designed by Mifflin (1977). The Keyzer algorithm is guaranteed to converge if the equilibrium problem is specified in the appropriate way. This means that production is considered as given (which is reasonable for

[12] See the discussion of "near separability" in Chapter 7.

most agricultural products), and that domestic demand in any year depends on Cobb–Douglas or linear expenditure system utility functions.[13] The algorithm has been used only on test problems, but it is planned to solve the world food model which the International Institute for Applied Systems Analysis (IIASA) is building.

Mifflin's algorithm has also been used to solve the test problems presented in Scarf (1973). The authors let the algorithm run until the precision achieved matches that of Scarf's calculations, in the sense of the maximum norm. Although it is difficult to compare the results of calculations done on different computers, it appears that the order of magnitude of the cost is about the same as that of Scarf's calculations, so that the procedure proved expensive for these problems. It does not have global convergence properties, but a "ball of attraction" local convergence result holds.[14] Use of the method in preference to Scarf's may however be justified for problems with many dimensions for, unlike Scarf-type procedures, the number of iterations of Mifflin's (1978) method is not closely linked to the dimensionality of the search. In judging the results, it must also be realized that this is experimental work with a new algorithm the efficiency of which can perhaps be increased substantially (Scarf's calculation, to which the results of the Mifflin algorithm are compared, also used an early version of his algorithm).

11.9. Appendix: Notes on the computer program

11.9.1. Introduction

During the early stages of the computations, namely the adjustment of the model (1973–74), use was made of the linear programming code Ophelie written in the mid-1960s for the Control Data 6600 computer. Ophelie had the advantage of including parameterization possibilities which were not currently available on the more recent and efficient code, Apex. Indeed, parameterization is a very useful device during the construction of a model since it makes it possible to examine at a relatively low cost, the possibility

[13] See Geary (1950–51) for the specification of these utility functions and Stone (1954) for the first application to demand estimation.

[14] The number of iterations is smaller than that reported by Scarf, but individual iterations cost more computer time than those of the Scarf procedure.

frontier of the model, and the way the different substitutions which are built in can operate.

The first general equilibrium solutions reported in Ginsburgh and Waelbroeck (1976a) have been computed "by hand" in the sense that the excess budgets were calculated outside of the computer based on the solution of each linear program (function evaluation). On the basis of these "hand" computations, a new linear program, with revised welfares, was set up (revision) and resubmitted to the computer. It was only after some experience had been gained on the model and the algorithms that we decided to program the whole procedure.

Before describing the program it is useful to go into some detail concerning the Apex code described at full length in CDC (1972).

11.9.2. The Apex computer code in general

Essentially, Apex can be thought of as a FORTRAN-written computer program, solving linear programming problems, almost entirely in-core.[15] It consists of a series of subroutines, the main ones of which (for our needs at least) are: INPUT, REVISE, BCDOUT, SELECT, LIST, EQLIST, BASISIN (or CRASH), PRIMAL, BASISOUT, and OUTPUT. Each of these subroutines is concerned with a specific action and will now be briefly described.[16]

INPUT: This subroutine reads in the data of the model, written in a specific way, and constructs the files necessary for processing.

REVISE: This subroutine allows changing the data of the original model, without actually changing anything in the original input deck. The REVISE file only contains information about the coefficients which are changed in, added to, or deleted from the original file.

[15] The dimension of the problem which can be handled can be deduced from the following formula giving the amount of central memory (CM) required for a run: $CM = 10m + 0.65p + 0.5n + 3(m/n)p + 12\,000$, where m is the number of rows, n the number of columns (including the right-hand sides), and p the number of nonzero coefficients in the constraint matrix and the right-hand sides. For our problem we had CM = 24 500 out of the 64 000 memory length usually available on a CDC 6400. However, it should be noted that when using some special perturbation techniques (in the case of almost singularities, or ill-conditioned matrices caused by normalization problems) this field length is usually too small.

[16] Our aim is not to describe the exact way a program has to be written, but only to give the general structure. They syntactic details can be found in CDC (1972).

BCDOUT: Files created by the INPUT and possible REVISE subroutines are converted back into card images, thereby creating a new data deck. This subroutine is useful if the user desires a corrected revised input deck for further use.

SELECT: Several SET instructions specify the direction of optimization and which equation and vectors should be chosen as objective function, right hand side and bounds set. These instructions are followed by a call of the SELECT subroutine which completely builds up the problem to be solved.

LIST and EQLIST: LIST gives a list of the constraints and/or variables of the model, including name, type ($=, \leqslant, \geqslant, \ldots$), number of coefficients; also upper and/or lower bounded variables are given, together with the value of the bound. The second subroutine, EQLIST, provides the user with a printout of the constraints. Both these subroutines are very useful to check whether the problem is error-free.

CRASH or BASISIN: The CRASH subroutine generates a starting basis if no other (better) basis is available to start with. On the other hand, BASISIN instructs the computer to read an existing advanced basis currently residing on some specific file.

PRIMAL: This is the central subroutine of Apex. It solves the linear program (or informs the user that the problem is infeasible or unbounded).

BASISOUT: This subroutine saves the current optimal basis of the problem. This basis can then be resubmitted to Apex, in another run, by the BASISIN subroutine.

OUTPUT: This final subroutine prepares the solution report. It has two[17] main options: the solution can be printed and/or it can be cast into a FORTRAN-readable file.

Apex is constructed in such a way that each of the subroutines can, loosely speaking, be extracted and called as a subroutine from a main FORTRAN program written by the user. On the other hand, Apex can be used as such

[17]It has more than two options, but only two are of interest to us.

by simply submitting to the code any linear program and specifying how the problem should be solved; this will be called an Apex Control Program, or simply an Apex Program.[18]

In the first option the user writes his own FORTRAN program and calls, when and if needed, one or more of the Apex subroutines, exactly in the same way as he would call them in a usual program (the instruction in the main FORTRAN program is simply CALL XXX, where XXX is the subroutine required).[19] For instance, the data of a problem can be modified, according to the results of a first optimization, and the newly created problem can be submitted in the same run to be reoptimized. The structure of such a run would require a FORTRAN program to be written, calling several Apex subroutines, checking the results of the first optimization, revising the data of the problem according to these results, and recalling Apex subroutines to optimize and print the output. Clearly, as is the case with every program, provided there is sufficient core the problem can reside in central memory during the whole run. This simplifies the management of various external files (since very few will exist) and reduces the computing time since the program has direct access to all the data at each moment. Of course, there is no free lunch and this way of using Apex requires much more programming work and skill; in fact, it amounts to updating and recompiling the partly FORTRAN-written Apex-I program, which can be relatively time and money consuming during the focusing needed for every computer program.

In the second option, Apex and the user-written FORTRAN program remain isolated, and the communication between both is made through external files, usually disks. The example problem given in the preceding paragraph would be treated in the following way. A first Apex run would solve the problem and write the solution on a disk; a FORTRAN user program would read this solution from the disk, revise the data, and write a revised file in card images; this last file, together with the original data would then be resubmitted to Apex for a second optimization. The difference with the first option is that, necessarily, external files have to be created, even if the dimension of the problem does not need them; this means that there will be a file management problem and also that the run will take more time since files have to be written to and read from external files.

[18] There is still another possibility in which user-written FORTRAN subroutines can be called from a main Apex Program.

[19] Initially, of course, some interfacing is necessary.

Figures 11.1 and 11.2 attempt to capture the essential features of both options.

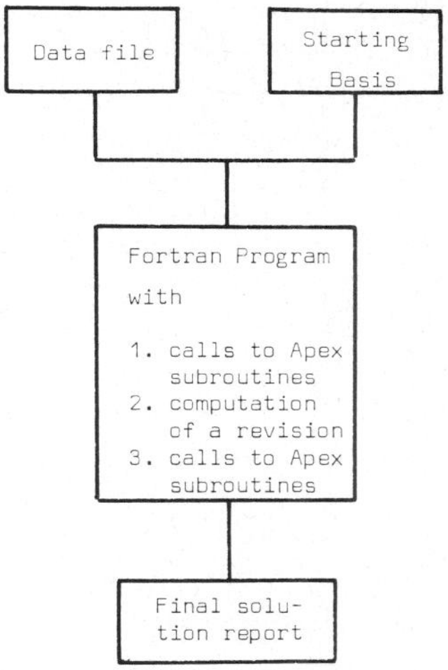

Figure 11.1. Scheme of the computer program, option 1.

Despite its less-efficient behavior, we chose the second option. The main reason was that we were experimenting with a genuine approach which meant a large number of changes in the user-written program (i.e. the algorithms described in Chapter 5 and in the main text of this chapter); since each change had to be tried out, much computer time would have been spent in updating and recompiling each time the user-written program was coupled with the Apex subroutines.

The program we have written therefore consists of a series of {Apex→ user-written→Apex} iterations, linked through external files. We now briefly sketch the structure of both the Apex and the user-written programs, before discussing the link between them. To be complete, we also briefly describe the structure of the data deck, the data revisions deck, and the initial basis deck.[20]

[20] In the MPS format; there are other formats which can be used. This one, however, is the most common.

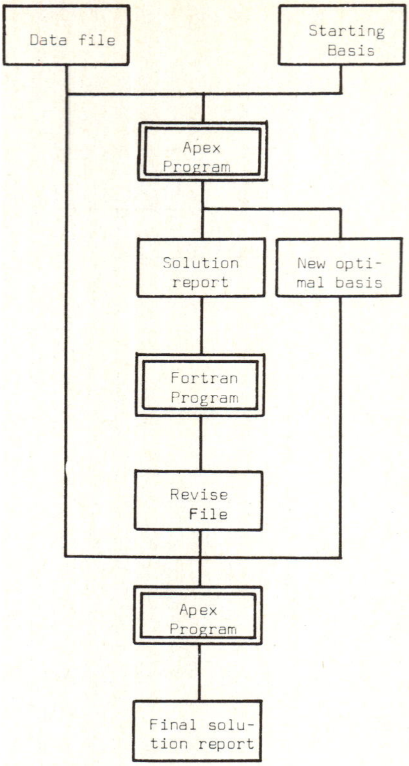

Figure 11.2. Scheme of the computer program, option 2.

11.9.3. The data deck

The deck is divided into four sections which appear in the following order.

(a) The ROWS section which specifies the names of the constraints and their type.

(b) The COLUMNS section which specifies the coefficients of the constraints matrix; each coefficient is located by a row name and a column (variable) name.

(c) The RIGHT-HAND-SIDE section in which the cards define the right-hand-side values for the constraints.

(d) The BOUNDS section (optional) which indicates the variables that are bounded and the values of the bounds.

Each section starts with a header card. The first card of the deck is the name header, punched in the following format:[21]

col. 1–4: NAME
col. 15–24: name of the problem (alphanumeric)

The *rows section* starts with the header card:

col. 1–4: ROWS

The following cards describe all the rows—constraints and objective function(s)—as follows:

col. 3 : constraint type: N for free row (objective function)
E for equality
G for greater or equal
L for less or equal
col. 5–14: rowname (alphanumeric)

The *columns section* starts with the header card:

col. 1–7: COLUMNS

The following cards describe the coefficients of the constraints matrix and the objective function(s):

col. 5–14: name of the column (variable)
col. 15–24: name of the row (constraint)
col. 25–34: value of the coefficient

Notice that zero coefficients do not have to be specified and that all coefficients referencing the same variable must follow each other (in any order).

The *right-hand-side section* starts with the header

col. 1–3: RHS

[21]In what follows we use capital letters for the letters which are actually punched and small letters in all other cases.

The following cards contain the values and are punched as follows:

col. 5–14: right-hand-side name[22] (alphanumeric)
col. 15–24: name of the row (as defined in the rows section)
col. 25–34: value of the element

The *bounds section* starts with the header

col. 1–6: BOUNDS

The following cards contain the values and specify the type of bound:

col. 2–3: type of bound UP: $0 \leqslant x_j \leqslant \bar{u}_j$
LO: $0 < \underline{u}_j \leqslant x_j$
FR: $-\infty \leqslant x_j \leqslant \infty$
FX: $x_j = c_j$
MI: $x_j \leqslant 0$
col. 5–14: bounds' set name[23] (alphanumeric)
col. 15–24: name of the column (variable)
col. 25–34: value of the bound for types UP, LO, and FX

The final card of the data deck is:

col. 1–6: ENDATA

11.9.4. The (optional) revision deck

Instead of manually changing the cards of the data deck, the user can construct a revision deck which, merged with the original data deck, produces a new (revised) data deck.[24]

Four directives can be used: AFTER, BEFORE, DELETE, and MODIFY. The deck is organized in the same way as the data deck; it contains the same header cards, namely ROWS, COLUMNS, RHS, and BOUNDS,

[22] Several RHS vectors can be specified, one after the other. However, all the coefficients pertaining to one vector must have the same RHS name and follow each other (in any order).

[23] Footnote 22 applies with bounds' sets instead of RHS sets.

[24] This new deck can be saved on a file (disk or even cards) by the BCDOUT instruction. Of course, when the EDIT software is available corrections can be made without using REVISE.

each of which is followed by the corrections; and the first header card is again a NAME card and the last one an ENDATA card.

The directives are written as follows.

(a) The AFTER directive:

col. 3–7: AFTER

or { col. 3–7: AFTER
col. 15–24: name of a row, column, right-hand-side set, and bounds' set }

The first option inserts new elements or vectors after the last previously existing element or vector. The second option inserts new elements or vectors after the element or vector referred to in col. 15–24.

(b) The BEFORE directive:

col. 3–8: BEFORE

or { col. 3–8: BEFORE
col. 15–24: name of a row, column, right-hand-side set, and bounds' set }

The first option inserts new elements or vectors before all existing elements or vectors; the second option inserts them before the element or vector referred to in col. 15–24.

(c) The MODIFY directive:

col. 3–8: MODIFY

This directive modifies an existing vector (in the rows section) or element (in the other sections).

(d) The DELETE directive:

col. 3–8: DELETE

This instruction deletes an existing vector (in the rows and columns section) or the whole set (in the RHS and bounds sections).

Each of these directives is followed by cards (or card images) written in the same format as for the data deck on which the directive acts.

11.9.5. The (optional) initial basis deck

Since this deck is usually provided by the computer, let us simply say that it consists of:

(a) a header card

col. 1–4: NAME
col. 15–24: name of the basis

(b) a series of cards stating the names of the variables (including slacks) which are basic and nonbasic; and

(c) a final card

col. 1–6: ENDATA

11.9.6. The Apex Control Program

With the information given in sections 11.9.2–11.9.5, it is easy to see how an Apex Program can be constructed.[25]

Each subroutine is called by a macro instruction punched on a card in the following format:

col. 1–10: used for an optional (alphanumeric) label to which another instruction can send
col. 11–20: name of the subroutine
col. 21–30, 31–40, 41–50, 51–60, 61–70: reserved for optional parameters, which are generally (except for the case of the SET verb):
col. 21–30: a name to be found on or to be given to a header card of either the data, the revision or the initial basis deck
col. 31–40: the name of the external file on which the deck resides or on which it has to be written

For the special SET instruction, the following applies:

col. 1–10: optional label
col. 11–20: SET
col. 21–30: conventional name: KNDIR: direction of optimization
KNOBJ: objective function
KNRHS: right-hand-side
KNBND: bounds

[25] Here also we restrict our attention only to the material we need. It should be noted that, if the control program is not too long or complex, it can be created by Apex itself using a single control card.

col. 31–40: contains the direction of optimization (MAX or MIN) for KNDIR and the names of the objective function, the right-hand-side and the bounds' set to be used in the run

We should also add that almost every instruction of this type is followed by a so-called BRANCH card which instructs the computer what to do in the case where something abnormal happens, for instance if the name of the header card does not correspond to the one mentioned in columns 21–30 of the preceding instruction. Since this has nothing to do with the logic of our program, we do not want to enter into the details, although the instructions are compulsory.

The logical steps of the program are: (1) read the data of the problem; (2) read a possible revision deck; (3) save the revised data (optional); (4) print the list of variables, bounds, and equations (optional); (5) specify the objective function, the direction of optimization, the RHS set, and the bounds set; (6) read a starting basis or (6′) ask the computer to set up a basis; (7) solve the model; (8) save the new basis (optional); (9) print or (9′) write on a disk or (9″) print and write on a disk the results; (10) terminate. For this simple scheme, the program will be written as follows:

```
    (1)  INPUT        ANYNAME      TAPE1
    (2)  REVISE       ANYNAME      TAPE7
    (3)  BCDOUT       ANYNAME      TAPE13
    (4)  LIST
         EQLIST
    (5)  SET          KNDIR        MAX (or MIN)
         SET          KNOBJ        OBJFNAME
         SET          KNRHS        RHSNAME
         SET          KNBND        BNDNAME
         SELECT
    (6)  BASISIN      ANYNAME      TAPE3
or  (6′) CRASH
    (7)  PRIMAL
    (8)  BASISOUT     ANYNAME      TAPE4
    (9)  OUTPUT       FULL
or  (9′) OUTPUT       SPECIAL      TAPE12
or  (9″) OUTPUT       FULL/SPEC    TAPE12
    (10) EXIT
```

Two remarks are in order. The first concerns the name appearing in the second field of the card (specified here as ANYNAME) when a file is read or created. If there is only one set in the file (a unique data set, or revise set, or starting basis set), the name can be replaced by a $ sign in column 20;[26] the same applies if a file is created, i.e. if no name is specified but a $ sign is punched in column 20, the file is automatically given the name of the existing problem. The second remark concerns the file name appearing in the third field; actually, any name can be used provided the interfacing with the computer control program is correctly written. The names we have given are those assigned by default by the Apex Program; this means implicitly that if those names are used in the computer control program, they do not have to be specified in the Apex Control Program. They are automatically assigned and the third field in the card can remain blank.

11.9.7. Structure of the solution file created by Apex

As already mentioned, a FORTRAN readable file of the solution can be provided by the Apex Control Program. This file is written on TAPE12.

Each solution file contains first two header records[27] divided into seven words; the seventh word of the first record gives the value of the objective function; the others contain information on the problem handled, like the name of the problem, of the objective function, etc.

The following records contain the solution. A seven-word record is written for each constraint and variable. Each constraint record contains the following information:

Word	Type	Information
1	alphanumeric	name of the row
2	real	value of the left-hand side
3	real	value of the slack
4	real	RHS lower limit
5	real	RHS upper limit
6	real	value of the dual variable
7	octal	special word

[26] In fact, if a $ sign is punched, the first set of the file is taken into consideration if there are several sets present on the file.

[27] Generally speaking, each (un)formated WRITE statement in FORTRAN defines a record. Likewise, a record can be read by an (un)formated FORTRAN READ statement.

Each variable record contains the following:

Word	Type	Information
1	alphanumeric	name of the column
2	real	level of the variable
3	real	corresponding objective function coefficient
4	real	lower bound on the variable
5	real	upper bound on the variable
6	real	marginal value[28]
7	octal	special word

In both cases the seventh word contains information on the states of the row or column variable, which are of no interest to us. A final seven-word record is written to indicate the end of the file. It contains the following:

Word	Type	Indication
1	alphanumeric	$$END$$bbb
2–7	—	zeros

All these records can be read as follows:

```
READ(12) (WORD(J), J=1,7)
```

The whole FORTRAN program to read the output file is very simple to write. One of the possible forms is given here:

```
          PROGRAM(INPUT,OUTPUT,TAPE12)
          REWIND 12
C         READING IS DONE IN A DO LOOP
          DO 200 I=1,100 000
          READ(12) (WORD(J), J=1,7)
          IF(WORD(1).EQ.10H$$END$$bbb) GO TO 900
C         TREATMENT OF THE INFORMATION
          ...
    200   CONTINUE
    900   CONTINUE
          ...
          CALL EXIT
          END
```

[28] By marginal value is meant the corresponding "$z_j - c_j$" value of the simplex criterion. Note that for a bound the "$z_j - c_j$" value is the shadow price.

Note that the seventh word of record 3 and the following (the so-called special word) cannot be treated as such. Special subroutines are necessary to disassemble the word (see CDC, 1972, appendix B).

11.9.8. The user-written FORTRAN program

Let us recall that the purpose of this program is to read the solution of the linear program, change specific coefficients, construct a revise file, and submit a revised problem to a new Apex run.

Actually, there are two types of programs which had to be written:

(a) a program 1 which leads from the near equilibrium to the first "equilibrium" iteration; and

(b) a program 2 leading from one "equilibrium" iteration to the next; this program contains options for the various computational procedures.

The two programs could have been written as a unique program. In fact, they differ very little from each other; they simply construct different revisions of the data.

Programs 1 and 2 make use of five external files:

INPUT: we did not use it, but information can be read from the INPUT file.

OUTPUT: after each function evaluation the program prints the value of exports, imports, their prices, the *ad valorem* tariffs, the balances of payments, and any other relevant information

TAPE7: on which the REVISE file is written by program 2

TAPE12: from which program 2 has to read the solution of the linear program

TAPE15: contains the tariff structure if prices are equal to 1 (since they will be updated by the formula $p_{ij}t_{ij}$, where p_{ij} is the price of imports of commodity j in country i and t_{ij} is the tariff); it also contains information on the choice of the computational procedure and the different parameters needed (e.g. the adjustment speed parameters)

The main FORTRAN instructions of the programs are the following:

```
PROGRAM FTN (INPUT, OUTPUT, TAPE7, TAPE12,
             TAPE15)
```

```
              ...
C             READING THE TARIFFS AND THE INSTRUCTIONS
C             CONCERNING THE CHOSEN
C             COMPUTATIONAL PROCEDURE (TAPE15)
              REWIND 15
              READ (15,1)...
      1       FORMAT
C             READING THE SOLUTION FILE OF APEX (TAPE12)
              REWIND 12
C             READING OF THE HEADER RECORDS
              DO 100 I=1,2
      100     READ(12) (WORD(K), K=1,7)
C             READING OF DUAL VARIABLES
              DO 101 I=1,M
      101     READ(12) A, A, A, A, A, DUAL(I), A
C             READING OF PRIMAL VARIABLES
              DO 102 I=1,N
      102     READ(12) A, PRIMAL(I), A, A, A, A, A
C             CHOICE OF THE COMPUTATIONAL PROCEDURE
              ...
C             COMPUTATIONS
              ...
C             PRINTING OF SELECTED RESULTS
              ...
C             STOP ITERATIONS IF RESULTS OF TWO
C             SUCCESSIVE FUNCTION EVALUATIONS
C             ARE CLOSE ENOUGH
              ...
C             CONSTRUCTION OF THE REVISE FILE (TAPE7)
              REWIND7
              WRITE(7,2)
              WRITE(7,3)
              ...
              WRITE(7,90)
      2       FORMAT(4HNAME, 10X, 7HANYNAME)
      3       FORMAT(7HCOLUMNS)
              ...
      90      FORMAT(6HENDATA)
              CALL EXIT
              END
```

The only remark concerns the way to stop the whole procedure when an approximate fixed point has been located. A very easy way of doing this, although not the most elegant, is to introduce in the program a READ statement which reads nonexistent data.

11.9.9. The computer control program

This program links together the different steps of the procedure and manages the various files. It is written in the SCOPE control language but can easily be adapted, e.g. to NOS.

The program involves five existing permanent files (the Apex program, the two FORTRAN programs, the data, and an advanced basis) and creates three permanent files at the end of the run which can be used in a later run (a new data set, a revision, and a new advanced basis). Nine other files (including INPUT and OUTPUT) are created during the run. These files will now be described in some detail.

(a) *Permanent files* (*input*)

APEX: is a permanent file containing the Apex code

DATA: contains the data of the LP problem

BASIS: contains a good starting basis

FTN1: contains the object deck of the FORTRAN user-written program 1 ensuring the transition from the near equilibrium to the first equilibrium

FTN2: contains the object deck of the FORTRAN user-written program 2 leading from one "equilibrium" to the next

(b) *Other files*

TAPE1: is a copy of the DATA file for the near equilibrium solution; after that, it contains the problem in the form requested for the equilibrium iterations

TAPE3: is a copy of the BASIS file for the near equilibrium solution; after that, it contains the latest basis obtained from the preceding optimal solution

TAPE4: the Apex Control Program writes the optimal basis on TAPE4, which is then copied on TAPE3 for the next run

TAPE7: contains the REVISE deck which describes the variant to be computed; after that, it contains the corrections leading from one equilibrium to the other

TAPE12: the Apex Control Program writes the FORTRAN-readable solution of the linear program on TAPE12

TAPE13: contains the result of the BCDOUT subroutine constructing revised data files
TAPE15: contains the tariffs and specific information on the computational procedure to be used

(c) *Permanent files (output)*
TAPE21: contains the data deck, ready for new iterations on the same problem, if necessary
TAPE24: contains the latest basis
TAPE27: contains the latest revise

The program itself is concerned with the execution of Apex and user programs and the handling of the various files attached to and created by the run. The job control program is now given in extensive form:[29]

```
JOB( )
COMMENT. ATTACHING THE PERMANENT FILES TO THE
JOB
ATTACH(APEX,APEXIA,ID=PUBLIC)
ATTACH(DATA,DATA,ID=DATA)
COPY(DATA,TAPE1)
ATTACH(BASIS,BASIS,ID=BASIS)
COPY(BASIS,TAPE3)
ATTACH(FTN1,FTN1,ID=FTN1)
ATTACH(FTN2,FTN2,ID=FTN2)
COMMENT. COPYING ON TAPE 15 SPECIFIC PARAME-
TERS RELATED TO THE COMPUTATIONAL PROCEDURE
TO BE USED
COPYBR(INPUT, TAPE15)
COMMENT. COPYING ON TAPE7 A POSSIBLE REVISE
DECK(VARIANT)
COPYBR(INPUT, TAPE7)
COMMENT. SOLVING THE NEAR EQUILIBRIUM
REWIND(APEX,TAPE1,TAPE3,TAPE7)
RFL(100 000)
APEX.
COMMENT. TRANSITION FROM NEAR EQUILIBRIUM TO
EQUILIBRIUM
```

[29]Under SCOPE, which is somewhat different from NOS.

```
       REDUCE.
       REWIND(TAPE7,TAPE12,TAPE15,FTN1)
       FTN1(INPUT,OUTPUT,TAPE7,TAPE12,TAPE15)
       COMMENT. FIRST EQUILIBRIUM COMPUTATION
       REWIND(TAPE4,TAPE13)
       COPY(TAPE4,TAPE3)
       COPY(TAPE13,TAPE1)
       REWIND(APEX,TAPE1,TAPE3,TAPE4,TAPE7,TAPE12)
       RFL(100000)
       APEX.

(+)    COMMENT. TRANSITION FROM EQUILIBRIUM TO
       EQUILIBRIUM
       REDUCE.
       REWIND(TAPE7,TAPE12,TAPE15,FTN2)
       FTN2(INPUT,OUTPUT,TAPE7,TAPE12,TAPE15)
       COMMENT. EQUILIBRIUM COMPUTATION
       REWIND(TAPE4)
       COPY(TAPE4,TAPE3)
       REWIND(APEX,TAPE1,TAPE3,TAPE4,TAPE7,TAPE12)
       RFL(100000)

(++)   APEX.
       ...
       COMMENT. THE SEQUENCE OF CARDS STARTING WITH
       (+) AND ENDING WITH (++) IS REPEATED FOR EACH
       FUNCTION EVALUATION[30]
       ...
       COMMENT. LAST COMPUTATION OF EXCESS BUDGETS
       AND OTHER RESULTS
       REDUCE.
       REWIND(TAPE7,TAPE12,TAPE15,FTN2)
       FTN2(INPUT,OUTPUT,TAPE7,TAPE12,TAPE15)
       EOR Card
       Cards containing the tariffs and parameters related to the computa-
       tional procedure
       EOR Card
       Revise file
       EOR Card
```

[30] This formulation can be handled in a nicer way under NOS.

```
        Apex Control Program: Near Equilibrium Computation
        EOR Card

        Apex Control Program: First Equilibrium Computation
(+)     EOR Card
(++)    Apex Control Program: Equilibrium Computation
        ...
        COMMENT. THE SEQUENCE STARTING WITH (+) AND
        ENDING WITH (++) IS REPEATED FOR EACH FUNC-
        TION EVALUATION
        ...
        EOR Card
        COMMENT. SAVING OF IMPORTANT FILES
        REQUEST(TAPE21,*PF)
        REQUEST(TAPE24,*PF)
        REQUEST(TAPE27,*PF)
        REWIND(TAPE1,TAPE4,TAPE7)
        COPY(TAPE1,TAPE21)
        COPY(TAPE4,TAPE24)
        COPY(TAPE7,TAPE27)
        CATALOG(TAPE21,DATA1,ID=DATA1)
        CATALOG(TAPE24,BASIS1,ID=BASIS1)
        CATALOG(TAPE27,REVISE,ID=REVISE)
        COMMENT. SAVING OF THE OUTPUT FILE, IF OUTPUT
        RESIDES ON TAPE12
        REQUEST (TAPE28,*PF)
        REWIND (TAPE12)
        COPY (TAPE12,TAPE28)
        CATALOG (TAPE28,OUTPUT,ID=OUTPUT).
        EOF card
```

CHAPTER 12

Results

This chapter describes the results of experiments with two versions of GEM. Both are "demonstration models", the basic framework of which is by now quite out of date. However, it is still largely identical to that of the "international model", originally built in 1972–3. But since that time our work has focused on developing more rigorous and more flexible specifications, and verifying whether successive versions of our algorithm could solve the resulting system. We have not sought to recalibrate the model to make it fit actual development or even to exploit newly available data on the world economy.

In particular, the "base" or "unchanged tariffs" case assumes unchanged policies, whereas policies did indeed change a great deal over the period. Comparisons between this and free trade projections are thus comparisons between two hypothetical situations. Also, none of the simulations takes account of the 1973 increase in oil prices. The model, we felt, did not include a good enough representation of the energy sector or of the oil-exporting countries to be used for such an assessment. Although some calculations of the impact of higher energy prices were made, we decided not to present them here.

Readers should feel free therefore to judge the results in terms of their gut feeling about how the world economy should behave. But they should not expect the model to replicate the world which is depicted by today's statistical yearbooks.

Some readers will obviously have different feelings about how the world economy behaves. The two versions of GEM crystallize opposing views. The first version, termed hereafter as the "low elasticities version", reflects the opinion which is still widely held today that the exports and imports of developing countries are not very responsive to prices, even in the long run. This implies that world demand imposes a severe constraint on growth for individual developing countries, and even more for the developing world as a whole, so that the strategy of development has to be designed within the straitjacket defined by access to foreign exchange. It is this view of the world which has inspired the import substituting policies still pursued by many countries. Over the years the striking export success of a number of countries which adopted outward oriented policies has however convinced a growing number of economists that world markets are very flexible in the long run. This led us to build a second "high elasticities version" to reflect this other and possibly more realistic view of the world.

The two versions of GEM should be regarded as two different models. We discovered, as we built up a high elasticities version of GEM, that pervasive changes were needed. To reflect the vision of the elasticity optimists it proved necessary to redesign the utility functions of the developed world, the import substitution mechanism in developing countries, and to replace the model's putty–clay by putty–putty production functions. More than a thousand coefficients were changed. The models became so different that pairwise comparisons of their solutions would be pointless.[1]

12.1. The world economy according to the two GEMs

The solutions of GEM define complete sets of equilibrium prices and quantities. It would be tedious to discuss in detail all these results. For this reason we decided to build up a set of national accounts for each solution of the model, and to focus comments on these aggregated data. National accounts are presented both in constant and in current prices. The reader should keep in mind that the "current" prices in a general equilibrium model depend on the normalization rule adopted (in GEM this rule sets the domestic prices of the Middle East and developed countries region equal to unity). Constant price aggregates are evaluated in terms of the prices of the free trade solution.

The values of the main national accounting aggregates in the "unchanged tariffs" solution are given in table 12.1. As described by the model, the economies of Latin America and Asia are roughly equal in size, and those of Africa and the Middle East are a third and a fifth as large, respectively. The last figure would of course be much larger if the model took account of today's oil prices and not those of 1970. The GNP of developed countries is three to four times that of the developing world.[2]

[1] Such comparisons are in any event difficult since the prices used to evaluate the constant price aggregates produced by the two models are not identical.

[2] This GNP is 10 percent lower in the high elasticities than in the low elasticities version of the model. This is mainly due to our choice of value of the exogenous "supply of domestic resources" in that area, and does not result from the working of the model.

Table 12.1
Macroeconomic variables in the unchanged tariffs solution (current prices, billions dollars).

	Low elasticities version					High elasticities version				
	Latin America	Asia	Africa	Middle East	Developed	Latin America	Asia	Africa	Middle East	Developed
Consumption	267.0	209.3	87.4	[a]	[a]	261.0	271.5	81.0	[a]	[a]
Investment	69.5	44.8	19.0	[a]	[a]	72.2	60.2	19.9	[a]	[a]
Exports	24.6	30.4	19.1	29.4	88.7	26.4	26.1	16.2	37.4	80.5
Imports	34.2	38.7	22.2	16.4	80.6	39.7	38.8	21.4	17.2	69.1
GNP	326.9	245.8	103.2	63.2	2769.7	319.9	319.0	95.6	71.2	2475.8

[a] Not defined in the model.

Table 12.2
Relation between the "constant prices" of the model and 1970 prices (indices 1970 prices = 1).

	Consumption	Investment	Exports	Imports	GNP
Latin America					
Low elasticities version	0.991	0.824	0.993	1.111	0.871
High elasticities version	1.065	1.077	1.188	1.252	1.051
Asia					
Low elasticities version	0.828	0.708	0.958	1.115	0.780
High elasticities version	1.203	0.923	1.258	1.254	1.144
Africa					
Low elasticities version	0.832	0.841	1.028	1.118	0.811
High elasticities version	1.039	1.173	1.241	1.270	1.048

Allowing for population, these figures imply a much higher *per capita* GNP in Latin America than in Asia and Africa. The share of trade in GNP is rather low in Latin America as a result of that region's long standing import substitution policies. It is low also in Asia because of the weight of the large inward oriented countries of South Asia. It is high in Africa and even higher in the Middle East, reflecting the large size of the exports oriented enclave sectors in these two regions. The share of trade in GNP is low in developed countries, since the model covers only these countries' trade with the developing world.

All national account aggregates are evaluated at endogenously generated prices. It is useful to relate these to the prices of the 1970 base year of the model. This is done in table 12.2, for the prices of the free trade solution of GEM (used to evaluate the constant prices aggregates discussed in this chapter). The table does not give the prices for the Middle East and developed countries regions. Domestic prices in these regions are equal to unity because they serve as numeraire.

It is seen that the prices generated are not far from those of the 1970 base year, which are of course much below today's prices. To convert the model's prices into those of today, it would be necessary to roughly double all high elasticities version constant price aggregates, and to multiply by 2.5 these magnitudes in the low elasticities version.[3]

Table 12.3 describes the sector breakdown of GNP at factor prices, and of exports and imports in Latin America, Asia, and Africa (hereafter

[3]The fact that the high elasticities price level is higher than the low elasticities level has no particular significance, given the pervasive differences between the two models.

Table 12.3
Contribution of agriculture, mining and oil, manufacturing, and other sectors to factor price GNP and trade in the unchanged tariffs solution (current prices, billions dollars).

	Low elasticities version			High elasticities version		
	Factor price value added	Exports	Imports	Factor price value added	Exports	Imports
Latin America						
Agriculture	35.8	7.5	3.7	38.4	11.1	6.6
Mining and oil	15.6	10.1	1.3	8.8	10.3	10.4
Manufacturing	91.9	7.0	29.2	109.5	4.9	22.7
Other industries	163.8	—	—	136.9	—	—
GNP factor prices	307.3	—	—	293.7	—	—
Total trade		24.6	34.2		26.4	39.7
Asia						
Agriculture	102.1	8.7	7.2	138.4	9.2	8.9
Mining and oil	5.7	1.6	1.5	2.5	2.3	5.7
Manufacturing	68.6	20.0	30.0	95.5	14.6	24.2
Other industries	55.3	—	—	66.5	—	—
GNP factor prices	231.7	—	—	302.9	—	—
Total trade		30.4	38.7		26.1	38.8
Africa						
Agriculture	24.2	6.9	2.7	24.5	7.0	1.4
Mining and oil	5.7	6.1	0.2	2.0	6.3	3.9
Manufacturing	27.1	6.0	19.4	30.0	2.8	16.1
Other industries	35.7	—	—	26.3	—	—
GNP factor prices	92.7	—	—	82.9	—	—
Total trade		19.1	22.2		16.2	21.4

referred to as "the three developing regions"). Table 12.3 illustrates the higher degree of industrialization in Latin America and the low share of "mining and oil" in Asia, whose manufacturing sector is substantially more export oriented than that of the other regions because this area includes the export oriented economies of Korea, Singapore, and Taiwan. Its agricultural production, on the other hand, is largely absorbed by domestic consumption.

Table 12.4 provides a condensed view of world markets. It illustrates the dominating role of developed countries as importers of primary commodities and as exporters of manufactured goods, and that of the Middle East in the oil export trade. The intra trade of developing countries is not large, though it is not negligible. The main link between the economies of developing countries results from their common dependence on markets in

Table 12.4

World exports and imports in the unchanged tariffs solution (current prices, billions dollars).

	Low elasticities version					High elasticities version				
	Three developing areas	Middle East	Intra trade developing	Developed countries	World trade	Three developing areas	Middle East	Intra trade developing	Developed countries	World trade
Exports										
Primary products	28.8	0.5	10.5	6.5	35.8	32.0	0.4	12.8	7.9	40.3
Oil	12.3	27.1	2.9	0.4	39.8	14.2	36.2	18.5	1.6	52.0
Manufactured goods	33.0	1.8	9.3	81.8	116.6	22.4	0.7	5.5	70.7	93.8
Total	74.1	29.4	22.7	88.7	192.2	68.6	37.4	36.8	80.2	186.1
Imports										
Primary products	14.1	2.9	10.5	18.8	35.8	17.7	3.0	12.8	19.6	40.3
Oil	2.5	0.8	2.9	36.5	39.8	19.2	0.9	18.5	31.9	52.0
Manufactured goods	78.5	12.6	9.3	25.5	116.6	63.0	13.2	5.5	17.6	93.8
Total	95.1	16.3	22.7	80.8	192.2	99.9	17.2	36.8	69.1	186.1

developed countries and on supplies from those countries more than from direct trade links.

Both versions imply that the economy of Latin America is somewhat more dynamic than those of Asia and Africa. This reflects our interpretation of the results of, for example, Chenery and his associates (1968, 1975), in their work on the patterns of economic development, which suggests that savings rates rise and capital coefficients fall with income at an early stage of growth. Table 12.5 gives the saving rates assumed for the three regions, and the marginal productivity of capital in the base case. The lower productivity in Africa, according to GEM, results mainly from our choice of production functions, implying lower efficiency than in other regions and thus reflecting the inadequate size of the domestic market and poor leadership in many countries of the continent. In Asia we were somewhat less pessimistic in specifying production functions, although the specification does take account of the low dynamism of South Asia and Indonesia. The marginal productivity of capital is also held in check by the diminishing returns in agriculture. In Latin America, productivity is also held in check by the diminishing returns implied by the excessive emphasis on import substitution.

The base case, which implies "unchanged policies" in 1970–80, does not, as has been said, reflect the shift to more outward oriented policies which have taken place in a large number of countries in that decade. The very high effective protection rates shown in table 12.6 are roughly in line with the findings of Balassa (1971) and Little, Scitovsky and Scott (1970). Protection of manufacturing is particularly strong, but import competing sectors of agriculture also receive substantial protection. Rates are highest in Latin America, whose import substitution policies have been pushed furthest.

Table 12.7 describes the income distribution implied by the model in the unchanged tariffs solution. It should be noticed that, for three reasons, GEM should not be expected to reproduce income distribution patterns

Table 12.5
Savings and interest rates in the three developing regions in the unchanged tariffs solution.

	Low elasticities version		High elasticities version	
	Saving rate (%)	Interest rate (%)	Saving rate (%)	Interest rate (%)
Latin America	0.22	0.20	0.22	0.15
Asia	0.17	0.18	0.17	0.17
Africa	0.18	0.17	0.18	0.11

Table 12.6
Effective protection rates by industries in the unchanged tariffs solution.

	Low elasticities version			High elasticities version		
	Latin America (%)	Asia (%)	Africa (%)	Latin America (%)	Asia (%)	Africa (%)
Tropical noncompeting[a]	−0.01	−0.01	−0.01	−0.03	—	−0.20
Tropical competing[a]	0.77	0.46	0.47	0.74	0.47	0.46
Cereals[a]	0.75	0.46	0.46	0.74	0.47	0.45
Agricultural raw materials[a]	0.81	0.49	0.49	0.94	0.50	0.49
Mining	0.98	1.13	0.62	0.85	0.96	0.85
Oil	1.82	3.14	0.84	1.90	2.67	0.83
Food products	1.59	1.48	1.18	1.51	2.42	1.01
Textiles	1.26	0.99	0.71	1.26	1.01	0.76
Chemicals	0.86	0.67	1.43	0.72	0.45	1.03
Nonmetallic products	0.32	0.15	−0.27	0.20	0.10	−0.35
Basic metals	0.96	0.47	0.78	0.77	0.42	0.63
Machinery	0.90	0.50	0.75	0.64	0.37	0.57
Other manufactures	1.01	0.65	1.08	0.70	0.53	0.89
Construction	−0.24	−0.14	−0.21	−0.36	−0.15	−0.38
Services	−0.01	−0.05	−0.02	−0.03	−0.08	−0.07

[a]In agriculture the model distinguishes production on fertile and marginal land: value added per unit of output is higher on fertile land. The coefficients given refer to effective protection of fertile land production.

data as usually defined: (a) GEM has no public sector so that public as well as private capital is assumed to bear interest; (b) the model reflects the functional distribution of income, *stricto sensu*, more faithfully than in usual national accounts data, for example the reward of capital in GEM includes that of human capital; and (c) the remuneration of self-employed workers is completely split into wage, interest, and rent components; farm

Table 12.7
Income distribution in the unchanged tariffs solution (current prices, billions dollars).

	Low elasticities version			High elasticities version		
	Latin America	Asia	Africa	Latin America	Asia	Africa
Labor income	130.7	115.8	42.7	128.6	150.5	42.1
Capital income	172.9	100.9	49.6	151.6	120.6	38.1
Import substitution rent	1.4	2.6	0.4	11.4	13.7	1.5
Ricardian rent in agriculture	2.3	12.4	0	2.2	18.1	1.2
GNP factor prices	307.3	231.7	92.7	293.7	302.9	82.9

rents are split into true Ricardian rent, and interest on the capital stock made available to the farmer by the landlord. Thus, the shares of labor and agricultural rent are much smaller than is implied by national accounts calculations of the usual type, while the share of capital is larger than usual.

12.2. The functioning of GEM

The equations of GEM were described in Chapter 9. It may however be useful to recall briefly some of the model's main characteristics.

The model differs from the classical equilibrium model of tariff theory in three ways.

(1) The most important difference is that saving is assumed to be a constant proportion of income instead of being determined optimally by the intertemporal maximization of utility. As a result, changes of tariffs affect the increase in the capital stock if they change the ratio of consumption to investment prices. This introduces into the model a "dynamic" impact of tariffs which, we think, is realistic.

(2) The price of oil is set exogenously by producers. This is treated by introducing a compensatory levy equal to the difference between the exogenous price and the cost of production. In two industries—basic metals and non metallic minerals—market shares are assumed to be set by cartel agreements. Prices are not constant, however, but are equal to an average of the marginal costs of exporters, weighted by market shares.

(3) The utility function, finally, reflects the psychological cost of moving between activities as well as the satisfaction derived from the consumption of commodities. This is GEM's way of allowing for the "adjustment costs" widely discussed in theoretical papers on tariff policies.

It is interesting to summarize the properties of GEM by coefficients which describes its overall properties. Table 12.8 gives estimates of key parameters, obtained from the aggregate data, which hopefully provide a clearer picture of the model's functioning than can be obtained from a perusal of its many coefficients. Since almost all of the model's variables are jointly dependent, the coefficients were estimated by an instrumental variables approach. The reader will notice in particular the high international price elasticities assumed in the high elasticities version. These are higher than those suggested by econometric estimates. This reflects our feeling that in the long run—which is what the model represents—countries can achieve large changes in trade shares without much change in relative

Table 12.8
Characterization of the aggregate properties of the two versions of GEM.

	Low elasticities version	High elasticities version
Price elasticity of import demand of developed countries		
Primary commodities (except oil)	−1.2	−3.8
Manufactured goods	−1.8[a]	−5.9[a]
Elasticity of substitution of export of developing regions versus other developing regions		
Primary commodities	9.5	4.3
Manufactured goods	0.8	6.3
Supply elasticity in developing regions with respect to the ratio of the sector value added price to the price of factor price GNP[b]		
Latin America agriculture	0.7	0.7
Asia agriculture	0.5	0.5
Africa agriculture	0.6	0.6

[a]Weighted average of the elasticities assumed for different products in building up the model.

[b]The supply elasticity for mining and manufacturing is not given because it is very high and hence cannot be measured satisfactorily. Changes in the price weights used in calculating price indices, by changing the term $\Delta \log p$ in the definition $\Delta \log q / \Delta \log p$ of the elasticity, have a large impact on the estimate.

prices. The striking trade gains achieved by Germany, Japan, and some Far Eastern developing countries did not lead to a lasting deterioration of their export prices.

12.3. Some remarks on the application of GEM to the study of tariff policies

The next four sections of this chapter are devoted to an evaluation of alternative tariff policies. These policies are caricatures of those which might be realistically considered by governments. The "unchanged tariffs" assumed in one solution, which implies complete rigidity of trading policies in developing countries after 1970, are possible only in a strangely fossilized world; the "complete elimination of import tariffs in Latin America" is even less likely, as are the other combinations of zero or reduced tariffs.

We suggest that the reader should think of "unchanged tariffs" as a description of the world as it might have been had not a number of developing countries begun to shift to more outward oriented trade policies, and of "elimination of tariffs in Latin America" as describing a situation in which an important group of developing countries, not necessarily all situated in one continent, reduce tariffs more quickly and completely than has happened in practice. All the policies studied are extreme; they would not be adopted in practice in a world in which government policy evolves as a result of a slow process of compromises and of trial and error.

GEM was designed as a tool to demonstrate the applicability of a new approach. In this spirit it seemed appropriate to study its mechanisms in some detail. Accordingly, the comments in this chapter will seek to do much more than say "if this measure is adopted such and such consequences will result"; we shall attempt to go at some depth into the model's working to describe exactly how each result is produced.

12.4. Adjustment of trade to tariff reductions in developing countries

Reducing tariffs in a country makes foreign goods more attractive to its citizens. This increases imports and forces the country to reduce export prices to stimulate exports and check the growth of imports. This adjustment is achieved through a reduction in the equilibrium exchange rate.

The exchange rate is normally defined as the rate at which the currencies of two countries are exchanged. In a general equilibrium model, in which there is no money, this definition is not applicable, and in fact there is no unique way of defining the exchange rate. In GEM this is defined as the ratio of the price index of labor and putty capital to that of domestic resources in developed countries.

Table 12.9 describes the adjustment of trade in three developing areas to the removal of import tariffs in Latin America, and in the three developing regions. In both versions of the model a substantial reduction of the exchange rate is required to keep the balance of payments in equilibrium. What most distinguishes the responses of the two models is the much greater increase of trade in the high than in the low elasticities version. It is interesting to note that in the former version, Asia and Africa's balances of payments are adversely affected by a tariff cut in Latin America, so that they have to devalue slightly, whereas in the latter they benefit from that cut and can revalue. In the high elasticities version the gain which these

Table 12.9
Adjustment of trade, prices, and exchange rates to tariff cuts in Latin America and in the three developing regions (billions of dollars or indices).

	Low elasticities version			High elasticities version		
	Unchanged tariffs	No tariffs, Latin America	No tariffs, developing regions	Unchanged tariffs	No tariffs, Latin America	No tariffs, developing regions
Latin America						
Export value	24.6	28.4	28.0	26.4	54.2	54.9
volume	22.0	28.3	29.7	26.6	59.8	59.7
Import value	34.2	37.9	37.4	39.7	67.7	68.4
volume	33.1	37.0	38.0	39.9	69.1	69.4
Price exports	1.115	1.003	0.943	0.992	0.906	0.919
Exchange rate	1.212	0.963	0.914	1.015	0.864	0.901
Asia						
Export value	30.4	30.3	32.5	26.1	27.7	47.2
volume	25.6	26.1	35.2	27.1	29.0	52.0
Import value	38.7	38.4	40.6	38.8	40.2	59.8
volume	37.4	37.9	41.5	39.1	41.4	61.4
Price exports	1.186	1.160	0.923	0.966	0.957	0.908
Exchange rate	1.125	1.109	0.899	0.901	0.924	0.896
Africa						
Export value	19.1	18.3	18.4	16.2	16.6	25.9
volume	16.9	16.6	19.6	16.8	17.4	28.2
Import value	22.2	21.6	21.7	21.4	22.4	31.2
volume	21.5	21.3	22.1	21.5	22.6	31.7
Price export	1.129	1.105	0.936	0.960	0.955	0.917
Exchange rate	1.217	1.170	0.894	0.921	0.925	0.868
World trade price index	1.059	1.035	0.969	1.057	1.063	0.879

regions derive from cheaper supplies of Latin American goods outweighs the loss caused by enhanced competition from Latin America on third markets.

Table 12.10 gives a more detailed picture of the adjustment of exports. Latin America adjusts to unilateral removal of its tariff barriers by increasing sharply its exports of primary commodities, largely at the expense of Asia. In the latter region these commodities are produced under fairly strongly increasing costs. Asia replaces the foreign exchange earnings from primary exports by increasing sharply exports of manufactured goods, where competition from Latin America is less intense. Africa, whose export structure resembles that of Latin America, and which also produces agricultural goods at fairly constant costs, responds to the Latin American policy shift by a balanced adjustment of exports of primary commodities, oil, and manufactured goods. The move to free trade by Asia and Africa helps Latin America in the high elasticities case by improving its export/import prices ratio (see table 12.15). This relieves the pressure on its balance of payments and enables it to reduce the high cost exports of the diminishing returns agricultural sector.

Tariff cuts affect imports in two ways in the model. They increase the share of "foreign goods" in domestic use, as compared with "home goods",[4] both because of the responsiveness to prices of the consumption of different goods and because of the complex structural changes caused by the tariff cuts. This mechanism is quite weak. Of much greater importance is the impact of lower tariffs on the competitiveness of import substituting production of foreign goods which brings about a reduction in that production and a corresponding increase in imports of foreign goods.

Table 12.11 illustrates these mechanisms. It is seen that the tariff elasticity of domestic consumption of foreign goods is extremely low. We feel that GEM does not give a true picture of this aspect of economic mechanisms. The impact of tariff cuts on production of import substituting industries is rather small in the low elasticities version, but quite large in the other version. The impact is greatest in Latin America, which has the highest level of protection, and smallest in Africa, which has both lower import duties and a clear comparative disadvantage in producing the goods which it imports.

[4] In GEM (see Chapter 9) each of the three developing regions is assumed to be capable of producing "home goods", used domestically or exported, and "foreign goods", which replace imports.

Table 12.10

Adjustment of exports and exchange rates of the three developing areas, and of imports of developed countries, to tariff cuts in developing areas (billions of dollars or indices).

	Low elasticities version			High elasticities version		
	Unchanged tariffs	No tariffs, Latin America	No tariffs, developing regions	Unchanged tariffs	No tariffs, Latin America	No tariffs, developing regions
Latin America						
Primary commodities value	10.04	13.34	11.44	13.14	28.09	22.44
volume	8.90	13.21	12.60	13.62	31.35	24.93
price	1.128	1.010	0.908	0.965	0.896	0.900
Oil value and volume[a]	7.57	7.71	7.77	8.29	8.37	8.61
Manufactures value	6.97	7.35	8.79	4.94	17.76	23.88
volume	5.46	7.41	9.33	4.67	19.63	26.20
price	1.277	0.992	0.942	1.059	0.905	0.911
Exchange rate	1.212	0.963	0.914	1.015	0.864	0.901
Asia						
Primary commodities value	9.11	6.60	7.76	9.90	2.60	7.02
volume	7.86	6.03	8.63	10.20	2.87	7.65
price	1.159	1.095	0.899	0.970	0.907	0.918
Oil value and volume[a]	1.27	1.30	1.30	1.60	1.74	1.78
Manufactures value	20.03	22.43	23.42	14.64	23.38	38.40
volume	16.49	18.82	25.27	15.25	24.35	42.54
price	1.215	1.192	0.927	0.960	0.960	0.903
Exchange rate	1.125	1.109	0.899	0.901	0.924	0.896
Africa						
Primary commodities value	9.62	8.35	8.98	8.98	7.89	12.67
volume	8.49	7.70	9.94	9.65	8.64	14.14
price	1.133	1.085	0.903	0.931	0.913	0.897
Oil value and volume[a]	3.48	3.56	3.58	4.33	4.72	4.79
Manufactures value	5.97	6.44	5.81	2.84	4.02	8.42
volume	4.92	5.34	6.09	2.84	4.05	9.30
price	1.213	1.206	0.954	1.000	0.993	0.905
Exchange rate	1.217	1.170	0.894	0.921	0.925	0.868

[a] Value and volume are equal since the price is exogenously set equal to unity.

Table 12.11

Adjustment of consumption of foreign goods and imports to tariff reductions in Latin America and in the three developing regions (billions of dollars, constant prices).

	Low elasticities version			High elasticities version		
	Unchanged tariffs	No tariffs, Latin America	No tariffs, developing regions	Unchanged tariffs	No tariffs, Latin America	No tariffs, developing regions
Latin America						
Average tariff rate	0.492	0	0	0.62	0	0
Consumption foreign goods	38.50	39.49	41.50	83.34	89.39	89.88
Share in constant market prices GNP	0.150	0.151	0.159	0.297	0.302	0.303
Imports	33.12	37.05	38.10	39.91	69.13	69.94
Import substituting production	5.39	2.44	3.40	43.44	20.06	19.93
Asia						
Average tariff rate	0.360	0.357	0	0.415	0.414	0
Consumption foreign goods	47.74	48.25	50.09	80.65	81.68	86.69
Share in constant market prices GNP	0.234	0.236	0.243	0.252	0.255	0.261
Imports	37.37	37.95	41.47	39.06	41.45	61.45
Import substituting production	10.37	10.31	8.62	41.58	40.23	25.24
Africa						
Average tariff rate	0.338	0.337	0	0.420	0.410	0
Consumption foreign goods	23.68	23.41	23.35	32.20	32.57	34.07
Share in constant market prices GNP	0.295	0.293	0.290	0.356	0.357	0.359
Imports	21.55	21.32	22.09	21.50	22.65	31.71
Imports substituting production	2.13	2.10	1.26	10.70	9.92	2.37

The by now classical way of assessing the impact of tariffs on the competitivity of import substituting activities is to calculate the "effective rate of protection". This is obtained by dividing the import tariff on a good (net of import tariffs on the inputs of importable goods required for its production) by the value added in producing that good, evaluated at world prices.[5]

It is well known that this formula is valid only in the "small country case" in which a country has no power to influence the world prices of the goods which it imports and exports. If supply and demand elasticities are less than infinite, the imposition of tariffs will affect the equilibrium exchange rate, so that export and import prices will change. The drop of value added in import substituting activities will be less than the formula predicts: the effective tariff formula overstates the protection enjoyed by import substituting activities. Value added per unit will rise in export activities. The shift of the equilibrium exchange rate improves the competitivity of import substituting activities and helps them to adjust to the enhanced competition from foreign producers; it also increases the incentive to export.

This mechanism is too abstract to be well grasped by public opinion, a fact which is an important aspect of the political economy of protection. Much resistance to tariff reductions results from an exaggerated view of their impact on import substituting activities: it is argued that the survival of whole slices of the country's production capacity depends on the maintenance of high tariff barriers. Pressure for higher protection is likewise enhanced by an exaggerated view of the gains which will result for the industries which seek protection.

Finally, there is not enough understanding of the impact of tariffs on the profitability of export activities. Exporters, who do not realize just how large the increases of domestic costs which tariffs generate are likely to be, do not oppose protection as strongly as they would if they understood their interest.

A second mechanism, which has drawn less attention from theorists, reflects the impact of import tariffs on the efficiency of the economic system and hence on the prices of production factors. When protection is

[5] In the classical formulation of the concept, input coefficients are assumed to be fixed. Let $a^{\mathrm{h}}_{i,j}$ and $a^{\mathrm{f}}_{i,j}$ be the amounts of "home" and "foreign" goods of type i required to produce one unit of good j; let τ_i be *ad valorem* tariff rates, p^{f}_i world prices of foreign goods, and p^{h}_i domestic prices of home goods. The domestic prices of foreign goods are $p^{\mathrm{f}}_i(1+\tau_i)$. The value added per unit of import substitutable goods, evaluated at world prices, is $v^*_j = p^{\mathrm{f}}_j - \Sigma a^{\mathrm{h}}_{i,j} p^{\mathrm{h}}_i - \Sigma a^{\mathrm{f}}_{i,j} p^{\mathrm{f}}_i$. The net tariff protection enjoyed by import substituting industries is $\tau^*_j = p^{\mathrm{f}}_j \tau_j - \Sigma a^{\mathrm{f}}_{i,j} p^{\mathrm{f}}_i \tau_i$. Thus, the effective tariff rate is τ^*_j / v^*_j. For these concepts, see Balassa (1965), Basevi (1966), Corden (1966), and Johnson (1965).

eliminated the real reward of these factors improves. As a result, profit margins in import substituting activities are squeezed *more* than would happen if the real reward of the factors of production did not change. Thus, when world markets are highly perfect the effective tariff formula may *understate* and not overstate the protection enjoyed by import substituting activities. The simulation of the high elasticities version illustrates this possibility.

Table 12.12 describes the impact of tariffs on the profitability of import substituting and of export industries.

The impact of tariffs on the profitability of export and of import substituting activities depends on the assumed price elasticities in world trade. In the low elasticities version—which paradoxically corresponds to the view of the world of advocates of import substituting policies—half of the protection granted to industries is eroded away by the subsequent general adjustment of prices. The effective protection formula provides a better estimate of the true protection level in the high elasticities version of GEM.

It is interesting to note that in Asia the effective protection formula actually slightly understates the level of protection in the high elasticities version. As explained above, this reflects the impact of free trade on the efficiency of the economy and hence on the real reward of labor and capital.

The shifts in international specialization which result from tariff cuts are revealed by table 12.13 which describes the net exports of the main categories of goods. The table confirms the trends noted in the discussion of the exports data. The adoption of free trade by Latin America leads that region to specialize in the production of primary commodities. Much of this shift is negated when other developing areas join Latin America in the move to free trade.

Note that the changes in domestic demand and in net exports which take place when Latin America moves to free trade are mutually offsetting: that region's status as a net exporter of primary commodities is enhanced. But the move to free trade generates an increased dynamism in the domestic economy, in particular an increase in investment; this increases demand for machines so that the manufacturing sector does not suffer. This is illustrated by table 12.14.[6]

[6]The readers may be surprised by the sharp fall in constant prices value added of the oil industry in the high elasticities model. This is due to the opposite changes of output of the high value added import substituting sector and of the low value added export sector when tariffs are removed. As a result, value added drops sharply, although production does not change very much.

Table 12.12

Adjustment of indexes of value added per unit of output in import and export industries to tariff cuts in Latin America and in the three developing regions (indices[a] free trade solution = 1).

	Low elasticities version				High elasticities version			
	Unchanged tariffs	No tariffs, Latin America	No tariffs, developing regions	Effective tariff prediction	Unchanged tariffs	No tariffs, Latin America	No tariffs, developing regions	Effective tariff prediction
Latin America								
Index of price of value added per unit of output in export industries	0.969	1.029	0.992	0.971	0.881	1.009	0.984	0.884
Index of price of value added per unit of output in import substituting industries	1.373	1.079	1.097	1.836	1.582	1.186	1.218	1.959
Asia								
Index of price of value added per unit of output in export industries	0.962	1.000	1.003	0.945	0.976	0.929	1.001	0.944
Index of price of value added per unit of output in import substituting industries	1.275	1.264	1.105	1.560	1.569	1.518	1.130	1.530
Africa								
Index of price of value added per unit of output in export industries	0.954	0.956	0.994	0.974	0.936	0.937	0.997	0.975
Index of price of value added per unit of output in import substituting industries	1.246	1.265	1.100	1.764	1.604	1.561	1.168	1.666

[a] The export and import substitution industries' value added price indices are weighted by unchanged tariffs solution exports and values added in import substitution, respectively. Both indices are deflated by the price index of GNP at factor prices.

Table 12.13

Adjustment of net exports of major industry groups in the three developing areas to tariff reduction in Latin America and in the three developing regions (billions of dollars, constant prices).

	Low elasticities version			High elasticities version		
	Unchanged tariffs	No tariffs, Latin America	No tariffs, developing regions	Unchanged tariffs	No tariffs, Latin America	No tariffs, developing regions
Latin America						
Primary industries except oil	5.47	9.41	7.60	6.53	18.75	13.00
Oil	6.56	6.24	6.41	−1.83	−5.83	−5.40
Manufactures	−23.09	−24.37	−22.40	−18.03	−23.20	−17.79
Total	−11.06	−8.72	−8.39	−13.31	−9.29	−10.20
Asia						
Primary industries except oil	1.21	−0.65	1.43	0.49	−7.65	−5.25
Oil	0.01	0.02	−0.39	−3.63	−3.57	−4.02
Manufactures	−12.95	−11.17	−7.31	−8.88	−1.27	−0.22
Total	−11.73	−11.80	−6.28	−12.01	−12.49	−9.49
Africa						
Primary industries except oil	6.04	5.24	7.41	8.07	6.96	12.23
Oil	3.38	3.46	3.48	0.47	0.88	0.29
Manufactures	−14.07	−13.41	−13.37	−13.23	−13.08	−15.98
Total	−4.65	−4.71	−2.47	−4.69	−5.24	−3.47

Table 12.14

Changes in constant prices value added and domestic demand in Latin America as a result of a move to free trade by that region (billions of dollars, constant prices).

	Low elasticities version				High elasticities version			
	Value added		Domestic final demand		Value added		Domestic final demand	
	Unchanged tariffs	No tariffs, Latin America	Unchanged tariffs	No tariffs, Latin America	Unchanged tariffs	No tariffs, Latin America	Unchanged tariffs	No tariffs, Latin America
Primary products except oil	34.3	37.1	17.1	16.8	43.7	57.0	22.8	23.0
Oil	10.9	10.8	3.6	3.7	4.2	1.8	3.7	4.0
Manufacturing	74.8	76.0	111.2	113.8	94.2	94.5	132.1	138.5
Nontraded goods	133.0	133.3	136.7	136.5	134.1	137.5	135.2	139.6
Total	253.0	257.2	268.6	270.8	276.2	290.9	293.8	305.0

Finally, we discuss the impact of a unilateral move to free trade in developing countries on their terms of trade. As explained above, the removal of tariffs forces developing countries to cut export prices in order to generate the exports needed to pay for increased imports. This worsens their terms of trade. Therefore part, or all, of the increase in output generated by the economically efficient free trade policies will be lost by the region which has removed tariffs, and given to the rest of the world. Other countries derive a free ride gain from the free trade policies of their partners.

The terms of trade may be measured in several ways. We show two in table 12.15. One is the ratio of export to import prices—the most usual definition. The second, the "gross terms of trade", is also quite familiar; it is the difference between the current relative prices and constant prices current balances of payments.[7] Constant prices GNP minus the gross terms of trade indicator can then be used as a measure of the ability of the economy to purchase goods. This concept is ambiguous and can lead to paradoxes.[8] But for the solutions of GEM we feel that it is a useful rough indicator of the impact of the terms of trade on the international distribution of purchasing power.

As shown in table 12.15, the impact of tariff reductions by developing countries on their GNP and purchasing power is quite different in the two

[7]The measure is based on the following model, which is simpler than GEM but approximates its pattern of price behavior. Let PX_i, PE_i and PM_i be production, export and import prices in solution $i=0,1$, and AID_i be the amount of aid in real terms; let X_i, E_i and M_i be production, exports, and imports in these solutions. Let solution 0 be the base, so that $PX_0=PE_0=PM_0=1$. Assume $PX_1=PE_1$ (export prices = production prices). For balance of payments equilibrium we need $E_iPE_i+AID_iPM_i=M_iPM_i$ $(i=0,1)$. Then gross domestic product is X_i+AID_i. Clearly, we then have gross domestic expenditure $X_0+M_0-E_0=X_0+AID_0$ in the base solution; for solution 1 we have gross domestic expenditure at constant prices

$$X_1+M_1-E_1=X_1+E_1PE_1/PM_1-E_1+AID_1=X_1+AID_1+E_1(PE_1/PM_1-1),$$

where $E_1(1-PE_1/PM_1)$ is the "gross terms of trade loss" of table 12.15, and the gross domestic expenditures level compatible with balance of payments equilibrium, equal to $X_1+AID_1+E_1(PE_1/PM_1-1)$, is the "purchasing power" given in the table.

[8]This is because the measure is sensitive to the choice of base solution. If solution 1 is chosen as the base of the price indices, then export and import prices in solution 0 are $1/PE_1$ and $1/PM_1$. The gross terms of trade gain is $E_0(PM_1/PE_1-1)$. It is clear that $E_0(PM_1/PE_1-1)\neq E_1(1-PE_1/PM_1)$; the difference between the two measures can be substantial if, as happens in the high elasticities model, the level of exports varies substantially between solutions. This can lead to paradoxical conclusions when "purchasing power" increases if one of the solutions is chosen as a base and decreases if the other solution is the base. Our use of the "compensating transfer" concept below meets this objection to some extent.

Table 12.15

Adjustment of GNP, the terms of trade, and purchasing power in the three developing areas to tariff reduction in Latin America and in the three developing regions (billions of dollars or indices).

	Low elasticities version			High elasticities version		
	Unchanged tariffs	No tariffs, Latin America	No tariffs, developing regions	Unchanged tariffs	No tariffs, Latin America	No tariffs, developing regions
Latin America						
GNP constant market prices	257.5	262.1	261.3	280.4	295.8	296.1
Gross terms of trade gain or loss[a]	1.5	−0.7	−1.0	−0.1	−4.2	−3.2
Purchasing power[b]	259.0	261.4	260.3	280.3	291.6	292.9
Ratio export/import prices	1.080	0.981	0.960	1.276	0.958	0.975
Asia						
GNP constant market prices	204.3	204.1	206.1	319.7	320.7	332.0
Gross terms of trade gain or loss[a]	3.4	3.6	−1.9	−0.7	0	−3.1
Purchasing power[b]	207.7	207.7	204.3	319.0	320.7	328.9
Ratio export/import prices	1.144	1.147	0.943	0.972	0.987	0.932
Africa						
GNP constant market prices	80.3	79.8	80.5	90.5	91.1	94.9
Gross terms of trade gain or loss[a]	1.5	1.4	−0.9	−0.6	−0.6	−1.8
Purchasing power[b]	81.8	81.2	79.6	89.9	90.5	93.1
Ratio export/import prices	1.093	1.088	0.953	0.965	0.965	0.933

[a] Current price minus constant price balance of payments.
[b] GNP at constant prices plus gross terms of trade loss.

versions of GEM. In the low elasticities case, Latin America improves both its GNP and purchasing power by cutting tariffs unilaterally, but it does so at the expense of other developing countries. As a single region it behaves somewhat like the "small country" of international trade theory. That is to say, it faces fairly high price elasticities of demand for its exports, and can finance by additional exports its increased imports without having to cut export prices drastically. Other developing countries, however, suffer terms of trade losses as a result of the enhanced competition from Latin American exporters, and find their purchasing power reduced as a result. The three developing areas cannot of course be regarded as a "small country". They are confronted by a lower price elasticity of demand. When all three areas together cut tariffs, the resulting terms of trade loss is so large that it absorbs most of the gain in efficiency caused by the move to free trade. In the low elasticities version, cutting tariffs is a beggar-your-neighbor policy for individual developing countries; each gains only at the expense of its fellows; the true beneficiary is the developed world.

The low elasticities version, although representing a fairly widespread view of how the world works, in our view strongly underestimates the flexibility of international trade. The more realistic high elasticities version fortunately paints a much rosier picture of the impact of tariff cuts. Not only do tariff cuts in one region lead to a substantial increase in GNP, but they actually improve slightly the terms of trade and GNP of other developing areas. What happens is that Asia and Africa gain more by being able to buy cheap Latin American goods than they lose by having to face more intense competition from Latin America in third markets.

12.5. A world without import tariffs

Free trade occupies a central place in international trade theory since it is the institutional setting which enables the world to reach optimal efficiency. It was of course desirable to run a free trade solution of the two GEMs. It was decided that the best approximation to free trade would be obtained by eliminating all import tariffs, but maintaining export tariffs. For oil and nonferrous metals these "tariffs" are interpreted as rents allowing for the true value of low-cost nonrenewable resources. The rather low export tariffs on tropical noncompeting foods (coffee, cocoa, tea) reflect the monopoly enjoyed by producers of these goods which we felt would continue even if there was a worldwide move to free trade.

The way efficiency can be measured is shown in fig. 12.1 which, for the sake of simplicity, describes a closed economy producing two goods that

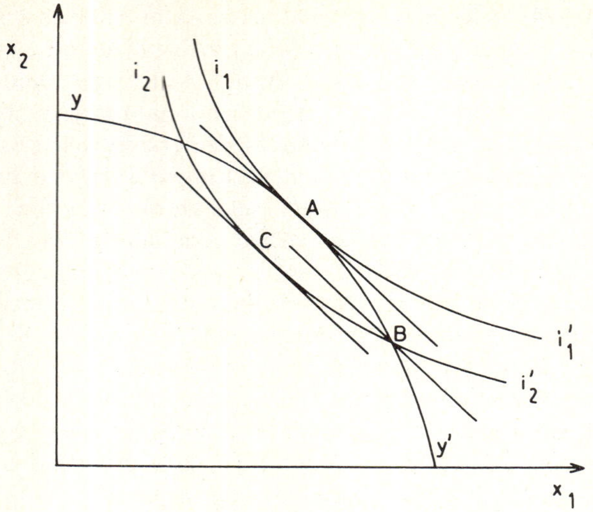

Figure 12.1. Measuring the efficiency of world trade.

are purchased by consumers whose preferences can be represented by a social welfare function. In the figure yy' is the production possibility curve in this economy, and $i_1 i_1'$ and $i_2 i_2'$ are indifference curves of the social welfare function. In the absence of price distortions, the economy is in equilibrium at A: supply equals demand for both goods, and consumers use the whole of the income earned by enterprises. If there were price distortions—an indirect tax for example—the system might well find itself in equilibrium at $B=(x_{21}, x_{22})$.

A monetary measure of the loss of efficiency may then be derived as follows. Let p_1, p_2 be the free trade equilibrium price. GNP in the free trade situation, evaluated at free trade prices, is equal to $\text{GNP}_1 = p_1 x_{11} + p_2 x_{12}$. In the tax-ridden situation, GNP at free trade prices drops to $\text{GNP}_2 = p_1 x_{21} + p_2 x_{22}$; the loss is equal to $\text{LOSS}_1 = \text{GNP}_1 - \text{GNP}_2$.

The difference between the two values of GNP is not a complete description of the cost of the tax distortion, for consumers would be as happy at $C=(x_{31}, x_{32})$ as at B, and spend even less. If $\text{COST} = p_1 x_{31} + p_2 x_{32}$, then the extra spending $\text{LOSS}_2 = \text{GNP}_2 - \text{COST}$ is a further loss to agents in this economy, and reflects the distortions of consumption patterns caused by the indirect tax.

The total loss, $\text{LOSS}_1 + \text{LOSS}_2$, can then be interpreted as the maximum amount which consumers would be willing to pay to secure elimination of the tax distortions. This measure will be used in this section to evaluate the efficiency cost of import restrictions.

In GEM the stock of capital is endogenous since the model describes equilibrium at the end of a ten-year period. Any increase in efficiency will generate additional savings, which in turn generate additional capital. It is also assumed in GEM that consumers save a constant fraction of their income at current prices; if the price of investment goods falls relative to that of consumption goods real investment will therefore rise and (at least in the short run) consumption will decrease.

The second mechanism is quite strong in the model, as table 12.16 illustrates. Because a large proportion of investment goods are traded goods, their relative price tends to fall when tariffs are reduced. This causes a rise in real investments which is enhanced by the automatic reinvestment of a part of the pure welfare gains. We feel that this "dynamic impact of tariffs" is a realistic phenomenon. However, it is worth emphasizing that the resulting increase in output is not due to improved efficiency of the economy, but to the greater thriftyness implied by the model's assumptions about savings behavior. Such an increase in thrift could be obtained in other ways, e.g. by generating more public savings.

Table 12.17 describes these three impacts of import tariffs on output and welfare in the three developing areas. The largest component is the "dynamic" impact of tariffs on the rate of accumulation. In the low elasticities case the more classical "pure welfare gains" are quite small.

The gains from improved consumption efficiency are not large in any version of the model. This is because it has been assumed that consumption is quite insensitive to price, in the high as well as in the low elasticities versions, so that tariffs do not lead to a large misallocation of consumer expenditures. The size of this component is probably underestimated in the model as it is presently formulated.

The utility functions of Middle East oil-producers and developed countries are linear. Hence, for those regions there is no "gain from improved consumer allocation". Initial resources in developed countries are constant in the model. Hence, the GNP gains which they realize when the world moves to free trade are entirely due to a more efficient allocation of resources in production. In the Middle East, on the other hand, the production functions in the oil and nonoil sectors are linear, so that there is no reason for misallocation of resources in production. GNP changes therefore reflect the capital accumulation which, by assumption, is closely related to the oil export earnings of these countries.

Table 12.16

Adjustment of investment and capital accumulation in the three developing regions to a general move to free trade (billions of dollars, constant prices or ratios).

	Low elasticities version		High elasticities version	
	Unchanged tariffs	No import tariffs	Unchanged tariffs	No import tariffs
Latin America				
Ratio of consumption to investment prices	0.961	1	0.867	1
Investment	53.7	57.6	56.8	68.5
Ratio of investment to domestic demand	0.200	0.212	0.193	0.219
Asia				
Ratio of consumption to investment prices	0.967	1	0.862	1
Investment	37.1	39.0	53.2	62.6
Ratio of investment to domestic demand	0.171	0.181	0.160	0.180
Africa				
Ratio of consumption to investment prices	0.966	1	0.877	1
Investment	14.8	15.8	16.84	19.92
Ratio of investment to domestic demand	0.174	0.182	0.177	0.197

Table 12.17
Sources of the gain derived by the three developing areas from a general move to free trade (billions of dollars, constant prices or ratios).

	Low elasticities version		High elasticities version	
	Gain	% of unchanged tariffs factor prices GNP	Gain	% of unchanged tariffs factor prices GNP
Latin America				
Increase in available resources	4.0	1.60	10.8	3.90
Gain from improved production efficiency	0.5	0.21	7.5	2.73
Gain from improved consumption efficiency	0.5	0.20	0.3	0.10
Total	5.0	2.01	18.6	6.73
Asia				
Increase in available resources	1.8	0.88	9.7	3.03
Gain from improved production efficiency	0.9	0.42	5.5	1.73
Gain from improved consumption efficiency	0.4	0.22	0.7	0.20
Total	3.1	1.52	15.9	4.96
Africa				
Increase in available resources	0.7	0.91	2.4	2.74
Gain from improved production efficiency	0.2	0.22	2.2	2.54
Gain from improved consumption efficiency	0.3	0.38	0.3	0.38
Total	1.2	1.61	4.9	5.66

Table 12.18 summarizes the gains for the world.

Many empirical studies of the welfare cost of tariffs disregard the "gain from improved allocation of consumption", and consider only the impact of lower trade barriers on GNP, i.e. the gains which result from the "increase in production resources" and from the "improvement in productive efficiency" terms.

We have investigated how the choice of price weights influences this term. This is done in table 12.19 which provides data on GNP both at market and at factor prices. The constant market prices GNP is the better indicator of welfare, because it is market and not factor prices which are proportional to marginal utilities. The factor prices data, on the other hand, match the way in which economic activity is perceived by producers, since it is value added which is the source of factor rewards.

It turns out that the weights which we have used to evaluate constant prices GNP imply a conservative estimate of the impact of tariffs on market prices GNP. "Unchanged tariffs" prices weights would have led to a higher impact on GNP from the adoption of free trade than the "no impact tariffs" weights which we have used. This is because the items of expenditure which increase most when tariffs are removed are those which

Table 12.18

Sources of the GNP gains derived by Middle East oil-producers, developed countries and the three developing areas from a general move to free trade (billions of dollars, constant prices or ratios).

	Low elasticities version		High elasticities version	
	Gain	% of unchanged tariffs factor prices GNP	Gain	% of unchanged Tariffs factor prices GNP
Middle East oil-producers				
Gain in GNP	1.2	1.7	3.8	5.3
Developed countries				
Gain in GNP	3.3	0.1	2.7	0.1
Three developing areas				
Gain in GNP	8.1	1.5	38.1	5.6
Gain in developing countries from improved consumption efficiency	1.2	0.3	1.3	0.2
World				
Total gain	13.8	0.37	45.9	1.42

Table 12.19

Constant prices GNP gain from a general move to free trade, measured at "unchanged tariff" and at "free trade" prices (indices unchanged tariffs solution = 1).

	Low elasticities version		High elasticities version	
	Unchanged tariffs price weights	No import tariffs price weights	Unchanged tariffs price weights	No import tariffs price weights
Latin America				
Constant market prices GNP index	1.024	1.019	1.079	1.068
Constant factor prices GNP index	1.013	1.018	1.011	1.066
Asia				
Constant market prices GNP index	1.021	1.014	1.048	1.048
Constant factor prices GNP index	1.006	1.013	1.013	1.048
Africa				
Constant market prices GNP index	1.013	1.012	1.077	1.058
Constant factor prices GNP index	1.005	1.010	1.022	1.053

were taxed most heavily; price weights which include taxes thus lead to a high estimate of the growth of output. The discrepancy between the two sets of indices is however not very large (of the order of 1 percent).

Weighting by factor prices leads to opposite and much larger differences. It is very interesting to observe that in the high elasticities model the removal of tariffs has virtually no impact on value added if this is weighted at factor prices of the "unchanged tariffs" solution. This impact is quite large when the price weights used reflect the "no import tariffs" equilibrium. The explanation of this phenomenon is as follows. The removal of tariffs leads to a precipitous decline of output of industries whose value added was artificially swollen by tariff protection, and to an expansion of export activities whose value added was squeezed by the antiexport bias implied by the high exchange rate which protection causes. So it is not surprising that "unchanged tariffs" price weights lead to a low estimate of the impact of free trade on output.

We feel that this observation helps to explain why production indices often suggest that the economic performance of countries after a tariff cut is quite poor. Production indices are usually base weighted Laspeyres indices; and just after a tariff has been eliminated these will give excessive weight to sectors which are shrinking and underweight those which are expanding.

12.6. The prices of factors and the Stolper–Samuelson theorem

Since the article by Stolper and Samuelson (1941), the impact of tariffs on income distribution has attracted a great deal of attention. GEM does not satisfy the assumptions of the theorem. It of course does not satisfy the rather curious assumptions required by rigorous proofs in the many goods many factors case. It may be conjectured that these are not too important in practical cases. A more important discrepancy is that the regions in GEM do not satisfy the crucial "small country assumption" of perfectly elastic demand for exports and supply of imports. Also, the supply of one factor—capital—is not fixed, since the model covers a ten-year period over which part of accrued welfare gains are reinvested. It is worthwhile, however, to examine, in the spirit of the theorem, the relation between tariffs and income distribution.

It is possible to identify four "factor prices" in the model: wages; the rental prices of capital existing at the beginning of the period; an index of agricultural rents; and an index of the price of the specialized factors (entrepreneurs, skilled labor, etc.) engaged in import substitution. The theorem predicts that the price of the factor intensively used in import substituting activities will drop relative to all other prices when protection is removed, so that its real reward will fall. Since it would be tedious and somewhat irrelevant to undertake all the required pairwise comparisons, we have compared the prices of factors with the price index of GNP.

Stolper and Samuelson do not discuss how tariffs are spent. Since their argument is entirely in terms of relative prices, it appears appropriate to assume that tariffs are redistributed to producers in a nondistorting way, i.e. in proportion to their income. Therefore the figures in table 12.20 describe the response to tariffs of factor prices adjusted for this redistribution.

The table shows that the reward of the specialized factors engaged in import substitution does indeed fall drastically when tariffs are removed. This illustrates the disappearance of the high rents which accrue to protected entrepreneurs when a country moves to free trade. As import substituting activities tend to be capital intensive, there is a presumption that the price of capital will fall also. This occurs in the low but not in the high elasticities case. Agricultural rents and the wage rate do rise as expected.

The explanation of this discrepancy between the two versions is probably an income effect, as can be seen in table 12.21. Import substitution rents are fairly large in the high elasticities version. Their virtual disappearance when the economy moves to free trade releases a substantial income which accrues to other factors, including capital. In that version the reduction of tariffs also induces a sharp increase in exports of manufactured goods, many of which are rather capital-intensive also.

It should be noticed that in table 12.21 the amount of capital which receives a reward is larger in the free trade than in the unchanged tariffs version, because some of the welfare and other gains are reinvested. The quantities of other factors are the same in both solutions. It is interesting to consider the price of newly invested capital—the interest rate—equal to the rental rate divided by the price index of capital. As the relative price of capital goods drops when protection is removed, the interest rate moves more favorably than the rental rate: it is existing capital, locked into initial capacities, which suffers while the interest rate, which measures the incentive to create new capital, increases in both versions of GEM.

12.7. Toward a new international tariff order

Thus far we have discussed policy alternatives without regard to political feasibility. The "no tariffs Latin America" solution is the least unrealistic if

Table 12.20

Adjustment of real factor prices in developing countries to tariff cuts in developing countries and to a general move to free trade (indices or ratios).

	Low elasticities version			High elasticities version		
	Unchanged tariffs	No tariffs developing countries	No import tariffs	Unchanged tariffs	No tariffs developing countries	No import tariffs
Latin America						
Real wage index adjusted for redistribution of tariffs	1	1.049	1.057	1	1.053	1.055
Interest rate	1	1.020	1.045	1	1.155	1.219
Index of real rental price of capital adjusted for redistribution of tariffs	1	0.986	0.981	1	1.020	1.019
Asia						
Real wage index adjusted for redistribution of tariffs	1	1.024	1.049	1	1.053	1.055
Interest rate	1	1.022	1.034	1	1.160	1.228
Index of real rental price of capital adjusted for redistribution of tariffs	1	1.073	0.979	1	1.029	1.031
Africa						
Real wage index adjusted for redistribution of tariffs	1	1.000	1.034	1	1.019	1.021
Interest rate	1	0.977	1.034	1	1.243	1.342
Index of real rental price of capital adjusted for redistribution of tariffs	1	0.973	0.963	1	1.093	1.088

Table 12.21

Adjustment of real income of production factors in developing countries to tariff cuts in developing countries and to a general move to free trade (factor incomes adjusted for redistribution of tariffs, billions of dollars).

	Low elasticities version			High elasticities version		
	Unchanged tariffs	No import tariffs, developing regions	No import tariffs	Unchanged tariffs	No import tariffs, developing regions	No import tariffs
Latin America						
Income of wage earners	107.7	110.1	110.5	121.1	128.3	128.9
Income of capital owners	142.4	143.9	144.3	142.7	155.3	158.1
Agricultural rents	1.9	2.1	2.5	2.6	5.6	6.8
Import substituting rents	1.1	0.4	0.2	10.8	2.2	0.8
Total	253.1	256.5	257.5	277.2	291.4	294.7
Asia						
Income of wage earners	101.7	103.5	104.9	158.6	167.9	168.7
Income of capital owners	88.6	89.7	89.8	127.1	138.8	142.1
Agricultural rents	10.9	10.8	10.6	18.6	19.3	20.8
Import substituting rents	2.3	1.4	1.0	14.1	5.3	3.2
Total	203.5	205.5	206.3	318.4	331.3	330.3
Africa						
Income of wage earners	35.5	35.2	35.6	44.0	44.9	45.1
Income of capital owners	40.8	40.5	40.9	39.8	43.7	44.3
Agricultural rents	0.4	1.3	1.3	1.4	1.5	1.8
Import substituting rents	0.3	0.1	0.1	1.6	0.1	0
Total	77.0	77.1	77.9	86.8	90.2	91.2

it is interpreted as representing a shift to outward oriented policies by a significant group of developing countries. But neither a general move towards free trade by developing countries, nor the elimination of obstacles to trade by both the developing and developed worlds, seems likely.

Our guess is that if a Tokyo round encompassing both developed and developing countries is organized some day, the agenda will specify a larger percentage reduction in tariffs for developed than for developing countries. Protection levels are lower today in the former, so that equal proportional cuts would seem unfair to developing countries. The latter also are unlikely to renounce the right to using tariffs to foster infant industries.

This suggests solving the model for a "negotiated tariff cut", involving the complete elimination of obstacles to trade by developed countries, and the halving of protection in developing countries. The consequences of such an event are compared in table 12.22 to those of the *status quo*, and of theory's ideal goal of free trade.

It is seen that according to the low elasticities version, free trade is hardly a desirable goal for developing countries. Their production does rise as a result of the elimination of tariffs; but this gain is almost completely offset by the deterioration of their terms of trade. Developed countries and Middle East oil-producers are the real gainers since both their productivity and their terms of trade improve: it is these areas which capture almost all of the increase of world GNP.

Free trade, on the other hand, is quite attractive to developing countries in the high elasticities version. Production rises substantially and only a small fraction of this increase is dissipated via the terms of trade. Developed countries benefit both from greater efficiency and from improved terms of trade. Efficiency accounts for two-thirds of their gain, the terms of trade for the rest.

A negotiated tariff cut is much preferable for developing countries in the low elasticities versions, but free trade is best in the other version. It should be remembered that in the high elasticities version even a unilateral move to free trade by developing is far better than the present policies of high protection. As expected, the terms of trade are better for developing countries with the negotiated cut than under free trade while GNP is lower; it is the balance of the two effects which translates into a sharp gain in the low elasticities version, and into a small loss in the other version. Free trade is best for the developed world in both versions since both their GNP and their terms of trade worsen if developing countries halve their tariffs instead of eliminating them completely.

It is also interesting to consider the impact on developing countries of concessionary tariff preferences of the type which have been advocated by

Table 12.22

Adjustment of GNP, purchasing power, and the terms of trade to a general move to free trade, and to a negotiated tariff cut (billions of dollars, constant prices).

	Low elasticities version			High elasticities version		
	Unchanged tariffs	No import tariffs	Negotiated tariff cut	Unchanged tariffs	No import tariffs	Negotiated tariff cut
Latin America						
GNP market prices	257.5	262.3	260.4	280.4	299.4	292.0
Gross terms of trade	1.5	0	2.0	0	0	0.9
Purchasing power	259.0	262.3	262.4	280.4	299.4	293.0
Loss from misallocation of consumption	0.5	0	0	0.3	0	0.1
Asia						
GNP market prices	204.3	207.0	206.3	319.7	335.0	330.2
Gross terms of trade	3.4	0	3.5	−0.7	0	0.7
Purchasing power	207.7	207.0	209.9	319.0	335.0	331.0
Loss from misallocation of consumption	0.4	0	0	0.7	0	0.2
Africa						
GNP market prices	80.3	81.4	81.7	90.5	95.7	94.2
Gross terms of trade	1.5	0	1.7	−0.6	0	−0.1
Purchasing power	81.8	81.4	83.4	89.9	95.7	94.1
Loss from misallocation of consumption	0.3	0	0	0.3	0	0
Three developing areas						
GNP market prices	542.1	550.7	548.4	690.6	730.1	716.4
Gross terms of trade	6.4	0	7.2	−1.3	0	1.5
Purchasing power	548.5	550.7	555.7	689.3	730.1	717.9
Loss from misallocation of consumption	1.2	0	0	1.3	0	0.3
Middle East oil producers						
GNP market prices	63.2	64.3	63.4	71.2	75.0	73.0
Gross terms of trade	−0.7	0	−0.7	−0.4	0	−0.9
Purchasing power	62.5	64.3	62.7	70.8	75.0	72.1
Developed countries						
GNP market prices	2769.7	2773.4	2771.9	2475.8	2478.5	2478.1
Gross terms of trade	−5.6	−12.5	−6.4	1.7	0	−0.7
Purchasing power	2764.0	2760.9	2765.5	2477.6	2478.5	2477.5

Remark: no "loss from misallocation of consumption" is given for oil-producing and developed countries. Given the structure of GEM, this variable is zero for these areas.

Table 12.23
Adjustment of GNP, purchasing power, and the terms of trade to unilateral tariff reductions by developed countries (billions of dollars, constant prices).

	Low elasticities version			High elasticities version		
	Unchanged tariffs	No tariffs developed	True generalized preferences	Unchanged tariffs	No tariffs developed	True generalized preferences
Latin America						
GNP market prices	257.5	258.6	258.3	280.4	283.4	282.2
Gross terms of trade	1.5	2.6	2.3	−0.1	0.7	0.3
Purchasing power	259.0	261.2	260.6	280.4	284.0	282.5
Loss from misallocation of consumption	0.5	0.2	0.2	0.2	0.3	0.3
Asia						
GNP market prices	204.3	205.4	205.2	319.7	322.7	322.4
Gross terms of trade	3.4	5.4	5.1	−0.7	0.9	0.4
Purchasing power	207.7	210.8	210.3	319.0	323.6	322.7
Loss from misallocation of consumption	0.4	0.0	0.0	0.7	0.4	0.4
Africa						
GNP market prices	80.3	81.3	81.0	90.5	91.7	91.4
Gross terms of trade	1.5	2.6	2.3	−0.5	0.1	0.0
Purchasing power	81.8	83.9	83.3	89.9	91.9	91.4
Loss from misallocation of consumption	0.3	0.0	0.0	0.3	0.2	0.3
Three developing areas						
GNP market prices	542.1	545.3	544.5	690.6	697.8	696.0
Gross terms of trade	6.4	10.6	9.7	−1.3	1.7	0.7
Purchasing power	548.5	555.9	554.2	689.3	699.5	696.7
Loss from misallocation of consumption	1.2	0.2	0.2	1.2	0.9	1.0
Middle East oil-producers						
GNP market prices	63.2	63.2	63.2	71.2	71.4	71.4
Gross terms of trade	−0.7	−1.3	−1.2	−0.4	−1.3	−1.2
Purchasing power	62.5	61.9	62.0	70.8	70.1	70.2
Developed countries						
GNP market prices	2769.7	2770.4	2769.8	2475.9	2476.3	2474.4
Gross terms of trade	−5.6	−9.2	−8.5	1.7	−0.4	0.6
Purchasing power	2764.0	2761.1	2761.3	2477.6	2475.9	2475.0

UNCTAD. The generalized system of preferences (GSP) which emerged after protracted negotiations was so hedged with reservation clauses that it offered little of value to developing countries. The original hopes were for a much more ambitious scheme suppressing tariffs for a wide list of manufactured goods. We have run simulations for policy options that go beyond the hopes of the most sanguine advocates of the GSP: a "true generalized system of preferences" under which tariffs are eliminated for all developing countries' exports to the developed world, even for such sensitive items as textiles. Under the other option, even agricultural tariffs are eliminated.

For the developing countries a zero tariffs policy has a more favorable impact on output than true generalized preferences, for two reasons. The first is that because of the inefficiency of agriculture in Europe and Japan, free trade would bring a significant increase in efficiency. Also, cutting tariffs on manufactured goods, for which protection is low, while high agricultural tariffs are maintained, would make the protection pattern more distorting than it was.

Table 12.23 shows that these policies would indeed be of value to the developing world. Using our rule of thumb that one of the model's constant price dollars is worth 2–2.5 1979 dollars, it is seen that the benefit to developing countries would be about half of the yearly amount of aid which these countries are receiving today.

Developed countries lose substantially less than the amount which is gained by their developing partners: aid through tariff preferences is cheaper than classical forms of aid because the reduction of protection is a positive sum game. The developed countries' obvious reluctance to follow this route reflects their fear of the political costs of the adjustment which accompanies the expansion of trade, and perhaps also political considerations, since classical aid is easier to use to exert political pressure than the assistance which is extended via tariff preferences.

It is striking that in the high elasticities version, developing countries stand to gain much more from eliminating their tariffs unilaterally than if developed countries were to grant them free access to their markets for all goods (compare tables 12.15 and 12.22). An emphasis on *quid pro quo* bargaining is obviously misplaced in that version.

12.8. Equilibrium adjustment to a fall of GNP in developed countries

To what extent is the welfare of developing countries dependent upon the prosperity of the developed world? The question has different answers according to whether what is considered is short- or long-run adjustment.

In the short run, disequilibrium phenomena dominate the adjustment process. A sudden recession in developed countries would cause sharp falls in raw material prices; developing countries would have no time to reallocate resources, and to develop new types of export earnings and import substituting activities. As a result their GNP would inevitably fall rather sharply. The long-run impact would be smaller. After a number of years, developing countries would gradually adjust to the situation and their output would therefore recover, although probably not to the level achieved before the fall of output in the developed world.

GEM is capable of describing the long-run adjustment only. It should be stressed that what it describes is the end-point of an ideal and frictionless

Table 12.24
Adjustment of trade, prices, and exchange rates of the three developing areas to a drop in developed countries' GNP (billions of dollars or indices).

	Low elasticities version		High elasticities version	
	Unchanged tariffs, high developed GNP	Unchanged tariffs, low developed GNP	Unchanged tariffs, high developed GNP	Unchanged tariffs, low developed GNP
Latin America				
Exports value	24.6	23.7	26.4	26.0
volume	22.0	22.0	26.6	26.4
Imports value	34.2	33.1	39.7	39.3
volume	33.1	32.5	39.9	39.5
Price exports	1.115	1.074	0.992	0.988
Price imports	1.032	1.020	0.996	0.995
Exchange rate	1.212	1.100	1.015	1.013
Asia				
Exports value	30.4	29.2	26.1	24.7
volume	25.6	26.3	27.1	25.6
Imports value	38.7	37.4	38.8	37.4
volume	37.4	36.6	39.1	37.8
Price exports	1.186	1.110	0.966	0.965
Price imports	1.037	1.022	0.994	0.993
Exchange rate	1.125	1.021	0.901	0.900
Africa				
Exports value	19.1	16.1	16.2	15.1
volume	16.9	14.7	16.8	15.6
Imports value	22.2	19.4	21.4	20.3
volume	21.5	19.1	21.5	20.4
Price exports	1.129	1.096	0.960	0.959
Price imports	1.032	1.020	0.995	0.994
Exchange rate	1.217	1.155	0.921	0.920

adjustment. In the real world the final state reached by the economy would bear the mark of the stresses and strains which preceded the return to equilibrium.

The striking fact which emerges from table 12.24 is that the impact of a 10 percent drop in GNP of developed countries is surprisingly small, even in the low elasticities model. The variables listed in the table are those which would be affected most sharply by such a drop. It turns out that imports drop by 2–3 percent in volume and export prices by 3–6 percent. In the high elasticities version the effect is even smaller. This underlines a remark made in a conversation by T. N. Srinivasan, commenting on views of A. Lewis, that economists tended to exaggerate the importance to developing countries of prosperity in the developed world: with appropriate policies, developing countries would suffer only minimally if their developed partners were to "sink into the sea".

This result is confirmed by recent experience: developing countries which responded to high oil prices and low world demand by allowing the

Table 12.25
Adjustment of net exports of major industry groups in the three developing areas to a drop in developed countries' GNP (billions of dollars, constant prices).

	Low elasticities version		High elasticities version	
	Unchanged tariffs, high developed GNP	Unchanged tariffs, low developed GNP	Unchanged tariffs, high developed GNP	Unchanged tariffs, low developed GNP
Latin America				
Primary industries, except oil	5.47	6.26	6.53	7.06
Oil	6.56	5.82	−1.83	−2.46
Manufactures	−23.09	−22.55	−18.03	−17.81
Total	−11.06	−10.47	−13.33	−13.21
Asia				
Primary industries, except oil	1.21	2.12	0.49	0.20
Oil	0.01	−0.07	−3.63	−3.53
Manufactures	−12.94	−12.35	−8.88	−8.63
Total	−11.73	−10.31	−12.01	−11.96
Africa				
Primary industries, except oil	6.04	4.63	8.07	7.78
Oil	3.38	3.07	0.47	0.11
Manufactures	−14.07	−12.03	−13.23	−12.65
Total	−4.65	−4.33	−4.69	−4.76

Table 12.26
Adjustment of GNP, the terms of trade, and purchasing power in the three developing areas to a drop in developed countries' GNP (billions of dollars or indices).

	Low elasticities version		High elasticities version	
	Unchanged tariffs, high developed GNP	Unchanged tariffs, low developed GNP	Unchanged tariffs, high developed GNP	Unchanged tariffs, low developed GNP
Latin America				
GNP constant market prices	257.5	256.1	280.4	280.0
Gross terms of trade	1.5	1.0	−0.1	−0.2
Purchasing power	259.0	257.1	280.3	279.8
Ratio export/import prices	1.080	1.053	1.276	1.272
Asia				
GNP constant market prices	204.3	203.4	319.7	319.0
Gross terms of trade	3.4	2.1	−0.7	−0.9
Purchasing power	207.7	205.5	319.0	318.1
Ratio export/import prices	1.144	1.086	0.972	0.970
Africa				
GNP constant market prices	80.3	79.1	90.5	89.8
Gross terms of trade	1.5	1.1	−0.6	−0.6
Purchasing power	81.8	80.1	89.9	89.2
Ratio export/import prices	1.093	1.075	0.965	0.965

price mechanism to adjust the pattern of production and trade, succeeded in maintaining a virtually unchanged rate of economic growth. It is worth remarking, of course, that there is a major difference between the disappearance of a region and a 10 percent decline in its output. If the developed world were truly to suffer the watery fate of the Atlantis of the ancients, it would cease to be a source of the many capital goods which developing countries cannot yet produce: this would change drastically the production functions of developing countries.

The "10 percent sinking into the sea" assumed in the solution of GEM would however change the pattern of specialization of the developing world (table 12.25). Oil exports would be most strongly affected, because the income elasticity of demand for oil is high and the price elasticity of demand is low. Because of the high elasticity of demand for manufactured exports, these would lose on the whole compared with primary commodities.

This impression that the prosperity of the developed world has little impact on that of the developing countries is confirmed by table 12.26, which describes the equilibrium response of their GNP and purchasing power to the drop of output in developed countries. The elasticities of GNP with respect to that of the developed world exceed 0.1 in only one case (Africa in the low elasticities version); they are often much lower. As the gross terms of trade deteriorate slightly purchasing power drops slightly more than GNP. However, in no case does that variable's elasticity with respect to the GNP of developed countries amount to as much as 0.25 (Africa in the low elasticities version again).[9]

[9]The larger loss suffered by Africa is a second-best phenomenon. That area reacts to declining demand abroad by resorting to import substitution, so that both exports and imports drop significantly. As both exports of primary products and imports have prices which are distorted by tariffs, the social cost of this reduction of trade is substantial.

Mathematical appendix

In this Appendix we briefly survey the mathematical results we use in the book. For the sake of simplicity we do not state the most general results since these are not needed in our context.

A.1. The Kuhn–Tucker–Uzawa theorems

Let $x \in X^0 \subset \mathfrak{R}^n$ and $f : X^0 \to \mathfrak{R}$, $g : X^0 \to \mathfrak{R}^m$; $b \in \mathfrak{R}^m$.

Definition 1. Mathematical program (M). Find $\bar{x} \in X$ such that $f(\bar{x}) = \max_{x \in X} f(x)$, $\bar{x} \in X = \{x \mid x \in X^0,\ g(x) \leqslant b\}$.

This definition encompasses the usual one in which $X^0 = \Omega^n$ is the n-dimensional non-negative orthant. The problem M is then: find $\bar{x}$ such that $f(\bar{x}) = \max f(x)$, $\bar{x} \in X = \{x \mid x \geqslant 0,\ g(x) \leqslant b\}$, or alternatively, $\max f(x)$ s.t. $x \geqslant 0$, $g(x) \leqslant b$.

Definition 2. Slater's condition. Let $X^0 \subset \mathfrak{R}^n$ and convex. Let g be a convex vector function on X^0. The convex region $X = \{x \mid x \in X^0,\ g(x) \leqslant b\}$ is said to satisfy Slater's condition if there exists a point $\tilde{x} \in X^0$ such that $g(\tilde{x}) < b$.

Note that if $X^0 = \Omega^n$, Slater's condition implies the existence of an $\tilde{x}$ such that $\tilde{x} > 0$, $g(\tilde{x}) < b$.

Definition 3. Lagrangian function. The function $L(x, u) = f(x) + u \cdot [b - g(x)]$, $u \in \mathfrak{R}^m$ is called a Lagrangian function and the elements of u are Lagrange or Kuhn–Tucker multipliers, or dual variables.

Definition 4. Saddle-point problem 1 (SP 1). Find $\bar{x} \in X^0$, $\bar{u} \in \Omega^m$ such that

$$L(x, \bar{u}) \leqslant L(\bar{x}, \bar{u}) \leqslant L(\bar{x}, u)$$

for all $x \in X^0$, $u \in \Omega^m$.

Definition 5. Saddle-point problem 2 (SP 2). Find $\bar{x} \in X^0$, $\bar{u} \in \Omega^m$ such that

$$L_x(\bar{x}, \bar{u}) = 0,$$

$$L_u(\bar{x}, \bar{u}) \geqslant 0; \qquad \bar{u} \cdot L_u(\bar{x}, \bar{u}) = 0; \qquad \bar{u} \geqslant 0,$$

where L_x and L_u are partial derivatives of $L(\cdot)$ with respect to x and u. It is assumed here that f and g are differentiable on X^0. If $X^0 = \Omega^n$, the conditions for the saddle-point problem can be written in the more symmetrical form:

$$L_x(\bar{x}, \bar{u}) \leqslant 0; \qquad \bar{x} \cdot L_x(\bar{x}, \bar{u}) = 0; \qquad \bar{x} \geqslant 0$$

$$L_u(\bar{x}, \bar{u}) \geqslant 0; \qquad \bar{u} \cdot L_u(\bar{x}, \bar{u}) = 0; \qquad \bar{u} \geqslant 0$$

Theorem 1. Characterization of M by SP 1 [Kuhn–Tucker–Uzawa].

(a) If $(\bar{x}, \bar{u})$ is a solution of SP 1, then $\bar{x}$ is a solution of M.

(b) Let $X^0 \subset \mathcal{R}^n$ be convex, $-f$ and g be convex on X^0 and let g satisfy Slater's condition. If $\bar{x}$ is a solution of M, $\bar{x}$ and some $\bar{u} \in \Omega^m$ will solve SP 1, and $\bar{u} \cdot [b - g(\bar{x})] = 0$.

Proof. Mangasarian (1969, pp. 74–80).

Theorem 2. Characterization of M by SP 2 [Kuhn–Tucker].

(a) Let $\bar{x} \in X^0 \subset \mathcal{R}^n$ be convex and open, and $-f$ and g be differentiable and convex on X^0. If $(\bar{x}, \bar{u})$ is a solution of SP 2, then $\bar{x}$ is a solution of M.

(b) Let $X^0 \subset \mathcal{R}^n$ be convex and open and $-f$ and g be differentiable on X^0; let g satisfy Slater's condition. Then if $\bar{x}$ is a solution of M, $\bar{x}$ and some $\bar{u} \in \Omega^m$ will solve SP 2.

Proof. Mangasarian (1969, pp. 94–110).

Remark. Relation between SP 1 and SP 2.

(a) Let $X^0 \subset \mathcal{R}^n$ be convex and open and f and g be differentiable on X^0; let $u \in \Omega^m$. If $(\bar{x}, \bar{u})$ is a solution of SP 1, it is also a solution of SP 2.

(b) Let $X^0 \subset \mathcal{R}^n$ be convex and open and $-f$ and g be differentiable and convex on X^0; let $u \in \Omega^m$. If $(\bar{x}, \bar{u})$ is a solution of SP 2 it is also a solution of SP 1.

Remark. Problem M is presented as a maximization problem under less or equal inequality constraints. The minimization problem will be written: find $\bar{x}$ such that $f(\bar{x})=\min_{x\in X} f(x)$, $\bar{x}\in X=\{x\,|\,x\in X^0,\ g(x)\geqslant b\}$.

To characterize the optimal solution, we require the same conditions as for theorems 1 and 2 except that f and $-g$ will have to be convex instead of concave.

A.2. Duality

Let $x\in X^0\subset\mathfrak{R}^n$, X^0 convex and open; let $f: X^0\to\mathfrak{R}$, $g: X^0\to\mathfrak{R}^m$ be differentiable on X^0; $b\in\mathfrak{R}^m$.

Definition 6. Dual program (D). Find x^* and $u^*\in\Omega^m$ such that

$$L(x^*,u^*)=\min_{(x,u)\in Y} L(x,u),$$

$$(x^*,u^*)\in Y=\{(x,u)\,|\,x\in X^0,\ u\in\Omega^m,\ L_x(x,u)=0\}.$$

Note that if $X^0=\Omega^n$, we end up with a set Y defined by

$$Y=\{(x,u)\,|\,x\in\Omega^n,\ u\in\Omega^m,\ L_x(x,u)\leqslant 0\}.$$

Theorem 3. Duality theorem [Wolfe]. Let $X^0\subset\mathfrak{R}^n$ be convex and open; let $-f$ and g be differentiable and convex on X^0 and g satisfy Slater's condition. If $\bar{x}$ is a solution of M, there exist multipliers (or dual variables) $\bar{u}\in\Omega^m$ such that $(\bar{x},\bar{u})$ is a solution of D and $f(\bar{x})=L(\bar{x},\bar{u})$.

Proof. Mangasarian (1969, p. 115).

Lemma 1. Euler's theorem on homogeneous functions. Let $h(x)$ be differentiable and homogeneous of degree $r>0$. Then $\bar{x}\cdot h_x(\bar{x})=rh(\bar{x})$ where $h_x(\bar{x})$ is the Jacobian of h at $\bar{x}$.

Theorem 4. Duality for homogeneous programs. Let all conditions of theorem 3 be satisfied and let f and g be homogeneous of the same degree $r>0$. Then $f(\bar{x})=\bar{u}\cdot b$.

Proof. Using theorem 2, we have $L_x(\bar{x},\bar{u})=0$. Clearly $L_x(\bar{x},\bar{u})\cdot\bar{x}=0$. But

$$L_x(\bar{x},\bar{u})\cdot\bar{x}=\left[f_x(\bar{x})-\bar{u}\cdot g_x(\bar{x})\right]\cdot\bar{x}$$
$$=f_x(\bar{x})\cdot\bar{x}-\bar{u}\cdot g_x(\bar{x})\bar{x}.$$

By homogeneity of f and g, $f_x\cdot\bar{x}=rf(\bar{x})$ and $g_x\cdot\bar{x}=rg(\bar{x})$. Hence

$$L_x(\bar{x},\bar{u})\cdot\bar{x}=r\left[f(\bar{x})-\bar{u}\cdot g(\bar{x})\right]=0.$$

Since $r>0$, $f(\bar{x})=\bar{u}\cdot g(\bar{x})$. But then

$$f(\bar{x})=L(\bar{x},\bar{u})=f(\bar{x})+\bar{u}\cdot\left[b-g(\bar{x})\right]=\bar{u}\cdot b.$$

where the first equality is a consequence of theorem 3. Q.E.D.

Remark. Interpretation of Lagrange multipliers: let all conditions of theorem 4 be satisfied. Then at the point $(\bar{x},\bar{u})$ it can be shown that the multipliers $\bar{u}$ are equal to the usually upper hemicontinuous derivatives of $f(\bar{x})$ with respect to the right-hand side of the constraints b.

A.3. Linear programming

Let $x\in X^0=\Omega^n$ and let $f: X^0\to\mathfrak{R}$ and $g: X^0\to\mathfrak{R}^m$ be linear.

Definition 7. Linear program (LP). Find $\bar{x}\in X$ such that $c\cdot\bar{x}=\max_{x\in X}c\cdot x$, $\bar{x}\in X=\{x\mid x\geqslant 0,\ Ax\leqslant b\}$. Since $-f$ and g are linear, they are convex, differentiable and homogeneous of degree 1. Hence, theorem 2 leads to the following conclusions.

Theorem 5. Complementary slackness. If $\bar{x}$ is a solution of LP then

$$c-\bar{u}\cdot A\leqslant 0;\qquad (c-\bar{u}\cdot A)\cdot\bar{x}=0;\qquad \bar{x}\geqslant 0,$$
$$b-A\bar{x}\geqslant 0;\qquad \bar{u}\cdot\left[b-A\bar{x}\right]=0;\qquad \bar{u}\geqslant 0,$$

where $(c-\bar{u}\cdot A)\cdot\bar{x}=0$ and $\bar{u}\cdot[b-A\bar{x}]=0$ are the so-called complementary slackness conditions.

Proof. Apply theorem 2. Q.E.D.

Using definition 6 for the dual program, this can be stated as: find x^* and u^* such that

$$L(x^*, u^*) = \min_{(x,u)\in Y} L(x, u),$$

$$(x^*, u^*) \in Y = \{(x, u) | x \geqslant 0, u \geqslant 0, c - \bar{u} \cdot A \leqslant 0\}.$$

From theorems 3 and 4 we know that $L(x^*, u^*) = L(\bar{x}, \bar{u}) = c \cdot \bar{x} = \bar{u} \cdot b$. Hence, we can define

Definition 8. Dual of a linear program. Find $\bar{u} \in U$ such that $\bar{u} \cdot b = \max_{u\in U} u \cdot b$, $\bar{u} \in U = \{u | u \geqslant 0, u \cdot A \geqslant c\}$.

Theorem 6. Duality theorem of linear programming. A pair of feasible solutions (x, u) is optimal if and only if $c \cdot \bar{x} = \bar{u} \cdot b$.

Proof. Apply theorems 4 and 5.

We do not enter into computational details. We will, however, need a basic theorem used in devising algorithms:

Theorem 7. Consider an LP with n variables and m constraints which has at least one solution. There exists a solution with at most m positive variables.

Proof. Gass (1964, p. 50).

A.4. The vector maximization problem

Let $x \in X^0 \subset \mathfrak{R}^n$, $f_1, f_2, \ldots, f_p : X^0 \to \mathfrak{R}$, $g : X^0 \to \mathfrak{R}^m$; $b \in \mathfrak{R}^m$.

Definition. Vector maximum. $\bar{x} \in X = \{x | x \in X^0, g(x) \leqslant b\}$ is said to be a vector maximum if there exists no other $\tilde{x} \in X$ such that $f_i(\tilde{x}) \geqslant f_i(\bar{x})$, $i = 1, 2, \ldots, p$, with the strict inequality holding for at least one i.

Theorem 8. If $\bar{x} \in X$ is a solution to the vector maximization problem, then $f_1(\bar{x}) = \max f_1(x)$ subject to $x \in X$ and $f_2(x) \geqslant f_2(\bar{x}), \ldots, f_p(x) \geqslant f_p(\bar{x})$.

Proof. Assume the assertion to be false. There exists an $\tilde{x}\in X$ and an index q such that

$$f_i(\tilde{x}) \geqslant f_i(\bar{x}), \qquad i=1,2,\ldots,p,$$

$$f_q(\tilde{x}) > f_q(\bar{x}), \qquad i=q.$$

But then $\bar{x}$ is not a solution to the vector maximization problem as assumed. Q.E.D.

References

Adams, F. G. and J. R. Berhman (1976), *Econometric Models of World Agricultural Commodity Markets: Cocoa, Coffee, Tea, Wool, Cotton, Sugar, Wheat, Rice*, Cambridge, Mass.: Ballinger.

Adams, F. G. and S. A. Klein (1978), *Stabilizing World Commodity Markets*, Lexington, Mass.: Lexington Books.

Adelman, I. and S. Robinson (1978), *Income Distribution Policy in Developing Countries, A Case Study of Korea*, London: Oxford University Press.

Adelman, I. and E. Thorbecke, eds. (1966), *The Theory and Design of Economic Development*, Baltimore: Johns Hopkins University Press.

Arrow, K. J. (1974), "Stability Independent of Adjustment Speed", in: G. Horwich, ed., *Trade, Stability and Macroeconomics, Essays in the Honor of L. A. Metzler*, New York: Academic Press.

Arrow, K. J. and A. C. Enthoven (1961), "Quasi-Concave Programming", *Econometrica* 29, 779–800.

Arrow, K. J. and F. Hahn (1971), *General Competitive Analysis*, San Francisco: Holden Day.

Arrow, K. J. and L. Hurwicz (1958), "On the Stability of the Competitive Equilibrium I", *Econometrica* 26, 522–52.

Arrow, K. J. and L. Hurwicz (1960), "Competitive Stability Under Weak Gross Substitutability: The Euclidean Distance Approach", *International Economic Review* 1, 38–49.

Arrow, K. J., H. D. Block and L. Hurwicz (1959), "On the Stability of the Competitive Equilibrium II", *Econometrica* 27, 82–109.

Arrow, K. J., L. Hurwicz and H. Uzawa, eds. (1958), *Studies in Linear and Nonlinear Programming*, Stanford, Calif.: Stanford University Press.

Arrow, K. J., S. Karlin and P. Suppes, eds. (1960), *Mathematical Methods in the Social Sciences*, Stanford, Calif.: Stanford University Press.

Balassa, B. (1965), "Tariff Protection in Industrial Countries: An Evaluation", *Journal of Political Economy* 73, 573–94.

Balassa, B. (1971), *The Structure of Protection in Developing Countries*, Baltimore: Johns Hopkins University Press.

Ball, R. J., ed. (1973), *The International Linkage of National Economic Models*, Amsterdam: North-Holland.

Barten, A. P. (1969), "Maximum Likelihood Estimation of a Complete System of Demand Equations", *European Economic Review* 1, 7–73.

Barten, A. P. (1970), "Some Reflections on the Relation Between Private Consumption and Collective Expenditure in an Expending Mature Economy", in: J. Paelinck, ed., *Programming for Europe's Collective Needs*, Amsterdam: North-Holland, 82–98.

Basevi, G. (1966), "The United States Tariff Structure: Estimates of Effective Protection of United States Industries and Industrial Labor", *Review of Economics and Statistics* 48, 147–60.

Behrman, J. R. (1968), *Supply Response in Underdeveloped Agriculture*, Amsterdam: North-Holland.

Bhagwati, J. N. and P. Desai (1970), *India: Planning for Industrialisation*, London: Oxford University Press.

Blackorby, C., R. Boyce and R. Russel (1978), "Estimation of Demand Systems Generated by the Gorman Polar Form; A Generalisation of the S-Branch Utility Tree", *Econometrica* 46, 345–78.

Blitzer, C. R., P. B. Clark and L. Taylor, eds. (1976), *Economy-Wide Models and Development Planning*, London: Oxford University Press.

Bruno, M. (1966), "A Programming Model for Israel", in: I. Adelman and E. Thorbecke, eds., *The Theory and Design of Economic Development*, Baltimore: Johns Hopkins University Press.

CDC (1972), *Apex-I Reference Manual*.

Charnes, A., C. B. Garcia and C. E. Lemke (1977), "Constructive Proofs of Theorems Relating to F(x) = y, with Applications", to appear in *Mathematical Programming*.

Chenery, H. B. and W. J. Raduchel (1971), "Substitution in Planning Models", in: H. B. Chenery, ed., *Studies in Development Planning*, Cambridge, Mass.: Harvard University Press.

Chenery, H. B. and M. Syrquin (1975), *Patterns of Development, 1950–1970*, London: Oxford University Press.

Chenery, H. B. and L. Taylor (1968), "Development Patterns: Among Countries and Over Time", *Review of Economics and Statistics* 50, 391–416.

Chenery, H. B. and H. Uzawa (1958), "Non-Linear Programming and Economic Development", in: K. J. Arrow, L. Hurwicz and H. Uzawa, eds., *Studies in Linear and Non-Linear Programming*, Stanford, Calif.: Stanford University Press.

Chenery, H. B. and R. Watanabe (1958), "International Comparisons of the Structure of Production", *Econometrica* 26, 487–521.

Chenery, H. B., H. Elkington and C. Sims, (1970), "A Uniform Analysis of Development Patterns", Harvard University: Economic Development Report no. 148 (July).

Clark, P. B. (1970), *Planning Import Substitution*, Amsterdam: North-Holland.

Corden, W. M. (1966), "The Structure of a Tariff System and the Effective Protection Rate", *Journal of Political Economy* 74, 221–37.

Corden, W. M. (1971), *The Theory of Protection*, Oxford: Clarendon Press.

Dantzig, G. B. (1963), *Linear Programming and Extensions*, Princeton: Princeton University Press.

Dantzig, G. B., B. C. Eaves and D. Gale (1979), "An Algorithm for a Piecewise Linear Model of Trade and Production with Negative Prices and Bankruptcy", *Mathematical Programming* 16, 190–209.

Day, R. H. (1963), *Recursive Programming and Production Response*, Amsterdam: North-Holland.

Debreu, G. (1951), "The Coefficient of Resource Utilization", *Econometrica* 19, 273–92.

Debreu, G. (1959), *Theory of Value*, New York: Wiley.

Debreu, G. (1974), "Excess Demand Functions", *Journal of Mathematical Economics* 1, 15–21.

Diewert, W. E. (1973), "On a Theorem of Negishi", *Metroeconomica* 25, 119–35.

Dixon, P. B. (1975a), *The Theory of Joint Maximization*, Amsterdam: North-Holland.

Dixon, P. B. (1975b), "The Computation of Economic Equilibria: A Joint Maximization Approach", paper presented at the Third World Conference of the Econometric Society, Toronto.

Drèze, J. (1975), "Existence of an Exchange Equilibrium under Price Rigidities", *International Economic Review* 16, 301–20.

Duloy, J. H. and R. D. Norton (1973), "CHAC, a Programming Model of Mexican Agriculture", in: L. M. Goreux and A. S. Manne, eds., *Multi-Level Planning: Case Studies in Mexico*, Amsterdam: North-Holland, 291–337.

Eaves, B. C. (1970), "An Odd Theorem", *Proceedings of the American Mathematical Society* 26, 509–13.

Eaves, B. C. (1971), "Computing Kakutani Fixed Points", *Siam Journal of Applied Mathematics* 21, 236–44.

Eaves, B. C. (1972), "Homotopies for Computation of Fixed Points", *Mathematical Programming* 3, 1–22.

Eaves, B. C. and R. Saigal (1972), "Homotopies for Computation of Fixed Points on Unbounded Regions", *Mathematical Programming* 3, 225–37.

Eaves, B. C. and H. Scarf (1976), "The Solution of Systems of Piecewise Linear Equations", *Mathematics of Operations Research* 1, 1–27.

Eckaus, R. S. and K. S. Parikh (1968), *Planning for Growth: Multisectoral, Intertemporal Models Applied to India*, Cambridge, Mass.: MIT Press.

Fisher, F. M., P. H. Cootner and M. Baily (1972), "An Econometric Model of the World Copper Industry", *The Bell Journal of Economics and Management Science* 3, 568–609.

Fromm, G. and L. R. Klein (1969), "Solutions of the Complete System", in: J. S. Duesenberry, G. Fromm, L. R. Klein and F. Kuh, eds., *The Brookings Model: Some Further Results*, Amsterdam: North-Holland, 363–421.

Gale, D. (1960), *The Theory of Linear Economic Models*, New York: McGraw-Hill.

Gale, D. and H. Nikaido (1965), "The Jacobian Matrix and Global Univalence of Mappings", *Mathematische Annalen* 159, 81–93.

Gantmacher, F. R. (1960), *The Theory of Matrices*, vol. 1, New York: Chelsea Pub.

Garcia, C. B. (1976), "A Hybrid Algorithm for the Computation of Fixed Points", *Management Science* 22, 606–13.

Garcia, C. B. (1977), "Continuation Methods for Simplicial Mappings", in: S. Karamardian, ed., *Fixed Points and Applications*, New York: Academic Press, 149–63.

Garcia, C. B. and F. J. Gould (1976a), "An Improved Scalar Generated Homotopy Path for Solving $f(x)=0$", Report 7633, Center for Mathematical Studies in Business and Economics, University of Chicago.

Garcia, C. B. and F. J. Gould (1976b), "An Algorithm Based on the Equivalence of Vector and Scalar Labels in Simplicial Approximation", Report 7626, Center for Mathematical Studies in Business and Economics, University of Chicago.

Garcia, C. B. and F. J. Gould (1977), "Relations Between Complementary Pivoting Algorithms and Local and Global Newton Methods", Report 7735, Center for Mathematical Studies in Business and Economics, University of Chicago.

Garcia, C. B. and W. I. Zangwill (1976), "Determining All Solutions to Certain Systems of Nonlinear Equations", Report 7712, Center for Mathematical Studies in Business and Economics, University of Chicago.

Gass, S. I. (1964), *Linear Programming*, New York: McGraw-Hill.

Geary, R. C. (1950–51), "A Note on 'A Constant Utility Index of the Cost of Living'", *Review of Economic Studies* 18, 65–66.

Ginsburgh, V. and J. Waelbroeck (1974a), "Computational Experience with a Large General Equilibrium Model", Center for Operations Research and Econometrics, University of Louvain.

Ginsburgh, V. and J. Waelbroeck (1974b), "Linear Programming and General Equilibrium Theory", Center for Operations Research and Econometrics, University of Louvain.

Ginsburgh, V. and J. Waelbroeck (1975a), "A General Equilibrium Model of World Trade, Part 1: Full Format Computation of Economic Equilibria", Cowles Foundation Discussion Paper 412, Yale University.

Ginsburgh, V. and J. Waelbroeck (1975b), "A General Equilibrium Model of World Trade, Part 2: The Empirical Specification", Cowles Foundation Discussion Paper 413, Yale University.

Ginsburgh, V. and J. Waelbroeck (1976a), "Computational Experience with a Large General Equilibrium Model", in: J. and M. Los, eds., *Computing Equilibria: How and Why*, Amsterdam: North-Holland.

Ginsburgh, V. and J. Waelbroeck (1976b), "Linear Programming Formulation of International Trade Mechanisms and Trade Theory", in: H. Glesjer, ed., *Quantitative Studies of International Economic Relations*, Amsterdam: North-Holland, 73–90.

Ginsburgh, V. and J. Waelbroeck (1977), "A General Equilibrium Model of World Trade, Part 3: Some Calculations of the Impact of Tariffs on World Trade and Welfare", Center for Operations Research and Econometrics, University of Louvain.

Ginsburgh, V. and J. Waelbroeck (1979), "A Note on the Simultaneous Stability of Tâtonnement Processes for Computing Equilibria", *International Economic Review* 20, 367–80.

Glejser, H., ed. (1976), *Quantitative Studies of International Economic Relations*, Amsterdam: North-Holland.

Goldberger, A. S. and T. Gamaletsos (1970), "A Cross Country Comparison of Consumer Expenditure Patterns", *European Economic Review* 1, 357–400.

Goldfeld, S. M. and R. E. Quandt (1972), *Nonlinear Methods in Econometrics*, Amsterdam: North-Holland.

Goreux, L. M. (1977), *Interdependence in Planning, Multilevel Programming Studies of the Ivory Coast*, Baltimore: Johns Hopkins University Press.

Goreux, L. M. and A. S. Manne, eds. (1973), *Multi-Level Planning: Case Studies in Mexico*, Amsterdam: North-Holland.

Gorman, W. M. (1953), "Community Preference Fields", *Econometrica* 21, 63–80.

Grandmont, J. M. (1977), "The Logic of the Fix-Price Method", *The Scandinavian Journal of Economics* 79, 169–86.

Hahn, F. H. (1958), "Gross Substitutes and the Dynamic Stability of General Equilibrium", *Econometrica* 26, 169–70.

Hansen, T. (1968), "On the Approximation of a Competitive Equilibrium", Ph.D. Dissertation, Yale University.

Hansen, T. and H. Scarf (1969), "On the Applications of a Recent Combinatorial Algorithm", Cowles Foundation Discussion Paper 272, Yale University.

Harris, J. R. and M. P. Todaro (1970), "Migration, Unemployment and Development: A Two-Sector Analysis", *American Economic Review* 60, 126–42.

Hazell, P. B. R. (1971), "A Linear Alternative to Quadratic and Semivariance Programming for Farm Planning Under Uncertainty", *American Journal of Agricultural Economics* 53, 53–62.

Heady, E. O. and J. L. Dillon (1961), *Agricultural Production Functions*, Ames, Iowa: Iowa State University Press.

Hirsch, M. W. (1963), "A Proof of the Nonretractibility of a Cell into Its Boundary", *Proceedings of the American Mathematical Society* 14, 364–65.

Houthakker, H. S. (1957), "An International Comparison of Household Expenditure Patterns, Commemorating the Centenary of Engel's Law", *Econometrica* 25, 532–51.

Houthakker, H. S. (1975), "The Calculation of Bilateral Trade Patterns in a Ricardian Model With Intermediate Products and Barriers to Trade", Harvard Institute of Economic Research.

Johnson, H. G. (1965), "The Theory of Tariff Structure, with Special Reference to World Trade and Development", in: *Trade and Development*, Geneva: Institut Universitaire des Hautes Etudes Internationales.

Jorgenson, D. W. and L. Lau (1977), "Statistical Tests of the Theory of Consumer Behavior", in: H. Albach, E. Helmstädter and R. Henn, eds., *Quantitative Wirtschaftsforschung: Wilhelm Krelle zum 60. Geburtsdag*, Tübingen: J. C. B. Mohr, 383–94.

Junz, H. B. and R. R. Rhomberg (1965), "Prices and Export Performance in Industrial Countries 1953–63", *IMF Staff Papers* 12, 224–69.

Karamardian, S. (1977), *Fixed Points and Applications*, New York: Academic Press.

Karlin, S. (1959), *Mathematical Methods and Theory in Games, Programming and Economics*, London: Pergamon Press.

Kellog, R. B., T. Y. Li and J. Yorke (1975), "A Constructive Proof of the Brouwer Fixed Point Theorem and Computational Results", Institute for Fluid Dynamics and Applied Mathematics, University of Maryland.

Kellog, R. B., T. Y. Li and J. Yorke (1977), "A Method of Continuation for Calculating a Brouwer Fixed Point", in: S. Karamadian, ed., *Fixed Points and Applications*, New York: Academic Press, 133–47.

Konno, H. (1976), "A Cutting Plane Algorithm for Solving Bilinear Programs", *Mathematical Programming* 11, 14–27.

Koopmans, T. C., ed. (1951), *Activity Analysis of Allocation and Production*, New York: Wiley.

Kravis, I. B. and R. E. Lipsey (1971), *Price Competitiveness in World Trade*, New York: National Bureau of Economic Research.

Kravis, I. B., Z. Kennessey, A. Heston and R. Summers (1975), *A System of International Comparisons of Gross Products and Purchasing Power*, Baltimore: Johns Hopkins University Press.

Kuhn, H. W. (1968), "Simplicial Approximation of Fixed Points", *Proceedings of the National Academy of Sciences (USA)* 61, 1238–42.

Kuhn, H. W. and J. C. McKinnon (1975), "The Sandwich Method for Finding Fixed Points", *Journal of Optimization Theory and Applications* 17, 189–204.

Kuhn, H. W. and A. W. Tucker (1951), "Nonlinear Programming", in: *Proceedings of the Second Berkeley Symposium on Mathematical Statistics and Probability*, Berkeley: University of California Press, 181–92.

Labys, W. C. (1975), "Commodity Modelling: Survey and Prescriptions", Geneva: Institut Universitaire des Hautes Etudes Internationales.

La Salle, J. and S. Lefschetz (1961), *Stability by Lyapunov's Direct Method with Applications*, New York: Academic Press.

Lamel J., J. Richter and W. Teufelsbauer (1972), "Patterns of Industrial Structure and Economic Development: Triangulation of Input-Output Tables of ECE Countries", *European Economic Review* 3, 47–63.

Leamer, E. E. and R. M. Stern (1970), *Quantitative International Economics*, Boston, Mass.: Allyn and Bacon.

Lemke, C. E. (1965), "Bimatrix Equilibrium Points and Mathematical Programming", *Management Science* 11, 681–89.

Lemke, C. E. and J. T. Howson (1964), "Equilibrium Points of Bimatrix Games", *Siam Journal of Applied Mathematics* 12, 413–23.

Linneman, H. and Assoc. (1973), *Moira: A Model of International Relations in Agriculture*, Amsterdam: North-Holland.

Little, I., T. Scitovsky and M. Scott (1970), *Industry and Trade in Some Developing Countries, a Comparative Study*, London: Oxford University Press.

Lluch, C., A. A. Powell and R. A. Williams (1977), *Patterns in Household Demand and Saving*, London: Oxford University Press.

Los, J. and M. Los, eds. (1976), *Computing Equilibria: How and Why?*, Amsterdam: North-Holland.

Maizels, A. (1971), *Exports and Economic Growth of Developing Countries*, Cambridge: Cambridge University Press.

Maizels, A., L. F. Campbell-Boross and P. B. W. Rayment (1971), *Exports and Economic Growth of Developing Countries*, Cambridge: Cambridge University Press.

Malinvaud, E. (1953), "Capital Accumulation and Efficient Allocation of Resources", *Econometrica* 21, 323–68.

Mangasarian, O. (1969), *Nonlinear Programming*, New York: McGraw-Hill.

Manne, A. S. (1963), "Key Sectors of the Mexican Economy", in: A. S. Manne and H. Markovitz, eds. *Studies in Process Analysis*, New York: Wiley.

Manne, A. S. (1970), "Sufficient Conditions for Optimality in an Infinite Horizon Development Plan", *Econometrica* 38, 18–38.

Manne, A. S. (1974), "Multisector Models for Development Planning: A Survey", *Journal of Development Economics* 1, 43–69.

Manne, A. S., H. P. Chao and R. Wilson (1977), "Computation of Competitive Equilibria by a Sequence of Linear Programs", Department of Operations Research, Stanford University.

Manne, A. S. and H. M. Markowitz, eds. (1963), *Studies in Process Analysis: Economy-Wide Production Capabilities*, New York: John Wiley.

Manne, A. S. and T. E. Weisskopf (1970), "A Dynamic Multi-Sectoral Model for India, 1967–75", in: A. Carter and A. Brody, eds., *Applications of Input-Output Analysis*, Amsterdam: North-Holland.

Mantel, R. R. (1968), "Toward a Constructive Proof of the Existence of Equilibrium in a Competitive Economy", *Yale Economic Essays* 8, 155–200.

Mantel, R. R. (1971), "The Welfare Adjustment Process: Its Stability Properties", *International Economic Review* 12, 415–30.

Mantel, R. R. (1974), "On the Characterization of Aggregate Excess Demand", *Journal of Economic Theory* 9, 348–53.

McDougall, G. D. A. (1951), "British and American Exports: A Study Suggested by the Theory of Comparative Costs", *Economic Journal* 61, 697–724.

McDougall, G. D. A. (1952), "British and American Exports: A Study Suggested by the Theory of Comparative Costs", *Economic Journal* 62, 487–521.

McFadden, D., A. Mas-Colell, R. Mantel and M. K. Richter (1975), "A Characterization of Community Excess Demand Functions", *Journal of Economic Theory* 9, 361–74.

McKenzie, L. (1960), "Matrices with Dominant Diagonals and Economic Theory", in: K. J. Arrow, S. Karlin and P. Suppes, eds., *Mathematical Methods in the Social Sciences*, Stanford, Calif.: Stanford University Press, 47–62.

McKenzie, L. W. (1976), "Why Compute Economic Equilibria", in: J. Los and M. Los, eds. *Computing Equilibria, How and Why?*, Amsterdam: North-Holland, 3–19.

Mennes, L. B. M. (1973), *Planning Economic Integration Among Developing Countries*, Rotterdam: Rotterdam University Press.

Merrill, O. H. (1972), "Applications and Extensions of an Algorithm that Computes Fixed Points of Certain Upper Semi-Continuous Point to Set Mappings", Ph.D. Dissertation, Department of Industrial Engineering, University of Michigan.

Mifflin, R. (1978), "An Algorithm for Constrained Optimization with Semismooth Functions", International Institute for Applied Systems Analysis.

Nataf, A. (1953), "Possibilité d'Agrégation dans le Cadre de la Théorie des Choix", *Metroeconomica* 5, 22–30.

Negishi, T. (1960), "Welfare Economics and Existence of an Equilibrium for a Competitive Economy", *Metroeconomica* 12, 92–97.

Negishi, T. (1972), *General Equilibrium and International Trade*, Amsterdam: North-Holland.

Nerlove, M. (1958), *The Dynamics of Supply: Estimation of Farmers' Response to Price*, Baltimore: Johns Hopkins University Press.

Nikaido, H. (1968), *Convex Structures and Economic Theory*, New York: Academic Press.

Nugent, J. B. (1970), "Linear Programming Models for National Planning: Demonstration of a Testing Procedure", *Econometrica* 38, 831–55.

Ortega, J. M. and W. C. Rheinboldt (1970), *Iterative Solutions of Nonlinear Equations in Several Variables*, New York: Academic Press.

Osterrieth, M. (1978), "The Impact of Less Developed Countries' Trading Position on World Agricultural Prices", *European Economic Review* 11, 87–98.

Papanek, G. (1972), "The Effect of Aid and Other Resource Transfers on Savings and Growth in Less Developed Countries", *Economic Journal* 82, 934–51.

Quirk, J. and R. Saposnik (1968), *Introduction to General Equilibrium Theory and Welfare Economics*, New York: McGraw-Hill.

Saigal, R. (1976), "On Paths Generated by Fixed Points Algorithms", *Mathematics of Operations Research* 1, 359–80.

Saigal, R. and M. J. Todd (1976), "Efficient Acceleration Techniques for Fixed Point Algorithms", Center for Operations Research and Econometrics, University of Louvain.

Santhanam, K. V. and R. H. Patil (1972), "A Study of the Production Structure of the Indian Economy: An International Comparison", *Econometrica* 40, 159–76.

Sandee, J., (1960), *A Demonstration Planning Model for India*, Bombay: Asia Publishing House.

Scarf, H. (1960), "Some Examples of Global Instability of the Competitive Equilibrium", *International Economic Review* 1, 157–72.

Scarf, H. (1967a), "The Approximation of Fixed Points of a Continuous Mapping", *Siam Journal of Applied Mathematics* 15, 1328–43.

Scarf, H. (1967b), "On the Computation of Equilibrium Prices", in: W. Fellner et al., *Ten Economic Studies in the Tradition of Irving Fisher*, New York: John Wiley, 207–30.

Scarf, H. with the collaboration of T. Hansen (1973), *The Computation of Economic Equilibria*, New Haven: Yale University Press.

Scarf, H. (1977), "The Computation of Equilibrium Prices: An Exposition", Cowles Foundation Discussion Paper 473, Yale University.

Shamir, S. (1979a), "The Dynamic Shift Algorithm. A Homotopy Fixed Point Algorithm with a Dynamic Triangulation Having an Arbitrary Grid Refinement Factor", Systems Engineering Program, Department of Engineering, Stanford University.

Shamir, S. (1979b), "A Homotopy Fixed Point Algorithm with an Arbitrary Integer Refinement Factor", Systems Engineering Program, Department of Engineering, Stanford University.

Shoven, J. B. (1974), "A Proof of the Existence of a General Equilibrium with ad Valorem Commodity Taxes", *Journal of Economic Theory* 8, 1–25.

Shoven, J. B. and J. Whalley (1974a), "General Equilibrium with Taxes: A Computational Procedure and Existence Proof", *Review of Economic Studies* 40, 475–89.

Shoven, J. B. and J. Whalley (1974b), "On the Computation of Competitive Equilibrium on International Markets with Tariffs", *Journal of International Economics* 4, 341–54.

Singh, I. and C. Y. Ahn (1978), "A Dynamic Multicommodity Model of the Agricultural Sector, a Regional Application in Brazil", *European Economic Review* 11, 155–80.

Smale, S. (1976), "A Convergent Process of Price Adjustment and Global Newton Methods", *Journal of Mathematical Economics* 3, 107–20.

Sonnenschein, H. (1973), "Do Walras' Identity and Continuity Characterize the Class of Community Excess Demand Functions?," *Journal of Economic Theory* 6, 345–54.

Stern, J. J. and J. D. Lewis (1977), "Employment Patterns and Income Growth", Harvard Institute for International Development.

Stolper, W. F. and A. P. Samuelson (1941), "Protection and Real Wages", in: *The Collected Scientific Papers of P. A. Samuelson*, Cambridge, Mass.: The MIT Press, 1966.

Stone, R. (1954), "Linear Expenditure Systems and Demand Analysis: An Application to the Pattern of British Demand", *The Economic Journal* 64, 511–27.

Taylor, L. (1976), "Theoretical Foundations and Technical Implications", in: C. R. Blitzer, P. C. Clark and L. Taylor, eds., *Economy-Wide Models and Development Planning*, Oxford: Oxford University Press, 33–109.

Tims, W. (1975), "Possible Effects of Trade Liberalization on Trade in Primary Commodities", Bank Staff Working Paper no. 193 (January).

Todaro, M. P. (1971), *Development Planning: Models and Methods*, Nairobi: Oxford University Press.

Todd, M. J. (1976a), *The Computation of Fixed Points and Applications*, New York: Springer-Verlag.

Todd, M. J. (1976b), "On Triangulations for Computing Fixed Points", *Mathematical Programming* 10, 322–46.

Todd, M. J. (1976c), "Orientation in Complementary Pivot Algorithms", *Mathematics of Operations Research* 1, 54–66.

Todd, M. J. (1977), "On the Jacobian of a Function at a Zero Computed by a Fixed Point Algorithm", Center for Operations Research and Econometrics, University of Louvain.

Trzeciakowski, W. (1971), "Systems of Indirect Management in a Planned Economy", Cowles Foundation Discussion Paper 312, Yale University.

Tweeten, L. G. and C. Leroy Quance (1969), "Positivistic Measures of Aggregate Supply Elasticities: Some New Approaches", *American Economic Review* 59, 175–83.

USDA (1978), "Alternative Futures for World Food in 1985", US Department of Agriculture Report no. 146.

Uzawa, H. (1958), "The Kuhn–Tucker Theorem in Concave Programming", in: K. J. Arrow, L. Hurwicz and H. Uzawa, eds., *Studies in Linear and Nonlinear Programming*, Stanford, Calif.: Stanford University Press.

Van der Laan, G. and A. J. J. Talman (1979), "A Restart Algorithm for Computing Fixed Points without an Extra Dimension", *Mathematical Programming* 17, 74–84.

Von Neumann, J. (1945), "A Model of General Economic Equilibrium", *Review of Economic Studies* 13, 1–9.

Waelbroeck, J., ed., (1976), *The Models of Project Link*, Amsterdam: North-Holland.

Watanabe, T. (1961), "A Test of the Constancy of Input-Output Coefficients Among Countries", *International Economic Review* 2, 340–50.

Weisskoff, R. (1971), "Demand Elasticities for a Developing Economy: An International Comparison of Consumption Patterns", in: H. B. Chenery, ed., *Studies in Development Planning*, Cambridge, Mass.: Harvard University Press, 322–58.

Weisskopf, T. E. (1971), "Alternative Patterns of Import Substitution in India," in: H. B. Chenery, ed., *Studies in Development Planning*, Cambridge, Mass.: Harvard University Press, 95–121.

Weisskopf, T. E. (1972), "The Impact of Foreign Capital Inflow on Domestic Savings in Underdeveloped Countries", *Journal of International Economics* 2, 25–38.

Westphal, L. E. (1969), "Multisectoral Project Analysis Employing Mixed Integer Programming", in I. Adelman, ed., *Practical Approaches to Development Planning: Korea's Second Five-Year Plan*, Baltimore: Johns Hopkins University Press.

Wilmuth, R. J. (1973), "The Computation of Fixed Points", Ph.D. Dissertation, Department of Operations Research, Stanford University.

Wilson, R. (1978), "The Bilinear Complementarity Problem and Competitive Equilibria of Linear Economic Models", *Econometrica* 46, 87–103.

Wolfe, P. (1963), "Methods of Nonlinear Programming", in: L. Graves and P. Wolfe, eds., *Recent Advances in Mathematical Programming*, New York: McGraw-Hill.

Wolsey, L. A. (1974), "Convergence, Simplicial Paths and Acceleration Methods for Simplicial Approximation Algorithms for Finding a Zero of a System of Nonlinear Equations", Center for Operations Research and Econometrics, University of Louvain.

Author index

Subject index